DICTIONARY OF
AMERICAN BOOK
COLLECTORS

Dictionary of American Book Collectors

DONALD C. DICKINSON

GREENWOOD PRESS

New York • Westport, Connecticut • London

Allen County Public Library
Ft. Wayne, Indiana

Library of Congress Cataloging in Publication Data

Dickinson, Donald C.
  Dictionary of American book collectors.

  Bibliography: p.
  Includes index.
  1. Book collectors—United States—Biography—
Dictionaries. I. Title.
Z989.A1D53 1986   002'.075'0922 [B]   85-5580
ISBN 0–313–22544–3 (lib. bdg. : alk. paper)

Library of Congress Catalog Card Number: 85-5580
ISBN: 0–313–22544–3

First published in 1986
Greenwood Press, Inc.
88 Post Road West, Westport, Connecticut 06881

Printed in the United States of America

The paper used in this book complies with the
Permanent Paper Standard issued by the National
Information Standards Organization (Z39.48–1984).
10 9 8 7 6 5 4 3 2 1

In memory of
My mother, Stella B. Dickinson, 1899–1983
and
My father, Charles W. Dickinson, 1898–1984

Contents

Abbreviations for Works Cited Frequently

AB	*AB Bookman's Weekly*
ABC	*American Book Collector*
ARLC	*Annual Report: The Library of Congress*
BBPL	*Bulletin of the Boston Public Library*
BC	*The Book Collector*
BNYPL	*Bulletin of the New York Public Library*
Cannon	Carl Cannon, *American Book Collectors and Collecting from Colonial Times to the Present* (New York: H. W. Wilson, 1941; reprint, Westport, Conn.: Greenwood Press, 1976)
CB	*Current Biography*
DAB	*Dictionary of American Biography*
DALB	*Dictionary of American Literary Biography*
DANB	*Dictionary of American Negro Biography*
Everitt	Charles P. Everitt, *The Adventures of a Treasure Hunter* (Boston: Little, Brown & Co., 1951)
Farnham	Luther Farnham, *A Glance at Private Libraries* (Boston: Crocker and Brewster, 1855)
Goodspeed	Charles E. Goodspeed, *Yankee Bookseller* (Boston: Houghton Mifflin Co., 1937)
Granniss	Ruth S. Granniss, "American Book Collecting and the Growth of Libraries," in *The Book in America* (New York: Bowker, 1939)

Grolier 75	*Grolier 75: A Biographical Retrospective to Celebrate the Seventy-fifth Anniversary of the Grolier Club in New York* (New York: Grolier, 1959)
HLB	*Harvard Library Bulletin*
HuLB	*Huntington Library Bulletin*
JAMA	*Journal of the American Medical Association*
JHMAS	*Journal of the History of Medicine and Allied Sciences*
NCAB	*National Cyclopedia of American Biography*
NYT	*New York Times*
PAAS	*Proceedings of the American Antiquarian Society*
PAPS	*Proceedings of the American Philosophical Society*
PBSA	*Papers of the Bibliographical Society of America*
PLC	*Princeton Library Chronicle*
PMHS	*Proceedings of the Massachusetts Historical Society*
PW	*Publishers Weekly*
QCHS	*Quarterly of the California Historical Society*
QJLC	*Quarterly Journal of the Library of Congress*
QNLBCC	*Quarterly Newsletter of the Book Club of California*
Randall	David A. Randall, *Dukedom Large Enough* (New York: Random House, 1969)
SCLC	*Special Collections in the Library of Congress: A Selective Guide*, compiled by Annette Melville (Washington, D.C.: Library of Congress, 1980)
Wolf and Fleming	Edwin Wolf II with John Fleming, *Rosenbach: A Biography* (Cleveland: World, 1960)
Wynne	James Wynne, *Private Libraries of New York* (New York: E. French, 1860)
YLG	*Yale Library Gazette*

Abbreviations for Major American Book Auction Companies

American Art	American Art Association, 1886–1929
American Art-Anderson	American Art Association—Anderson Galleries, 1929–1934
Anderson	Anderson Auction Company, 1903–1915 The Anderson Galleries, 1915–1929
Bangs	Cooley and Bangs, 1837–1838 Bangs, Richards and Platt, 1839–1848 Bangs, Platt and Co., 1849–1850 Bangs, Brother, 1851–1858 Bangs, Merwin, 1858–1876 Bangs and Co., 1876–1903
Birch	Thomas Birch and Sons, 1864–1890
Butterfield	Butterfield and Butterfield, 1865–
California Book Auction	California Book Auction Galleries, 1956–
Freeman	Samuel T. Freeman and Co., 1903–1933
Heartman	Charles F. Heartman Auction Company, 1913–1934
Henkels	Stan V. Henkels, 1883–1934
Leavitt	George A. Leavitt, 1857–1892
Leonard	Leonard and Company, 1852–1918
Libbie	Charles F. Libbie, 1878–1919

For a more detailed list of American auction houses and their locations the user is referred to: "List of American Book Auction Houses," in *American Book Auction Catalogues 1713–1934, A Union List* by George L. McKay (New York, 1937), pp. xvii–xxxii.

Merwin	Merwin Clayton Sales Company, 1904–1912
	Merwin Sales Company, 1912–1915
Metropolitan	Metropolitan Art Association, 1914–1915
Parke-Bernet	Parke-Bernet Galleries, 1937–1964
Rains	Rains Auction Rooms, 1932–1938
Sabin	Joseph Sabin and Co., 1860–1861
Sotheby's	Sotheby Parke Bernet, 1964–1984
	Sotheby's, 1984–
Thomas	M. Thomas and Sons, 1828–1906

Preface

The purpose of this book is to present biographical information on 359 significant American book collectors who died before December 31, 1984. The only previous work on this subject, Carl Cannon's *American Book Collectors and Collecting*, published in 1941, is still valuable but difficult to use for reference purposes because of its essay format. More recent information can only be found by searching through a maze of journals, memoirs, reports, and auction records. This book brings that information together for easy consultation.

As with any biographical source book that attempts to select a few names from the multitude, various criteria had to be applied. Clearly, the most important measure of a book collector's stature rests in the quality and depth of the materials collected. This evaluation is not always easy to come by. In some cases reports and bibliographies issued by institutional libraries identify these outstanding collections, but in others one must go to the auction records and to booksellers' catalogs. The size of the collection may or may not be a factor. A well-selected library of 500 titles may outrank a 10,000-volume miscellany. Further, the unity of materials collected—how the books complement one another—is frequently a more important criterion than size. Elmer Belt's splendid Leonardo da Vinci library at the University of California at Los Angeles is a prime example of a carefully constructed, interlocking collection. In addition, the presence of certain designated rarities, such as the *Bay Psalm Book* or the Shakespearean folios, has traditionally been a measure of a collection's reputation. Provenance also plays a part in determining significance. Books from the distinguished libraries of Morris L. Parrish, Thomas W. Streeter, and Robert Hoe III, for example, carry their own credentials. Finally, the physical condition of books and manuscripts is of such importance to both collectors and libraries that it is unlikely that a library made up of worn or mutilated copies could be designated a significant collection.

Generally, the men and women represented in this survey formed libraries distinguished by the quality, unity, and superior physical condition of the materials they collected as well as the importance those materials had to other collectors and/or to institutional libraries. In addition to these general criteria, a few special considerations were applied in the process of selecting candidates. No one was included on the basis of general eminence alone. Most Presidents of the United States and many important writers have owned substantial working libraries, but few of these individuals can be classified as collectors. However, Thomas Jefferson, with his lifelong devotion to books and his significant role in the founding of the Library of Congress, is included, as is the avid reader and collector John Adams. Further, this survey is limited to the personal or private collector as opposed to the institutional collector. On that basis, such notable figures as Lyman C. Draper (Wisconsin Historical Society), Clarence S. Brigham (American Antiquarian Society), and William A. Jackson (Harvard University), all of whom developed extraordinary scholarly libraries for their institutions, are not included. Since collectors are often eclectic in their tastes, it was difficult in some cases to separate those who concentrated on books from those who gathered prints, portraits, and drawings. Where books seemed to predominate, the collector was considered. With regret, this meant the exclusion of such remarkable collectors as I. N. P. Stokes and Louis V. Ledoux, who concentrated on prints. Philip D. Sang and James M. Osborn, on the other hand, have been included on the basis of their interest in books as well as in graphic and manuscript materials.

This dictionary may in some cases reflect the available record rather than the true stature of the individual collector. Because some collectors have enjoyed more publicity than others, their entries are likely to be fuller than those of their colleagues who worked quietly and out of the public eye. Therefore, the length of the entries does not necessarily reflect the importance of the collector. Finally, as with any biographical reference work of this scope, some worthy collectors will have been overlooked. The author would be glad to know of such omissions for a future edition.

The information provided in the narrative discussions is intended to identify the collector's chief areas of interest, to describe how those interests developed, and, where possible, to indicate the influence the collector and collection may have had. This approach should be useful to librarians, collectors, curators, and individuals in the book trade who wish to identify prominent American collectors. When a sketch mentions another collector who is discussed in a separate entry, an asterisk (*) is placed after the name as a cross reference. Sale prices have been included selectively in order to give a sense of book values at a particular time. They are samples only and in no way constitute a price guide. In the same way, individual titles within a particular library have been mentioned to give a sense of the collection as a whole. The sketches have been written for both the interested amateur and the advanced scholar.

Each entry consists of three complementary sections: a brief biographical synopsis, a narrative discussion, and a selective bibliography. The biographical information includes birth and death dates as this information was found to be available in standard sources. Educational background has been limited to notation of earned degrees. The auction sale information given under "Collection Disposition" was gathered from George McKay's *American Book Auction Catalogues 1713–1934* and William Hallam Webber's privately printed *An Alphabetical List of the Named Book Auction Sales as Recorded by the American Book Prices Current from the Beginning of 1935 to August 1982* and includes the names of auction houses and sale dates. Only the first day of the sale is given, although in many cases sales continued over several days. In the bibliographic notes, Part A entries include both printed catalogs of the collection and selected books and articles by the collector about his own collection or collecting in general. Part B entries provide secondary references about the collector. In order to conserve space, no more than six representative citations have been included in Part A. Notices of obituaries are included only when more substantive information is lacking.

Many librarians, curators, and bookdealers have contributed unselfishly to the preparation of this text. I am particularly indebted to a number of people who examined the draft list of collectors and made comments and suggestions. They include:

W. H. Bond, Librarian Emeritus, The Houghton Library, Harvard University, Cambridge, Massachusetts

Herbert Cahoon, Curator of Autograph Manuscripts, The Pierpont Morgan Library, New York, New York

Thomas P. Clarke, Consultant, Sotheby Parke Bernet, Inc., New York, New York

Glen Dawson, Dawson's Book Shop, Los Angeles, California

Frances Hamill, Hamill and Barker, Chicago, Illinois

Paul S. Koda, The School of Library and Information Science, Catholic University of America, Washington, D.C.

Herman W. Liebert, Librarian Emeritus, The Beinecke Rare Book and Manuscript Library, Yale University, New Haven, Connecticut

Marcus A. McCorison, Director and Librarian, American Antiquarian Society, Worcester, Massachusetts

Ellen Shaffer, Curator, Silverado Museum, Saint Helena, California

Madeleine B. Stern, Rostenberg and Stern, New York, New York

Decherd Turner, Director, Harry Ransom Humanities Research Center, University of Texas, Austin, Texas

In addition, I am grateful for the assistance and encouragement provided by William R. Cagle (Indiana University, Lilly Library), Edwin H. Carpenter (Pasadena, California), James Gilreath (Library of Congress), Lucille V. Miller (Ventura, California), Father William Monihan (University of San Francisco),

Lawrence Clark Powell (Tucson, Arizona), Robert Rosenthal (University of Chicago), Judy H. Sahak (Scripps College), Wilbur J. Smith (Los Angeles, California), Daniel Traister (University of Pennsylvania), Alexander D. Wainwright (Princeton University), Edwin Wolf II (Library Company of Philadelphia), and Jake Zeitlin (Zeitlin and Ver Brugge). I could not have located many of the facts in this volume without access to materials in the library of the Grolier Club of New York, nor could I have interpreted them without the cordial assistance of Robert Nikirk and his library staff. I appreciate the support provided by the University of Arizona in granting me a sabbatical leave for the fall term of the 1981-1982 academic year and for providing travel funds through the Humanities Research Grants Committee. I owe special thanks to Herman W. Liebert, who read drafts of the sketches of the Yale collectors, and to my colleague Margaret F. Maxwell, who read several portions of the text. The work could not have been completed without the aid of a number of graduate assistants, including Jean Dickinson, Hiroshi Nakajima, Mark Labdon, George Pilling, Robert Sorgenfrie, and especially Jean Heiss, who helped correct the draft. The final typing was accomplished with devotion by Patricia Walz and Adela Zubiate-Rodarte. My final and deepest thanks goes to my family, who tolerated and even expressed interest in American book collectors over a prolonged period of time. In the last analysis, the author takes full responsibility for the text. The preparation of this volume has been both a pleasure and a challenge.

DICTIONARY OF
AMERICAN BOOK
COLLECTORS

Introduction

Book collecting in America has had a long and diverse history. In the beginning, during colonial times, collecting was entirely the preserve of the wealthy. Collectors were almost without exception upper-class professionals—physicians, clergymen, politicians, and landowners. These men brought books with them from England and, once settled on their Virginia plantations or in their Boston pulpits, ordered titles from dealers in London and Paris. The eighteenth-century libraries of William Byrd of Virginia, Thomas Prince of Boston, and James Logan of Philadelphia were typical of what could be done at that time with money and taste. Byrd's collection, for example, included history, religion, philosophy, European literature, and well-edited versions of the Greek and Roman classics. Logan went beyond these traditional fields and added landmarks from the various scientific disciplines. The Prince library was composed chiefly of theological works and philosophy.

An emphasis on collecting works on European history and culture prevailed until the middle of the nineteenth century, when a few individuals started to pay more attention to American history. By 1865 three active and well-informed collectors—John Carter Brown, James Lenox, and George Brinley—had formed distinguished libraries of Americana. These men took collecting seriously, understood the international book market, and had a thorough knowledge of bibliography. Working with London-based dealers like Obadiah Rich and Henry Stevens, they bought books, pamphlets, and maps that traced the opening of the American continent and the growth of the individual colonies.

While Brinley, Lenox, and Logan were completing their impressive libraries, a new breed of collector began to emerge. These men had different interests from their aristocratic forebears and came from a wider social and professional milieu. Rush C. Hawkins, a military man, collected incunabula; George Ticknor, a Harvard professor, brought together a great library of Spanish and Portuguese literature; Thomas Dowse, a leather-dresser, concentrated on New England history. In his *Private Libraries of New York*, published in 1860, James Wynne described fifty-one collections brought together by a diverse group of lawyers, doctors, and merchants. By the beginning of the 1880s, Charles W. Frederickson and Thomas P. Barton had formed splendid Shakespearean libraries, while William H. Arnold and Charles B. Foote began to show what might be done with American literature.

One factor that had a strong influence on nineteenth-century collecting was the expansion of the auction business. While a few firms could trace their beginnings back to the early decades of the century, major growth in this area occurred after 1850. The New York firm of George A. Leavitt first offered books for sale in 1857, and Boston auctioneer Charles F. Libbie began his business early in 1878. In the forefront of all this activity stood New York bookseller Joseph Sabin. His influence on book collecting in America during the last decades of the nineteenth century was pervasive. In addition to his chief calling as a bookseller, he was active as an auctioneer, an editor, and a bibliographer. The first twelve volumes of the *Dictionary of Books Relating to America* are a monument to Sabin's energy and knowledge. In addition, he compiled the superb catalog for the William Menzies sale of 1876 and presided over the first three sessions of the George Brinley sales held between 1879 and 1881. For many bibliophiles the high point of the century came on Thursday evening, April 7, 1881, when Sabin sold the Brinley copy of the Gutenberg Bible to New York lawyer Hamilton Cole for $8,000.

While the increased activity of the auction houses aided in the dispersal of books, the emergence of book clubs provided an important setting for socialization and the exchange of information on the book arts. The constitution of the Grolier Club of New York, written in 1884, declared the purpose of that organization to be the "literary study and promotion of the arts pertaining to the production of books, including the occasional publication of books, designed to illustrate, promote and encourage those arts." In the ten years following the formation of the Grolier Club, similar societies sprang up in Boston (the Club of Odd Volumes, 1886), Cleveland (the Rowfant Club, 1892), Philadelphia (the Philobiblon Club, 1894), and Chicago (the Caxton Club, 1895). Through exhibitions, publications, and lectures these organizations provided a stimulating environment for collectors, publishers, bibliographers, and librarians.

Perhaps the most influential collector of the post–Civil War era was industrialist and first president of the Grolier Club, Robert Hoe III. His distinguished library of English and European literature was augmented by impressive gatherings of manuscripts and early printing. The sale of the Hoe library, which took place between 1911 and 1912 and netted almost $2 million, was a landmark occasion. As with the Brinley sale thirty years earlier, the most dramatic moment came with the sale of the Gutenberg Bible. The irrepressible New York bookdealer George D. Smith secured the prize for Henry E. Huntington with a bid of $50,000. Book collecting in America had come of age.

Before Huntington's name had become a byword in the auction rooms, John Pierpont Morgan and Henry Clay Folger had been making major purchases both in England and in America. Morgan, with the first-rate bibliographical advice of his shrewd and scholarly librarian Belle da Costa Greene, bought outstanding collections of manuscripts, early printing, and literature. Working quietly, Folger constructed one of the world's greatest Shakespeare libraries. In 1924 the Morgan collections became a public institution under a board of trustees, and eight years later the handsome Folger Shakespeare Library opened its doors to scholars.

While a number of dealers helped Morgan and Folger amass their collections, none was more knowledgeable and important than A. S. W. Rosenbach. With his infectious optimism, sure sense of the market, and rich knowledge of books and manuscripts, he was able to buy and sell rarities at prices unheard of by his competitors. Between 1920 and 1940 Rosenbach established himself in many minds as the greatest bookseller of them all. Some of his success can be attributed to his wide range of devoted friends, many of whom were also good customers. Among his supporters from academia were such prominent figures as Chauncey Brewster Tinker of Yale and Randolph P. Adams of the William L. Clements Library at the University of Michigan. Other supporters included the enthusiastic A. Edward Newton and a galaxy of distinguished private collectors: Herschel V. Jones, John Hinsdale Scheide, Lessing J. Rosenwald, Estelle Doheny, Carl H. Pforzheimer, Frank J. Hogan, Owen D. Young, Harry E. Widener, and William M. Elkins. Many of these collectors also ordered from Gabriel Wells and Lathrop Harper in New York, Charles Sessler in Philadelphia, Charles Goodspeed in Boston, Ernest Dawson in Los Angeles, and the firms of Quaritch and Maggs in London, to mention only a few of the better-known shops.

Although the secondhand-book trade had become geographically diversified by the 1920s, the book auction business remained centered in New York and London. When important libraries came on the market, their sale was usually conducted under the auspices of the American Art Association or the Anderson Galleries. In 1929 the Anderson Galleries obtained the Jerome Kern library and staged what was called the sale of the century. Kern, an extraordinarily successful popular composer, had started to collect rare books and manuscripts around 1915 and in ten years had amassed one of the great high-point libraries of the century. He owned mouth-watering rarities by Poe, Dickens, Hardy, Lamb, Shelley, Keats, and most of the other nineteenth- and twentieth-century English and American literary giants. By 1929, having grown tired of the world of books, he decided to sell. In a never-to-be-forgotten buying spree, dealers and collectors vied with each other to secure the Kern rarities. Prices spiraled upward until buyers paid ten to twenty times Kern's original purchase prices. When it was all over, Kern had netted some $1,739,000 on an original investment of $500,000. It was a high water mark and would remain so for many years.

In the decade following the Kern sale, the period of the economic depression, rare book prices dropped to mere fractions of their worth. Even auctions of the well-publicized libraries of such enthusiastic connoisseurs as A. Edward Newton and Frank J. Hogan failed to stir much interest. About this same time, however, another type of collector began to make an impression on the American antiquarian book market—the scholarly buyer with a knowledge of bibliography and a determined preference for perfect copies. The astute Samuel Johnson collectors Donald and Mary Hyde represented this approach, as did Lessing J. Rosenwald, Arthur Houghton, Morris L. Parrish, and Carroll A. Wilson. Perhaps the publication in 1934 of John Carter and Graham Pollard's analytical *An Enquiry into the Nature of Certain Nineteenth Century Pamphlets,* an unmasking of the Thomas J. Wise forgeries, made collectors a bit more cautious. In any case, by 1940 book collecting in America had taken another step toward maturity.

While many collectors arranged to sell their libraries at auction, others channeled their books directly to public institutions through gift or purchase. Starting with John Harvard's gift to the newly founded college in Cambridge, Massachusetts, in 1638, the record of support provided to American libraries by knowledgeable collectors has been long and honorable. Although no brief list can begin to reveal the extent of distinguished institutional collections started by private individuals, the names of Edward E. Ayer (Newberry Library), Edwin J. and Frederick W. Beinecke (Yale University), James Ford Bell (University of Minnesota), Elmer Belt (University of California at Los Angeles), Albert A. Berg (New York Public Library), John Carter Brown (Brown University), Alfred C. Chapin (Williams College), William L. Clements (University of Michigan), DeCoursey Fales (City College of New York), Horace H. Furness, Sr. (University of Pennsylvania), Wilmarth S. Lewis (Yale University), Josiah K. Lilly (Indiana University), George Herbert Palmer (Wellesley College), Morris L. Parrish (Princeton University), Lessing J. Rosenwald (Library of Congress), Henry R. Wagner (Yale University, Huntington Library, Pomona College), and Harry E. Widener (Harvard University) will serve to indicate the range and significance of this movement.

The diversity that characterized collecting in the first fifty years of the twentieth century was magnified and extended during the next thirty-five years. Collectors turned their attention to children's books, science fiction, westerns, detective fiction, and ethnic materials. Bibliographies were developed on many of these topics, making the collector's task easier. Auctions continued to flourish. The Thomas W. Streeter sale of western Americana (1966-1969), with net receipts of over $3 million, was an obvious landmark. Influential dealers like Hans P. Kraus scoured the international market to bring early printed works and rare manuscripts to the attention of affluent collectors. On another level, C. Glenn Carrington, a New York social worker with only a modest income and working independently, built a remarkable library on black culture.

Book collecting continues to flourish in America in spite of fluctuating economic factors, unfavorable tax laws, and problems associated with the channels of distribution. The pleasures that attracted William Byrd, Thomas Prince, and James Logan in the eighteenth century still exert a powerful magnetic force. In his essay "American Book Collectors," in *Book Collecting and Scholarship*

(Minneapolis: University of Minnesota Press, 1954), historian Louis B. Wright sounded an appropriate note of praise for American collectors. "The United States," he said, "owes a vast debt to book collectors, a debt far greater than the average citizen realizes. For the devoted book collectors of our country have contributed enormously to the cultural development of the nation and they have made possible scholarship and learning which we could not have had without their libraries. They deserve to rank with the founders of colleges and universities as public benefactors."

A

ADAM, Robert B. (b. July 7, 1863, Loughborough, Scotland; d. April 11, 1940, Buffalo, N.Y.). *Collection Disposition:* Anderson, February 15, 1926; Yale University; Rosenbach Foundation.

The son of a Scottish schoolteacher, Adam came to the United States in 1872. He settled in Buffalo, New York, with his uncle Robert Adam and eventually adopted the uncle's name. The elder Adam was a prosperous collector of works by Robert Burns, Samuel Johnson, John Ruskin, and other major English literary figures, and soon he imbued his nephew with bookish tastes. Together they worked on extra-illustrating such sets as George B. Hill's editions of Boswell's *Life of Johnson* and *Johnsonian Miscellanies*. After the death of his uncle in 1904, Adam sold the Burns books and manuscripts to A. S. W. Rosenbach* and gave his notable Ruskin and James Hogg materials to Yale. All this was necessary to make room for books and manuscripts by Johnson and his circle. In 1921 Adam issued a one-volume catalog of his Johnson holdings but immediately began to plan for a more ambitious work. Eight years later his catalog was published in four volumes by the Oxford University Press with an introduction by A. Edward Newton*. Hard times fell on Adam during the depression, and for a number of years his books rested in a bank vault as security for a loan. In 1948 the entire collection was sold to Johnson collectors Donald and Mary Hyde*.

Throughout his collecting life Adam was a respected member of the inner circle of bookmen who were customers of Rosenbach. This amiable group included at that time such bibliophiles as Jerome Kern*, Charles Osgood, Chauncey Brewster Tinker*, and Newton. Adam's Johnson collection was recognized by these connoisseurs as perhaps the finest in private hands in the United States. In all matters relating to books and collections, Adam was a generous and knowledgeable individual. His catalogs and his gifts to Yale assure him a secure place among notable collectors of the early twentieth century.

10 ADAMS, JOHN

Bibliography

A. *Catalogue of the Johnson Collection* (Buffalo, 1921); *The R. B. Adam Library Relating to Dr. Samuel Johnson and His Era* (Oxford, 1929); *Works, Letters, and Manuscripts of James Hogg* (Buffalo, 1930).

B. Cannon, 223-224; *Grolier 75*, 121-123; Wolf and Fleming, 209-211, 242-243; Robert French, "The R. B. Adam Collection of Ruskin," *YLG*, July 1929, 1-7; Frederick Pierce, "James Hogg, the 'Ettrick Shepherd'," *YLG*, January 1931, 37-41.

ADAMS, John (b. October 19, 1735, Quincy, Mass.; d. July 4, 1826, Quincy, Mass.). *Education:* A. B., Harvard College, 1755. *Collection Disposition:* Boston Public Library; Boston Athenaeum; Adams Mansion.

From the time he was a young man, books played an important part in Adams' life. He learned both Greek and Latin and enjoyed the works of Herodotus, Thucydides, and Tacitus in the original. Besides the historians, he read and collected the complete works of the classical poets and philosophers—Plato, Homer, Aristotle, Ovid, Lucretius, Cicero, and Marcus Aurelius. He owned legal texts to support his professional practice, and standard treatises on government and history to provide background reading. Adams had standard works on English history and comparable volumes for Spain, Russia, the Netherlands, Sweden, Portugal, and France. While living in Paris, Adams acquired a diverse collection of books by the leading political thinkers of the day—Bolingbroke, Rousseau, Voltaire, Turgot, and Condorcet. It is quite likely, as suggested by Zoltán Haraszti, that the Adams library of eighteenth-century social philosophy may have been the best in America. Adams was a great reader, and the extant copies of his books show margins and flyleaves covered with notes and arguments. If social philosophy took first place in the Adams library, religion ran a close second. He owned the writings of the early church fathers, eighteenth-century tracts and sermons, and a wide selection of Bibles. A note in the published catalog of his library indicates that he occasionally borrowed theological books from the Thomas Prince* collection in the Old South Church, and since several of the "Adams' books" contain the Old South bookplate, it seems obvious that he borrowed without always remembering to return. The study of religious controversy, he once wrote Thomas Jefferson*, had occupied his thoughts for more than sixty years.

When Adams left Washington, D.C., in 1801 and returned to Quincy, his library became his solace and reward. It supplied him with a flood of references and opinions, which he communicated regularly and forcefully to his friends Benjamin Rush and Jefferson. In 1822, wishing to establish a Greek and Latin school in Quincy, he gave the town his books, "excepting a few that I shall reserve for my consolation in the few days that remain to me." After several transfers, some 3,000 books were moved to the Boston Public Library to make them more accessible to scholars. Other volumes remained in the Adams Mansion in Quincy, and a few went to the Boston Athenaeum. With catholic tastes and an inquiring mind, Adams built one of the largest personal libraries in colonial New England.

Bibliography

B. *DAB* 1, 72-82; *NCAB* 2, 1-5; Zoltán Haraszti, *John Adams and the Prophets of Progress* (Cambridge, Mass., 1952), 14-24; A. S. W. Rosenbach, *A Book Hunter's Holiday* (Boston, 1936), 139-142.

ADLER, Elmer (b. July 22, 1884, Rochester, N.Y.; d. January 11, 1962, San Juan, P.R.). *Collection Disposition:* Princeton University; La Casa del Libro, San Juan.

The *Dictionary of American Biography* identified Adler's various vocations as collector, printer, publisher, and bibliophile. He was also a teacher and a curator. While managing advertising for the family clothing business, Adler developed a taste for beauty in the printed word. This took a more serious form in 1920, when he arranged a successful exhibition on the history of printing at the Rochester Memorial Art Gallery. Two years later Adler moved to New York and launched the Pynson Printers, a small company dedicated to quality graphic work. Adler's own library, including samples from five centuries of fine printing, served as a reference collection for the brave new venture. After an uncertain beginning the Pynson Printers developed a host of important friends. Commissions came from Alfred A. Knopf and H. L. Mencken. Designers and graphic artists provided critical acclaim in the typographical journals. One of the most important products of the Pynson Printers was *The Colophon: A Book Collector's Quarterly*, issued from 1930 to 1940 and again from 1948 to 1950. *The Colophon*, with its Adlerian emphasis on quality, was an aesthetic success but a commercial failure. When the war forced it to cease publication, Adler went to Princeton to carry on his crusade for tasteful printing. There, with the support of the Friends of the Library, he established the Department of Graphic Arts, the basis of which was the Adler book and print collection, rich with examples from the shops of Peter Schoeffer, Wynkyn de Worde, Aldus Manutius, Nicolas Jenson, John Baskerville, and Bruce Rogers. He arranged seminars, gave lectures, and organized exhibitions for students and faculty on the history of the book, graphic processes, and book collecting.

The last stage of Adler's quest for aesthetic graphic expression took place in Puerto Rico. While visiting in San Juan he was asked for advice on the directions that might be taken in the development of fine printing in that country. The bait was more than Adler could resist. For the last seven years of his life he was the guiding spirit for a new printing museum in San Juan called La Casa del Libro. He gave books and manuscripts, urged his friends to do the same, and involved the government and local businesses in a variety of support activities. Within four years La Casa del Libro had a representative collection of some 4,000 volumes of fine printing, with emphasis on Spanish history and culture. Through his varied contributions over a period of forty years, Adler is remembered as an energetic promoter of all that is associated with quality in the graphic arts.

Bibliography

A. "So You're a Collector!" *The Colophon*, January 1932; "Adventure by Design," *PLC*, November 1943, 27-29; *An Informal Talk at the University of Kansas* (Los Angeles, 1954).

B. Paul Bennett, *Elmer Adler in the World of Books* (New York, 1964); Philip Duschnes, "Elmer Adler—Visionary," *AB*, August 20, 1962, 627-628; Al Hine, "Bookman in San Juan," *Harper's*, February 1962, 25-27; Paul Johnson, "Elmer Adler: The Pynson Printers," *PW*, March 7, 1931, 1183–1189; Lawrence Thompson, "Forty Mercer Street," *PLC*, November 1940, 27-34; John Winterich, "Man About the House," *PLC*, November 1947, 13-16.

ALDIS, Owen F. (b. June 6, 1852, Saint Albans, Vt.; d. August 5, 1925, Paris, France). *Education:* A.B., Yale University, 1874; J.D., Columbia University, 1876. *Collection Disposition:* Yale University.

After practicing law for a short time, Aldis moved to Chicago and founded a successful real estate firm. His book-collecting activities began around 1890 and focused on American literature. In order to develop his collection along systematic lines, Aldis placed the bulk of his orders in the hands of P. K. Foley, noted Boston bookseller. Foley's *American Authors 1795-1895* provided the bibliographical information Aldis required to build his library. The avid collector and knowledgeable dealer worked together in perfect harmony. Aldis prepared extensive want lists which Foley used to develop advertisements for newspapers and journals. Foley often shipped as many as 100 books a month to his Chicago customer. Beginning in 1909 Aldis shifted some of his business to Walter Hill of Chicago, principally to take advantage of the Jacob C. Chamberlain* and Frank Maier* auctions. Shortly after these sales, Aldis, whose eyesight was failing, decided to turn his collections over to Yale University. The gift was not without conditions, however, since Aldis wanted nothing less than first-class treatment for his treasures. He requested a separate room, a curator, and specially built protective shelving. Beyond that, Aldis wanted all the American literature in the library moved to one location to supplement his collection. Although the Yale staff was understandably reluctant to make such a move, they did transfer certain authors into the designated Aldis area. As a result, the American literature collection took on great depth and strength. Such authors as Cooper, Whitman, and Lowell were represented by their complete works and by an extensive body of pertinent criticism. Aldis understood the importance of research materials for the working scholar. His contributions gave Yale a strong start in the formation of one of the country's greatest holdings of American literature.

Bibliography

B. *NCAB* 44, 292; Donald Gallup, "Aldis, Foley, and the Collection of American Literature at Yale," *PBSA*, 1st Q 1943, 41-49.

ALLAN, John (b. February 26, 1777, Kilbarie, Scotland; d. November 19, 1863, New York, N.Y.). *Collection Disposition:* Bangs, May 2, 1864.

Allan came to the United States from Scotland at the age of seventeen. He followed a career as an import agent for woolens and whiskey. His collecting specialties included Robert Burns, Thomas Dibdin, American history, and extra-illustrated books. One of his choice rarities was a magnificent morocco-bound copy of John Eliot's "Indian Bible," one of the few with a dedication from the compiler. Among fellow collectors Allan was known to have a genuine passion for his hobby. On one occasion, according to an anecdote, collecting may have saved his life. Seriously ill with quinsy, Allan was shocked to overhear his friends talking about how they would divide up his library when he died. Allan's rage was so complete that it burst the threatening abscess in his throat, causing the fever to subside. This was just as his friends had planned. When Allan died several years later his library was carefully cataloged by bookseller Joseph Sabin and sold by Bangs auction house in New York. His Eliot Bible, the first to be sold at auction in the United States, brought $850, while an extraordinary extra-illustrated copy of *Knickerbocker History of New York* went for $1,250. In all, the sale netted a very satisfactory $40,000. Allan was an enthusiastic amateur collector more interested in highly decorative formats than in bibliographic niceties.

Bibliography

B. Wynne, 1-14; Evert Duyckinck, *Memorial to John Allan* (New York, 1864).

ALTSCHUL, Frank (b. April 21, 1887, San Francisco, Calif.; d. May 29, 1981, San Francisco, Calif.). *Education:* A.B., Yale University, 1908. *Collection Disposition:* Yale University.

Throughout his professional life Altschul was closely associated with international trade and economics, first as a partner in the banking firm of Lazard Frères and later as a writer and president of the Council of Foreign Relations. His other side was literary and bibliographic. While a student at Yale he was influenced by the dynamic English professor Chauncey Brewster Tinker* and became deeply interested in book collecting and printing. He started with the English novelist George Meredith but soon enlarged his interests to include incunabula and French illustrated books from the sixteenth to the eighteenth centuries. Many of his important purchases were made through the Rosenbach firm in Philadelphia, an organization which he served as a financial adviser. Frequently the dual roles of Rosenbach customer and Rosenbach adviser worked to Altschul's advantage. In 1923, for example, when Rosenbach purchased the famous Roederer library of French illustrated books, Altschul was given first choice from the collection as a reward for securing a loan through Lazard Frères.

Not satisfied with merely gathering a personal collection, Altschul became one of the most energetic supporters of the Yale Library. In 1924, after hearing a Tinker speech exhorting the alumni to help secure rare books, Altschul established an endowment fund in his own name and organized an active support group called the Yale Library Associates. Seven years later he turned over his extensive collection of Meredith books, manuscripts, and letters to the library. Over the years his support never wavered. His gifts of incunabula and early printing— among which were Euclid's *Elements*, printed by Erhard Ratdolt in 1482, and Geoffroy Tory's magnificent *Champfleury* (1529)—form a distinguished section of the Beinecke Rare Book and Manuscript Library at Yale. He also acquired contemporary works. His collection representing the modern French book arts was notable for its inclusion of such masters as Auguste Lepère, Jacques Beltrand, and François-Louis Schmied. Individual volumes in this collection were distinguished for their excellence in typography and their decorated hand-bindings. Altschul also presented Yale with the complete working archive of the Overbrook Press, a printing establishment he owned and directed for more than twenty-five years. Along with those books he included his extensive personal library, which consisted of the outstanding products of the British and American fine press movement of the twentieth century. This included long runs of the books of the Kelmscott, Doves, Nonesuch, Gregynog, and Cuala presses, as well as representative works by such eminent designers as Bruce Rogers, D. B. Updike, and W. A. Dwiggins. Because of his varied interests and unlimited enthusiasm, it would be difficult to isolate Altschul's chief contribution to Yale. It is enough to say that he collected and gave with great generosity and good taste.

Bibliography

A. *A Catalogue of the Altschul Collection of George Meredith in the Yale University Library* (New Haven, 1931); *The Overbrook Press Bibliography 1934–1959* (Stamford, Conn., 1959); "Laudemus Vivos Gloriosos" (reprint of letter to Chauncey Brewster Tinker suggesting the founding of a library support group), *YLG*, October 1964, 90–92.

B. Wolf and Fleming, passim; Thomas Marston, "Early Printed Books from the Collection of Frank Altschul," *YLG*, January 1959, 87–90; Wyman Parker, "The Altschul Book Bequest," *YLG*, April 1983, 138–144; Dale Roylance and Donald Gallup, "The Altschul Collection: The Arts of the French Book 1838–1967," *YLG*, October 1969, 45– 102; Norman Strouse, "The Overbrook Press: An Example of Collecting in Depth," *QNLBCC*, Summer 1976, 51–64.

AMES, Oakes (b. 1874, North Easton, Mass.; d. 1950, Boston, Mass.). *Education:* A.B., A.M., Harvard University, 1898, 1899. *Collection Disposition:* Harvard University.

From his early college days Ames had been intensely interested in flowering plants. Although his father and grandfather had been successful businessmen, Ames chose to devote his life to teaching and research. His Harvard career spanned forty years and included appointments as Louis Agassiz Professor of Botany and director of the Botanical Museum and the Arnold Arboretum. His own specialty was the scientific study of orchids, an area in which he developed a large library and wrote voluminously. He built a herbarium at his home, a collection containing 64,000 specimens, which with photographs, drawings, and books he turned over to Harvard in 1938. His other collection, books and paintings on economic botany, also went to Harvard. In addition to purely scientific studies, he enjoyed literary works and fine printing. Ames' appreciation for quality bookmaking and his love of reading were pleasantly displayed in "Notes on My Library" and "More Notes on My Library," two charming entries from his journals. Books, were, in his words, "crystalized products of the human brain...to teach the generation that is and the generation to be what is best in life."

Bibliography

A. "Notes on My Library" and "More Notes on My Library," in *Jottings of a Harvard Botanist* (Cambridge, Mass., 1979), 105-111.

B. Pauline Ames Plimpton, "Introduction," in *Jottings of a Harvard Botanist* (Cambridge, Mass., 1979), 1–26.

AMORY, Harcourt (b. 1854; d. November 26, 1925, Boston, Mass.). *Education:* A.B., Harvard University, 1876. *Collection Disposition:* Harvard University.

All Amory's collecting energy went into obtaining the works of nineteenth-century English satirist and mathematician Lewis Carroll. At one time Amory had planned to create carved wooden figures based on the drawings in *Alice in Wonderland* for a toy theater. For that purpose he secured a copy of the rare 1865 edition. Later he turned his attention to Carroll bibliographic rarities, letters, manuscripts, and memorabilia. To fill out the Carroll collection, Amory obtained all the scientific papers and books written under Carroll's real name, Charles Lutwidge Dodgson. Eventually Amory's holdings went to Harvard, providing that institution with one of the finest Carroll collections in the United States.

Bibliography

A. *The Harcourt Amory Collection of Lewis Carroll in the Harvard College Library*, compiled by Flora Livingston (Cambridge, Mass., 1932).

B. "Lewis Carroll," in *The Houghton Library 1942–1967* (Cambridge, Mass., 1967), 76–79; *NYT*, November 28, 1925, 15.

ANDREWS, William Loring (b. September 9, 1837, New York, N.Y.; d. March 21, 1920, New York, N.Y.). *Collection Disposition:* Anderson, April 18, 1921; Yale University.

As a young man, Andrews entered the family leather business, but he retired at the age of forty to write and to pursue his collecting interests. He was devoted to a variety of forms and formats: illuminated manuscripts, maps, prints, fine bindings, illustrated books, and early Aldines and Elzevirs. Andrews also had a lifelong consuming interest in all aspects of the history of New York City. Along with several other members of the Grolier Club, Andrews founded the Society of Iconophiles, a group imbued with a deep feeling of pride for New York. The purpose of this organization was to preserve and record the history of the city by means of pictures and other graphic representations. Andrews' own library provided a number of rare maps and texts, which the Society published in handsome limited editions. In addition to his collecting activities, Andrews was a prolific writer. Between 1865 and 1908 he published thirty-six books, each a study of some aspect of bibliography, collecting, or iconography. The books were written with style and enthusiasm and were carefully executed on rag paper with fine typography and tasteful copperplate illustrations. The finished products were in the highest quality of the bookmaker's art of that time. As one of the most active and articulate collectors of the 1880s, Andrews enjoyed the personal association of those who shared his interests. He was one of the founding members of the Book Fellows' Club in 1881 and three years later helped organize the Grolier Club of New York.

As with any serious collector, Andrews gave considerable thought to the eventual disposition of his library. In *Gossip About Book Collecting* he put his decision in writing: the books that had given him so much pleasure were, on his death, to be distributed in a way that would cheer the hearts of other collectors. Six months before he died, the collection was sold to New York bookseller James Drake and passed from his hands to the Anderson Galleries. Andrews' writing and personal enthusiasm for books gave an important new status to collecting and bibliography.

Bibliography

A. *Gossip About Book Collecting* (New York, 1900); *Jean Grolier and his Library* (New York, 1892); *The Old Book Sellers of New York and Other Papers* (New York, 1895); *Sextodecimos et Infra* (New York, 1895); "Vagaries of Book Collecting," *The Lamp*, March 1903, 102-209; *Catalogue of the William Loring Andrews Collection of Early Books in Yale University* (New York, 1913).

B. *DAB* 2, 299; *NCAB* 13, 347; Cannon, 144-146; *Grolier* 75, 15-17; Robert Nikirk, "Two American Book Collectors of the Nineteenth Century: William Loring Andrews and Beverly Chew," in *Book Buying and Book Selling* (Chicago, 1978); "In Memoriam William Loring Andrews," *Yearbook of the Grolier Club* (New York, 1921).

ARENTS, George (b. May 7, 1885, New York, N.Y.; d. December 14, 1960, New York, N.Y.). *Collection Disposition:* New York Public Library; Syracuse University.

After completing his junior year at Columbia University, Arents joined the American Tobacco Company, where his father was an executive officer. Subsequently he held major offices in the International Cigar Company and the American Machine and Foundry Company. Early in his career Arents began to collect books, periodicals, pamphlets, and manuscripts on all phases of the history of tobacco. These publications spanned the centuries and contained information from all parts of the world. Many items in the collection document the spread of smoking in the late sixteenth century and the resulting controversy over harmful effects on the body. The debate raged in the seventeenth century, as shown by such publications as King James' *A Counterblaste to Tobacco* (1604) and the pro-tobacco tracts of such well-known literary figures as Ben Jonson and Sir

John Beaumont. In addition to these fiery declarations, the collection held a wide variety of materials on tobacco-growing and the tobacco trade. As if to balance the serious content of the collection, Arents also gathered over 125,000 cigarette cards and countless drawings, prints, and sketches relating to smoking. In 1943 the entire archive was turned over to the New York Public Library along with a sizable endowment for continuing support. The library provided the collection with special rooms, a curator, and a series of carefully documented bibliographies.

In addition to the vast tobacco library, Arents gave the New York Public Library a unique collection of books originally issued in parts. The guiding principle here was prior appearance of the books as serials in a newspaper or magazine. A large portion of the titles represent the work of such well-known Victorians as Trollope, Scott, and Dickens. Arents also had a good collection of the nineteenth-century English caricaturists, with representative works by Rowlandson, Leech, and "Phiz." In addition to the handsome gifts presented to the New York Public Library, Arents gave generously to Syracuse University. A book-collecting medal is named in his honor, as is the university library's rare book room. Arents' contributions to libraries were many and varied, but preeminent among them was the development of the tobacco collection. He will be remembered as an intelligent collector who documented one of man's most prevalent social habits.

Bibliography

A. *Tobacco: Its History Illustrated by the Books, Manuscripts, and Engravings in the Library of George Arents Jr.*, edited by Jerome Brooks (New York, 1937–1943); "Book Collecting—As I Have Found It," *BNYPL*, April 1954, 162–166; "Where There's Smoke, There's Literature," *PBSA*, 1st Q 1941, 145–150.

B. *NCAB* E, 334; Jerome E. Brooks, "The Library Relating to Tobacco Collected by George Arents," *BNYPL*, January 1944, 3–15; Sarah Dickson, "The Arents Collection of Books in Parts and Associated Literature," *BNYPL*, June 1956, 267–280; Helmut Lehmann-Haupt, "English Literature in the Collection of George Arents," *The Colophon*, February 1940, 23–47; "Arents Tobacco Collection," in *Guide to the Research Collections of the New York Public Library*, compiled by Sam Williams (Chicago, 1975), 293–295.

ARMOUR, George Allison (b. 1855, Chicago, Ill.; d. June 8, 1936, Princeton, N.J.). *Education:* A.B., Princeton University, 1877. *Collection Disposition:* American Art—Anderson, April 22, 1937.

Upon graduating from Princeton, Armour studied law but never entered practice. He was much more interested in collecting books and manuscripts. In 1895 he was one of fifteen prominent Chicago citizens active in the founding of the Caxton Club, an organization devoted to the appreciation of fine printing. His literary tastes clustered around the works of Spenser, Shakespeare, Milton, Wordsworth, and Shelley. For example, he acquired Keats' own set of Shakespeare with the poet's marginal notes and comments. He also collected works from the Kelmscott and Doves presses, fine bindings, and books designed by Bruce Rogers.

He was a friend of Chicago collector John Henry Wrenn*, through whom he became acquainted with Thomas J. Wise. Although he bought some books from Wise, he avoided the fabricated first editions sold by the nefarious bibliographer to other American collectors. Armour's valuable library was dispersed after his death at auction in New York.

Bibliography

B. *Letters of Thomas J. Wise to John Henry Wrenn*, edited by Fannie E. Ratchford (New York, 1944), passim; Andrew A. West, "The Armour Library," in *American Art Association Catalogue 4323* (New York, 1937); *NYT*, June 9, 1936, 24.

ARMSTRONG, A. Joseph (b. March 29, 1873, Louisville, Ky.; d. March 31, 1954, Waco, Tex.). *Education:* A.B., A.M., Wabash College, 1902, 1904; Ph.D., University of Pennsylvania, 1908. *Collection Disposition:*Baylor University.

In 1912 Armstrong was hired as head of the Department of English at Baylor University in Waco, Texas. Through previous experience at Illinois Wesleyan and Georgetown College in Kentucky, he had established himself as an able teacher and a Robert Browning enthusiast. As early as 1905 he began to build a personal library of Browning materials: books, pamphlets, critical material, volumes from Browning's own library, and even furniture from Browning's home. In 1918, when the materials began to outgrow his shelves, Armstrong presented the collection to the Baylor Library, there establishing a "Browning Room." Armstrong's advocacy of the Baylor collection spread through his promotion of Browning societies, his own publications, extensive correspondence with other Browning scholars, and worldwide travel. He focused so much attention on the Texas depository that many important volumes came in the form of gifts. The 1923 senior class provided the funds for the purchase of an important series of Browning's letters, and a Waco businessman gave the library money to buy the first edition of *Pauline*, a long-sought rarity. By 1940 the collection had again outgrown its facility, and Armstrong began to promote the idea of a separate library building. Through the support of Baylor alumni and the board of trustees, a handsome "Armstrong-Browning Library and Museum" was dedicated in 1951. This structure, with carved bronze entrance doors, stained-glass windows, and a sizable gathering of Browning books, manuscripts, and letters, is a tribute to both the collector and the poet.

Bibliography

B. *NCAB* 46, 20; Lois Douglas, *Through Heaven's Back Door* (Waco, Tex., 1951); Cherie Rayburn, "Baylor and Browning," *The Baylor Line*, September 1980, 16–19.

ARNOLD, William H. (b. March 18, 1854, Poughkeepsie, N.Y.; d. January 2, 1923, Nutley, N.J.). *Collection Disposition:* Bangs, January 30, May 7, 1901; Anderson, November 10, 1924.

In order to understand Arnold fully, one must recognize his contributions as a bookdealer, author, collector, and bibliographer. According to his autobiographical *Ventures in Book Collecting*, he worked in the book trade for many years with little interest in personal collecting. All this changed in 1888, when he moved to New York and joined the Grolier Club. There he was exposed to the influence of a number of knowledgeable bookmen. He started to obtain catalogs from all over the world and to buy first editions of prominent American and British literary figures: Thoreau, Emerson, Holmes, Whittier, Tennyson, and the Brownings. He bought only books in fine condition, preferring those in original bindings. In *First Report of a Book Collector*, published in 1897, Arnold described the joys of collecting and the ways of bookdealers and auctioneers. Along with printed first editions, Arnold managed to accumulate a number of significant letters and manuscripts, particularly those of Irving, Keats, and Shelley. His collecting acumen was confirmed when he offered his rarities at auction in 1901 and received many times the original purchase prices. Hawthorne's *Fanshawe*, for example, which Arnold had obtained for $200, sold for double that price, while the manuscript of Emerson's *Threnody* returned ten times Arnold's original investment. As soon as his first library was sold, Arnold took up collecting again with renewed vigor. This time he concentrated on autographed material, manuscripts, and limited "trial editions" by such noted figures as Kipling, Keats, and Tennyson. The Tennyson collection gave him the most pleasure and was perhaps the most distinguished gathering in his library. Many of these precious acquisitions came to him through negotiations with British bibliographer Thomas J. Wise. Arnold's praise for Wise, to whom he referred as his "dear old friend," seems ironic today in view of John Carter and Graham Pollard's *Enquiry*, which exposed Wise as a consummate forger and thief. It was Wise who wrote the flattering "Foreword" to *Ventures in Book Collecting*, Arnold's second book, and Wise who provided faked "trial copies" for the collection. A year and a half after Arnold's death, the Anderson Galleries issued a sumptuous sale catalog of the library enlivened with an introduction by the notable collector Robert B. Adam*. The sale was a success and returned a record $148,723 to the Arnold estate.

Bibliography

A. *First Report of a Book Collector* (New York, 1897); *Ventures in Book Collecting* (New York, 1923).

B. Cannon, 172–176; Ernest Dressel North, "Notes of Rare Books," *The Book Buyer*, March 1901, 134–135; April 1901, 226–227.

ASAY, Edward (b. 1825, Philadelphia, Pa.; d. ?). *Collection Disposition:* Bangs, December 18, 1871; private sale to Theodore Irwin, 1881.

The few known facts concerning Asay's background indicate that he was a minister who turned to law and achieved considerable prominence in that profession. By the time he was forty Asay had gathered a library of some 4,500 volumes on American history and English literature. Among the more important items in his collection were the four Shakespeare folios and eleven of the rare quartos. He also had strong holdings of Dante, Spenser, Milton, and Ben Jonson. When the Chicago fire swept away many important collections Asay was in Europe, but by great good fortune he had stored his books in a safe in New York under the care of bookdealer Joseph Sabin. Shortly after his return to the United States, Asay put his books up for auction. This did not remove him from the market, however; his name continued to appear on sales records as a buyer of Americana and English literature. He was particularly active at the William Menzies* sale of 1876. Five years later, because of increased business pressures, he was forced to sell his library to Theodore Irwin* of Oswego, New York. In his day, Asay was known as one of Chicago's leading collectors.

Bibliography

B. David Gray, "Bibliophilism: The Rare and Unique Books in the Library of Mr. E. G. Asay of Chicago," *American Bibliopolist*, November-December 1874, 165–169; February 1875, 56–59; Robert Rosenthal, "Three Early Book Collectors of Chicago," *Library Quarterly*, July 1983, 371–383.

ASPINWALL, Thomas (b. May 23, 1786, Brookline, Mass.; d. August 11, 1876, Boston, Mass.). *Education:* A.B., Harvard University, 1804. *Collection Disposition:* private sale to Samuel L. M. Barlow, 1863; Leonard, June 3, 1879.

Although Aspinwall's collecting career covered only twenty years, he amassed an impressive library of Americana. In 1815, at the age of twenty-nine, he was appointed American consul at London, and from that vantage point he built his collection. It was a time when materials relating to America were readily available prior to the period of intense competition from such avid collectors as John Carter Brown* and James Lenox*. Aspinwall owned a 1493 "Columbus Letter," a long run of the "Jesuit Relations," and many early New England tracts and legislative journals. He listed all these rare materials in a catalog issued in Paris in 1833, a date that in effect signaled the end of his active buying career. After he returned to the United States, Aspinwall sold the most important portions of his library to New York collector Samuel L. M. Barlow*. This transaction was managed by the famous bibliographer Henry Harrisse*, who brought around 200 items, the cream of the collection, to Barlow's home in the summer of 1864. This was fortunate, because the remainder of the library, some 3,700 volumes, was destroyed in a warehouse fire at Bangs, Merwin and Co., on September 19. A sale of the remaining Aspinwall books took place in Leonard's auction rooms in Boston three years after his death.

Bibliography

B. *Appleton's Cyclopedia of American Biography* 1, 111; Cannon, 103–104.

AUERBACH, Herbert S. (b. October 4, 1882, Salt Lake City, Utah: d. March 19, 1945, Salt Lake City, Utah). *Education:* B.S., M.S., Columbia University, 1905, 1906. *Collection Disposition:* Parke-Bernet, October 27, 1947.

Endowed with an impressive combination of determination and intelligence, Auerbach successfully pursued a number of careers: banking, politics, engineering, merchandising, and writing. As a hobby he began to collect books and manuscripts on the history of Utah, especially items that reflected the Mormon influence. Taking his source material from interviews with pioneers, letters, and early diaries, he wrote a series of well-documented articles on state history for the *Utah Historical Quarterly*. His personal library was particularly strong in primary materials—early newspapers, almanacs, and immigrants' guides. His copy of *The Mormon Way Bill of 1851* by Joseph Cain and Arier Brower was unique in its detailed description of North American Indian culture. He also acquired rare editions of Joseph Smith's works, early Salt Lake City municipal documents, and Californiana. In addition to his own frequent scouting trips, Auerbach relied on bookdealers Charles Everitt and Edward Eberstadt. In the final disposition of his books, Auerbach was specific: they were to be sold at auction to give other collectors the same pleasure he had derived from them. At the sale the standard works on western American history stirred little enthusiasm from the bidders, but the Mormon items drew a satisfactory return. The *Mormon Way Bill*, for example, brought an astounding $3,500, the high water mark of the sale. In his area of specialization Auerbach developed a notable collection that few could challenge.

Bibliography

B. J. C. Alter, "Herbert Auerbach," *Utah Historical Quarterly*, July 1945, v-viii; "The Auerbach Sale," *QNLBCC*, Winter 1947, 21–23.

AVERY, Samuel Putnam (b. March 17, 1822, New York, N.Y.; d. August 11, 1904, New York, N.Y.). *Collection Disposition:* Columbia University; New York Public Library; Grolier Club of New York; Bangs, January 30, 1867; Leavitt, June 3, 1884; Anderson, November 10, 1919.

After working for the American Bank Note Company for several years, Avery opened his own engraving firm in New York. His excellent work brought him to the attention of such leaders of the art world as William Walters and Cornelius Vanderbilt. Walters began to supply Avery with consignments of European prints and paintings, some of the first to appear for sale at auction in the United States. As a result of his growing reputation as a connoisseur, Avery was appointed American art commissioner for the Paris Exposition of 1867. Following that event, he was chosen as one of the General Committee members for the development of the Metropolitan Museum of Art and asked to serve as one of the original trustees of the New York Public Library. While associated with the library, he was instrumental in founding the Department of Prints and gave his massive personal collection to that department. He supported the development

of the Architecture Library at Columbia University in New York with an
endowment and the gift of a large number of books from his personal library.
The Avery Architecture Library is considered by many to be the foremost collection
in the country. It is not surprising that Avery, a sophisticated and loyal New
Yorker, was one of the founding members of the Society of Iconophiles, a small
group of Grolier Club members interested in preserving the history of the city
through collecting and commissioning prints and books. Avery's interest in the
book arts centered on fine bindings. He owned such curiosities as the *Chronological
Handlist of the Various Editions of "The Compleat Angler"* bound in sharkskin
and Theodore Deck's *La Faience* in a binding studded with pottery. Other
bindings in his library were commissioned by Jean Grolier, Diane de Poitiers,
and Marguerite de Valois. Avery's gifts to libraries established him as one of
the chief art patrons at the turn of the century.

Bibliography

A. *Diaries 1871–1882* (New York, 1979); *A Handbook of the S. P. Avery Collection
of Prints and Art Books in the New York Public Library* (New York, 1901); *Catalogue
of the Ellen Walters Avery Collection of Books* (New York, 1897); *Avery Architectural
Library Catalog* (New York, 1968, 1975, 1977).

B. *DAB* 1, 445; *NCAB* 1, 159; *Grolier 75*, 1–3; Henri Pene DuBois, *Four Libraries
of New York* (New York, 1892); Grolier Club, *Editorials and Resolutions in Memory of
Samuel P. Avery* (New York, 1905); Harry Lydenberg, *History of the New York Public
Library* (New York, 1923), 381–384; Russell Sturgis, "Samuel Putnam Avery," *Columbia University Quarterly*, December 1904, 14–23.

AYER, Edward E. (b. November 16, 1841, Kenosha, Wis.; d. May 3, 1927,
Pasadena, Calif.). *Collection Disposition:* Field Museum of Natural History;
Newberry Library.

In August 1861 Ayer joined the First California Cavalry and was assigned
almost immediately to duty in Tucson, Arizona. It was there on the desert frontier
that Ayer was first exposed to books and to the pleasures of reading. In the
office of a silver mine near the Mexican border, an unlikely spot to improve the
mind, he found a weatherbeaten copy of W. H. Prescott's *The Conquest of
Mexico*. This exposure to Prescott's great work, as Ayer remembered in later
years, brought history into focus and led him to read a variety of historical
studies. Slowly Ayer began to accumulate a library. In 1903 he bought the
important James Pilling collection on North American Indian linguistics. This
purchase provided Ayer with an impressive library of biblical texts and hymnals
translated into the various Indian languages. In addition to materials on Native
Americans, Ayer gathered books and manuscripts on the native peoples of Hawaii
and the Philippines. His collecting zeal led to the acquisition of numerous trade
records, diaries, and early newspapers. As the books and manuscripts overflowed
Ayer's home, he transferred them regularly to the Newberry Library in Chicago,
where he served as a trustee. In 1910 the Newberry Library set aside special

rooms for the materials, and in the following year it dedicated the entire collection as "The Edward Ayer Collection on the North American Indian." The Ayer collection included early exploration, Indian warfare, Spanish government affairs in the Southwest, linguistics, art, and culture. Much of the development of the library was based on careful examination of Thomas Field's* *An Essay Towards an Indian Bibliography*. According to Frank Lockwood, Ayer's biographer, Field's work was a constant source of information and of almost daily use in suggesting likely authors and titles.

In addition to his interests in native peoples, Ayer gathered pewter, vases, fossils, and bird specimens, which he presented to the Field Museum in Chicago. He also collected books on ornithology and for a time authorized the museum to purchase all the research material that came to their attention relating to that subject. In 1924 the Field Museum published a highly regarded bibliography based on Ayer's gifts. Despite the diversity of his interests, Ayer never wavered in his enthusiasm for Indian materials. Shortly before his death he authorized publication of a comprehensive guide to the Newberry collections. Ayer's books and manuscripts not only enriched Chicago-area libraries but have served as an international resource for scholarly investigation of the American Indian.

Bibliography

A. "How I Bought My First Book," *Newberry Library Bulletin*, December 1950, 143–145; *Catalogue of the Edward E. Ayer Ornithological Library* (Chicago, 1926); *Indian Linguistics in the Edward E. Ayer Collection* (Chicago, 1941); *A Checklist of Manuscripts in the Ayer Collection* (Chicago, 1937); *List of Narratives of Indian Captivities* (Chicago, 1930).

B. *DAB* 1, 44; *NCAB* 20, 37; Cannon, 125–131; J. Christian Bay, *Edward Everett Ayer 1841–1927* (Chicago, 1927); Frank Lockwood, *The Life of Edward E. Ayer* (Chicago, 1929); Donald Wilhelm, "A Lumberman Bibliophile," *The Outlook*, August 25, 1915, 997–1001.

B

BALL, Elisabeth (b. December 26, 1897, Muncie, Ind.; d. April 29, 1982, Muncie, Ind.). *Education:* B.S., Vassar College, 1917. *Collection Disposition:* Free Library of Philadelphia; American Antiquarian Society; Pierpont Morgan Library; Indiana University (Lilly Library); Ball State University.

There is little doubt that Ball inherited her interest in children's books from her father. He developed a fine library of English and continental juveniles based on purchases from the C. T. Owen collection and from the Kirkor Gumuchian 1930 sale catalog, *Les Livres de l'Enfance.* From this base she built one of the country's most important collections of children's books. At first, following her father's lead, she concentrated on English and European titles, but later she added many American imprints. In both subject matter and format her purchases ran a gamut that encompassed catechisms, chapbooks, Bibles, grammars, fairy tales, and classic myths. On her shelves prosaic New England primers collided with swashbuckling adventure stories, while thumb Bibles fought for space with illustrated folios. When the Pierpont Morgan Library mounted large exhibitions of children's books in 1957 and 1975, Ball was listed as one of the chief lenders. In 1964 she gave a substantial portion of her collection to the Morgan and established a fund for continued purchases. In a further demonstration of generosity, she purchased the Gillett G. Griffin collection of American children's books for the Morgan Library. Earlier she had contributed a collection of hornbooks to the Free Library of Philadelphia and her own American imprints to the American Antiquarian Society. On her death the George and Frances Ball Foundation presented the remainder of her children's books, some 8,500 volumes, to the Lilly Library of Indiana University, while an assorted collection of first editions went to the Bracken Library at Ball State University in Muncie. Her library of children's books was recognized as preeminent by experts in this country and abroad. The catalog accompanying the 1975 Morgan exhibition stated, ''Since the disposal of the late Edgar Oppenheimer's* library . . . there can be no question of the supremacy of that formed by Miss Ball.''

Bibliography

A. ''The Moving Market or Cries of London Town,'' in *Bibliophile in the Nursery*, edited by William Targ (Cleveland, 1957), 193–207.

B. ''Elisabeth Ball,'' *PAAS*, April 1983, 43–45; Elizabeth Johnson and Judith Endelman, ''Lilly Library's Elisabeth Ball Collection,'' *AB*, November 12, 1984, 3417–3422; Correspondence with William R. Cagle, Librarian at Lilly Library, 1984; William R. Cagle, *Annual Report of the Lilly Librarian 1983–1984* (Bloomington, Ind., 1984), 3–8.

BALLARD, Ellis A. (b. June 4, 1861, Athens, Ohio; d. June 13, 1938, Philadelphia, Pa.). *Education:* A.B., LL.B., University of Pennsylvania, 1881, 1883. *Collection Disposition:* Parke-Bernet, January 21, 1942.

Immediately following his graduation, Ballard began an active law practice in Philadelphia. As a collector, Ballard was noted for his interest in the works of British storyteller Rudyard Kipling. According to Philadelphia bibliophile Barton Currie*, it was Ballard's rigorous legal training that enabled him to concentrate on Kipling with such single-minded devotion. Many collectors start with a favorite author, Currie noted, but as time goes on they are lured into a variety of other interests. In Ballard's case, Kipling supplied enough inspiration and challenge for a lifetime. Although Ballard had always enjoyed reading the colorful Kipling tales, it was not until 1896 that he began to collect in earnest. Part of his enthusiasm can be attributed to his friendships with Currie and the irrepressible author-bookman A. Edward Newton*. It may have been Newton who suggested that Ballard place himself in the hands of Philadelphia bookdealers Porter and Coates for Kipling first editions. The advice was bad. These early ''firsts'' turned out to be spurious, as Ballard discovered later when he became more sophisticated at the book-collecting game.

The final Ballard collection contained not only books but also magazines, newspapers, letters, and manuscripts from all periods of Kipling's writing career. Ballard attempted to gather all states of printing and all binding variants in order to produce a complete publication profile for each item. The library was particularly strong in works from the so-called ''Indian period'' of Kipling's production and included long runs of rare newspapers and pamphlets. Among these publications were *The Week's News*, *The Pioneer Mail*, and the *Indian Railway Series* which carried the first appearance of many of Kipling's best-known tales and poems. Very little published over Kipling's name during this period was missing. When Ballard brought together a number of these fugitive pieces for a private publication in 1936, critics noted that it was the first time they had ever appeared in book form. In the course of his collecting career, Ballard acquired many outstanding presentation copies, photographs, letters, and manuscripts. One of the charming rarities within this group was the copy of Kipling's first book, *Schoolboy Lyrics*, with a presentation inscription to his mother. In 1935 Ballard issued a detailed catalog of his collection in which he included a rich assortment of personal notes on provenance, cost, and condition. It is one of the most readable catalogs ever produced.

Although Ballard understood the fine points of collecting, he put personal enjoyment ahead of bibliographic minutia. He could quote from the ballads and poems by the hour and delighted in reading Kipling's tales to his children and grandchildren. Four years after Ballard died his library was put up for sale at Parke-Bernet in New York. Unfortunately the timing of the sale, just a month after the Pearl Harbor attack, was disastrous. For institutional buyers, such as the Pierpont Morgan Library, it was an opportunity to secure bargains. The well-annotated Ballard catalog stands as an impressive record of what a determined one-author collector can achieve.

Bibliography

A. *Catalogue: Intimate and Descriptive of My Kipling Collection, Books, Manuscripts, and Letters, with Reproductions of Rarities, How I Got Them, Why I Prize Them, and What I Failed to Get, with Inferences and Opinions Solely My Own and Probably Wrong* (Philadelphia, 1935).

B. Wolf and Fleming, passim; Barton Currie, *Fishers of Books* (Boston, 1931), 101–102.

BANCROFT, Hubert Howe (b. May 5, 1832, Granville, Ohio; d. March 2, 1918, San Francisco, Calif.). *Collection Disposition:* University of California at Berkeley; Bangs, February 7, 1900.

After working in bookstores in Buffalo and San Francisco, Bancroft decided in 1856 to open his own book business. The firm prospered. By 1870 he required a five-story building to house all the printing, binding, and sales operations. As one of his first publication efforts, Bancroft brought together all the books and pamphlets he could find having to do with California. This collection became the working material for *The Pacific States Almanac* (1862). Gradually he enlarged his collecting to include Alaska, Mexico, the Southwest, and the Midwest. In 1862 and again in 1866–1867, Bancroft traveled to Europe, spending most of his time hunting books in the shops of Madrid, Rome, Paris, and London. In 1868 he commissioned London publisher Joseph Whitaker to act as his agent at the José Andrade library auction. Andrade, a prominent Mexico City publisher, had collected early imprints and books about native culture over a period of forty years, and his 6,000-volume library was considered one of the best in private hands. Whitaker did his work so well that nearly half the books and manuscripts went to Bancroft. In 1876 the collector acquired the E. George Squier* library of newspapers, books, pamphlets, and manuscripts on the history of Central America. The third great sale by which Bancroft augmented his library occurred in 1880 and represented the property of José Ramirez, a federal judge in Durango. On this occasion Bancroft asked the well-known Henry Stevens of London to represent his bids but unwisely failed to specify any limits. Materials that Bancroft thought would cost $12,000 ran three times that figure. Bancroft consoled himself when he realized the values these prices implied for his own growing collection. In 1869, before the additions from the Squier or Ramirez auctions, Bancroft had some 16,000 volumes; by 1881, he had 35,000 and by 1890 over 50,000. He was ever patient and watchful and, as he put it in *Literary Industries*, built his collection by "lying in wait for opportunities." In the meantime Bancroft enlarged his publishing operations. He purchased a new building on Merchant Street and set the vast Bancroft literary factory into operation. A crew of assistants, researchers, and editors combed archives, interviewed pioneers, indexed manuscripts, and wrote the texts that carried Bancroft's name. In many cases his contribution was limited to planning the contents and writing the introductions.

As early as 1885 Bancroft began to make plans for the disposition of his library. Both the state of California and the University of California at Berkeley were approached, but the price of $250,000 struck both as prohibitive. In order to settle the matter, Bancroft asked distinguished historian Reuben Gold Thwaites to act as a consultant. After considering all the manuscripts, indexes, and catalogs, Thwaites estimated the market value at $315,000, although the real value to the state, he claimed, would be much more. Based on Bancroft's offer to supply $100,000 as evidence of goodwill, the regents of the university approved the purchase for $250,000. In his autobiography Bancroft modestly described his collection as containing "heaps and heaps of diamonds—and sawdust. Good gold and genuine silver . . . mixed with refuse and debris." This realistic appraisal does not diminish the fact that the Bancroft library was one of the most important acquisitions ever made by the University of California library system. Bancroft's varied roles as historian, publisher, collector, and editor all focused in the formation of a great research library.

Bibliography

A. *Literary Industries* (San Francisco, 1890).

B. *DAB* 1, 570–571; *NCAB* 5, 112; Cannon, 96–103; Flora Apponyi, *The Libraries of California* (San Francisco, 1878), 13–60; Harry Clark, "The Production, Publication, and Sale of the Works of Hubert Howe Bancroft" (Ph.D. dissertation, Berkeley, 1969); George W. Cole, "Book Collectors as Benefactors of Public Libraries," *PBSA*, 3rd and 4th Q 1915, 53–55; Warren Howell, "Exploring California Book Trade History," *AB*, January 8, 1979, 256–258; Lawrence Clark Powell, "Hubert Howe Bancroft," in *Bibliographers of the Golden State* (Berkeley, Calif., 1967), 13–14.

BARLOW, Samuel L. M. (b. June 5, 1826, Granville, Mass.; d. July 10, 1889, Glen Cove, N.Y.). *Collection Disposition:* American Art, February 3, 1890.

A native intelligence, tact, and good judgment all contributed to the success of Barlow's New York legal practice. In 1847 he achieved his first great victory by settling the various claims that arose from the treaty concluding the war with Mexico. Fifteen years later, in his best-known case, he won a settlement of $9 million against Jay Gould for mismanagement of the Erie Railroad. Although Barlow had started to collect Americana before he met bibliographer Henry Harrisse* in 1863, his serious involvement can be measured from that date. Barlow was consistently generous in allowing the sometimes irascible Harrisse the complete freedom of his library, an openhandedness that Harrisse repaid with bibliographical advice. In 1863 Harrisse urged Barlow to buy the distinguished Thomas Aspinwall* library, which included, among other rarities, a 1493 Latin "Columbus Letter" and a fine set of the "Jesuit Relations." The bulk of the purchase was destroyed in a warehouse fire, but fortunately Harrisse had brought some of the choicest items directly to Barlow. In 1864, with the Aspinwall books providing substance, Harrisse issued one of the scarcest of all collectors catalogs, a four-copy edition of *Biblioteca Barlowiana*. This was followed in 1866 by two important publications financed by Barlow, *Notes on Columbus* and the renowned *Bibliotheca Americana Vetustissima*. With continued guidance from Harrisse, Barlow amassed other important historical works, including a variety of editions of the travels of Vespucci and Cortez and a rich assortment of Canadian history. In 1883, after the library had been appraised, Barlow considered giving it to a New York institution at half the estimated value, but nothing ever came of these plans. The close relationship between Barlow and Harrisse continued into the decade of the 1880s, based on their mutual appreciation for Americana. The 1890 catalog, for the sale after Barlow's death, included an extended introduction by Harrisse with a detailed explanation of the development of the collection and a warm tribute to Barlow. The sale of the books at the American Art Association brought the estate nearly $85,000, a satisfactory return by any standards. The largest private buyer was Brayton Ives*, who secured the Cortez and Vespucci letters. The chief institutional buyers were the Lenox Library of New York and the Boston Public Library. In anticipation of the sale, the Boston City Council set aside $25,000 expressly for library purchases. That amount enabled Boston to obtain a number of rarities, including the "Columbus Letter" of 1493 and the early records of the Massachusetts General Court. This success must have pleased the editor of the *Boston Critic*, who promoted the sale by reminding readers that many of the books came from the Boston library of Thomas Aspinwall* and that if justice were to be served the books should return to his native city. The editorial went on to predict that unless some "grasping millionaire" seized the books Boston would be successful.

Biographical sketches of Barlow describe him as a shrewd bon vivant who loved show dogs, art, whist, paintings, and rare books. He was fortunate in his friendship with Harrisse, since that relationship resulted in many important acquisitions for his collection. The Barlow sale was an important event in the New York book world, some claiming it approached the George Brinley* auction in importance. The quality of his sale catalog and the Harrisse bibliographies established Barlow as one of the leading nineteenth-century collectors of Americana.

Bibliography

A. *Biblioteca Barlowiana* (New York, 1864).

B. *DAB* 1, 613–615; *NCAB* 3, 259–260; Cannon, 104–105; Randolph Adams, "Henry Harrisse, Bibliographer," in *Three Americanists* (Philadelphia, 1939), 1–33; Arnold Growall, *Henry Harrisse: Biographical and Bibliographical Sketch* (New York, 1899); "The Barlow Sale," *The Critic*, February 1, 1890, 55; February 15, 1890, 80, 85–86, Joseph Rosenblum, "Two Americanists: Samuel L. M. Barlow and Henry Harrisse," *ABC*, March/April 1985, 14–25.

BARTON, Thomas P. (b. 1803, Philadelphia, Pa.; d. April 5, 1869, Barrytown, N.Y.). *Collection Disposition:* Boston Public Library.

Barton's early years were spent in the diplomatic service in France, and it was there that he developed a taste for collecting. By the time he returned to the United States in 1832, he had already acquired a library of historical and literary rarities. He was particularly interested in English drama and had a notable Shakespearean collection, including all the folios and a large number of the early quartos. Writing in 1881, Shakespearean scholar Horace Furness* declared the Barton collection the finest in America. The real importance of the collection, according to Furness, came in the extensive amount of ephemera present: newspapers, contemporary reviews, and playbills. This was working material for the scholar. In addition to the English literary holdings, Barton collected French and German drama and continental history. By 1860, when James Wynne surveyed New York private libraries, the Barton collection of 15,000 items was recognized as one of the finest in the city. In many cases the books displayed the handsome bindings of Payne and Riviere. By Barton's will the library was to be placed in an institution that would keep all the books together and provide users with a printed catalog. The Boston Public Library wanted the collection desperately, but Joseph Sabin's appraisal of $50,000 made that out of the question. When Mrs. Barton lowered the price to $34,000, the trustees came up with the funds. Although many other American collectors followed Barton in an enthusiasm for Shakespeare, his role as a pacesetter was significant.

Bibliography

B. *DAB* 1, 23–24; *NCAB* 14, 365; Cannon, 318–319; Wynne, 59–96; Horace Furness, "The Barton Library," *Annual Report of the Boston Public Library* (Boston, 1881); H. G. Wadlin, *The Public Library of the City of Boston* (Boston, 1911), 128–132; "The Barton Library," *BBPL*, July-September 1921, 173–177.

BASSLER, Harvey (b. April 21, 1883, Myerstown, Pa.; d. March 14, 1950, Downingtown, Pa.). *Education:* A.B., M.S., Albright College, 1903, 1910; E.M., Lehigh University, 1908; Ph.D., Johns Hopkins University, 1913. *Collection Disposition:* Lehigh University; Franklin and Marshall College; American Museum of Natural History.

During the period 1920–1932, while Bassler was working in Peru as chief geologist for Standard Oil, he collected more than 10,000 specimens of local amphibians and reptiles. This was the same kind of determined effort he later applied to book collecting. First he acquired a large library on jungle flora and fauna. Later he turned his scholarly attention to Pennsylvania history. He became particularly attracted to the colorful books, broadsides, and manuscripts of the Pennsylvania Dutch. In 1946 he enhanced his growing collection with the purchase of some 3,500 volumes from another private collector and became owner of one of the finest Pennsylvania Dutch collections in the country. Franklin and Marshall College gave him storage space for his archive and appointed him as a special library consultant on Pennsylvania history. After his death the entire Pennsylvania Dutch collection went to the college. His scientific books and journals were divided equally between Lehigh University and the American Museum of Natural History.

Bibliography

B. Lee Edson, "The Collector," *The Lamp*, Winter 1982, 13–15; Alfred Shoemaker, "In Memoriam," *The Pennsylvania Dutchman*, April 1950, 1.

BEINECKE, Edwin J., Sr. (b. January 6, 1886, New York, N.Y.; d. January 21, 1970, Mount Kisco, N.Y.) *Collection Disposition:* Yale University.

After two years at Yale, Beinecke dropped out and took a job in the construction business. After World War I he entered the family-owned Sperry and Hutchinson Company and was responsible for its growth and development for forty years. Aroused by Yale's indefatigable Chauncey Brewster Tinker*, Beinecke's collecting began with Samuel Johnson, after which he turned to Robert Louis Stevenson. The Jerome Kern* sale of 1929 provided some of his earliest rarities. With keen interest and ample means, Beinecke made his Stevenson collection internationally preeminent. A six-volume catalog published between 1951 and 1964 described the rich holdings in detail. In addition to the books, Beinecke acquired large holdings of Stevenson manuscripts and letters, partly from the files of the Scribner publishing house in New York. The collection also included Stevenson criticism and hundreds of books from his private library.

Around 1955 Beinecke began to buy papyri, early illuminated manuscripts, and incunabula for Yale. At the same time he became deeply concerned with Yale's collections. With other members of the family, Beinecke decided to support construction of a new library building for rare materials at Yale. The Beinecke Rare Book and Manuscript Library, completed in 1963, fulfilled this dream. "The Beinecke" has been acknowledged as one of the most beautiful libraries in the world. Having built the building, Beinecke and his family proceeded to supply it with rarities of all kinds. Although any brief listing of the Beinecke gifts would necessarily fall short of indicating the library's riches, some outstanding titles demand attention. In 1964, for example, Beinecke authorized the purchase of an entire H. P. Kraus catalog of papyri. To this he added leaves from a fourth-century Greek Book of Kings, two eighth-century leaves from the Gospel of Mark, and a splendid illuminated Bible prepared for Cardinal Albergati in 1428. Beyond the manuscript period, Beinecke added a large number of incunabula, including Cicero's *De Officiis* (1465), the first dated printing of a classical author; examples of the imprints of Sweynheym and Pannartz and Caxton; and the first edition of the *Codex Justinianus* (1475). Later centuries were not neglected, as evidenced by manuscripts and books on navigation and discovery; the prayer book used by Sir Thomas More during his imprisonment; 300 tracts by Luther and his contemporaries; and a copy of John Donne's poems owned by Charles Lamb and annotated by Coleridge. Other riches included the original manuscript of Byron's "The Prisoner of Chillon" and some twenty volumes of the diaries of British composer Sir Arthur Sullivan. Shortly after the collector's death the Yale Library was able to secure a collection of over 200 incunabula from a private collector in Belgium and designated them the "Edwin John Beinecke Memorial Collection." This was a fitting tribute to one of the great American collectors. The Beinecke legacy is a splendid building and a rare book and manuscript collection that placed Yale in the first rank among scholarly libraries of the world.

Bibliography

A. *A Stevenson Library Catalogue of a Collection of Writings By and About Robert Louis Stevenson, Formed by Edwin J. Beinecke*, compiled by George McKay (New Haven, 1951–1964).

B. *NCAB* 57, 330; Herman W. Liebert and Thomas E. Marston, "The Edwin J. Beinecke Memorial Collection," *YLG*, October 1970, 37–52; Wilmarth S. Lewis, "Address at the Dedication of the Beinecke Rare Book and Manuscript Library," *YLG*, April 1964, 123–126; Marjorie Wynne, "The Edwin J. Beinecke Collection of Robert Louis Stevenson," *YLG*, January 1952, 117–136.

BEINECKE, Frederick W. (b. April 12, 1887, New York, N.Y.; d. July 30, 1971, Great Barrington, Mass.). *Education:* Ph.B., Yale University, 1909. *Collection Disposition:* Yale University.

Until he had reached his mid-sixties, Frederick Beinecke, brother of Edwin*, was occupied with the family-owned Sperry and Hutchinson Company. Once started as a collector of western history, Beinecke proceeded with great energy. The 1953 *Yale Library Gazette* noted some of Beinecke's first gifts to the Yale Collection of Western Americana, a record it continued to carry with impressive regularity until the time of his death. The Beinecke contributions to the western collections were carefully planned to augment the materials already given by

William Robertson Coe*, Henry R. Wagner*, Thomas W. Streeter*, and Winlock Miller*. Where they had emphasized the Pacific Northwest, the Middle West, and Texas, Beinecke supplied documentation of the settlement and colonization of the Spanish Southwest. The *Yale Library Gazette* of January 1960 provided details on one of his major gifts, an extensive collection of manuscripts, maps, books, pamphlets, and broadsides having to do with the Mexican War of 1846–1848. This archive of over 900 items presented both the American and Mexican sides of the conflict. Other strong areas of the Beinecke western collection focused on the history of the early missions in Mexico, Arizona, and California, the Civil War in the West, and Texas and California history. Although the Southwest was Beinecke's primary interest, he also supplied Yale with a number of significant titles in the history of the Pacific Northwest and the Great Plains. After his death an endowment to Yale guaranteed continued growth of the western Americana collection.

Bibliography

A. *A Catalogue of the Frederick and Carrie Beinecke Collection of Western Americana* (New Haven, 1965).

B. Archibald Hanna, "Additions to the Beinecke Collection," *YLG*, July 1961, 24–27; July 1963, 14–25; January 1965, 135–136; Archibald Hanna, "Frederick W. Beinecke, 1887–1971," *YLG*, October 1971, 65–66; Jerry Patterson, "The Mexican War 1846–1848: A Collection of Contemporary Materials Presented by Frederick W. Beinecke, 1909," *YLG*, January 1960, 94–123.

BELL, James Ford (b. August 16, 1879, Philadelphia, Pa.; d. May 7, 1961, Minneapolis, Minn.). *Education:* B.S., University of Minnesota, 1901. *Collection Disposition:* University of Minnesota.

After graduating from the University of Minnesota, Bell began a lifelong career in the family milling business in Minneapolis. Beginning in the 1920s, Bell gathered print and manuscript materials relating to the development of world trade. This emphasis was based on his personal interest in the historical efforts of nations to improve their political standing through commerce. He concentrated on maps, books, charts, and globes that described trade routes to the Americas and to the Orient—man's earliest attempts to push back geographic and economic frontiers. He was primarily interested in those efforts as they touched on the discovery and exploration of the Americas, but he also collected records of trade and exploration in Europe and Asia. The Bell collection boasted first printings of classic travel narratives of such explorers as Hakluyt, Drake, Ptolemy, Wadsemüller, and Mandeville. Bell owned the Latin edition of the first "Columbus Letter" as well as travel accounts by Vespucci and Cartier. One of the high points in his library was a splendid set of the "Jesuit Relations," purchased from the Rosenbach Company. As Bell's collecting interests moved to inland America, he added titles by Champlain, Hennepin, Charlevoix, and Robert

Rogers. He also acquired the archives of the Hudson Bay Company and the Selkirk Community.

Bell was adamant in his insistence on pristine original condition. The authentic spirit of the author's times, he believed, could be conveyed only by handling first editions in fine condition. His favorite bookdealers—H. P. Kraus, A. S. W. Rosenbach*, Henry Stevens, and Francis Edwards—understood his point of view and supplied him with distinguished copies. Bell's interpretation of world trade was very broad and encompassed not only the traditional accounts of exploration but also maritime law, missionary journals, and company archives. In 1953, in accordance with a long-held plan, the James Ford Bell Room was dedicated at the University of Minnesota Library as a permanent home for the collection. Speaking on that occasion, Bell emphasized his hope that students would find the manuscripts, books, and maps a key to understanding the past. "This library," Bell declared, "contains bound fragments of time." The James Ford Bell Library has provided students with an opportunity to deepen their understanding of both European expansion and American settlement.

Bibliography

A. *The James Ford Bell Library: An Annotated Catalog of Original Source Materials Relating to the History of European Expansion 1400–1800* (Boston, 1981); "Bound Fragments of Time," in *Book Collecting and Scholarship* (Minneapolis, 1954).

B. *DAB* 7, 46; *NCAB* 6, 216; Theodore Blegen, "A Glorious Court," in *Book Collecting and Scholarship* (Minneapolis, 1954); John Parker, *James Ford Bell and His Books* (n.p., n.d.).

BELT, Elmer (b. April 10, 1893, Chicago, Ill.; d. May 17, 1980, Los Angeles, Calif.). *Education:* B.A., M.A., M.D., University of California at Berkeley, 1916, 1917, 1920. *Collection Disposition:* University of California at Los Angeles; Occidental College.

The same virtues that made Belt a renowned urologist and teacher—his commitment, enthusiasm, and persistence—aided his career as an outstanding book collector. During his student days Belt came upon the graceful and explicit artwork of the Italian master Leonardo da Vinci. The da Vinci drawings of the human figure, unlike the illustrations in most medical texts, were accurate and alive. Belt was so attracted to this man and his work that over a period of forty years he built one of the foremost collections of Vinciana in the world. In his autobiographical *Books and the Imagination*, veteran Los Angeles bookdealer Jake Zeitlin described his early involvement with Belt. The collector wanted every item in Ettore Verga's *Bibliografia Vinciana* (1930) and told Zeitlin he could have exclusive hunting rights based on fair treatment and a $200-a-month limit. This happy arrangement lasted for more than forty years. In order to satisfy Belt's wide-ranging enthusiasm, Zeitlin obtained books from da Vinci's own library, variant editions of his writings, sketches, original manuscripts, letters, and biographical texts. Everything was germane. In addition to Zeitlin's help,

Belt had the good fortune to find a highly intelligent assistant in the person of Kate Steinitz, a former patient. Deeply devoted to Belt and to the study of da Vinci, Steinitz was the ideal collection manager. She cataloged the books, wrote articles, mounted exhibits, and in general provided the organization necessary to make the archive useful.

While Belt was actively working on the da Vinci library, he built several other distinguished collections. In the late 1950s he presented a gathering of the novels of W. Weir Mitchell and a collection by and about Florence Nightingale to the University of California at Los Angeles (UCLA) Biomedical Library. His personally inscribed books and letters from novelist Upton Sinclair went to Occidental College, while books on whaling and those by D. H. Lawrence found their way to UCLA shelves. It was the Leonardo collection, however, that was preeminent. In 1960, fulfilling a carefully thought out plan, Belt announced the gift of his magnificent collection to UCLA, where it would, he hoped, act as a stimulant for teaching and research. The dissertations and studies produced from the "Elmer Belt Library of Vinciana" justified the collector's highest expectations. For Belt, book collecting was much more than a leisurely avocation. He made intelligent use of bookdealers, studied bibliography, and worked hard to secure perfect copies. His scholarly collecting activities and his generosity to UCLA place his name high on any list of distinguished American collectors.

Bibliography

A. *Surgeon and Bibliophile: Elmer Belt*, (Los Angeles, 1983); *Leonardo the Anatomist* (Lawrence, Kans., 1955); *Catalogue of the Incunabula in the Elmer Belt Library of Vinciana* (Los Angeles, 1971); "Leonardo da Vinci's Library," *QNLBCC*, Fall 1949, 84–88; *The Elmer Belt Florence Nightingale Collection Presented to the University of California* (Los Angeles, 1958); "Jake Zeitlin, Master at Filling Libraries," in *A Garland for Jake Zeitlin* (Los Angeles, 1967), 69–74; "The Joy of Kate Steinitz," *Wilson Library Bulletin*, January 1970, 514–517.

B. Robert Vosper, "A Tribute to Elmer Belt," *UCLA Librarian*, July-August 1980, 50–51; Jake Zeitlin, *Books and the Imagination: Fifty Years of Rare Books*, (Los Angeles, 1980), 290–297.

BEMENT, Clarence S. (b. April 11, 1843, Mishawaka, Ind.; d. January 27, 1923, Philadelphia, Pa.). *Collection Disposition:* American Art, February 28 and March 29, 1923.

At an early age Bement entered the family machine tool company in Philadelphia. He remained in that business for his entire working career, rising eventually to the position of president. He had the acquisitive disposition of a born collector and the means to satisfy his many interests. First he concentrated on minerals, gathering one of the most important collections in the world, then he turned to books and finally to coins and medals. His book collection was based on his fastidious tastes for illuminated manuscripts, early prayer books, and large paper editions of eighteenth- and nineteenth-century literary classics. As a customer of Philadelphia bookdealer Moses Polock, Bement became acquainted with the elderly man's literate and energetic nephew A. S. W. Rosenbach*. When Rosenbach decided to begin a book business for himself, Bement agreed to help launch the fledgling venture with his fine library. He gave his books to Rosenbach on consignment, an extraordinarily useful arrangement for the new businessman. The Bement library was well known to turn-of-the-century bibliophiles, so Rosenbach had a ready market when he made the books available for sale. Eventually many items found their way into the libraries of Harry E. Widener* and John Pierpont Morgan* and helped establish strong credentials for the new Rosenbach Company. The final Bement sales brought to the market the press books and monuments of literature that the collector had gathered so assiduously. The fruits of his labor contributed to the growth of the Pierpont Morgan Library in New York and the Widener Library at Harvard.

Bibliography

B. *DAB* 1, 173; Wolf and Fleming, passim; A. S. W. Rosenbach, *Books and Bidders* (Boston, 1927), 18–19.

BEMIS, Frank B. (b. 1861, Boston, Mass.; d. March 10, 1935, Boston, Mass.). *Collection Disposition:* private sale to A. S. W. Rosenbach, 1935.

Because of his extreme reticence, little was known about the library formed by Boston banker Frank Bemis during his lifetime. The best overall account of his collecting habits can be found in Charles Goodspeed's *Yankee Bookseller*. According to Goodspeed, Bemis worked with a great variety of dealers and built his library of American and English literature one volume at a time. He took advantage of auction sales, securing notable first editions of the work of Shakespeare, Spenser, Keats, Blake, and several of the nineteenth-century New England poets. One of the American literary treasures in his collection was the first edition of *Evangeline* inscribed by Longfellow to Hawthorne. He also had a copy of *Tamerlane*, the rarest of all Poe items, secured from the Frederick Halsey* sale. Goodspeed attributed much of Bemis' understanding of book values and bibliography to his close friendship with Harold Murdock, director of the Harvard University Press. Philadelphia bookdealer A. S. W. Rosenbach* also played an important part in encouraging Bemis and furthering his collecting enthusiasms. Sometime before his death Bemis had arranged for the proceeds from the sale of his collection to go to the Children's Hospital of Boston. The trustees in charge of the estate sold the library to Rosenbach, who in turn passed the books along to his favorite customers. The Bemis collection was gathered with intelligence and a clear sense of direction. Its strength was a tribute to the collector and to a number of scholarly bookdealers.

Bibliography

B. *Grolier 75*, 105–106; Goodspeed, 146–150; Wolf and Fleming, passim.

BENDER, Albert (b. 1866, Dublin, Ireland; d. March 4, 1941, San Francisco, Calif.). *Collection Disposition:* Mills College, University of San Francisco, Occidental College, Stanford University, University of California at Berkeley.

The son of a Dublin rabbi, Bender came to San Francisco as a teenager and found employment as a clerk in an insurance firm. He worked his way up and eventually established Albert Bender and Company as one of the largest insurance organizations in California. As his business prospered, Bender developed a passion for collecting and a reputation for generosity. It was said that he regarded himself as a channel through which precious books and paintings found their way to institutions of higher education. Beginning in 1920, Bender gave a rich variety of books and manuscripts to Mills College, Stanford University, the University of California, and the University of San Francisco. His collecting interests included fine press books as well as first editions and autographed copies of Whitman, Bierce, Jeffers, Harte, and Yeats. His interest in Mills College may have been sparked by President Aurelia Reinhardt, a confirmed Dante collector, who understood Bender's enthusiasms. His gifts to Mills included Johnson's Dictionary, a Baskerville Bible, a sixteenth-century Book of Common Prayer, and other volumes influential in the development of Western humanistic thought. When the Albert Bender Room was dedicated at Mills in 1929, San Francisco's distinguished printer John Henry Nash praised the depth and value of the collection.

Throughout his life Bender carried on an extensive correspondence with numerous literary figures, among whom were Irish authors James Stevens and Oliver Gogarty and American poets Carl Sandburg and Robinson Jeffers. On Bender's death the Mills College Library received this manuscript archive and the major portion of his personal library. Stanford received the Kelmscott Chaucer and a few other choice items as a culmination of the many gifts presented to them during the collector's lifetime. In 1970, on the fiftieth anniversary of the founding of the Bender Room, James D. Hart, director of the Bancroft Library, commented on the donor's great generosity and his unremitting support of the arts. Although Bender did not have a university education, he understood the importance of rare books as a stimulus for learning. For his enthusiastic support of cultural endeavors in the Bay area, Bender was appropriately dubbed "Saint Albert of San Francisco."

Bibliography

B. Monroe Deutsch, "Saint Albert of San Francisco," *Menorah Journal*, Spring-Summer 1955, 43–49; James D. Hart, *The Scholar and the Book Collector*, Address delivered on October 29th, 1970 on the 50th Anniversary of the Founding of the Albert M. Bender Collection (Oakland, Calif., 1971); Oscar Lewis, *To Remember Albert M. Bender* (Oakland, Calif., 1973); Flora Reynolds, "Albert Bender and the Mills College Library," *California Librarian*, October 1977, 6–16.

BENTLEY, William (b. June 22, 1759, Boston, Mass.; d. December 29, 1819, Salem, Mass.). *Education:* A.B., Harvard College, 1777. *Collection Disposition:* Allegheny College; American Antiquarian Society.

At the age of twenty-three Bentley was appointed minister of the Unitarian East Church of Salem, Massachusetts. His broad interests included theology, natural history, philosophy, and linguistics. He wrote articles on antiquarian topics for the *Salem Register* and corresponded with the leading intellectual figures of his day. Thomas Jefferson* once tried to persuade him to accept the presidency of the University of Virginia, but Bentley refused. His library reflected a number of his scholarly enthusiasms and consisted of historical and scientific texts, the classics in Greek and Latin, and standard works in theology and philosophy. It was, in short, a library well suited to an institution of higher learning. This fact was not lost on Timothy Alden, a close friend of the collector who was planning to start a college for boys in Meadville, Pennsylvania. An agreement was drawn, and after Bentley's death some 700 books were transported from Salem across the mountains to Meadville to form the basis of the Allegheny College library. Thanks to Bentley's gift and a collection presented by James Winthrop*, Allegheny College opened its doors in 1823 with one of the finest libraries in the colonies.

Bibliography

A. *The Diary of William Bentley* (Salem, Mass., 1805–1819).

B. *DAB* 1, 207; *NCAB* 10, 220; Edwin Wolf, "Some Books of Early New England Provenance in the 1823 Library of Allegheny College," *PAAS*, April 1963, 13–44.

BENZ, Doris L. (b. 1907; d. April 1984, Lynn, Mass.). *Education:* Radcliffe College, 1930. *Collection Disposition:* Christie's, November 16, 1984.

As the only daughter of a wealthy New England businessman, Benz was able to indulge her tastes for beautiful books and manuscripts. She made many of her purchases from James F. Drake in New York and from the shops of Maggs and Quaritch in London. Her interests ranged from fine printing and binding to association copies, letters, and manuscripts. She owned fore-edge paintings, Sangorski and Sutcliffe bindings, Kate Greenaway drawings, and examples of the work of the Doves, Cresset, and Kelmscott presses. The important English authors of the sixteenth through the nineteenth centuries were all well represented in her collection. Since Benz's books had never been shown in exhibitions, few dealers or curators knew of their existence. When the collection came on the market in 1984, its richness took the book world by surprise. The chief beneficiary was the Dartmouth College Library. In 1982 Benz altered her will to designate Dartmouth as the recipient of the proceeds of the sale. It was an unusually thoughtful procedure. The Dartmouth Library received unrestricted funds while collectors and dealers had the opportunity of adding to their stock.

Bibliography

B. "Foreword," *Christie's Catalogue* (New York, 1984).

BERG, Albert A. (b. August 10, 1872, New York, N.Y.; d. July 1, 1950, New York, N.Y.). *Education:* A.B., City College of New York, 1891; M.D., Columbia University, 1894. *Collection Disposition:* New York Public Library.

Books played an important part in Berg's life from his student days at City College. To help pay his tuition, he worked as a shelver in the college library. In that environment he became an avid reader and a collector. The advance of his professional career was paralleled by an increased devotion to collecting. By 1938 he and his older brother Henry had formed a collection of 3,000 volumes with emphasis on the great writers of English and American literature. Since they believed that the collection should be available to a wider public, they approached officers of the New York Public Library, offering the books and funds for further acquisitions. In the midst of these negotiations Henry died, and the gift, as accepted by the trustees in February 1940, was turned into a memorial. At this point the most important phase of the collection's development began. In only fifteen months the Berg collection grew from 3,000 items to well over 30,000, with the acquisition of two major private libraries. The first of these, obtained through Mitchell Kennerley, president of the Anderson Galleries, was the superb literature collection of William T. H. Howe*, president of the American Book Company. Howe had gathered first editions and manuscripts from many of the outstanding English and American authors of the nineteenth and twentieth centuries. No sooner had the Howe library arrived at the New York Public Library than Kennerley suggested that Berg add the Owen D. Young* books to his growing cache. Young, onetime president of General Electric Company, had built an impressive library of books and manuscripts based on his interest in major English and American literary figures. After extensive legal maneuvers, Berg and Young agreed to make a joint gift of the distinguished 15,000-volume collection to the New York Public Library. This unprecedented cultural event was given front-page coverage in the *New York Times* of May 5, 1941. Berg continued to make major major gifts throughout his lifetime and on his death provided the library with a generous endowment for future purchases. The Berg collections, occupying separate rooms in the New York Public Library, have made that institution a national center for literary research.

Bibliography

A. *Catalogue of the Berg Collection* (Boston, 1969).

B. Cannon, 226–227; *Grolier 75*, 188–190; John Gordon, "A Doctor's Benefaction: The Berg Collection at the New York Public Library," *PBSA*, 3rd Q 1954, 303–314; *NYT*, May 5, 1941, 1; *Guide to the Research Collections of the New York Public Library* (Chicago, 1975), 79–80.

BEROL, Alfred C. (b. October 5, 1892, New York, N.Y.; d. June 14, 1974, Danbury, Conn.). *Education:* A.B., Harvard University, 1913. *Collection Disposition:* Columbia University; Harvard University.

Shortly after his release from the armed forces at the end of World War I, Berol joined the Eagle Pencil Company, founded by his grandfather. He rose to the position of president and later chairman of the board, serving in those capacities from 1946 to 1972. His interest in library and bibliographic societies included memberships in the Grolier Club of New York and the Friends of the Columbia University Library. Although Berol's collecting interests were diversified, they all reflected his enthusiasm for association books, autographs, and illustration. His first major collection focused on the work of English artist Arthur Rackham. Over a period of years, Berol built up an astonishing array of watercolors, original paintings, sketchbooks, letters, and illustrated first editions. He presented a portion of this collection to Columbia University in 1956 and followed with generous supplementary gifts on an annual basis. In the early 1960s he gave Columbia and Harvard a number of colonial documents and letters from the hands of such important figures as Washington, Jay, and Hamilton. His fine collection of Daniel Press books went to Harvard, and an impressive collection of American sheet music went to Columbia. Special Collections Curator Kenneth Lohf estimated the size of the sheet music collection alone to be 20,000 items. In 1970 the Columbia University trustees paid tribute to Berol's generosity by awarding him their first Distinguished Service Citation.

Bibliography

A. "Foreword" to *The Centenary of Arthur Rackham's Birth* (New York, 1967).

B. Kenneth Lohf, "Alfred Berol in Memoriam," *Columbia Library Columns*, November 1974, 43–45; Kenneth Lohf, "The Arthur Rackham Centenary," *Columbia Library Columns*, February 1968, 43–45; Correspondence with Kenneth Lohf, July 1982; Patrick McGuire, "An Ardent Lewis Carroll Collector," *ABC*, January/February 1985, 19–26.

BIDDLE, Moncure (b. October 27, 1882, Philadelphia, Pa.; d. September 30, 1956, Philadelphia, Pa.). *Education:* A.B., Harvard University, 1905. *Collection Disposition:* Free Library of Philadelphia; Parke-Bernet, April 29, 1952.

A member of an old and distinguished Philadelphia family, Biddle was trained for a career in investment banking. His chief hobby was collecting books and prints. While a cursory examination of the Biddle auction catalog might suggest that he was attracted only to illustrated works, that impression would be wrong. His holdings of Baskerville Press items were impressive, as was his collection of Bibles. He had both the "He" and "She" Bibles as well as the first complete English version printed in America, known familiarly as the "Aitkin Bible." Surpassing these in importance, however, was the Horace collection. Working with scholarly determination over a long period of time, Biddle amassed a collection of over 850 editions of Horace's works. These volumes were carefully chosen to illustrate various aspects of scholarly editing as well as the history of printing, binding, and illustration. Beginning in 1954 and continuing over the next several years, Biddle presented this distinguished collection to the Free Library of Philadelphia. The gift was augmented by other members of the Biddle family, then by support from the Free Library itself. It is now recognized as one of the notable Horatian collections in the country. Biddle also enjoyed sharing his love of books with fellow bibliophiles. Every year from 1932 to 1945 he issued a charming "Christmas Letter," to the delight of selected friends. These little monographs dealt with rare flower books, English translators of Horace, or any other topic that interested him at the time. They are delightful evidence of Biddle's joy in books and reading.

Bibliography

B. Merle Odgers, "Horace: Alive for Twenty Centuries," in *Four Talks for Bibliophiles* (Philadelphia, 1958); Ellen Shaffer, "The Rare Book Department, Free Library of Philadelphia," *PBSA*, 1st Q 1970, 5.

BIERSTADT, Edward Hale (b.?; d. December 19, 1896, New York, N.Y.). *Collection Disposition:* Bangs, April 5 and 19, 1897.

Although details of Bierstadt's early life are not readily available, much of his collecting activity seems to have centered around the Grolier Club in New York. He was elected treasurer shortly after the club was organized in 1884, and he enjoyed friendships with such notable founding members as Theodore Low DeVinne*, William Loring Andrews*, and Beverly Chew*. His bibliographic expertise found an outlet in contributions to one of the club's earliest publications, *Catalogue of Original and Early Editions of Some of the Poetical and Prose Works of English Writers from Langland to Wither* (1893). As a collector, Bierstadt concentrated on English and American literature from the seventeenth through the nineteenth centuries. Wisely, he avoided the high-priced Elizabethans in favor of more approachable nineteenth-century figures: William Morris, Swinburne, Hawthorne, Lowell, and Whittier. He was particularly devoted to Whittier and in 1895 published an extended bibliography of that author's works in *The Book Buyer*. A similar work on Lowell was pending at the time of his death. When the Bierstadt library was brought to auction, Ernest Dressel North, rare book columnist for *The Book Buyer*, described the contents in glowing terms. At the sale, buyers paid high prices for the American and English literature. George D. Smith, later known as the chief buyer for Henry E. Huntington* and Henry Clay Folger*, made a considerable number of purchases, gaining experience for later conquests. The Bierstadt library was a sound collection of literature gathered by an astute bibliographer.

Bibliography

A. "A Bibliography of the Original Editions of the Works of John Greenleaf Whittier," *The Book Buyer*, May-October 1895, 216–221, 268–274, 324–330, 382, 388, 432, 436, 498–499.

B. Beverly Chew, "The Bierstadt Library," in *Catalogue of the Library of the Late Edward Hale Bierstadt*, April 5, 1897; Ernest Dressel North, "Notes of Rare Books," *The Book Buyer*, April 1897, 290–291; May 1897, 398–399.

BISHOP, Cortlandt Field (b. 1870, New York, N.Y.; d. March 3, 1935, Lenox, Mass.). *Education:* A.B., A.M., Ph.D., L.L.B., Columbia University, 1891, 1892, 1893, 1894. *Collection Disposition:* American Art—Anderson, April 5, April 25, November 14, 1938, January 23, 1939, December 7, 1948, January 28, 1949.

As a member of a wealthy New York family, Bishop had the opportunity to travel widely and to develop his tastes in art and literature. He probably inherited some of his enthusiasm from his father, David Wolfe Bishop, a well-known figure in nineteenth-century New York art circles. Bishop's library included fine bindings, medieval manuscripts, incunabula, association copies, and rare editions of works of such luminaries as Dickens and Blake. One biographer has pointed out that Bishop may have been the only collector to have ever owned two copies of Castiglione's *Il Cortegiano* (1528) printed by Aldus and bound for Jean Grolier. Perhaps his most famous possession was the Marquess of Lothian copy of the tenth-century Anglo-Saxon manuscript known as the "Blickling Homilies." This historic document came to Bishop as a result of his ownership of the American Art Association and the Anderson Galleries, the two most important book auction firms in New York. He purchased a major interest in both the American Art Association (in 1923) and the Anderson Galleries (in 1927) and combined them in 1929. After the Lothian sale of 1932, certain great books, such as the "Blickling Homilies," were carried by the auction house and remained in Bishop's possession until his death.

Although it would be impossible in a short space to provide even a basic list of the high points in the Bishop library, one must note the 1462 Fust and Schoeffer Bible, the fourteenth-century Tickhill Psalter, the Caxton printing of Bonaventura's *Speculum Vitae Christi* (1490), Blake's *Songs of Innocense and of Experience* (1814) illuminated by the author, and Dickens' own reading copies of his stories and novels. The rare bindings in the library included examples of the work of all the most famous craftsmen of Europe and England. Under the direction of Mitchell Kennerley, former president of the Anderson Gallery, the Bishop books and manuscripts were listed for sale in the spring of 1938. The prices received in the first sessions were in line with the quality of the items offered, although not up to the inflated level Bishop had paid at the Lothian sale. A. S. W. Rosenbach* led the bidding and secured choice items for some of his favorite customers: John Hinsdale Scheide*, John Pierpont Morgan, Jr.*, and Lessing J. Rosenwald.* The final Bishop sales, held in Paris in 1948 and 1949, brought the estate an additional $300,000 but again disappointed the heirs. The prices Bishop paid in the decade of the 1920s reflected his personal wealth and position. Those prices simply could not be duplicated in the depressed economy of the 1930s. Bishop was an influential figure and a shrewd collector, an eminent personality in the book world in the early twentieth century.

Bibliography

B. *Grolier 75*, 178–179; Wolf and Fleming, passim; Wesley Towner, *The Elegant Auctioneers* (New York, 1970), passim; *Art News*, April 6, 1935, 13.

BITTING, Katherine Golden (b. 1869; d. 1937, Washington, D.C.). *Education:* B.S., M.S., Purdue University, 1889, 1891. *Collection Disposition:* Library of Congress.

A food chemist for the Department of Agriculture, Bitting collected books and pamphlets on all phases of gastronomy. At first she bought only those items related to her work, but later, after acquiring Vincaire's splendid *Bibliographie Gastronomique*, she became a true collector. With the aid of Parisian bookseller E. Nourry, she was able to obtain many of the European rarities listed in the Vincaire work. To these she added American and English texts on foods and food preparation, with particular emphasis on American regional cooking. Some of her books were written by renowned gourmets, but many were produced by government agencies and food manufacturers. Perhaps the most notable item in the Bitting library was the fifteenth-century Italian manuscript *Libro de Arte Coquinaria* by Maestro Martino, said to be the first printed cookbook. When Bitting died in 1937, her *Gastronomic Bibliography*, a listing of her own books and many others, was almost complete. It was published in 1939, the same year her husband began to give the gastronomy collection to the Library of Congress. Between 1939 and 1944 he presented the library with some 4,300 volumes, a substantial gift to the nation and a memorial to his wife. The Bitting collection is a unique index to an important phase of social history.

Bibliography

A. *Gastronomic Bibliography* (San Francisco, 1939; reprint, Ann Arbor, 1971).

B. *SCLC*, 41; Leonard Beck, "Two Loaf-Givers; or A Tour Through the Gastronomic Libraries of Katherine Golden Bitting and Elizabeth Robins Pennell," *QJLC*, Winter 1980, 35–63; Leonard Beck, *Two Loaf Givers* (Washington, D.C., 1984); Leonard Beck, "Praise Is Due Bartolomeo Platina: A Note on the Librarian-Author of the First Cookbook," *QJLC*, July 1975, 238–253.

BIXBY, William K. (b. January 2, 1857, Adrian, Mich.; d. October 29, 1931, Saint Louis, Mo.). *Collection Disposition:* Henry E. Huntington; Missouri Historical Society; George Washington University (Saint Louis); Bibliophile Society of Boston; Anderson, March 29, 1916, February 26, 1917; American Art—Anderson, April 4, 1934.

The story of Bixby's career reads like a Horatio Alger novel. At the age of sixteen he started working for the Great Northern Railroad. After a series of happy coincidences he became the protégé of the president of the railroad and was promoted to ever-increasing management responsibilities. By the time he was thirty-one, he was vice-president of the Missouri Car and Foundry Company, and shortly thereafter president of American Car and Foundry. He retired from business at the age of forty-eight to devote his time to collecting books and art objects. Of the many specialties in his library, he was particularly fond of manuscripts and inscribed copies that revealed the inner thoughts of well-known literary and historical figures. In 1905 he bought the manuscript journals of Major John André, the British officer involved in the Benedict Arnold treachery. In order to make this journal available to a wider audience of collectors, Bixby had it handsomely printed by the Bibliophile Society of Boston. Among other manuscripts he issued in this fashion were Shelley's *Notebooks*, edited by Harry Buxton Forman, the Charles Dickens–Maria Beadness *Private Correspondence*, edited by George Pierce Baker, and Nathaniel Hawthorne's letters to his fiancée, Sophia Peabody. During the period from 1910 to 1920, Bixby made important purchases from Philadelphia bookdealer A. S. W. Rosenbach*. These gems, which Rosenbach had obtained from the "Sentimental Library" of Harry B. Smith*, included Shelley's *Queen Mab* inscribed to Mary Godwin, Robert Burns' manuscript of "To Mary in Heaven," and Rudyard Kipling's "Recessional."In 1912 Bixby acquired an impressive archive of Thomas Jefferson* papers and letters, most of which he eventually gave to the Missouri Historical Society and to George Washington University in St. Louis.

As the collection grew, duplication was inevitable, and in 1916 and 1917 he joined Henry E. Huntington* to dispose of unwanted second copies at auction. These negotiations led to further housecleaning and to the sale of his most important literary manuscripts to Huntington. With space available, Bixby was ready to start buying again, and of course Rosenbach was again ready to sell. Bixby's second library was much like his first, full of notable literary and historical manuscripts and first editions. When his health failed in 1929, Bixby thought of Rosenbach again, this time to help with the final disposal of the library. Since he had sold the books to Bixby in the first place and knew their condition and value, Rosenbach was happy to take them back. In reviewing Bixby's collecting career, it is easy to sense his pleasure in handling choice documents, poems, and love letters. He understood the importance of original records and took pleasure in making them known to a wider public. In many ways he was an ideal collector.

Bibliography

A. "Some Fakes, Old and New," *Bibliographic Society Yearbook* (Boston, 1910).

B. *NCAB* 27, 23; Cannon, 310–311; *Grolier 75*, 82–84; Wolf and Fleming, passim; J. H. Schauinger, "William Bixby, Collector," *Book Collector's Packet*, March 1946, 9–16.

BLISS, Robert Woods (b. August 5, 1875, Saint Louis, Mo.; d. April 19, 1962, Washington, D.C.). *Education:* A.B., Harvard University, 1900. *Collection Disposition:* Harvard University (Dumbarton Oaks).

BLISS, Mildred W. (b. 1878; d. 1969). *Collection Disposition:* Harvard University (Dumbarton Oaks).

During a distinguished diplomatic career, Robert Bliss served in Puerto Rico, Russia, France, Sweden, and Argentina. In 1933, when he retired as ambassador to Argentina, he and his wife, Mildred, settled in Dumbarton Oaks, their estate outside Washington. There they determined to establish a research center for the study of Byzantine and medieval humanistic art. They had already begun to form a library of important books and journals several years earlier. By 1937 the collection numbered 2,000 volumes, and by 1940 it had increased to 10,000. Besides books, it also contained 5,000 photographs and long runs of journals, society proceedings, and transactions. The focus of the library was on materials that described Byzantine history and art from the founding of Constantinople in 326 to the fall of that city in 1453. By 1945 the collection had grown to an impressive 16,000 volumes. With the Blisses' support, The Dumbarton Oaks Center for Byzantine Studies sponsored lectures and symposiums and began to issue research publications on a regular basis. The library became known as an important resource center for Byzantine scholarship.

Beginning around 1945 Mildred Bliss began to collect rare books on gardening and landscape architecture. At that time many bookdealers were breaking up such books in order to sell individual plates. Mrs. Bliss wanted to preserve examples of the classic volumes in original condition. Her "Garden Library" covered the great European garden styles from the Renaissance to the twentieth century. In her will she stated: "Dumbarton Oaks is the home of the humanities, not a mere aggregation of books and objects of art . . . [and] gardens have their place in the humanistic order of life." By 1971 her library contained some 2,400 rare volumes on garden design and landscaping. The libraries of both Robert and Mildred Bliss are important humanistic archives.

Bibliography

B. *NCAB* 49, 448–449; Elizabeth Bland, "The Byzantine and House Collections," *HLB*, April 1971, 204–207; Merlin W. Packard, "The Library," *HLB*, January 1971, 33–35; John S. Thacher, "The Garden Library," *HLB*, April 1971, 211–212; William R. Tyler "Dumbarton Oaks, Introduction," *HLB*, January 1971, 25–27.

BODMAN, Harold C. (b. October 15, 1886, Chicago, Ill.; d. March 12, 1960, Santa Barbara, Calif.). *Education:* A.B., Harvard University, 1909. *Collection Disposition:* Claremont College.

After graduating from Harvard, Bodman served as an editor for several publishing companies. He retired from active business in 1930 and devoted himself to his investments, collecting, and travel. He moved to Italy in 1933, living there until the outbreak of World War II forced his return to the United States. During his travels, Bodman became entranced with the Italian countryside and bought a handsome villa that had once been the home of Poliziano, tutor of the children of Lorenzo de' Medici. Surrounded by the pervasive influence of the Italian Renaissance, Bodman began to collect the books and manuscripts of that period, among them Poliziano's own Greek and Latin verses and his translations of Plutarch and Epictetus. These works were augmented by representative editions of the writings of members of the Platonic Academy and also works by Dante, Petrarch, and Boccaccio. He owned handsome editions of books printed by Aldus Manutius and Nicolas Jenson. One of the most important of these, from the point of view of printing history, was a copy of Diogenes Laertius' *Vita et Sententiae Philosophorum*, printed by Jenson in 1475 in a typeface that became the model for Roman letters. Another high point in the collection was a fifteenth-century illuminated Book of Hours done for the Strozzi family of Florence. In 1956 Bodman presented his collection to the Honnold Library at Claremont College, where it was given a separate room and a professional curator. One of the last contributions he made to the collection before his death was the Miscomini 1488 printing of Homer's *Iliad* and *Odyssey* in Greek. As recounted in a brief history of the collection by Margaret Mulhauser, this particular edition had eluded Bodman for many years. It appeared once in a Sotheby catalog, in 1950, but the London antiquarian dealer Maggs acquired it first. Patience was rewarded. In 1959 the book came to the attention of David Magee, a San Francisco dealer, and he moved it directly from his shelves to Bodman's. With 170 incunabula and some 1,800 other early printings, the Bodman collection came to be recognized as a key West Coast resource for the serious study of the Italian Renaissance.

Bibliography

B. John M. Geerken, "Notes from the Fountainhead: The Bodman Collection and Italian Renaissance Studies in Claremont," *Honnold Library Record*, Spring 1974, 1–5; Margaret Mulhauser, "The Bodman Renaissance Collection," *Honnold Library Record*, Spring 1974, 6–8; Correspondence with Margaret Mulhauser, Bodman Collection Librarian, 1982.

BOLLINGER, James W. (b. April 10, 1867, Geneseo, Ill.; d. January 13, 1951). *Education:* B.A., LL.B., M.A., University of Iowa, 1888, 1889, 1893. *Collection Disposition:* University of Iowa.

In 1925, after the press of his professional legal career had slackened somewhat, Bollinger began to collect books. He had always been interested in the Civil War period and now decided to concentrate on Lincoln. By 1931 he had some 1,800 items in his library, a figure that he had doubled twenty years later when the collection went to the University of Iowa. Although the library consisted chiefly of books and pamphlets, Bollinger also had pictures, letters, and memorabilia. He was active in the associations concerned with Lincoln studies, and in 1943 he served on the five-man Lincoln Bibliography Committee of the Lincoln Life Foundation. The Bollinger Lincoln collection is one of the prized scholarly archives in the Special Collections Department of the University of Iowa.

Bibliography

B. Robert A. McCown, "James W. Bollinger as a Collector of Lincoln," *Books at Iowa*, April 1982, 3–14; *Bollinger Lincoln Lectures* (Iowa City, 1953).

BORDEN, Matthew C. D. (b. July 18, 1842, Fall River, Mass.; d. May 27, 1912, New York, N.Y.). *Education:* A.B., Yale University, 1864. *Collection Disposition:* American Art, February 17, 1913, January 7, 1916.

With a fortune derived from textile manufacturing, Borden was able to indulge his taste for the beautiful by collecting books, paintings, and sculpture. He enjoyed finely printed and illustrated works as well as elaborate bindings. In many cases he destroyed original bindings in order to have his books prepared in sumptuous style by Zaehnsdorf, Gruel, and Rivière. He was also fond of extra-illustrated sets of Dickens and Thackeray. Occasionally he bought manuscripts, but the bulk of the library was represented in printed works. A year after his death the books were sold at auction by the American Art Association in New York. Although the catalog was handsomely done by Arthur Swann, prices were far below expectations. The Borden library was a typical rich man's diversion, without any particular subject strength.

Bibliography

A. *Catalogue of the Printed Books, Manuscripts, Autograph Letters Collected by M. C. D. Borden* (New York, 1910).
B. *NCAB* 11, 441; Cannon, 225.

BORNEMAN, Henry S. (b. November 22, 1870, Allentown, Pa.; d. January 13, 1955, Philadelphia, Pa.). *Education:* A.B., LL.B., University of Pennsylvania, 1892, 1894. *Collection Disposition:* Free Library of Philadelphia; Parke-Bernet, November 1, 1955.

During his distinguished legal career, Borneman was regarded as one of the leading East Coast practitioners. He was an organizer of the Temple University Law School and the first dean of that institution. As a collector, he was both knowledgeable and assiduous. He became particularly interested in collecting the colorfully hand-decorated manuscripts and books produced by the first German settlers in Pennsylvania. Most of these documents—school texts, children's books, birth and death certificates, bookplates, and house blessings—were intimately connected with the everyday life of the Pennsylvania farmers and their families. Frequently they were adorned with symbolic designs and elaborate calligraphic work, now famous as the earliest folk art in the United States. Borneman was one of the first to recognize the importance and charm of these ephemeral folk specimens and managed to acquire them cheaply from attics and church basements. When purchased by the Free Library of Philadelphia shortly after Borneman's death, the collection contained some 600 examples and represented the work of artists in all the early German settlements. These historic documents were only a portion of the larger Borneman library, which traced the history of illumination.

For this purpose, Borneman had acquired European manuscripts dating from the twelfth to the seventeenth centuries as well as texts in Arabic, Armenian, and Persian. In most cases the manuscripts were decorated with miniatures and embellished with ornamental pen and brush work. Flora B. Ludington, librarian of Mount Holyoke College and a frequent visitor in the Borneman home, wrote that each manuscript was carefully acquired to illustrate a specific style and period of illumination.

In addition to the Pennsylvania materials, the Borneman library was rich in other kinds of Americana—first editions of eminent nineteenth-century New England poets, Benjamin Franklin's printing, histories of the Freemasonry movement, and documents autographed by George Washington and William Penn. The English literature section of the library, while less fully developed than the American section, boasted important series of letters, books, and manuscripts by Lamb and Blake. Borneman also had runs of the publications of the Vail, Essex House, and Kelmscott presses. This was a library that reflected the collector's good taste as well as his interest in preserving the record of early culture in Pennsylvania.

Bibliography

A. *Pennsylvania German Illuminated Manuscripts* (Norristown, Penn., 1937); *Pennsylvania German Bookplates: A Study* (Philadelphia, 1953).

B. Frances Lichten, *Fraktur: The Illuminated Manuscripts of the Pennsylvania Dutch* (Philadelphia, 1958); Flora B. Ludington, "Foreword," *Parke-Bernet Catalog* (New York, 1955); Ellen Shaffer, "Illuminators, Scribes, and Printers: A Glimpse of the Free Library's Pennsylvania Dutch Collection," *Pennsylvania Folklife*, Fall 1958, 19–27.

BRAISLIN, William C. (b. July 1, 1865, Burlington, N.J.; d. December 3, 1948). *Education:* A.B., Princeton University, 1887; M.D., Columbia University, 1890. *Collection Disposition:* Anderson, April 2, 1923; March 21 and April 4, 1927.

While following an active career in medicine, Braislin gathered an impressive personal library. His two chief interests were ornithology and American history. The history collection was the stronger, with emphasis on accounts of Indian captivity and overland travel. The ornithology collection was dispersed at auction in 1923, the historical materials in 1927. In both cases, the auction returns were satisfactory.

Bibliography

B. *NCAB* 37, 170; Cannon, 274–275.

BRASCH, Frederick E. (b. December 18, 1875, Mobile, Ala.; d. October 26, 1967, Mountain View, Calif.). *Collection Disposition:* Stanford University.

Although he did not graduate from grammar school, Brasch was able to feed his intellectual appetites with an intensive reading program at the San Jose City

Library. His application in the sciences was such that he was admitted to Stanford University as a special student and completed several years of university study. After working for a short time in a bookstore, he decided to become a librarian and moved through a series of responsible positions at the John Crerar Library in Chicago and the James J. Hill Reference Library in Saint Paul. In 1924 he was appointed assistant chief of the Smithsonian Division of the Library of Congress; the following year he was made chief. The Washington, D.C., location gave Brasch the opportunity he had been looking for to build a strong personal book collection on the history of science. With low wartime prices prevailing, he began to acquire a large number of books and pamphlets by and about the leading seventeenth- and eighteenth-century chemists, astronomers, and mathematicians, especially Sir Isaac Newton. He believed that the proper way to study the history of sciences was through a close examination of the writings of men of genius like Newton, Lavoisier, and Galileo. Early in his collecting career Brasch notified Stanford library officers that he wished to leave his personal library to the university in gratitude for the opportunity given him as a young man. In 1941, in order to help the university celebrate its fiftieth anniversary, Brasch gave the library ten of his choicest rarities. Seven years later Brasch moved to Palo Alto as Stanford's consultant in bibliography, a post that gave him ample opportunity to use the collection and to make additions when rare volumes became available. Raynard C. Swank, director of Stanford libraries, characterized Brasch as a patient and devoted scholar, one to whom the university community owed both affection and gratitude.

Bibliography

A. *An Essay on Sir Isaac Newton and Newtonian Thought* (Palo Alto, Calif., 1962).

B. John Y. Cole, "Frederick E. Brasch: Collector and Historian of Science," *Imprint*, April 1982, 9–12; "Frederick E. Brasch," *PAAS*, April 1968, 21–24.

BREAKER, William D. (b. 1867; d. May 20, 1953, New York, N.Y.). *Collection* Disposition: Rains Auction Rooms, November 26, 1935, April 7, 1937.

A *New York Times* reviewer identified the Breaker sale of 1935 as "an event that would lend distinction to any season." That comment could have been repeated for the 1937 sale, in which the remainder of the library was distributed. The proof was in the colonial history, American and English literature, early printing, and bindings, which Breaker had gathered so lovingly over a period of twenty years. He had made purchases at some of the great sales in the early part of the century, those of Henry Huth, Robert Hoe III*, Winston Hagen*, Samuel L. M. Barlow*, Herschel V. Jones*, and others. Among the high points in his library were the four Shakespeare folios, the 1649 "Cambridge Platform," Huth's copy of the Rome "Columbus Letter," Jean Grolier's own copy of an Aldine printing, the editio princeps of the *Imitatio Christi* (1473), and Eliot's "Indian Bible" of 1663. A survey of American letters would have revealed long runs of first editions of Longfellow, Hawthorne, Melville, and Lowell. Although a large number of the books carried distinguished provenance, others (like the copy of Holbein's "Dance of Death" bound in human skin) seemed to be merely curiosities. Bids exceeded expectations at both sales, with strong returns for classics of voyage and discovery and colonial history. Breaker acquired a diverse collection of recognized rarities at a time when the supply was good, and he sold them at a satisfactory level.

Bibliography

B. Philip Brooks, "Notes on Rare Books," *NYT*, November 24, 1935.

BREVOORT, J. Carson (b. July 10, 1818, New York, N.Y.; d. December 7, 1887, Brooklyn, N.Y.). *Education:* Diploma, Central School of Arts and Manufactures (Paris), 1838. *Collection Disposition:* New York State Fish Commission; Bangs, February 25, 1890.

At the age of twenty-six Brevoort traveled to Spain as the private secretary of Washington Irving. On returning to the United States in 1844, he took up a professional career in engineering and began to develop a library on American history. His own collection was based on the one developed by his father in the early 1800s. The elder Brevoort had studied at the University of Edinburgh and became acquainted with novelist Sir Walter Scott. From Scott he received a collection of early tracts, the working materials for a projected study of American history. When the book failed to materialize, Scott turned the collection over to Brevoort. This legacy of rare tracts and pamphlets formed the basis of Brevoort's library. In adding to his father's collection Brevoort concentrated on volumes that illustrated the exploration of America and its natural history. In all cases, Brevoort obtained the maps and charts that supplemented the textual accounts. Brevoort was an active supporter of the Astor Library in New York, serving as trustee for over twenty years and superintendent from 1876 to 1878. Joseph Sabin recognized Brevoort's contribution to American historical studies by dedicating the first volume of *Bibliotheca Americana* to him. The Brevoort library was a distinguished nineteenth-century historical collection.

Bibliography

B. *NCAB* 9, 193; Cannon, 106–107; Wynne, 105–124; Harry Lydenberg, *History of the New York Public Library* (New York, 1923), 63–65.

BREWER, Luther A. (b. December 17, 1858, Welsh Run, Pa.; d. April 28, 1933, Cedar Rapids, Iowa). *Education:* A.B., Gettysburg College, 1883. *Collection Disposition:* American Art, March 10, 1925; University of Iowa.

Addicted to collecting from youth, Brewer at first gathered English literature, fine printing, and association copies. In an essay written for the *Yearbook of the Bibliophile Society of Boston* in 1920, he declared an interest in the eighteenth-century Romantic poet and critic Leigh Hunt. When asked, "Why Leigh Hunt?" Brewer usually responded, "Why not?" Hunt was one of the most important literary figures of the early nineteenth century—a lover of books and an intimate of Shelley, Keats, Lamb, and Byron. Hunt edited a crusading journal, was sent to prison for an attack on the Prince Regent, went to Italy at the invitation of Byron and Shelley, and in 1828 published the controversial biography *Lord Byron and Some of His Contemporaries*. During the active auction period following World War I, Brewer found Hunt material readily available for reasonable prices. He commissioned bookdealers Walter M. Hill in Chicago and Maggs in London as his agents. Hill's purchases at the Buxton Forman sale of 1920 gave Brewer a splendid start. Because competition was limited, Brewer was able to locate not only first editions but also manuscripts and letters. He acquired several hundred letters sent by Hunt to his wife while imprisoned in Horsemonger Lane Jail from 1813 to 1815. The collection expanded to include books by members of Hunt's literary circle and books from his personal library. One of Brewer's own favorites was the copy of Hunt's *Wit and Humour* (1846) inscribed "To Mrs. Shelley (I mean 'Mary') from her affectionate friend L. H."

To the delight of his friends, each Christmas Brewer would issue a privately printed keepsake drawn from materials in his library. These pamphlets were a testimony to Brewer's love of books. In 1932 Brewer issued *My Leigh Hunt Library*, a thoroughly annotated description of his extensive holdings. Although he denied any standing as a bibliographer, the exhaustive notes in this work speak for themselves. A second volume, *My Leigh Hunt Library, the Holograph Letters*, came out five years after Brewer's death. The gallery-proof sheets of a final volume, *Huntiana and Association Books*, were destroyed in error before they had a chance to be issued. Brewer was a member of the school of collectors that emphasized the fun of the chase rather than financial gain. He collected because he enjoyed literature and liked to read.

Bibliography

A. "Delights of a Hobby," *Yearbook of the Bibliophile Society of Boston* (Boston, 1920); *The Joys and Sorrows of Book Collecting* (Cedar Rapids, 1928); *The Love of Books* (Cedar Rapids, 1923); *My Leigh Hunt Library* (Cedar Rapids, 1932); *My Leigh Hunt Library, the Holograph Letters* (Cedar Rapids, 1938).

B. J. Christian Bay, "Mr. Brewer's Collection of Leigh Hunt," in *My Leigh Hunt Library* (Cedar Rapids, 1932), vii-xxx; *NYT*, May 7, 1933, 31.

BRINLEY, George (b. May 17, 1817, Boston, Mass.; d. May 15, 1875, Hamilton, Bermuda). *Collection Disposition:* Leavitt, March 10, 1879, March 22, 1880, April 4, 1881, November 15, 1886; Libbie, April 18, 1893.

After spending his early years in Boston, Brinley moved to Hartford, Connecticut, where he established himself as an important landowner. He was a shrewd farmer, a domineering parent, and an avid bibliophile. By the time he was twenty-eight, Brinley had secured a large collection of American Indian materials owned by Boston bookseller Samuel G. Drake. Eight days before an announced auction, Brinley made private arrangements with Drake and took the entire lot. At the same time, he was buying energetically from the John Pickering and Gabriel Furman sales. Outside the auction rooms, his collecting techniques were original and effective. He found numerous rare pamphlets in the "waste paper" that had been turned over to paper mills for processing, and he also made a habit of traveling the back roads of New England in his buggy, trading pots and pans for books. Never one to limit himself to a single mode of supply, Brinley engaged the enterprising Henry Stevens of London to act as his agent for Americana as it appeared on the British book market. Since Stevens had already established business relations with John Carter Brown* and James Lenox*, two very energetic and knowledgeable collectors, Brinley's position was less than advantageous. In a number of cases, however, Brinley was able to secure fine items in spite of the competition. After Lenox and Brown had both refused John Winthrop's signed copy of the 1645 *Declaration of Former Passages and Proceedings Betwixt the English and the Narrow-gansets*, Brinley bought it for $50. When Lenox eventually decided it was worth owning, he had to pay four times the original price at the Brinley sale. The most dramatic instance of Brinley's intelligent book-scouting came with his purchase of more than 275 choice examples of the writing of Richard, Increase, and Cotton Mather* from Stevens after they had been refused by Brown, Lenox, and the British Museum. When the British Museum turned down a copy of the *Bay Psalm Book*, Brinley was quick to pick it up, although he called it a "dirty little book." In 1873 Stevens capped all his other transactions with Brinley by selling him the Erfurt copy of the Gutenberg Bible. In addition to these high points, Brinley held remarkable runs of early almanacs and colonial histories. Although he favored materials that dealt with the Northeast, he built sound holdings on the South, the Old Northwest, and Mexico, all of which gave his library breadth and importance.

The distribution of the Brinley library, at what has been referred to as the first great booksale in America, took place in New York from March 10, 1879, continuing in several sessions until April 1893. The catalog, carefully prepared by Brinley's old friend and bibliographic consultant James H. Trumbull, furnished a rich fare. Returns were excellent, with the Mather items bringing particularly high returns. At the third sale, Hamilton Cole* bought the Gutenberg Bible for $8,000, with Brayton Ives* as underbidder. It was a moment to remember. In an unusual directive, Brinley provided five historical societies and libraries with a $5,000 credit to be used against purchases at the sale. This generous act enabled the chosen institutions to make a number of significant purchases that otherwise would have been beyond their means. Brinley's reputation as a collector rests on his thorough understanding of Americana and his energy in obtaining important items. In Robert Roden's *Cambridge Press 1639–1692*, several rare tracts were annotated with the comment "Even Brinley could not find a copy." Those notes stand as an appropriate compliment to one of America's greatest collectors.

Bibliography

B. Cannon, 78–89; Randolph Adams, "George Brinley, Book Collector," in *Three Americanists* (Philadelphia, 1939), 35–67; Donald Engley, "George Brinley, Americanist," *PBSA*, 1st Q, 1966, 465–472; Marcus McCorison, "George Brinley, Americanist," *Gazette, Grolier Club*, 1980, 4–23; Kenneth Nebenzahl, "Reflections on the Brinley and Streeter Sales," *PBSA*, 2nd Q 1970, 165–175; William Reese, "George Brinley and His Library," *Gazette, Grolier Club*, 1980, 24–39; Henry Stevens, *Recollections of Mr. James Lenox of New York* (London, 1886).

BROWN, Dickson Q. (b. April 2, 1873, Pleasantville, Pa.; d. September 11, 1939, New York, N.Y.). *Education:* A.B., Princeton University, 1895. *Collection Disposition:* Princeton University; Parke-Bernet, May 22, 1939.

Trained as an engineer, Brown joined the firm of Tidewater Oil, a company of which his father was president. As an avocation he gathered an impressive collection of the works of the nineteenth-century English artist Thomas Rowlandson. In addition to some 2,000 prints, he had all of Rowlandson's published work as well as a complete library on the social and artistic history of the times. In 1928 he presented the bulk of the collection to Princeton and continued to make supplementary gifts up to the time of his death.

Bibliography

B. *NCAB* 14, 358–359; E. D. H. Johnson, "Special Collections at Princeton: The Works of Thomas Rowlandson," *PLC*, November 1940, 7–20.

BROWN, John Carter (b. August 28, 1797, Providence, R.I.; d. June 10, 1874, Providence, R.I.). *Education:* A.B., Brown University, 1816. *Collection Disposition:* Brown University.

As a member of an old and wealthy Providence mercantile family, Brown grew up in comfortable and cultivated surroundings. Although he was involved in some aspects of the family shipping business, he spent most of his life in travel and in developing his notable book collection. Early purchases, made in consultation with his older brother, included Bibles, Aldine press imprints, and extra-illustrated volumes. Brown's interest in Americana began to develop in the 1830s, after he had examined White Kennett's *Bibliothecae Americanae* and Obadiah Rich's *Bibliotheca Americanna Nova*, two of the earliest efforts at listing American imprints. The death of Brown's father in 1841 provided him with the means to pursue his collecting interests, while a friendship with New York bookseller John Russell Bartlett supplied an essential book trade connection. In 1844 Brown met Henry Stevens, just as that entrepreneur was about to launch his book business in London. The Stevens-Brown connection proved to be mutually advantageous, and it was not long before crates of books began arriving on the docks at Providence. In an early coup, Stevens secured the splendid Americana library of French historian Henri Ternaux-Compans. Between 1845 and 1847

Brown bought 1,500 volumes from Stevens, many from the Ternaux collection. Among the treasures received at this time were three editions of the "Columbus Letters," five editions of the "Cortez Letters," and long runs of the "Jesuit Relations." Although Brown and James Lenox* were often in competition for rare items, Stevens often provided the Providence collector with first choice. In some cases this worked well, but Stevens commented in *Recollections of James Lenox*, "Sometimes I found it difficult to prevent their colliding." Perhaps the most memorable instance of such a collision occurred when Brown bid 25 guineas and Lenox £25 on the "Columbus Letter" printed in Basel in 1493. Following his usual practice, and in spite of Lenox's anger, Stevens sent the volume to Brown. After a long and bitter correspondence, Brown finally gave the book to his New York rival in a rare gesture of bibliographic peacemaking.

When shelf space began to vanish in his home on Benefit Street, Brown constructed a fireproof book room, which served as the official library until a separate building could be erected on the university campus. Because of the increasing demands on the collection from a variety of students of Americana, Brown engaged Bartlett to prepare a comprehensive catalog. The bibliography began to appear in 1865 and continued to be issued until 1871.

After Brown died, his wife continued to build the library, although in different directions. She added a number of examples of early printing, Shakespeare folios, and several illuminated manuscripts. Brown's sons also added to the collection, improving the overall quality of many of the varieties. John Nicholas Brown, the oldest son, in particular took a deep interest in the library and in 1900, after adding many significant items, presented the library to the trustees of Brown University. The gift was accompanied by funds for a building and for continued collection development. The John Carter Brown Library is a national treasure for all those interested in the scholarly pursuit of American history.

Bibliography

A. *A Catalogue of Books Relating to North and South America in the Library of John Carter Brown of Providence, Rhode Island*, with notes by John Russell Bartlett (Providence, 1865–1871).

B. *DAB* 2, 136–137; *NCAB* 11, 402; Cannon, 64–72; Granniss, 309–310; Thomas Adams, "A Collector's Progress," *Gazette of the Grolier Club*, October 1968, 2–13; Henry Stevens, *Recollections of James Lenox of New York* (London, 1886); George P. Winship, *The John Carter Brown Library: A History* (Providence, 1914); Lawrence Wroth, *The First Century of the John Carter Brown Library* (Providence, 1946).

BURR, George Lincoln (b. January 30, 1857, Oramel, N.Y.; d. June 27, 1938, Ithaca, N.Y.). *Education:* A.B., Cornell University, 1881. *Collection Disposition:* Cornell University.

From the time he was a sophomore at Cornell, Burr was closely associated with Andrew Dixon White*, president of that institution. Starting as a student assistant, Burr quickly assumed responsibility for developing White's library.

After he graduated, Burr became White's private secretary, and in 1884 he traveled in Europe for the specific purpose of procuring books and manuscripts. He was particularly interested in materials relating to the inquisition, witchcraft, and persecution. Bookshops and libraries yielded treasures in response to his scholarly determination. Back home he became selector, cataloger, and bibliographer for what was to be one of the world's most outstanding libraries on witchcraft. He knew the book trade, understood values, and was an expert on European Renaissance and Reformation history. He was recognized internationally as an authority on the literature of witchcraft. As an avid collector, Burr had few rivals.

Bibliography

A. "A Witch-Hunter in the Book-Shops," *The Bibliographer*, December 1902, 431–446; "The Literature of Witchcraft," *American Historical Association Papers*, July 1890, 37–66.

B. *DAB* supp. 2, 75–76; *NCAB* 4, 479–480; Roland Bainton, *George Lincoln Burr: His Life and Selections from His Writings*, edited by Lois Gibbons (Ithaca, N.Y., 1943).

BURTON, Clarence M. (b. November 18, 1853, Whiskey Digging, Calif.; d. October 23, 1932, Detroit, Mich.). *Education:* B.S., LL.B., University of Michigan, 1873, 1874. *Collection Disposition:* Detroit Public Library.

Trained in the law, Burton practiced in Detroit and became familiar with the documentary records of that area. He used his knowledge of land titles to form the Burton Abstract and Title Company, the largest such organization in the city. As he worked with masses of family and business records he became more and more interested in local history. He started with materials on the history of Detroit but soon expanded his studies to include the entire Great Lakes region. As the collection grew, printed works took second place to manuscript records. He gathered reports, letters, maps, and diaries that reflected the day-to-day activities of engineers, ministers, educators, and businessmen—the first settlers of the Old Northwest. He obtained the papers of D. B. Woodbridge, Michigan's first delegate to Congress, and those of Lewis Cass, Michigan's first governor. Burton also acquired a distinguished set of the "Jesuit Relations," a comprehensive collection of the works of Father Gabriel Richard, Detroit's first printer, and lengthy runs of files of city directories and early newspapers. The library became far more than a hobby for Burton. It provided him with research materials for a series of well-edited books, pamphlets, and articles on local history. His comprehensive *City of Detroit 1701–1922*, for example, was a landmark for its time. In 1914, when the library had grown to 30,000 bound volumes, 40,000 pamphlets, and more than 500,000 manuscript items, Burton presented it to the city of Detroit. To this archive he added his residence, redesigned to serve as a library and museum. When the Detroit City Library was opened in 1921, it included a handsome area designated as the Burton Historical Collection. Today the library occupies expanded and comfortable quarters, its growth assured by a generous endowment from the founder.

Bibliography

B. *NCAB* 14, 284; Cannon, 259–261; Alice Dalligan, "Detroit's Master Archivist: Clarence M. Burton," *Detroit in Perspective*, Spring 1976, 145–158; "Clarence M. Burton," *Michigan History Magazine*, Winter 1933, 115–121; *The Burton Historical Collection of the Detroit Public Library* (Detroit, 1981).

BURTON, William E. (b. September 24, 1804, London, Eng.; d. February 10, 1860, New York, N.Y.). *Collection Disposition:* Sabin, October 8, 1860, January 22, 1861.

By the time he was twenty, Burton was acting in a British touring company and had established himself as a reputable comic actor. He came to the United States in 1834 and for a number of years created memorable roles in the Arch Street Theatre in Philadelphia. He turned to theater management, ran theaters in Baltimore and Washington, D.C., and finally opened his own house, the Burton Theatre, in New York. Throughout his active professional life, Burton managed to gather an impressive library. In 1848, when he moved from Philadelphia to New York, his collection numbered 12,000 volumes. Shakespeare was his principal interest, and to the quartos and folios he added a large library of critical and biographical material. He also had the chief works of Shakespeare contemporaries Thomas Decker, William Rowley, and John Marston. Like many other collectors of his time, Burton enjoyed owning extra-illustrated volumes that were expanded with engravings, prints, maps, and portraits. Burton's prize was an extra-illustrated edition of Shakespeare's works sumptuously illustrated in forty-two folio volumes. In another section of the library Burton provided space for the William Henry Ireland forgeries. Although Shakespeare predominated, the Burton library was also rich in English poetry of the seventeenth century, voyages and travel, and early printing from the Aldine and Elzevir presses.

When Burton died in 1860 the family arranged for the library to be cataloged and sold by bibliographer Joseph Sabin. This was Sabin's first New York sale, and it launched him on a long and successful career. The Burton sale was significant also for bringing the Shakespeare folios to auction in America for the first time. The collective bids on the four folios came to a little less than $700. According to the knowledgeable collector William Loring Andrews*, the Burton sale was the first great auction in New York. Burton's library reflected his professional interests and did credit to his collecting taste.

Bibliography

A. *Waggeries and Vageries* (New York, 1848).

B. *DAB* 2, 346–347; *NCAB* 2, 351; Cannon, 319–321; Wynne, 135–154; William L. Andrews, *Gossip About Book Collecting* (New York, 1900); William Keese, *William E. Burton* (New York, 1885).

BYRD, William (b. March 28, 1674, Westover, Va.; d. August 26, 1744, Westover, Va.). *Education:* Middle Temple, 1695. *Collection Disposition:* Sold to Isaac Zale, 1778, then auctioned by Robert Bell in Philadelphia, 1781.

Byrd was a gentleman-planter, a practical politician, and an amateur man-of-letters. As a young man Byrd spent much time abroad, studying first the classics, then business, and finally law. During this period he was exposed to a highly stimulating intellectual life and developed a taste for literature and the sciences. He read Latin, Greek, and Hebrew with equal facility. At the age of twenty-two he was elected to membership in the Royal Society, an honor bestowed on few Americans, certainly none of his age. Back in Virginia in 1704, Byrd assumed a variety of responsibilities connected with his 26,000-acre estate and the political affairs of the colony. He held office in the Council of State and served on numerous commissions, including one charged with settling the boundary between Virginia and North Carolina. On the literary side, he was a prolific letter writer and kept a detailed diary of all his personal and political activities. His reading was voluminous and eclectic, ranging over the sciences, poetry, theology, history, philosophy, and the classics. In order to stoke these intellectual fires he required a large personal library. In contrast to other colonial collectors like James Logan*, who concentrated on religion and moral philosophy, Byrd collected and read poetry and drama. Over a period of time he acquired many master works of English literature, including writings by Shakespeare, Jonson, Dryden, Bacon, Beaumont and Fletcher, and Chaucer. When it came to French authors, however, his taste was more for the philosophical writing of Descartes and Rousseau. In addition to literature, Byrd's library reflected a strong interest in Americana, including colonial history and the tales of voyage and discovery. In the fields of medicine and law he owned practical volumes one would expect to find on the shelves of a wealthy landowner of the time. In general, these were books chosen more for practical use than for show.

By 1778 the estate was in such serious financial trouble that the library and other household goods were put up for sale. Isaac Zale, a local iron merchant, bought the books *en bloc* for £2,000 pounds, then sent them to the Philadelphia auction house of Robert Bell, where they were distributed in a series of sales. In this way one of the finest colonial libraries was broken up and scattered beyond any hope of reconstruction. Byrd's library was a product of its time and as such constituted a remarkable artifact of eighteenth-century social history. Commentary by such authorities as Edwin Wolf II and Louis B. Wright have helped assure this remarkable collector a permanent place in colonial history.

Bibliography

B. *DAB* 3, 383–384; *NCAB* 7:247; Cannon, 15–26; Richard Beatty, *William Byrd of Westover* (Cambridge, Mass., 1932); Carl Cannon, "William Byrd II of Westover," *The Colophon*, n.s., Spring 1938, 291–302; G. R. Lyle, "William Byrd, Book Collector,"

ABC, May-June 1934, 163–165; July 1934, 208–211; Pierre Marambaud, *William Byrd of Westover* (Charlottesville, Va., 1971); Edwin Wolf, ''The Dispersal of the Library of William Byrd of Westover,'' *PAAS*, April 1958, 19–106; Louis B. Wright, *The First Gentlemen of Virginia* (San Marino, Calif., 1940).

C

CALDWELL, Edward (b. May 26, 1861, Bloom Township, Ill.; d. August 13, 1949, New York, N.Y.). *Education:* B.A., University of Michigan, 1886; M.E., Cornell University, 1888. *Collection Disposition:* Knox College.

In 1890 Caldwell entered the publishing business on the staff of *Electrical World*, a subsidiary of McGraw-Hill, and eventually became president of that company. In 1921 he wrote to the president of Knox College, where he had spent a year of undergraduate study, to propose development of a special book collection on the history of the Mississippi Valley. The collection, he suggested, might be called the "Finley Collection on the History and Romance of the Northwest," in honor of John Finley, former president of Knox and later editor of the *New York Times*. Caldwell enclosed a check in his letter and promised future support. Over the next twenty-five years Caldwell gave Knox College a steady stream of books for the Finley Library. Some of his gifts emphasized the early explorers—Champlain, Charlevoix, Hennepin, and Lewis and Clark—while others documented the history of Illinois. In addition to the books, Caldwell established an endowment fund and subsequently organized a Friends of the Library group. In 1957 the new addition to the library carried Caldwell's name in recognition of his considerable contributions to the college.

Bibliography

A. *A Catalogue of Books and Maps Belonging to the Finley Collection on the History and Romance of the Northwest* (Galesburg, Ill., 1928). "Books, Maps, and Views of Illinois One Hundred Years Ago," *Knox Alumnus*, February 1937, 26–28.

B. *NCAB* 38, 464; Everitt, 162–165.

CARRINGTON, C. Glenn (b. May 7, 1904, Richmond, Va.; d. June 12, 1975, New York, N.Y.). *Education:* B.A., Howard University, 1925; M.S., Columbia University, 1941. *Collection Disposition:* Howard University.

While he was attending Howard University in the 1920s, Carrington came under the influence of noted historian Alain Locke. Locke's belief in the African heritage and the importance of literary and historical records took root with Carrington, as it did with many other black students of that day. After obtaining a degree in social work, Carrington turned to book collecting as an avocation. His Brooklyn location gave him access to prominent black writers, artists, and musicians whose works soon overflowed the shelves in his small home. Carrington's library was built with diligence rather than with large sums of money. For a period of fifty years he rummaged through secondhand-book shops and wrote begging letters in order to form his collection on black life and culture. African art and American jazz were well represented, as were the achievements of black poets, novelists, and dramatists. Probably the outstanding literary segment in the library consisted of works by and about the black poet Langston Hughes. In addition to autographed first editions, Carrington had a number of Hughes' typed manuscripts and letters. Other holdings included the works of Carl Van Vechten and Countee Cullen and an impressive gathering of phonograph records and memorabilia from such jazz greats as Duke Ellington and Louis Armstrong. Carrington amassed some 2,000 books, 500 phonograph records, and over eighteen boxes of manuscripts, broadsides, letters, and sheet music. Early in 1974, following a long-cherished plan, Carrington opened negotiations with Howard University in order to place his materials in the Moorland-Spingarn Research Center. In 1977, two years after his death, the library was formally installed as part of the Center's research facilities. Carrington's devotion to the black heritage is well displayed in the gift to his alma mater.

Bibliography

A. *The Glenn Carrington Collection: A Guide to the Books, Manuscripts, Music, and Recordings*, compiled by Karen L. Jefferson (Washington, D.C., 1977).

B. Mary Ellen Perry, "Howard Gets Black Life Literary Collection," *Washington Star*, June 27, 1977, Section D.

CARSON, Hampton (b. February 21, 1852, Philadelphia, Pa.; d. July 18, 1929, Philadelphia, Pa.). *Education:* B.A., LL.B., University of Pennsylvania, 1871, 1874. *Collection Disposition:* Free Library of Philadelphia; Henkels, October 26, 1904.

By the time he was thirty, Carson had established himself as one of the leading trial lawyers in the East. He taught at the University of Pennsylvania Law School, became Pennsylvania's attorney general under Governor Samuel W. Pennypacker*, and held office as president of both the state and the national bar associations. He also found time to serve as a trustee of the Free Library of Philadelphia.

Carson's intense interest in history led him to assemble a large retrospective collection on the law. He focused on the common law, particularly as it developed in England in the sixteenth and seventeenth centuries. He owned yearbooks, abridgements, commentaries, statutes, reports, trial transcripts, biography, and history. Much of the collection served as a tool for Carson's own research and writing. In 1887 he published a treatise on the law of criminal conspiracies, and in 1891 he issued his major work, a definitive history of the Supreme Court of the United States with biographies of all the chief and associate justices. He also wrote historical studies for the state bar journal and bibliographic papers for the Philobiblon Club. His collection of books and articles was supplemented with an impressive array of manuscripts, letters, and prints. When the collection was turned over to the Philadelphia Free Library in 1927, the holdings consisted of 10,000 books, 100 manuscripts, 2,000 letters, and more than 10,000 prints and sketches.

Carson was particularly attracted to association volumes. In a talk to the Philobiblon Club in 1916, he described how books link the present to the past and illustrated his points with autographs and marginalia from his own library. His copy of Anthony Fitz-Herbert's *Abridgement*, for example, carried the signatures of Tench Francis, an early attorney general of Pennsylvania; John Dickinson, a signer of the U.S. Constitution; and Charles Chauncey, a notable eighteenth-century Philadelphia barrister. He also owned a long run of the fourteenth- and fifteenth-century *Year Books*, reports of actual cases tried in English courts. All the books and manuscripts were arranged on Carson's shelves in strict chronological order to emphasize his belief that the law was a steadily progressive science. The impressive array began with a thirteenth-century manuscript of the Magna Carta and concluded with a collection of the works of the eighteenth-century English jurist Sir William Blackstone. The Blackstone materials were extraordinary. Carson obtained English and American editions of the *Commentaries*, Blackstone's Patent of Precedence as king's counsel, his commission as a justice of the Court of Common Pleas, and letters, engravings, and portraits. The whole of the Carson library, as Philadelphia's Free Library Rare Book Curator Howell Heaney pointed out, was far greater than the sum of its parts. In addition to materials on the common law, it provided an impressive archive on the social environment of the sixteenth and seventeenth centuries.

In a talk delivered at the Free Library, Catherine Drinker Bowen explained how important the collection had been to her in writing *The Lion and the Throne*, her comprehensive biography of Sir Edward Coke. Carson lived in Philadelphia and built his library in that city. It is a matter of appropriate local pride that his books grace the Free Library and stand as a testimony to his respect for the history of the law.

Bibliography

A. *Catalogue of the Exhibits of the Hampton L. Carson Collection of Books, Documents, Portraits, and Autograph Letters Illustrative of the Growth of the Common Law* (Philadelphia, 1930); *Catalog of the Collection Illustrative of the Growth of the Common Law* (Boston, 1962).

B. *DAB* 11, 153–154; *NCAB* 3, 264; Catherine Drinker Bowen, "Sir Edward Coke and the Carson Collection," in *Four Talks for Bibliophiles* (Philadelphia, 1958), 39–58; Howell Heaney, "Rare Book Librarianship and Law Librarianship," in *Collecting and Managing Rare Law Books* (Dobbs Ferry, N.Y., 1981), 55–69.

CHAMBERLAIN, Jacob C. (b. July 3, 1860, Palmaner, India; d. July 28, 1905, New York, N.Y.). *Education:* A.B., 1882, Rutgers University. *Collection Disposition:* Anderson, February 16, November 4, 1909.

After graduating from Rutgers, Chamberlain joined the Thomas A. Edison Laboratories, where he became an active participant in the developing electrical industry. Since his time was completely given to this work until he was forty, his collecting activities were crowded into a brief five years. During those years however, he built one of the finest collections of American literature in the country. He began with the standard nineteenth-century figures such as Emerson, Hawthorne, Holmes, Longfellow, and Lowell but soon expanded his list to include nearly one-hundred authors in all. Whenever possible he obtained letters and manuscripts to enrich the printed record. Many times he was able to obtain these materials through direct negotiations with the author's family or friends. In the case of Longfellow, Chamberlain secured an important archive of intimate letters from George Greene, the poet's college friend. In 1900 Chamberlain increased the value of his library immeasurably by purchasing the entire American literature section from the Beverly Chew* collection. Chamberlain always insisted on original wrappers as a part of his interest in bibliographic accuracy. He believed in establishing the priority of editions by close examination of the author's letters and diaries. The 1904 exhibition of Hawthorne's first editions and manuscripts at the Grolier Club and the accompanying catalog were both his handiwork. The catalog served scholars as the standard Hawthorne bibliography for a number of years. Plans for similar exhibitions were cut short by his untimely death. Prices at the first Chamberlain sale were above average with the rare Poe items reaching record breaking levels. When Walter Wallace* obtained a presentation copy of *Al Aaraaf* for $2,900, the *New York Times* reminded readers that the same copy had been sold to Chamberlain eight years before at the Frederick French* sale for only $1,300. In a day when bibliographic equipment was somewhat primitive Chamberlain created his own checklists and formed a good library. Such distinguished collectors as Stephen Wakeman*, Walter Wallace* and W. T. H. Howe* obtained substantial portions of their collections from the two Chamberlain sales. In his iconoclastic memoir, *Adventures of a Treasure Hunter*, bookdealer Charles Everitt identified Chamberlain as one who cared much more for the literary value of books than for their potential market value. In Everitt's appropriate characterization, Chamberlain was "a true collector."

Bibliography

B. *NCAB* 24, 88; Cannon 176–178; Grolier 75, 99–101; Everitt 61–64; "News for Bibliophiles," *Nation*, February 11, 1909, 135, February 25, 1909, 190–191.

CHAPIN, Alfred C. (b. March 8, 1848, South Hadley, Mass.; d. October 2, 1936, Montreal, Can.). *Education:* A.B., Williams College, 1869; LL.B., Harvard University, 1871. *Collection Disposition:* Williams College.

After receiving his degree from Harvard, Chapin moved to New York and joined the legal staff of the Long Island Railroad. He used this base to enter politics, where he pursued a successful career at the municipal and state levels. He was first elected mayor of Brooklyn and later to the New York Assembly. In 1897 he gave up his political offices and began to devote himself to philanthropic efforts on behalf of Williams College. His interest in book collecting can be traced to 1915, when he was shown Eliot's "Indian Bible" and a number of other historical and literary rarities at James Drake's bookshop in New York. He bought the books for Williams but insisted they remain in New York until the college could erect a fireproof library building. The president and the trustees agreed, and Chapin continued to collect. In addition to help from Drake, Chapin now began to secure many historical rarities from the distinguished New York dealer Lathrop C. Harper. The focus of the collection had by this time settled on three main areas: incunabula, English literature, and Americana. Later, continental literature, Bibles, the history of science, and illustrated books would be added. With the help of Drake and Harper, Chapin was able to obtain rarities from several important libraries that came on the market between 1911 and 1925. He bought at the Robert Hoe III* and Henry E. Huntington* sales in New York and at the Huth and Britwell Court sales in London. By 1924, when the new Williams library opened its doors, Chapin was able to present faculty and students with a carefully selected rare book collection of over 9,000 volumes. He continued to supplement this gift, so that by the time of his death the total came to nearly 12,000 volumes. Early European printing was well represented and included more than 500 items from the fifteenth century. The jewel of this gathering was a perfect copy of Cicero's *De Oratore* printed at Subiaco by Sweynheym and Pannartz in 1465. The English literature section boasted the four Shakespeare folios, as well as important editions of the work of the other significant Elizabethan poets and dramatists. The American period of exploration and discovery was well documented with the narratives of Peter Martyr, Champlain, Lescarbot, and Hennepin, among others. Bibles and prayer books formed another rich section of the library, as did natural history and illustrated costume books.

Chapin made it clear from the start that he wanted the books used by undergraduates. This was to be no mere scholarly archive. The books and manuscripts would, he hoped, illuminate day-to-day class assignments and supply the raw material for papers and class projects. The original documents and first editions from his library would make it possible for students to approach historical and literary problems through the eyes of the participants. His wishes have been fulfilled. The gifts made it possible for undergraduates to work with original source materials and approach historical and literary problems directly. Chapin's gift provided students with a diverse and inviting record of Western humanistic thought.

Bibliography

A. *A Short Title List of the Chapin Library*, compiled by Lucy E. Osborne (Portland, Maine, 1939).

B. *NCAB* I, 525; Cannon, 205–208; Thomas R. Adams, "Chapin Library: An Idea," *Williams College Alumni Review*, May 1956, 23–26; H. Richard Archer, "The Chapin Library After Thirty-five Years," *QNLBCC*, Summer 1958, 51–57; Lucy E. Osborne, "The Chapin Library," *Library Journal*, February 15, 1924, 16–17; Lucy E. Osborne, *Alfred Clark Chapin* (Portland, Maine, 1937); Lucy E. Osborne, "Rare Books in a College Program," *Library Journal*, May 1, 1941, 27–28.

CHEW, Beverly (b. March 5, 1850, Geneva, N.Y.; d. May 20, 1924, Geneva, N.Y.). *Education:* A.B., Hobart College, 1869. *Collection Disposition:* Grolier Club; Henry E. Huntington Library; Anderson, December 8, 1924, January 5, 1925.

After graduating from college, Chew entered the banking business in New York. He proved to be a capable worker and rose over a short period of time from the level of junior accountant to that of vice-president. He had been a book collector since his student years at Hobart College, and the move to New York provided splendid new opportunities. At first he concentrated on the major nineteenth-century America literary figures, such as Lowell, Emerson, Thoreau, and Longfellow. For many years his Longfellow checklist, drawn up in 1885 for bookseller W. E. Benjamin, was considered the standard bibliographical source. Somewhat before the turn of the century, Chew began to buy editions of the British poets, particularly from the Jacobean and Caroline periods. In 1900 he decided it was impossible to collect both American and English literature and sold his Americana authors to his friend Jacob C. Chamberlain*. This left him free to concentrate on his favorite sixteenth- and seventeenth-century English authors: Shakespeare, Milton, Dryden, Pope, Donne, Crashaw, and others. The expertise Chew developed in close analysis of these authors was invaluable in the production of some of the Grolier Club's finest catalogs. His meticulous editing made the *Catalogue of Original and Early Editions . . . from Wither to Prior* (1905) and *The Poems of John Donne* (1895) outstanding productions.

As his library grew in stature, it attracted the attention of Henry E. Huntington*. In 1912, after turning down a number of overtures, Chew finally agreed to sell Huntington 2,000 choice titles, the bulk of his English literature collection. As soon as the books were packed off, Chew started buying again. This time he focused on lesser-known sixteenth- and seventeenth-century poets such as Edmund Waller, Humphrey Mosley, George Wither, and John Cleveland. In what turned out to be a satisfying turn of events, Chew was able to buy back some of his own books from Huntington as the railroad executive cleared his shelves of duplicates. It is therefore possible, as one biographer has pointed out, to identify books that have the remarkable Chew-Huntington-Chew provenance. In addition to general literature, Chew collected Bibles, American bindings up to 1850, silver and embroidered European bindings, bibliography, and prints.

Many of Chew's bibliographic activities centered around the Grolier Club of New York, where he was one of the most active members. He served on committees and was elected president of the club in 1892. Close friendships with such Grolier stalwarts as Theodore Low DeVinne*, Robert Hoe III*, Samuel P. Avery*, Marshall Lefferts*, and Winston Hagen* brought him into the center of American collecting activities. Throughout his life Chew gave many books and paintings to the Grolier Club. In his will he bequeathed the Club fifty-one fine bindings and a number of valuable oil portraits. In 1924 the sale of the Chew library attracted a large and enthusiastic group of buyers to the Anderson Galleries. Chew was one of the most respected collectors of his day, a status he earned with discerning bibliographic judgment and good taste. Librarian-bibliographer Henrietta Bartlett called him a "master spirit among collectors."

Bibliography

A. *Essays and Verses* (New York, 1926).

B. Cannon, 142–143; *Grolier 75*, 51–53; Granniss, 324–325; Henrietta C. Bartlett, "Introduction," in *Anderson Galleries Catalogue* (New York, 1924); Luther Livingston, "Library Formed by Beverly Chew," *The Nation*, October 31, 1912, 405; A. E. Newton, "Beverly Chew," in *Greatest Book in the World* (Boston, 1925), 424–443; Robert Nikirk, "Two American Book Collectors of the Nineteenth Century: William Loring Andrews and Beverly Chew," in *Book Selling and Book Buying* (Chicago, 1978), 99–118.

CHRYSLER, Walter P., Jr. (b. April 2, 1875, Wamengo, Kans.; d. August 18, 1940, Detroit, Mich.). *Collection Disposition:* Parke-Bernet, February 26, 1952, December 7, 1954, May 10, 1955.

At the age of thirty-five, Chrysler was manager of the Buick Motor Company in Detroit and was recognized as one of the leaders in the automobile industry. As a complement to his social and financial position, he began to acquire European impressionist paintings, rare books, and manuscripts. The Chrysler library focused on American literature, particularly the works of Clemens, Emerson, Harte, Hawthorne, Irving, Longfellow, and Poe. His Clemens collection was perhaps most distinguished of all and included manuscripts, letters, presentation first editions, and periodicals. Among his Emerson holdings was an essay written when the author was twelve years old and a student in the Boston Latin School. Chrysler was an active buyer at New York auctions, securing many of his rarities at the Morris Parrish* and John A. Spoor* sales of the late 1930s. The entire Chrysler library was dispersed at auction in a series of New York sales beginning in 1952.

Bibliography

B. *NCAB* D, 89; Randall, passim; *NYT*, August 19, 1940, I.

CHURCH, Elihu Dwight (b. 1835, New York, N.Y.; d. August 30, 1908, Westfield, Conn.). *Education:* A.B., City College of New York, 1855. *Collection Disposition:* Henry E. Huntington Library; Anderson, March 29, 1916.

Throughout his professional life, Church was involved in the family manufacturing business in New York. In the early 1880s he began to collect handsome folios illustrated by Bewick and Cruikshank. He also bought early Americana, securing examples from the Henry Stevens estate and from the Brayton Ives* sale. Reticent by nature, he insisted that his purchases be kept from public attention. The publication of his magnificent five-volume catalog in 1908 came as a surprise to historians and collectors. The *American Historical Review* of October 1908 compared the library favorably with the prestigious collections of James Lenox* and John Carter Brown*. The quality of the collection made up for its limited size—only 2,000 volumes. Working quietly at auctions in New York and London, Church had managed to obtain several "Columbus Letters," the *Bay Psalm Book*, and prime copies of Cortez, DeBry, Hulsius, Las Casas, Frobisher, and Vespucci. To this array he added colonial imprints representing the earliest presswork from Cambridge, Boston, and New York, and numerous pamphlets on Indian relations. It was not only the extraordinary items presented that drew universal praise but also the high quality of the catalog itself. Under the direction of bibliographers George Watson Cole and Henrietta Bartlett, the catalog provided students of American history with facsimile title page representations and copious notes.

In 1905, following another line of interest, Church bought the distinguished Rowfant library brought together by the English poet Frederick Locker-Lampson. From this small but well-coordinated cabinet library he kept a small number of rarities but sold the rest to Henry E. Huntington* and Winston Hagen*. After Church's death, legal complications forced the heirs to store the books in a New York warehouse for almost three years. George D. Smith, the agile New York bookdealer, saw an opportunity for a sale and brought the qualities of the Church library to Huntington's attention. The railway magnate, just on the threshold of his most active collecting period, decided to buy. On April 8, 1911, the *New York Times* reported one of the most important book transactions of the early part of the century, the sale of the Church library to George D. Smith. Church was a shrewd and enterprising collector who knew the value of books and understood the importance of working with the established book trade. His magnificent catalog remains his most enduring monument.

Bibliography

A. *A Catalogue of Books Relating to the Discovery and Early History of North and South America*, compiled by George Watson Cole (New York, 1907); *A Catalogue of Books Consisting of English Literature and Miscellanea . . . Forming a Part of the Library of E. D. Church* (New York, 1909); *Check List of Some of the Rarities in the Library of E. Dwight Church of New York City*, compiled by George Watson Cole (New York, 1903).

B. *Grolier 75*, 12–14; George Watson Cole, "Book Collectors as Benefactors of Public Libraries," *PBSA*, 1st Q 1915, 47–110; *NYT*, April 8, 1911, 12.

CLARK, William A., Jr. (b. March 29, 1877, Deer Lodge, Mont.; d. June 14, 1934, Salmon Lake, Mont.). *Education:* LL.B., University of Virginia, 1899. *Collection Disposition:* University of California at Los Angeles; University of Virginia.

As the youngest son of a Montana copper baron, Clark had the advantages of private schools and European travel. His father and his older brother Charles were collectors, and it is likely that their influence turned Clark toward rare and beautiful books. Until 1917 he had shown only desultory interest in building a personal library, acquiring a few conventional American first editions, but after that year he turned into a determined collector. He became acquainted with the bookdealers George and Alice Millard of Pasadena and through them began to gather an impressive collection of fine printing. He also began to obtain a wide range of English literature from the redoubtable New York dealer George D. Smith. By 1920 Clark felt he had accumulated enough distinguished volumes to warrant publication of a library catalog. For the detailed work involved he employed California bibliographer and bookseller Robert E. Cowan*. When Cowan's work was combined with the printing skill of John Henry Nash, the Clark catalogs were destined to have more than passing fame. With encouragement from the Millards and Smith, Clark's collecting interests gradually developed around Elizabethan and Jacobean drama. Through Smith he purchased over 100 Dryden items and was well on his way to developing one of the finest collections in the world. The Dryden texts were supported with manuscript material, letters, and a vast accumulation of criticism and biography.

Clark's Shakespeare holdings, made up of numerous folios and quartos, were impressive but not quite on the scale developed by Henry F. Huntington* or Henry C. Folger*. The Oscar Wilde collection, on the other hand, was first-rate. Some of this had come from Smith, some from A. S. W. Rosenbach*, and many from C. S. Millard, secretary to Wilde's executor. In 1928 Clark made one of his most important purchases with the acquisition of Wilde letters, manuscripts, and books offered by Dulau and Company. The Wilde holdings were virtually complete by the time they were presented to the University of California at Los Angeles.

With the aid of the bibliophile Seymour De Ricci, Clarke focused on French drama and bought fine editions of Corneille, Racine, Molière, and Ronsard. In 1923, frightened by a fire in his residence, Clark decided to construct a separate fireproof building in the West Adams district of Los Angeles. In 1926 he deeded it and the contents to the University of California, a splendid gift to the state. The endowment has allowed the collections to expand and the library to become a distinguished respository for literary research.

Bibliography

A. *The Library of William A. Clark Jr.* (San Francisco, 1920–1930).

B. *NCAB* 25, 301; Cannon, 215–218; *Grolier 75*, 198–200; Wolf and Fleming, passim; William D. Mangam, *The Clarks: An American Phenomenon* (New York, 1941); Lawrence Clark Powell, "From Private Collection to Public Institution: The William Andrews Clark Memorial Library," *The Library Quarterly*, April 1950, 101–108; Cora Edgerton Sanders, "The Beginnings of the Library," in *William Andrews Clark Memorial Library: Report of the First Decade 1934–1944* (Los Angeles, 1946), 13–17.

CLARY, William W. (b. October 15, 1888, Northfield, Minn.; d. October 13, 1971, Los Angeles, Calif.). *Education:* B.A., Pomona College, 1911. *Collection Disposition:* Honnold Library of Claremont Colleges.

After completion of his legal studies, Clary worked for the public defender in Los Angeles County and then joined the firm of O'Melveny and Myers, where he practiced until his death. Outside his active professional life, Clary devoted the major part of his time and energy to serving the Claremont Colleges. He was on the board of fellows for forty years and acted as a trustee at various times for Pomona, Harvey Mudd, and Pitzer colleges. According to Clary's own account, the first "collector's item" he ever bought was a copy of the 1831 New York second edition of Shelley's *Queen Mab*. This bargain in Ernest Dawson's ten-cent tray had an interesting history and was in fact the first edition printed in America. This book was the spark that led Clary to continue with Shelley over a period of fifty years.

In the late 1920s, along with W. Irving Way and Arthur Ellis, Clary joined a few other bibliophiles in the Los Angeles area to organize the Zamorano Club. It was through his acquaintance with Way, a former Chicago publisher, that Clary became interested in Andrew Lang, Bruce Rogers, William Morris, and Thomas Mosher. In the 1920s and 1930s Clary devoted considerable time to his Lang collection, developing strong holdings of the fairy tales, novels, poetry, and classics in translation. As the accumulation of books and pamphlets grew, Clary was drawn more and more to all things English. When in 1928 he became a trustee of the Claremont Colleges, which were organized somewhat on the Oxford plan, he decided to learn all he could about the venerable English institution. First Clary bought books on the history of Oxford University, then biographies of the more notable faculty. When he had accumulated some sixty books he turned them over to the Claremont Library, thinking that might be the end of the collection. It was only the beginning. Books led to books, and soon the collection included the writings of the various authors identified as the "Oxford Movement," poetry by Oxford graduates, printing from the Oxford University Press, and much more. The collection was never intended to be a rare book library, but rather a working tool for investigation of the history and traditions of the great university. In 1968 the collection, by then numbering 3,600 volumes, was cataloged in two handsome volumes and established in a separate room at the Honnold Library.

The Oxford collection took many intriguing tangents. In one of these Clary secured a manuscript archive of notebooks and correspondence of novelist Mary Augusta Ward (Mrs. Humphry Ward). Mrs. Ward's best-remembered work, *Robert Elsmere*, was set in the time of the Oxford religious controversies and elicited a barrage of criticism from such formidable figures as Prime Minister William Gladstone and philosopher Benjamin Jowett. All these documents, along with Mrs. Ward's correspondence with her publisher, Smith Elder, are housed in the Honnold Library.

The last collection formed by Clary focused on Milton and the variant editions of *Paradise Lost*. This text, interpreted in hundreds of ways with illustrations by countless distinguished artists, made for an intriguing bibliographic puzzle. Eventually the Milton collection took its place beside the Shelley and Lang titles in the Claremont Library. Clary collected with intelligence and purpose, to the great benefit of Claremont faculty and students.

Bibliography

A. *Fifty Years of Book Collecting* (Los Angeles, 1962); "An Oxford Collection," *BC*, Summer 1968, 177–189; *The William W. Clary Oxford Collection: A Descriptive Catalogue . . .* (Oxford, 1956); *A Supplementary Catalogue* (Oxford, 1965).

CLAWSON, John L. (b. March 17, 1865, Campbell, N.Y.; d. November 27, 1933, Buffalo, N.Y.). *Collection Disposition:* Merwin, January 28, 1915; Anderson, January 18, 1917, March 26, 1917, November 29, 1920, May 20 and 24, 1926.

After having grown up in central New York State, Clawson moved to Buffalo and eventually became senior partner in one of the largest dry goods firms in that city. His interest in book buying was dramatically brief. There is no record that he was an active collector before 1914, and by 1923 he had completed his library of Elizabethan literature. As bibliographer Seymour De Ricci pointed out, the scope of the collection, from 1550 to 1660, was narrow but the field was incredibly rich. Clawson had no intention of building a large library but was determined to form one of quality. A large number of important sixteenth-century books came on the market between 1918 and 1919 from the sale of the libraries of Winston Hagen* and Herschel V. Jones* and through the dispersal of Huntington duplicates. Working with A. S. W. Rosenbach*, Clawson obtained Shakespearean quartos, Milton first editions in original bindings, sixteenth-century morality plays, and Elizabethan poetry. By 1924, however, when his impressive catalog was issued, his enthusiasm had waned. According to Wolf and Fleming, it was as if the catalog had been a final statement. After that time he turned down all offers to buy. When the Clawson books came up for sale at the Anderson Galleries in 1926, little publicity was needed to attract the major figures in the book world. Rosenbach knew the collection intimately and bought heavily for his favored customers—Owen D. Young*, Henry C. Folger*, and Carl H. Pforzheimer*. Spending almost $200,000, Pforzheimer established himself as the top buyer. The total sale figure of $642,687 was ample vindication, if any was needed, of Clawson's shrewd good taste. The prices set at this sale established high-water-marks for years to come.

Bibliography

A. *A Catalogue of Early English Books in the Library of John L. Clawson* (Philadelphia, 1924).

B. Cannon, 221–223; Wolf and Fleming, passim; William A. Jackson, "John Clawson's Early English Books," in *To Doctor R* (Philadelphia, 1946), 97–119.

CLEMENTS, William L. (b. April 1, 1861, Ann Arbor, Mich.; d. November 6, 1934, Bay City, Mich.). *Education:* B.S., University of Michigan, 1882. *Collection Disposition:* William L. Clements Library of Americana; University of Michigan.

After graduating from the University of Michigan, Clements joined the family railroad machinery manufacturing business in Bay City. He assumed the presidency of the Industrial Works in 1895 and continued in that office until he retired thirty years later. Clements' interest in book collecting was kindled by a Bay City bibliophile-businessman, Aaron Cooke. Over a period of years, Cooke had formed an outstanding library of Americana, but in 1903, pleading poor health, he resigned all his public offices and turned over his collection to Clements. By 1910 Clements' interests were firmly set on collecting Americana, particularly materials that reflected the era of exploration and discovery. These interests were nourished by such prominent bookdealers as Lathrop C. Harper, George D. Smith, Robert Dodd, and Henry N. Stevens. They saw to it that Clements was kept informed of the availability of choice items of Americana. For example, it was Harper who helped Clements acquire the historical library of New York lawyer Newbold Edgar. This library contained numerous works by colonial poet Anne Bradstreet and tracts signed by famous Virginia colonial officer Captain John Smith. At the Robert Hoe* sale in New York and the Henry Huth sales in London in 1911, Clements had a further opportunity to enhance his collection. From the Huth library, for example, he bought the Latin translation of the "Columbus Letter" and Thomas Hariot's "Virginia" (1588), among some 150 other rarities. To be accurate, the Hariot eluded Clements at the sale, but later he was able to buy it directly from London bookdealer Bernard Quaritch. This unassuming little quarto, the first description in English of the first English colony, is one of the greatest rarities now in the Clements Library at the University of Michigan—where rarities are common.

After Clements was appointed to the board of regents at the University of Michigan in 1909, he began to devote a considerable amount of attention to the university library. Foremost in his mind was a plan to secure a proper place for his own books. In 1920 he outlined a program that not only provided for the transfer of his books and manuscripts to the university but also included erection of a building to house them. The William L. Clements Library of Americana was opened with appropriate fanfare on June 15, 1923.

Throughout the planning and building stages, Clements continued to add riches to the already impressive collections. Over a short period of time he acquired the letters of General Lewis Cass, manuscript accounts of the death of George

Washington, some 200 volumes documenting the French view of the American Revolution, and the papers and letters of the Earl of Shelburne. Then, working through French dealer Edouard Champion, he acquired the distinguished library of 17,000 volumes and 25,000 pamphlets belonging to historian Henry Vignaud.

During the last ten years of his life, Clements concentrated more on manuscripts than on printed books. In 1925 he obtained the papers of New York Governor George Clinton and those of Sir Henry Clinton, commander of English forces in the colonies. This archive of some 16,000 items contained the correspondence between Major John André and Benedict Arnold and included Arnold's letters to General Clinton. One of Clements' last great acquisitions, added four years before his death, was the manuscripts, letters, and diaries of British General Thomas Gage. Clements formed his library systematically, piece by piece, rather than through the amorphous *en bloc* technique employed, for example, by Henry E. Huntington* and Henry C. Folger*. For that reason his collection reflects the man more than do others gathered by his contemporaries. The Clements Library of Americana at the University of Michigan stands as one of the great depositories for the study of American history.

Bibliography

A. *The William L. Clements Library of Americana at the University of Michigan* (Ann Arbor, Mich., 1923).

B. *DAB*, Supp. 1, 179; *NCAB* B, 460; 42, 669; Cannon, 292–301; *Grolier 75*, 107–110; Randolph Adams, *The Whys and Wherefores of the William L. Clements Library* (Ann Arbor, Mich., 1930); William W. Bishop, "Some Recollections of William Lawrence Clements and the Formation of His Library," *The Library Quarterly*, July 1948, 185–191; Clarence Brigham, "William Lawrence Clements," *PAAS*, January 1936, 10–13; Margaret Maxwell, *Shaping a Library: William L. Clements as Collector* (Amsterdam, The Netherlands, 1973); James Shearer, "Bay City and the Clements Library," *Michigan History Magazine*, September 1954, 253–264.

COCHRANE, Alexander Smith (b. February 28, 1874, Yonkers, N.Y.; d. June 20, 1929, Saranac Lake, N.Y.). *Education:* B.A., Yale University, 1896. *Collection Disposition:* Yale University.

Before he offered Yale his Elizabethan rarities, little was known of Cochrane's book-collecting activities. As a wealthy New York industrialist, he had quietly taken advantage of opportunities to acquire rare books and manuscripts from some of the most important European and British auctions at the turn of the century. His favorites were the great Elizabethans—Shakespeare, Jonson, Marlowe, Sir Philip Sidney, and Spenser. Among the volumes he offered Yale were the first four Shakespeare folios, which he had purchased from the Henry Huth sale, a number of Shakespeare quartos, and a selection of distinguished editions of other Elizabethan and Jacobean dramatists. To these he added an array of pamphlets and critical material relating to the literary activities of the sixteenth century. In 1911 Cochrane founded the Elizabethan Club at Yale and presented his books as a basis for the library. In *A Census of Shakespeare's*

Plays in Quarto 1540–1709, Henrietta Bartlett and Alfred W. Pollard ranked the Elizabethan Club's library third in importance in the country, giving place only to the Henry C. Folger* and Henry E. Huntington* collections. Although small in number, the importance of the Cochrane gift remains beyond question.

Bibliography

B. *NCAB* 32, 479; Cannon, 333; A. E. Newton, *This Book Collecting Game* (Boston, 1928), 31.

COE, William Robertson (b. June 8, 1869, Worcestershire, Eng.; d. March 14, 1955, Palm Beach, Fla.). *Collection Disposition:* Yale University.

After arriving in the United States at the age of fourteen and completing his grammar school education, Coe joined an insurance firm in Philadelphia. He moved up quickly in the ranks of that organization and eventually served as president. His interest in the West and western literature may have stemmed from the pleasant associations formed in connection with his purchase of Buffalo Bill's Wyoming ranch around 1910. From that year Coe became deeply committed to a study of western lore and history, particularly the events surrounding settlement of the Pacific Northwest and the Louisiana Territory. In a significant early purchase, Coe obtained the western library of the Reverend Nathaniel S. Thomas, bishop of Wyoming. In this collection he secured religious tracts and land titles as well as letters and diaries of early western homesteaders and ranchers. As the collection developed, Coe found an ideal agent in scholarly New York bookdealer Edward Eberstadt. Eberstadt knew the book trade and was particularly knowledgeable about the fine points of western Americana. All this knowledge was placed at Coe's disposal in what turned out to be an ideal collector-dealer relationship. Among the Coe treasures were Lewis and Clark maps, Mormon church records, California gold rush diaries, land claims, town ordinances, and early northwestern imprints. More than other collectors, Coe was interested in the development of social institutions in the frontier communities. How and where did churches and business establishments begin? Documents in his collections often provided the answers.

After considering the facilities of several universities as a permanent home for his collection, Coe chose Yale because of its scholarly reputation and the evidence of its interest in western Americana. Materials from the Coe library began to arrive in New Haven in 1943 and continued to come in regular shipments until the time of his death. This gift, together with the contributions from Henry R. Wagner*, Winlock Miller*, Thomas W. Streeter*, and Frederick W. Beinecke*, laid the basis for "The Yale Collection of Western Americana." In a ringing tribute, Wagner once referred to the Coe library as the finest collection of western material in existence. The truth of that assessment can be appreciated by examining the 1948 issue of the *Yale Library Gazette* edited by Eberstadt; the 1952 *Catalogue of Manuscripts* edited by Mary Wirthington, and the four-volume *Catalog of the Yale Collection of Western Americana*.

In a totally different vein, Coe developed an outstanding library of ornithology. He organized it with the same careful attention to bibliographic detail that distinguished his western library. In addition to the monumental printed works by James Audubon and John Gould, Coe acquired a wide range of original oils and watercolors by such well-known illustrators as Thomas Howitt, Louis Fuertes, and Archibald Thornburn. One of the choice manuscripts in the collection was Audubon's 4,000-word letter to his wife, in which he sketched out for the first time the general plan of *The Birds of America*. The acquisition of this library moved Yale into the first rank for scholarly studies in ornithology. In the case of both the western collections and the ornithology materials, Coe set aside funds for the production of catalogs, employment of staff, and continued acquisitions— the ideal arrangement. Coe provided not only a rich archive of research materials but also the bibliographic support needed to assure the continued importance of the archive.

Bibliography

A. *Catalogue of Manuscripts in the Collection of Western Americana, Founded by William Robertson Coe* (New Haven, 1952); *Catalogue of the Yale Collection of Western Americana* (Boston, 1961); *Ornithological Books in the Yale University Library, Including the Library of William Robertson Coe* (New Haven, 1961).

B. *NCAB* G, 358; Edward Eberstadt, "The William Robertson Coe Collection of Western Americana," *YLG*, October 1948, 1–130; S. Dillon Ripley, "The Coe Ornithological Collection," *YLG*, October 1952, 66–70.

COLE, Hamilton (b. 1844, Claverack, N.Y.; d. October 29, 1889, New York, N.Y.). *Education:* A.B., Yale University, 1866. *CollectionDisposition:* Yale University; Bangs, April 7, 1890.

After graduating from college, Cole pursued a successful law career in New York, counting among his clients such important firms as American Express and Wells Fargo. He became a discriminating collector of early printing, book illustration, and books about books. In this last category he acquired an outstanding collection of the various editions of Richard de Bury's *Philobiblon*, including the first Cologne printing of 1473. Like many other collectors of his day, Cole expanded his favorite works by a process known as grangerizing, or extra-illustrating. In his hands a two-volume set of the Pickering edition of *The Compleate Angler* became a six-volume set with the addition of numerous portraits, prints, and watercolors. He extended a copy of Byron's *Childe Harold's Pilgrimage* from one volume to four with the insertion of over 360 portraits and pictures. A reviewer in the *New York Times* wryly compared such cut-and-paste activities to the depredations of Attila the Hun. Since Cole's chief interest was in book collecting, he naturally turned to the evocative treatises on that subject by British bibliophile Thomas F. Dibdin. Cole's collection contained first editions of Dibdin's works, with such highlights as an extra-illustrated octavo *Bibliomania* enlarged to a folio and printed on Whatman handmade paper. In the history of American

collecting, Cole is chiefly remembered as the purchaser of the George Brinley*
copy of the Gutenberg Bible. In 1881, when the Brinley library was brought to
auction, Cole outbid Brayton Ives* and secured the monument of printing for
$8,000. Later Cole sold the Bible to Ives, saying it did not fit his modest library
and that he had bought it only because of the bargain price. All Cole's books,
with the exception of the de Bury volumes, were dispersed at auction in the
spring of 1890. In an act of friendship Cole bequeathed his de Burys to Edward
Bement, who subsequently turned them over to Yale. The Cole library was a
typical late-nineteenth-century gathering by a wealthy man interested in book
history and book illustration.

Bibliography

B. Charles B. Hogan, "The Bement Collection of the Philobiblon," *YLG*, October
1931, 25–30; "Hamilton Cole and His Books," *NYT*, September 4, 1897, 5–6; "The
Hamilton Cole Library," *NYT*, March 9, 1890, 10.

COLEMAN, J. Winston (b. November 5, 1898, Lexington, Ky.; d. May 4,
1983, Lexington, Ky.). *Education:* B.S., M.S., University of Kentucky, 1920,
1929. *Collection Disposition:* Transylvania College.

After graduating from college Coleman worked briefly as a commercial
developer, but dissatisfaction with the business world led him to decide to devote
himself entirely to managing his Kentucky farm and to writing. Exposure to his
father's library, where he read Lewis Collins' *History of Kentucky*, kindled his
interest in state history. As he collected he found a number of important aspects
of Kentucky history that had been overlooked by traditional scholars. Based on
the texts and documents in his own growing library, Coleman decided to fill in
the blanks. He published pamphlets on dueling, the Freemasonry movement,
the slave trade, and early stagecoach routes. To these he added full-scale
biographies of Kentucky historians John Filson and Edward Troye and a
bibliography of early Kentuckiana. His most popular work, *Kentucky: A Pictorial
History*, was based on his own photographs taken with an ancient four-by-five
Graphic-View camera. In 1968 Coleman presented his collection of books,
pamphlets, photographs, and maps to the Transylvania College Library. The
purpose of the gift was to stimulate student interest in state history, a topic that
had absorbed his attention for over forty years.

Bibliography

A. *An Autobiographical Sketch* (Lexington, Ky., 1954); *Collected Writings* (Lexington,
Ky., 1969).
B. Lawrence Thompson, "J. Winston Coleman," *ABC*, January 1961, 3–4; Billy
Bevins, "J. Winston Coleman Jr., Kentucky's Greatest Amateur Historian," *Kentucky
Heritage*, Fall 1973, 6–9.

COLLAMORE, H. Bacon (b. 1894, Middletown, Conn.; d. September 28, 1975, Hartford, Conn.). *Collection Disposition:* Colby College; Free Library of Philadelphia; Indiana University; Trinity College; Yale University.

Throughout an active business career, Collamore gathered a number of impressive book and manuscript collections. He was particularly fond of modern poetry and made a special effort to acquire the works of such authors as Housman, E. A. Robinson, Frost, and Emily Dickinson. In the case of Housman, he developed an extraordinary collection of letters, first editions, and manuscripts, all of which he gave to the Lilly Library at Indiana University. Among the Housman books were an impressive number from the poet's own library bearing his handwritten annotations. Early in the 1920s Collamore began to collect E. A. Robinson and in the process established a delightful literary correspondence with the poet. He sent Robinson mystery fiction and received chatty letters and autographed first editions in return. Collamore presented a portion of his Robinson books to Colby College and later gave the letters and manuscripts to Trinity College. Perhaps Collamore's most important collection centered around the works of his friend Robert Frost. Again the poet and collector established a warm literary friendship. Frost appreciated Collamore's serious interest and sent him inscribed copies of all his books in their many variant states. Collamore bought some of the older titles from well-known New York bookdealer Mrs. Lewis Cohn.

While poetry was Collamore's first love, he never restricted himself to a single genre. He gave a collection of D. H. Lawrence books and manuscripts to Yale and a charming collection of Beatrix Potter watercolors, sketches, and first editions to the Free Library of Philadelphia. With this gift, as Ellen Shaffer noted, the Free Library became the official American headquarters of Flopsy, Mopsy, and Cottontail. In his bibliographic research, Collamore was as thorough as he was in his collecting activities. His article on binding variants in modern first editions in *The Colophon* was a model of painstaking research. He was appropriately described in a commemorative service held at Trinity College as "a bookman *par excellence.*"

Bibliography

A. *Edwin Arlington Robinson, A Bio-Bibliography: The H. Bacon Collamore Collection . . . Exhibited in the Trumbull Room of the Watkinson Library* (Hartford, Conn., 1969); *The Robert Frost Collection in the Watkinson Library* (Hartford, Conn., 1974); "Some Notes on Modern First Editions," *The Colophon*, Summer 1938, 354–358.

B. Reva Barez, "The H. Bacon Collamore Collection of D. H. Lawrence," *YLG*, July 1959, 16–23; John Carter, "A Footnote," in *A. E. Housman* (Bloomington, Ind., 1961), 33–37; Ellen Shaffer, "Collamore Collection of Beatrix Potter Goes to the Free Library of Philadelphia," *ABC*, April 1968, 11.

CONNOR, George Alan (b. 1895, Waterbury, Nebr.; d. 1973, Portland, Oreg.). *Collection Disposition:* University of Oregon.

Trained as a printer, Connor taught graphic arts in New York City, then in Europe and the Soviet Union. As a result of his travels abroad, Connor became interested in Esperanto and other artificial world languages. Soon he and his wife had become the chief American spokespersons for the promotion and use of Esperanto as the international language. He edited the *American Esperanto Magazine* and conducted tours throughout Western Europe and the Soviet Union. As his knowledge and enthusiasm for Esperanto grew, Connor built one of the world's outstanding libraries on that subject. Because of his position with the American Esperanto Society, Connor was able to secure many books and journals from foreign Esperanto societies on an exchange basis. His library included histories, biographies, grammars, songbooks, juveniles (called infano), and long runs of journals. Even recreational groups like the Boy Scouts had their own Esperanto magazines. In 1976, three years after Connor died, his wife gave the entire collection to the University of Oregon Library. That year the George Alan Connor Esperanto Collection was dedicated as a separate unit in the Special Collections Department. It is one of the most important archives for the study of international language.

Bibliography

A. *Catalog of the George Alan Connor Esperanto Collection*, compiled by Karin Smith and Susan Haake (Eugene, Oreg., 1978).

COOKE, Joseph J. (b. June 1, 1813, Providence, R.I.; d. July 8, 1881, Providence, R.I.). *Collection Disposition:* Leavitt, March 13, October 1, December 3, 1883; Redwood Library of Newport; Historical Society of Providence.

Although little is known of Cooke's early life, his collecting exploits are well documented through auction records. He was one of the principal buyers at the William Menzies* sale of 1876 and at the Peter Hastie sale a year later. According to Clarence Brigham, director of the American Antiquarian Society, Cooke's chief interest was Americana. He concentrated on the classic narratives of exploration and discovery and the diverse literature of the Revolutionary War period. He owned one of the rare Eliot "Indian Bibles," two sets of the DeBry "Voyages," and a cache of letters written by George Washington to General Joseph Reed. In addition, he had many Revolutionary War tracts and a collection of early Rhode Island and Providence printing. The entire library, which eventually numbered 25,000 items, was built in ten years. Although some of the books went to Newport and Providence libraries, the bulk were auctioned at Leavitt's in 1883. Before his death, Cooke decided to follow the George Brinley* plan and provided a $5,000 credit for each of ten libraries to be used against sale purchases. Even with these allowances the sale was disappointing. Cooke had apparently gathered books and pamphlets in whirlwind style without regard for condition. He is remembered as an accumulator with a somewhat unsophisticated taste for Americana.

Bibliography

B. Clarence Brigham, "Reminiscences of Some American Book Collectors," in *To Doctor R.* (Philadelphia, 1946), 46–47; Horatio Rogers, *Private Libraries of Providence* (Providence, R.I., 1878), 109–132; *Representative Men and Old Families of Rhode Island*, volume 2 (Providence, R.I., 1908), 891.

CORDELL, Warren N. (b. 1913, Terre Haute, Ind.; d. January 5, 1980, Highland Park, Ill.). *Education:* B.S., Indiana State University, 1933. *Collection Disposition:* Indiana State University.

In 1937 Cordell joined the A. C. Nielsen Marketing Research Company in Chicago and ten years later was appointed chief statistical officer. It was not until 1961 that he was able to devote time and energy to book collecting. Cordell had always been interested in words and their meanings, so when he started to collect it seemed natural to concentrate on English dictionaries. His first purchases were from John Fleming in New York and from Loudermilk's Bookshop in Washington, D.C. Prices were low and the competition was almost nonexistent. At first the books seemed to fall into place without much effort. Certainly any dictionary collector would want a respectable gathering of the Webster editions, variants of Johnson's *Dictionary of the English Language*, and Bailey's *Etymological Dictionary*. Cordell was working along those lines when he obtained a copy of a dictionary compiled by American lexicographer Joseph Worcester which included a seven-page "Catalogue of English Dictionaries." As Cordell studied the list of some 390 examples he became aware of the territory he was about to explore. It was the Worcester compilation that set Cordell on the road to dictionary bibliomania. His work took him to large cities around the world, where he found time to place his want list in the hands of knowledgeable dealers. He was careful to respond quickly to quotations and to buy as many items as possible in order to cement good business relationships. Dealers provided him with immediate preferential treatment. Among the high points in his collection were Randle Cotgrave's autographed copy of Hollyband's 1594 French-English dictionary and P. M. Roget's autographed first edition of the *Thesaurus*. Aside from these individual rarities, the Cordell collection was distinguished for its 200 separate editions of Samuel Johnson's *Dictionary* and all known editions of Bailey's *Etymological Dictionary*.

In 1969, prompted by a flash flood that destroyed some 200 books in his basement, Cordell made the first of four presentations to his alma mater, Indiana State University in Terre Haute. The university officers were planning a new library building and agreed to set aside a special room for the Cordell collection. By 1980, the year of his death, Cordell had given some 3,500 titles to the library. He believed that the English language was one of the most important cultural tools in the world and that dictionaries were the key to understanding that tool. The university supported that concept and established a Cordell Fellowship in Lexicography. The Cordell collection at Terre Haute is one of the richest resources for the study of English language dictionaries in the United States.

Bibliography

A. "Foreword," in *A Short Title Catalogue of the Warren N. and Suzanne B. Cordell Collection of Dictionaries 1475–1900*, compiled by Paul Koda (Terre Haute, Ind., 1975), ix-xix; "Excerpts from Colloquia on Dictionary Collecting," in *Papers on Lexicography in Honor of Warren N. Cordell* (Terre Haute, Ind., 1979), 157–162, 166–170.

B. Fred W. Hanes, "The History and Planned Development of the Cordell Collection," in *Papers on Lexicography in Honor of Warren N. Cordell* (Terre Haute, Ind., 1979), 153–156; Lawrence McCrank, "Warren N. Cordell," *Logophile: Friends of the Cunningham Memorial Library Newsletter*, March 1980.

COWAN, Robert E. (b. July 2, 1862, Toronto, Can.; d. May 29, 1942, Los Angeles, Calif.). *Collection Disposition:* University of California at Los Angeles; University of California at Berkeley.

In 1895, after spending a number of years as a clerk in a San Francisco bookstore, Cowan decided to go into business for himself. He concentrated on the history of California and built a solid reputation as a knowledgeable dealer. In 1897 he sold part of his collection to Collis P. Huntington, who wanted it as a gift for the University of California at Berkeley. With the proceeds of the sale, Cowan started buying more Californiana. His approach to the state literature was consistently scholarly and thorough. As early as 1897 he had called for a state bibliography. Seventeen years later he answered his own call with the publication of *Bibliography of the History of California and the Pacific West*. This first printed bibliography of the state was produced by the Book Club of California and handsomely printed by John Henry Nash.

In 1921 Cowan was invited to become librarian and cataloger for wealthy Los Angeles collector William A. Clark, Jr.*, then in the process of building his library of English literature. In the next eleven years Cowan prepared some half-dozen catalogs for Clark, resigning only when the depression reduced Clark's book funds. The same year he left Clark, Cowan issued his greatly revised and enlarged version of his bibliography, newly titled *A Bibliography of the History of California 1510–1930*. In the revision done with help of his son, Cowan listed some 4,700 titles, almost quadrupling the count of the earlier edition. After the publication of this magnum opus, Cowan decided to sell the contents to the University of California at Los Angeles (UCLA). Because Cowan's price of $50,000 was considered expensive, approval took three years. The Cowan library included, among other things, guides for gold-seekers, pamphlets on the Chinese question, documents on statehood, land claims, and early city directories, maps, and charters. Lawrence Clark Powell, who was appointed director in 1944, was assigned to catalog the Cowan books as his first professional task at UCLA. After turning over his books to the university, Cowan continued to collect Californiana and to produce bibliographies and articles. Los Angeles publisher Ward Ritchie characterized Cowan, with his Van Dyck beard and courtly manner, as "the king of the empire of Los Angeles bookmen." Cowan's legacy rests firmly on half a dozen bibliographies and on the choice volumes of western history in the Special Collections Department at UCLA.

Bibliography

A. *Bibliography of the History of California and the Pacific West* (San Francisco, 1914); *A Bibliography of the History of California 1510–1930* (Los Angeles, 1933); *Booksellers of Early San Francisco* (Los Angeles, 1953).

B. Cannon, 270–272; Robert G. Cowan, *California Bibliographers: Father and Son*, (Los Angeles, 1978); Warren Howell, "Exploring California Book Trade History," *AB*, January 8, 1979, 252–256; Frank Lundy, "The Cowan Library of California," *School and Society*, February 13, 1937, 234–235; Lawrence Clark Powell, "Robert Ernest Cowan," *Bibliographers of the Golden State* (Berkeley and Los Angeles, 1967), 15–23; Ward Ritchie, *Bookmen and Their Brothels* (Los Angeles, 1970), 4–6; Henry R. Wagner, "In Memoriam," *QCHS*, September 1942, 282–283.

COXE, Eckley B. (b. June 4, 1839, Philadelphia, Pa.; d. May 13, 1895, Drifton, Pa.). *Education:* B.S., University of Pennsylvania, 1858. *Collection Disposition:* Lehigh University.

As a mining engineer, Coxe acquired a large reference library. He had books, journals, and sets of transactions of the chief mining and engineering societies throughout the world. One of his early acquisitions was the scientific library of Julius Weisbach, his professor at the University of Freiberg. Coxe's entire library, some 7,500 items, was bequeathed to Lehigh University.

Bibliography

B. *DAB*, 2, 485–486; R. W. Haymond, "Notice of Eckley B. Coxe," *American Institute of Mining Engineers Transactions*, October 1895, 446–476.

COXE, John Redman (b. September 16, 1773, Trenton, N.J.; d. March 22, 1864, Philadelphia, Pa.). *Education:* M.D., University of Pennsylvania, 1794. *Collection Disposition:* Thomas, November 1, 1864.

At the age of twenty-one Coxe received his degree in medicine from the University of Pennsylvania under the guidance of the renowned Dr. Benjamin Rush. Like Rush, he was an experimenter and one of the first American physicians to advocate the use of vaccination. In the course of his research Coxe formed an impressive personal library. It was, according to his colleague Samuel Gross, the best collection of volumes on medical science in the country. The Coxe library also held a substantial number of sermons, Bibles, prayer books, and works on church history. A few months after his death the entire collection, estimated at 15,000 items, was sold at auction. Princeton University purchased the theological titles, and Gross bought the medical library.

Bibliography

B. *DAB* 4, 486–487; *NCAB* 22, 151; Samuel D. Gross, *Autobiography* (Philadelphia, 1887).

COYKENDALL, Frederick (b. November 23, 1872, Kingston, N.Y.; d. November 18, 1954, New York, N.Y.). *Education:* B.A., M.A., Columbia University, 1895, 1897. *Collection Disposition:* Columbia University.

Coykendall's professional life was composed of many strands. He was associated with the family-owned steamboat company and Columbia University Press and for twenty years served as chairman of the Columbia University Board of Trustees. He also devoted himself to book collecting and was widely respected for his published articles and carefully prepared author bibliographies. His collecting interests included the illustrator Arthur Rackham, novelist H. Rider Haggard, and poets John Masefield and Robert Bridges. In all cases, Coykendall collected manuscripts and letters as well as printed materials. In spite of his heavy business responsibilities he did a considerable amount of bibliographic work on authors he liked. His study of Matthew Lewis' novel *The Monk* was a model of careful research. Coykendall's bookish interests drew him into close association with members of the Grolier Club of New York, where he served in many capacities, including a term as president from 1935 to 1939. On his death his library was turned over to Columbia University. His bibliographies and his collections continue to serve scholarly investigators.

Bibliography

A. "A Note on *The Monk*," *The Colophon*, no. 1, 1935; *Arthur Rackham: A List of Books* (New York, 1922); *A Bibliography of Robert Bridges* (New York, 1933).

B. *NCAB* 45, 146; "In Memoriam," *Grolier Year Book*, 1955, 142–146; *NYT*, November 19, 1954, 22.

CROCKER, Templeton (b. September 2, 1884, San Francisco, Calif.; d. December 12, 1948, San Francisco, Calif.). *Education:* A.B., Yale University, 1908. *Collection Disposition:* California Historical Society; University of Virginia; University of California at Los Angeles.

With a fortune inherited from his grandfather, Crocker was able to indulge his interests in travel and collecting. Before he was thirty he had gathered libraries on California history and English literature. He purchased most of the Californiana from John Howell and the literature from Alice Millard and A. S. W. Rosenbach*. From Rosenbach he bought the second and third Shakespeare folios, along with first editions of books by Stevenson, Kipling, Tennyson, and Thackeray. Buying nineteenth-century English literature as he did, it was his fate to acquire a large number of the notorious forgeries of Thomas J. Wise. His Tennyson collection, sold to the University of Virginia after his death, was laden with these clever fabrications. In the California collection, however, every book and pamphlet was authentic and valuable. Over a period of thirty years he gathered western travel accounts, gold rush diaries, and early California imprints, maps, and newspapers. In addition to these printed works he owned a number of important nineteenth-century manuscripts on statehood. As a natural extension of his collecting activities, Crocker took an active part in local historical societies. He helped rejuvenate the California Historical Society by increasing membership, balancing the budget, and improving the journal. In order to enhance the research activities of the Society, he deposited his books and manuscripts in nearby rooms. In 1940, at the suggestion of collector and bibliophile Henry R. Wagner*, he turned them over entirely to the Society officers. In one final phase of his collecting Crocker gathered a large number of examples of the work of fifteenth-century Venetian printer Aldus Manutius. In 1961 the University of California at Los Angeles purchased this splendid gathering and designated it, in the name of the donors, the Ahmanson-Murphy Aldine Collection. Crocker was an enthusiastic and perceptive collector whose chief contribution was the construction of a remarkable library of Californiana.

Bibliography

A. *Catalogue of the Library of Charles Templeton Crocker* (Hillsborough, Calif., 1918); *The Templeton Crocker Collection of Seventy Books from the Aldine Press* (San Francisco, 1935); *The Ahmanson-Murphy Aldine Collection: A Checklist*, compiled by Brooke Whiting (Los Angeles, 1979).

B. Cannon, 272–273; Henry R. Wagner, "The Templeton Crocker Collection of California," *QCHS*, March 1940, 79–81; Henry R. Wagner, "Recollections of Templeton Crocker," *QCHS*, December 1949, 363–366.

CROESSMANN, Harley K. (b. ?, Du Quoin, Ill.; d. 1962, Du Quoin, Ill.). *Education:* Illinois College of Ophthalmology. *Collection Disposition:* Southern Illinois University.

Starting in 1925 and continuing for nearly forty years, Croessmann devoted himself to collecting everything he could find on James Joyce. Much of Croessmann's collecting was done through correspondence with such Joyce scholars as William York Tindall, Stuart Gilbert, and Richard Ellmann. In 1948 Croessmann's enthusiasms were sparked by a meeting with another avid Joyce collector, James F. Spoerri of Chicago. The real growth of Croessmann's library stemmed from that time. In the early 1950s Croessmann acquired one of his most treasured archives: the working papers of Joyce biographer Herbert Gorman. On the basis of these documents Croessmann wrote a brief paper for the *James Joyce Miscellany*, published by Southern Illinois University. Subsequently he deposited his Joyce materials at the university at Carbondale. The Croessmann library, including letters, rare editions, photographs, and translations, constitutes one of the outstanding Joyce collections in the United States.

Bibliography

B. *James Joyce 1882–1941: A Centenary Exhibit* (Carbondale, Ill., 1982), v–vii, 51–54.

CROWNINSHIELD, Edward A. (b. February 25, 1817, Boston, Mass.; d. February 20, 1859, Boston, Mass.). *Education:* A.B., Harvard College, 1836. *Collection Disposition:* Direct sale to Henry Stevens, 1859; Puttick and Simpson (London), July 12, 1860.

Born into a wealthy Boston family, Crowninshield was educated at the Round School by Joseph Cogswell and George Bancroft. He later matriculated at Harvard and went on to study law. Book collecting provided Crowninshield with a stimulating outlet for his varied intellectual interests. Strongly influenced by Bancroft and Cogswell, he concentrated on Americana, with a special interest in the period of discovery and colonization. He bought many books from Henry Stevens and was one of those who encouraged that energetic young Vermonter to establish a book business in London. Through Stevens and Boston bookdealer George Livermore*, Crowninshield acquired an exemplary library, a somewhat modified version of those built at approximately the same time by James Lenox*, John Carter Brown*, and George Brinley*. Besides such standard fare as Smith's "Virginia" and Hakluyt's "Voyages," the Crowninshield library boasted a pristine copy of the *Bay Psalm Book*. When Crowninshield died at the age of forty-two his books were turned over to Leonard's of Boston for auction. On receipt of the catalog, Stevens bought the lot before they could be put up for bids. He wanted to prove that in spite of the statements to the contrary the books he sold to Crowninshield had maintained their values. Negotiations were completed and Stevens acquired the library for $9,000. Before the books were shipped to England, Stevens gave Lenox, Brown, Charles Deane*, and a few other Americanists first choice. By the time the rest of the books were offered in London, he had recouped his entire investment and made a sizable profit. It was in connection with the Crowinshield sale that Stevens issued his famous *Guesses by a Yankee in London, May 26, 1860, on the Prices of Books and Autographs in the Crowninshield Catalogue*, a priced flyer issued to encourage bidding. Sir Thomas Phillipps, the insatiable British collector, invested over £670 in Crowninshield books, topping all other individual buyers. Stevens offered Crowninshield's *Bay Psalm Book* to the British Museum, but after five years of procrastination on the part of museum officers decided to look for an American buyer. He did not have far to look. George Brinley* had wanted this prize for some time and was happy to pay Stevens the required 150 guineas. That copy is now one of the treasured volumes in the Yale Library.

Bibliography

B. Cannon, 110–111; Farnham, 31–32; Charles Deane, "Memorial to Edward Crowninshield," *PMHS*, 1859, 356–359; Wyman Parker, in *Henry Stevens of Vermont* (Amsterdam, The Netherlands, 1963), 210–222; Henry Stevens, *Recollections of Mr. James Lenox of New York* (London, 1886), passim.

CRUMMER, LeRoy (b. April 15, 1872, Elizabeth, Ill.; d. January 1, 1934, Los Angeles, Calif.). *Education:* B.S., University of Michigan, 1893; M.D., Northwestern University Medical School, 1896. *Collection Disposition:* University of Nebraska at Omaha; University of Michigan Medical School; University of California Medical School at Berkeley.

After completing his medical education in Chicago, Crummer made several trips to Europe to study in the best clinics in Berlin, London, and Vienna. In 1906 he took over his father's practice in Omaha and continued there until 1929. At that time poor health forced him to move to Los Angeles. He contributed articles on heart disease to professional journals and taught in several medical schools.

Crummer traced his interest in book collecting to 1917, when he chanced to pick up an eighteenth-century Zurich edition of Sir Thomas Browne's *Religio Medici*. This started him on a successful quest for all the editions of that seminal work. He next obtained the medical classics mentioned in Sir William Osler's *Aequanimitas* (1889), those included in Mortimer Frank's translation of Choulant's *History and Bibliography of Anatomic Illustration* (1920), the works of Andreas Vesalius, and all variant issues of the fifteenth-century *Regimen Sanitatis*. In this process Crummer found himself in friendly rivalry with such notable collectors as Harvey Cushing*, Herbert Evans*, and Sir William Osler. In spite of this competition, Crummer's collection grew and became known particularly for its coverage of medical history in the first half of the sixteenth century. Crummer also devoted attention to French surgeon Ambroise Paré and English researchers William Harvey and Edward Jenner. Crummer's interest centered around the visual and led him to buy classic illustrated editions of Vesalius and Browne. He bought his first books from Walter Hill of Chicago, but as he became more sophisticated he established business relations with Paul Hoeber and Wilfred Voynich in New York, Maggs Brothers in London, and Davis and Orioli in Florence. Through the latter shop he obtained many rarities, including an unrecorded sixteenth-century Venice edition of Vesalius. Crummer was an energetic bibliographer, collector, and historian. He collected books he liked without regard for the fashions of the day. The results of his enthusiasms enhance a number of libraries.

Bibliography

A. "Essay on Collecting," in *Annals of Medical History*, 1928, 226–241; "The Dark Horse," *The Colophon*, vol. 1, part 3, September 1930.

B. A. G. Beaman, *A Doctor's Odyssey* (Baltimore, 1935).

CURRIE, Barton (b. March 8, 1877, New York, N.Y.; d. May 7, 1962, Merion, Pa.). *Collection Disposition:* Parke-Bernet, May 7, 1963.

As a reporter for several New York newspapers and later as editor of *Country Gentleman*, *Ladies' Home Journal*, and *World's Work*, Currie was deeply involved with the written word. He became interested in book collecting through the contacts he made with Philadelphia book entrepreneurs A. Edward Newton* and A. S. W. Rosenbach*. Currie collected authors he enjoyed, however, rather than those prescribed by other bibliophiles. In the autobiographical *Fishers of Books* he emphasized this by describing his enthusiasm for Conrad in spite of the negative opinions of Newton and Yale professor Chauncey Brewster Tinker*. Although Conrad was one of his early choices, Dickens and Thackeray were of equal interest. For some time Currie thought of himself as a one-author collector, buying Dickens rarities from Rosenbach and Gabriel Wells. When several Conrad manuscripts became available he took the bait. Later he became interested in Thackeray and acquired several special editions of *Vanity Fair*—one in parts, the other a presentation copy from the author to Charlotte Brontë. Then he became interested in the origin of the novel and bought first editions of Richardson's *Pamela* and Fielding's *Tom Jones*. With these trophies secure, he began to buy Trollope, Austin, Brontë, Cruikshank illustrations, a shelf of Lewis Carroll, and the manuscript of Sheridan's *School for Scandal*. This was clearly a case of unrestrained bibliomania. To supplement his English authors, and inspired by the pioneering literary purchases of his friend William T. H. Howe*, Currie began to add notable Americans such as Emerson, Longfellow, and Lowell. As he explained in his autobiography, these favorites replaced the limited, extra-limited, and super-limited editions of James Branch Cabell which he had once gathered. Currie condemned such artificially manufactured rarities. He was far more enthusiastic about the plain publishers' editions of the nineteenth-century New England poets or the works of Booth Tarkington. Currie had maintained a warm personal friendship with Tarkington over many years and formed a comprehensive collection of his works. In 1932 he published a Tarkington bibliography with a helpful historical introduction. In later years Currie was involved in writing and spent less time on collecting. The sale of his books in 1963 drew considerable attention from dealers and private collectors. The Conrad manuscripts in particular prompted record bids.

Bibliography

A. *Fishers of Books* (New York, 1931); *Booth Tarkington: A Bibliography* (New York, 1932).

B. *NYT*, May 9, 1962, 43; *Who Was Who in America*, vol. 4, 1961–1968, 22.

CUSHING, Harvey (b. April 9, 1869, Cleveland, Ohio; d. October 7, 1939, New Haven, Conn.). *Education:* A.B., Yale University, 1891; A.M., M.D., Harvard University, 1895. *Collection Disposition:* Yale University.

When Cushing joined the medical staff of Johns Hopkins in 1896 his collecting inclinations may have already been in place. Certainly he was adept at the varieties of scientific classification and careful analysis so essential for his surgical work. This kind of close attention to detail came to serve him well as he developed collecting specialties. Another positive influence came to Cushing from his association with the great surgeon-collector Sir William Osler. It was Osler who kindled Cushing's first major collecting interest and set him on the track of the works of the sixteenth-century anatomist Andreas Vesalius. This quest lasted for over forty years, resulting in the publication of a definitive bio-bibliography after Cushing's death. In 1912 Cushing moved to Boston and began a twenty-year period as head of surgery at Peter Bent Bringham Hospital, the most active part of his professional career. It was during this time that his collecting enthusiasms grew from a focus on anatomy to include the history of surgery and eventually the history of medicine in general. As his interests broadened, he began to buy books and manuscripts from knowledgeable European and British antiquarian dealers such as Bernard Quaritch, E. P. Goldschmidt, and E. Weil. Goldschmidt and Weil have both reported how they supplied Cushing with manuscripts and rare documents from the Admont and Melk monasteries in Austria. These related not only to Vesalius but also to early studies of astrology, mathematics, and medieval medical practice. Cushing was also interested in English medical history of the sixteenth and seventeenth centuries, which he supported with strong holdings of Robert Boyle, William Harvey, Nicholas Culpeper, and Edward Jenner. He also enjoyed the sixteenth-century translations by Jean Canappe and the small octavos of Ambroise Paré. In order to document modern scientific thought, Cushing acquired an extensive collection of the papers of Albert Einstein.

An intensive period of collecting began for Cushing after he retired from his appointment in Boston and returned to New Haven as Professor of Neurology and Director of Studies of the History of Medicine. It was there that he conceived the idea for the formation of a great library of medical history for Yale. This was not to be based on the Cushing collection alone, but would also take advantage of the other resources he knew were near at hand. In 1934 Cushing wrote to his old friends Arnold Klebs and John F. Fulton* suggesting that all three combine their private libraries in one great gift to Yale. The idea was inspired, for the three collections were unique and would produce few areas of duplication. Klebs had specialized in incunabula and in studies on smallpox and tuberculosis, while the Fulton library featured studies in physiology and experimental medicine. The university was quick to respond to the suggestion and set aside funds for building a medical library with a Cushing Historical Wing. In his collecting activities and in his bibliographical work, Cushing proved himself to be meticulous and determined. His biography of Osler and his other literary and medical publications ensure him a secure place as a medical historian. Beyond these contributions, he will be remembered for his devotion to learning and for the solid base he provided for one of the greatest medical libraries in the world.

Bibliography

A. *Life of Sir William Osler* (Oxford, 1925); *The Doctor and His Books* (Cleveland, 1927); *Bio-Bibliography of Vesalius* (New York, 1943); *The Harvey Cushing Collection of Books and Manuscripts* (New York, 1943).

B. *DAB*, Sup. 2, 137–140; *NCAB* 32, 402; *Grolier 75*, 167–168; L. M. Davey, "Harvey Cushing and the Humanities in Medicine," *JHM*, April 1969, 119–124; John Fulton, *Harvey Cushing* (Oxford, 1946); E. P. Goldschmidt, "A Doctor and His Books: Harvey Cushing and His Library," *JHM*, April 1969, 229–234; Geoffrey Jefferson, "Harvey Cushing and His Books," *JHM*, April 1969, 247–253; Elizabeth Thompson, *Harvey Cushing* (New York, 1950); E. Weil, "The Formation of the Harvey Cushing Collection," *JHM*, April 1969, 234–246; Madeline Stanton, "Harvey Cushing: Book Collector," *JAMA*, 1965, 141–144. "Dr. Harvey Cushing," *YLG*, January 1940, 33–40.

D

DALY, John Augustin (b. July 20, 1838, Plymouth, N.C.; d. June 7, 1899, Paris, France). *Collection Disposition*: Leavitt, October 14, 1878; American Art, March 20 and 28, 1900; Sotheby's (London), July 29, 1901; Anderson, April 27, 1925; Henkels, October 11, 1929.

Although Daly entered the theatrical world before he was twenty and continued in that profession until his death, he made his reputation not as an actor but as an impresario and a writer. He started by working as a critic for several New York newspapers, a part-time occupation he coupled with play-writing. Next he purchased a New York theater and organized several touring companies. His casts were of the first caliber and included such stars as Otis Skinner, John Drew, and Edwin T. Booth. In his travels Daly collected books, manuscripts, furniture, paintings, statuary, and silver, much of it focused on his interest in theater history. Since a considerable portion of Daly's reputation was founded on Elizabethan productions, it was not surprising that his book collection included many examples of the authors of that period. Daly owned the four Shakespeare folios, a large number of playbills and posters, and an archive of documents forged by William Henry Ireland. In the formation of his library, Daly exhibited the same flair and style that characterized his business endeavors. Many of his favorite volumes were expanded by extra-illustration, a process that involved the insertion of prints, letters, and watercolors into the text. The Daly copy of the Douay Bible, for example, was expanded to forty-one volumes, while his Irving and Marshall edition of *Shakespeare's Plays* was enlarged from eight to forty-two volumes. The Daly library prospered or languished in direct response to the owner's fluctuating financial status. In 1878 he had to sell over 1,000 volumes to satisfy creditors. Sadly, many of the books fell far below Daly's original buying prices.

A year after Daly's death the entire estate was placed up for auction at the

American Art Association. This time the books brought satisfactory prices, although the catalog itself was discredited by an English critic as "suitable only for the outer provinces." Daly's extra-illustrated sets brought substantial prices, with the Douay Bible going for $5,125 and Joseph Ireland's *Records of the New York Stage* achieving $6,125, the high-water-mark of the sale. Many of these extravagant prices were bid by George D. Smith, later to become known as the grand acquisitor for Henry E. Huntington* and Henry C. Folger*. The high prices paid at his auctions would certainly have pleased the flamboyant Daly.

Bibliography

B. *DAB* 3, 42–45; Cannon, 322–323; *Grolier 75*, 21–23; Joseph F. Daly, *The Life of Augustin Daly* (New York, 1917); "The Augustin Daly Library," *The Athenaeum*, March 24, 1900, 371.

DARLINGTON, William M. (b. May 1, 1815, Pittsburgh, Pa.; d. September 28, 1889, Pittsburgh, Pa.). *Education*: A.B., Jefferson College, 1835. *Collection Disposition*: University of Pittsburgh.

Although Darlington was a lawyer by profession, he devoted much of his life to historical study and writing. His primary interest was in exploration and settlement, particularly as those events affected his native Pennsylvania. As a historian, Darlington understood the importance of primary sources—letters, business records, and early diaries. He made these materials his special province and used them for a variety of publications. When he edited Christopher Gist's journals, the account of the travels of an eighteenth-century frontier scout, he was able to use his own maps and newspapers to report events as Gist himself would have known them. Darlington's collection of Pittsburgh materials was rich and varied. First he acquired standard histories and biographies, then he augmented that core with long runs of city directories, early periodicals, and maps. One of the strongest sections of the Pittsburgh archive covered the industrial growth of the city. Papers from various businesses and utilities provided documentation on the rise of Pittsburgh from a frontier town to an industrial metropolis. Like Clarence M. Burton,* Detroit's historian, Darlington was always alert to estate settlements as a means of obaining family records. Some of the most important letters, books, and records in his collection came from that source. Twenty years after Darlington's death his daughters presented the library of some 11,000 items to the University of Pennsylvania. Separate rooms were established and a staff was appointed to maintain and develop this excellent historical collection.

Bibliography

B. *NCAB* 16, 164; Anne Herbert, *Personal Memoirs of the Darlington Family at Guyasuta* (Pittsburgh, 1949); Ruth Salisbury, "Survey of the Darlington Memorial Library," *Western Pennsylvania Historical Magazine*, January 1964, 19–29.

DEANE, Charles (b. November 10, 1813, Biddeford, Maine; d. November 13, 1889, Cambridge, Mass.). *Collection Disposition*: Libbie, March 8 and 29, April 1, 1898.

Although he never received an earned university degree, Deane came to be respected by members of the scholarly community as a productive and accurate historian. He collected texts and manuscripts related to early American history and edited them for publication in the journals of the historical societies to which he belonged. Many volumes of the Proceedings of the Massachusetts Historical Society carried his notes and articles. His interests included the literature of voyage and discovery as well as accounts of early Virginia and New England history. No less an authority than Justin Winsor considered Deane's knowledge unequaled in these areas. Deane edited Governor Bradford's *History of the Plymouth Plantation* (1856), *The Letters of Phillis Wheatley* (1864), and numerous other colonial documents. He received many tributes and honorary degrees during his lifetime, and in 1878 he was elected to the prestigious London Society of Antiquarians. Among his colleagues Deane was known for his generosity and his knowledge of bibliographic detail. On his death, his books and pamphlets were auctioned in a series of sales at Libbie's in Boston.

Bibliography

B. *DAB* 3, 171–172; *NCAB* 3, 520; Cannon, 110–111; Farnham, 67–71; Justin Winsor, "Memoir of the Life of Charles Deane," *PMHS*, 1892, 45–89.

DeCOPPET, André (b. November 10, 1892, New York, N.Y.; d. August 1, 1953, Lausanne, Switz.). *Education*: A.B., Princeton University, 1915. *Collection Disposition*: Princeton University; Parke-Bernet, February 16, October 4, 1955, October 28, 1957, October 20, 1958.

Over a period of thirty years, DeCoppet, a New York broker, gathered an impressive collection of documents and books relating to French and American history. In 1934 he gave Princeton part of what had been the personal library of Napoleon Bonaparte as well as some 34,000 documents relating to the Napoleonic rule in Italy. In another important bequest DeCoppet gave Princeton his American historical manuscripts—3,700 letters and papers, including examples of the writing of Washington, Jefferson, Lincoln, and Wilson. The remainder of the DeCoppet library, chiefly literature, was dispersed in a series of New York auctions held between 1955 and 1958.

Bibliography

A. *The André DeCoppet Collection of American Historical Manuscripts: A Catalogue of an Exhibition in the Princeton University Library, May 16 to June 30, 1955* (Princeton, 1955).

B. R.M. Ludwig, "Looking Backward: Development of the Rare Books and Special Collections Since 1953," *PLC*, Spring 1975, 177; R. R. Palmer, "Beauharnais Archives," *PLC*, February 1942, 45–51.

DEERING, Frank C. (b. January 28, 1866, Saco, Me.; d. August 13, 1939, Saco, Me.). *Collection Disposition*: Newberry Library.

In a brief essay entitled "Adventures in Americana" bookdealer Michael Walsh identified Deering as a "collector from birth." Deering's chief interest was in the narratives of Indian captivities, and in that genre his collection was almost without peer. Many of the rarities on his shelves came through negotiations with Philadelphia bookseller A. S. W. Rosenbach*. Deering was one of those for whom Rosenbach obtained bargains at the William Breaker* sale of 1935. In addition to the books on Indians, Deering bought the classic fifteenth-century voyage and travel accounts and colonial histories. In 1967 the Newberry Library in Chicago bought the Deering collection in order to bolster their strong Edward E. Ayer* library. Almost three-fourths of the Deering books turned out to be duplicates, but according to Director Lawrence W. Towner, the unique titles made the purchase worthwhile. The Deering library added considerable strength to the Newberry's holdings.

Bibliography

B. Wolf and Fleming, passim; Lawrence W. Towner, *Every Silver Lining Has a Cloud: The Recent Shaping of the Newberry Library's Collections* (Chicago, 1970), 12–13; Michael Walsh, "Adventures in Americana," in *Four Talks for Bibliophiles* (Philadelphia, 1958), 83–96; A. E. Newton, *This Book Collecting Game* (Boston, 1928), 242-244.

DeGOLYER, Everitt (b. October 9, 1886, Greensburg, Kans.; d. December 14, 1956, Dallas, Tex.). *Education*: A.B., University of Texas, 1911. *Collection Disposition*: University of Texas at Austin; University of Oklahoma; Southern Methodist University; DeGolyer Foundation.

Before he was twenty-five, DeGolyer had established a reputation as a successful geologist by locating one of the most profitable oil deposits in North America. His managerial talents and acute interest in all facets of the petroleum business brought him continued advancement. He held executive offices in many of the petroleum societies and during World War II was appointed deputy petroleum administrator.

DeGolyer dated the beginning of his interest in book collecting to the time he purchased a "first edition" of Charles Dickens' *Pickwick Papers* at a London sale just before World War I. When the book turned out to be a handsomely bound reprint, DeGolyer decided to learn more about bibliography. After collecting English literature for a short time, he decided to concentrate on his own Southwest, particularly books that treated the American Indians, and the history of Mexico. In March 1924 he was fortunate to obtain the extensive Mexican history library of diplomat William B. Stevens. As DeGolyer's collecting interests centered more and more on western Americana, he developed an active business relationship with bookdealer Edward Eberstadt. According to one source, it was DeGolyer's purchases and loans that kept the Eberstadt firm solvent during the depression. DeGolyer also made regular purchases at that time from H. W. Caldwell in

Dallas, Jake Zeitlin in Los Angeles, and James Drake in New York. The pressure of an ever-increasing flow of books forced DeGolyer to look for institutional storage. Fortunately he did not have far to look. The officers of the University of Texas at Austin were happy to make room for the DeGolyer literary collections, giving him space at home to develop a new area of interest—the history of science. DeGolyer believed that this important field of study had been neglected by the academic community. At the University of Oklahoma, however, he found administrators and faculty who shared his enthusiasms. The collection, as they planned it, would support a series of courses focused on the writing and thinking of scientific theorists from early times to the twentieth century. DeGolyer would supply the landmark volumes to support the curriculum. As plans for the program moved forward, DeGolyer turned to Zeitlin and a few other history-of-science specialists to help him find the books. Soon first editions of Descartes, Bacon, Pascal, Euclid, and Borelli began to flow into the library at Norman, Oklahoma, making it one of the world's leading research centers for the study of the history of science.

DeGolyer's geology library, originally promised to the University of Oklahoma, was held back for personal research and after his death was deposited at Southern Methodist University. That institution also received the 40,000-volume DeGolyer collection of materials on Spanish and Mexican history. In addition to these deposits, DeGolyer's heirs placed a substantial number of books and manuscripts on the history of the Southwest in the library of the DeGolyer Foundation in Dallas. All three DeGolyer collections—geology, Southwest studies, and history of science—represented the collector's personal enthusiasms, his love of learning, and his respect for the past. By placing his books and manuscripts in public institutions, DeGolyer provided scholars with the tools for their continuing research. He was an astute and generous collector.

Bibliography

A. *The Library of the DeGolyer Foundation* (Dallas, 1964).
B. *NCAB* 43, 12; Lon Tinkle, *Mr. De* (Boston, 1970).

DePUY, Henry F. (b. April 12, 1859, Bath, N.Y.; d. October 19, 1924, Montreal, Can.). *Education*: A.B., Union College, 1883. *Collection Disposition*: Anderson, November 17, 1919, January 26, April 19, 1920, March 31, 1925.

In a letter published in the *New York Times*, DePuy recalled starting his book collection in 1890 with an emphasis on the Iroquois Indians. This led to tales of Indian captivity, American colonial history, and studies of the Constitution. Other topics that interested him included the Oneida and Selkirk communities, the anti-masonic movement, and early railroading. Although he never made an effort to secure manuscripts, he did acquire a few letters written by Benedict Arnold, Ethan Allen, and Aaron Burr. Until the time of his death, DePuy devoted himself to historical research and publication. In 1917 he issued his *Bibliographies of English Colonial Treaties with the Indians*, followed the next year by *An*

Early Account of the Establishment of Jesuit Missions in America. While working on these publications, DePuy moved from New York to Maryland and as a consequence sold some of his library. The sale brought $165,000 and was an unqualified success, with A. S. W. Rosenbach*, George D. Smith, and Lathrop Harper all securing important volumes. DePuy retained his Andrew Jackson materials and in 1922 brought out a selection of Jackson's letters. The letters themselves made up the principal part of the final sale of DePuy's effects. At the time of his death he was working on a bibliography of the work of Philadelphia's first printer, William Bradford. DePuy was a knowledgeable collector and a careful scholar. His published work is still used by those concerned with colonial history.

Bibliography

B. *NCAB* 20, 213; Cannon, 114–115; Wolf and Fleming, passim.

DeRENNE, Wymberley Jones (b. September 23, 1853, Newport, R.I.; d. June 23, 1916, New York, N.Y.). *Education*: LL.B., Columbia University, 1876. *Collection Disposition*: University of Georgia.

In 1891, after living in Europe for a number of years, DeRenne returned to the family estate in Georgia. Since his father had collected books and manuscripts on Georgia history it seemed appropriate to continue that effort. For twenty-five years he gathered any and all publications that touched on state history and the development of the Confederacy. He started, appropriately enough, with the narratives of the Native Americans who had inhabited the southeastern portion of the country before the first colonist arrived, then branched out to acquire early travel accounts and maps, the records of the trustees of the colony, acts and proceedings of the early legislatures, legal documents, sermons, and literary works. He also had the first products of Georgia presses. The Savannah material in the collection was particularly rich, with long runs of city directories and local newspapers. The collection provided an astoundingly complete picture of the colony and its early settlers. Another strong area of the DeRenne library covered the Civil War period. Perhaps the most important document from that era was the original manuscript of the Constitution of the Confederate states with the autographs of all the delegates. Other letters and diaries presented the events of the war years from the perspective of soldiers, journalists, clergymen, and lawyers.

As the collection grew, so did DeRenne's reputation with American and British bookdealers. Whenever Georgia material came on the market he frequently had first refusal. In 1907 a handsome oblong building was erected on the estate to provide a dignified, safe setting for the books. After the building was completed, DeRenne became more aware of the need for an accurate, descriptive catalog. One list was produced by bookdealer-bibliographer Oscar Wegelin, and in 1915 the collector engaged Leonard Mackall* to assume responsibility for a new catalog. Although DeRenne died shortly after this arrangement had been made, his son, who inherited the library, supported the project to its completion. The resulting three-volume catalog was a model of bibliographic accuracy and detail. In the late 1930s the family decided to transfer the library to a public institution, and the University of Georgia was the obvious choice. The DeRenne holdings remained in the state, providing southern historians and scholars with an unmatched historical archive.

Bibliography

A. *Books Relating to the History of Georgia in the Library of Wymberley Jones DeRenne of Wormsloe*, compiled and annotated by Oscar Wegelin (Savannah, 1911); *Catalogue of the Wymberley Jones DeRenne Georgia Library* (New York, 1931).

B. *NCAB* 18, 390–391; Cannon, 247–251; Leonard Mackall, ''The Founder and the Library,'' in *Catalogue of the Wymberley Jones DeRenne Georgia Library* (New York, 1931), xi-xx; ''Wymberley Jones DeRenne,'' *Georgia Historical Society Quarterly*, June 1918, 63–88.

DeVINNE, Theodore Low (b. December 25, 1828, Stamford, Conn.; d. February 16, 1914, New York, N.Y.). *Collection Disposition*: Anderson, January 12, 1920.

One of the foremost printers of his time, DeVinne was also well known for his writing and for his general support of the graphic arts. At the age of twenty-two he joined the printing firm of Francis Hart and rose through the ranks of that organization from compositor to foreman and finally, when Hart died in 1877, owner. After 1883 the firm was renamed Theodore DeVinne & Co. DeVinne was an exacting employer and demanded the finest efforts from his staff. Profitable contracts with *Century Magazine*, *St. Nicholas*, and *Scribner's Monthly* helped provide a steady income and enabled the firm to print private library catalogs and limited editions of the Grolier Club bibliographies. DeVinne was one of the founding members of the Grolier Club and served as its sixth president. His own private library consisted of the major works on typography, the manuals and histories of printing, specimen sheets, and over eighty examples of incunabula. He used his library and his wide-ranging knowledge of the graphic arts to write a series of monographs treating the history and development of printing. Such works as *The Invention of Printing*, *Notable Printers of Italy*, and *Title Pages as Seen by a Printer* were authoritative and well received.

When the DeVinne library was brought to auction in 1920, it offered buyers the most important collection on printing arts to be distributed in the United States up to that time. The Newberry Library of Chicago took full advantage of the opportunity and made substantial additions to their John M. Wing* Foundation on the history of printing. Although DeVinne was primarily a printer, his writing and collecting activities make him an important figure in the nineteenth-century world of books.

Bibliography

A. *The Invention of Printing* (New York, 1878); *Title Pages as Seen by a Printer* (New York, 1901); *Notable Printers of Italy During the Fifteenth Century* (New York, 1910); *The Practice of Typography* (New York, 1902–1904).

B. *DAB* 5, 263; *NCAB* 7, 67; Cannon, 191–192; *Grolier 75*, 4–7; Henry L. Bullen, *Theodore Low DeVinne, Printer* (New York, 1915); Carl Purlington Rollins, "Theodore L. DeVinne," *Signature*, n.s., 1950; Irene Tichenor, "Theodore L. DeVinne," *Gazette of the Grolier Club*, n.s., 1983–1984, 43–60.

DICKSON, Frederick S. (b. 1850; d. December 1, 1925). *Education*: A.B., Yale University, 1871. *Collection Disposition*: Yale University.

When Chauncey Brewster Tinker* made his famous speech to the alumni urging support of the Yale Library, he cited the names of three donors who had already made outstanding contributions: Owen F. Aldis*, William A. Speck*, and Frederick S. Dickson. It was Dickson who had provided the Yale Library with its outstanding collection of works by and about the English novelist Henry Fielding. The gift to Yale was appropriate because Dickson had been inspired to collect books in the first place by exposure to the teaching of Yale professor Thomas Lounsbury. Like other single-author collectors, Dickson aspired to own every edition of Fielding's plays, novels, and pamphlets wherever published. As Wilbur Cross pointed out in a tribute to Dickson, the collector found it most difficult to procure Fielding's plays since these were altered continually and each alteration constituted a new edition. For an avid collector of Dickson's mold, this kind of obstacle only made the search more intense. Dickson took a scholarly interest in Fielding's life as revealed through careful examination of publishing details. When it was asserted, for example, that Fielding was not read on the European continent, Dickson was able to prove otherwise by reference to the large number of translations issued through the end of the nineteenth century. By similar studies, Dickson was able to illuminate the complicated publication history of *Tom Jones* and other Fieding novels. When given to Yale, the total collection totaled some 2,000 volumes, with 150 editions of *Tom Jones* and 47 of *Joseph Andrews*. As Cross pointed out, Dickson came to live and have his being in Fielding, a situation that eventually brought great distinction to the Yale literature holdings.

Bibliography

B. Wilbur Cross, "The Fielding Collection," *YLG*, January 1927, 31–34.

DOHENY, Estelle (b. August 2, 1875, Philadelphia, Pa.; d. October 30, 1958, Los Angeles, Calif.). *Collection Disposition*: St. John's Seminary, Camarillo, Calif.; St. Mary's Seminary, Perryville, Mo.; Immaculate Heart College, Los Angeles, Calif.

Throughout her marriage, Doheny was closely associated with her husband's career as a pioneer California oil developer. In 1926 she became acquainted with avid book collector Frank J. Hogan* when he was retained as Mr. Doheny's chief legal counsel. Stimulated by Hogan's interest and prompted by Pasadena bookseller Alice P. Millard, Doheny turned her casual attraction for books into a serious collecting passion. First she was drawn to examples of the delicate art of fore-edge painting. This collection grew to be one of the most important in the world and supplied the substance for a historical bibliography by Carl Weber. Next, with the assistance of Los Angeles bookdealer Ernest Dawson and in friendly rivalry with Hogan, she began to gather the first editions of the works listed in Merle Johnson's *High Spots of American Literature* (1929). It was to Doheny's credit that she was able to secure the 200 rarities listed by Johnson before the more experienced Hogan completed his set. Another early collection centered on the history of California and the West, the area that had been crucial to the development of the Doheny oil fortune. In this case Doheny used the 1935 edition of Robert E. Cowan's* *Bibliography of the History of California and the Pacific West* as her chief buying guide. Then in 1931, following leads from collector and writer A. Edward Newton*, she began to acquire monuments of English literature. She was aided in her search by Millard and by Philadelphia bookdealer A. S. W. Rosenbach*. From Millard she obtained fine bindings and such treasures as the *Aeneid* written on vellum by William Morris and Graily Hewitt with miniatures by Edward Burne-Jones. Among many notable works, Rosenbach supplied a tenth-century manuscript bound in polychrome oak covers known as the Liesborn Gospels and the 1473 Gunther Zainer printing of *Imitatio Christi*. Among notable incunabula in the collection were the Old Testament volume of the Gutenberg Bible, Fust and Schoeffer's 1462 *Biblia Latina*, and Sweynheym and Pannartz's printing of *Lactantius* (1465), the first dated book printed in Italy.

As the size and importance of the collection grew, proper housing and protection became a concern. In 1939 Doheny solved this problem when she deeded over the library to the Roman Catholic archbishop of Los Angeles and engaged Wallace Neff to design a building for St. John's Seminary in Camarillo. On October 14, 1940, the Edward Laurence Doheny Memorial Library was dedicated with the Estelle Doheny collection of manuscripts and rare books installed on the second floor. The handsome three-volume catalog was one of the first major jobs of the Ward Ritchie Press. Doheny continued to add books to the St. John's library and to a lesser degree to St. Mary's Seminary in Missouri up to the time of her death. With innate good taste, Doheny formed one of the most impressive rare book and manuscript libraries in the United States.

Bibliography

A. *Catalogue of Books and Manuscripts in the Estelle Doheny Collection* (Los Angeles, 1940, 1946, 1955); *One Hundred Manuscripts and Books from the Estelle Doheny Collection in the Edward L. Doheny Memorial Library*, St. John's Seminary, Camarillo, California, exhibited for the Zamorano Club, May 6, 1960, compiled by Lucille V. Miller (Los Angeles, 1950).

B. *NCAB* 29, 238 (Edward Doheny); Wolf and Fleming, passim; Carey Bliss, "The Estelle Doheny Collection in the Edward Doheny Memorial Library," *QNLBCC*, Spring 1957, 35–43; Lucille V. Miller, "Edward and Estelle Doheny," *Ventura County Historical Society Quarterly*, November 1960, 3–20; Ward Ritchie, *The Dohenys of Los Angeles* (Los Angeles, 1974); Ellen Shaffer, "Reminiscences of a California Collector: Mrs. Edward Doheny 1875–1958," *BC*, Spring 1965, 49–59; Robert Schad, "The Estelle Doheny Collection," *The New Colophon* 3, 1950, 229–242; Carl Weber, *A Thousand and One Fore-Edge Paintings* (Waterville, Maine, 1949); Francis Weber, "The Estelle Doheny Collection of Western Americana," *The California Librarian*, January 1968, 41–45; Correspondence with Lucille V. Miller, former Director of the Doheny Library, May 1984.

DOWSE, Thomas (b. December 28, 1772, Charlestown, Mass.; d. November 4, 1856, Cambridge, Mass.). *Collection Disposition*: Massachusetts Historical Society.

With the small profits from his trade as a wool-puller and a leather-dresser, Dowse invested in books. As a twenty-eight-year-old journeyman leather-dresser earning $25 a month, he had already started his library. At that time, he once reported to George Ticknor,* he did not have a pair of boots but owned "several hundred good books, well bound." He was one of a small circle of Cambridge collectors, including Charles Deane* and George Livermore*, who accumulated sizable private libraries in the early years of the nineteenth century. The Dowse library contained the best translations of the Greek and Roman classics, a sampling of English and European literature, and many standard works in philosophy and religion. Shortly before his death Dowse began to think about the future of his books. After a discussion with Livermore, he decided to give them to the Massachusetts Historical Society. His only requirement, that the books be provided with a separate designated room, was quickly approved by the membership. In appreciation for the gift they commissioned Moses Wight to paint Dowse's portrait, a likeness that still hangs in the Society Library. Edward Everett's lengthy eulogy, delivered in December 1858 in Boston's Music Hall, stressed Dowse's humble origin, his modest nature, and his love of learning.

Bibliography

A. *Catalogue of the Private Library of Thomas Dowse, Presented to the Massachusetts Historical Society* (Cambridge, Mass., 1856).

B. *DAB* 3, 419–420; Farnham, 60–61; Edward Everett, "Eulogy on Thomas Dowse," *PMHS*, 1855–1858, 361–398; Walter Moir Whitehall, The Centenary of the Dowse Library," *PMHS*, 1959, 167–178.

DREER, Ferdinand Julius (b. March 2, 1812, Philadelphia, Pa.; d. May 24, 1902, Philadelphia, Pa.). *Collection Disposition*: Historical Society of Pennsylvania; Birch, May 28, 1889; Henkels, April 11, 1913.

After Dreer retired from his assaying business at the age of fifty, he devoted all his time to collecting and extra-illustrating. The latter pursuit, which was popular at the turn of the century, involved the insertion of plates, drawings, and letters into favorite volumes in order to increase their association value. Dreer was one of the chief practitioners of this hobby, building up elaborate expanded sets on banking, religion, architecture, and literature. In *The Amenities of Book Collecting*, A. Edward Newton* described his childhood delight in visiting the sumptuous Dreer library. In addition to books, Dreer had a collection of some 10,000 autographs and letters, an archive his heirs presented to the Pennsylvania Historical Society. When the library itself was brought to auction in 1913, George D. Smith was the chief buyer. He obtained the elaborate extra-illustrated sets for a fraction of what Dreer had given. By this time extra-illustrating had gone out of fashion and few buyers were willing to invest in Dreer's grandiose treasures.

Bibliography

A. *Catalogue of the Collection of Autographs Formed by Ferdinand Julius Dreer* (Philadelphia, 1890–1892).
B. *NCAB* 10, 206; A. Edward Newton, *The Amenities of Book Collecting* (Boston, 1918), 57–58.

DREXEL, Joseph W. (b. January 24, 1833, Philadelphia, Pa.; d. March 25, 1888, New York, N.Y.). *Collection Disposition*: New York Public Library.

Although he never attended a university, Drexel acquired an excellent humanistic education through travel and reading. By profession he was a banker and represented important financial interests in both Philadelphia and New York. He retired from business early to devote himself to collecting and to various philanthropies. His music library, numbering some 5,000 volumes and ranging over five centuries, included incunabula, eighteenth-century broadsides, and ballad operas. By Drexel's will this entire collection was given to the Lenox Library of New York, with the proviso that it be housed in separate quarters. Later it became the basis for the notable music department of the New York Public Library. Drexel proved his interest in Americana by his active buying at the William Menzies* and George Brinley* sales. Among other rarities, he owned a splendid set of the signers of the United States Constitution. The family kept the Americana and other general rarities after his death. Eventually they formed the basis of the collection of Drexel's grandson, Boises Penrose*.

Bibliography

A. *Catalogue of Joseph W. Drexel's Musical Library* (New York, 1869).
B. *DAB* 5, 457; *NCAB* 2, 377; Harry Lydenberg, *History of the New York Public Library* (New York, 1923), 118–119.

DURANT, Henry F. (b. February 20, 1802, Hanover, N.H.; d. October 3, 1881, Wellesley, Mass.). *Education*: A.B., Harvard University, 1841. *Collection Disposition*: Wellesley College.

A successful lawyer, minister, and philanthropist, Durant was a remarkably talented man. His first career, the law, brought him considerable financial reward as well as association with the eminent Boston jurist Rufus Choate. When he turned to the ministry, his eloquence assured him prominence in that field as well. He became interested in education for women when he and his wife served as trustees for the Mount Holyoke Seminary. Based on that experience, he decided to found a similar school in eastern Massachusetts. With Durant's backing, the first Wellesley College building was dedicated in September 1875. When the school opened it did so with his own well-selected private library of 10,000 volumes. Durant had started to collect books in college and later purchased Choate's comprehensive historical library. From 1860 to 1875 he made regular purchases from dealers in England and the United States. He was convinced that students and faculty needed research materials and to that end purchased long runs of scientific and literary periodicals. He also acquired Shakespeare and Milton collections, early editions of Chaucer, and sets of important continental authors. A year before his death, Durant bought the libraries of A. Owstein, a German clergyman, and William Medlicott, an English literary scholar. The Owstein books, purchased for an amazingly low price of $598, included several important incunabula, an assortment of Martin Luther tracts, Aldine and Elzevir printings, and early editions of the Augsburg Confession. Medlicott's books included early English ballads and French and English literature. The results of Durant's collecting provided Wellesley with a library of well-chosen volumes covering most of the disciplines of the humanities and social sciences. During the college dedication in 1875, Durant's contributions were recognized in a poem written by a freshman student:

> One myth-like tale shall rise from the far past dead,
> How on a night long kept with Memory's spark,
> The father of the college with glad looks,
> Stood smiling on his dear young friends, the girls
> And introduced them to his dear old friends, the books.

Bibliography

B. *DAB* 3, 541–542; *NCAB* 7, 327–328; Ethel Roberts, "Mr. Durant's Gifts to the Library," *The Wellesley Alumni Quarterly*, May 1923, 145–149; Ethel Roberts, *A Brief History of the Wellesley College Library* (Wellesley, Mass., 1936), 3–8.

DURRETT, Ruben T. (b. January 22, 1824, Huery County, Ky.; d. September 16, 1913, Louisville, Ky.). *Education*: LL.B., Louisville College, 1850. *Collection Disposition*: University of Chicago.

In the 1850s Durrett followed careers in both law and journalism. During the Civil War he was editor of the *Louisville Courier* but relinquished that obligation as his law practice grew. He also accepted a number of civic responsibilities, helping to found the Filson Club and the Louisville Public Library. With his family roots deep in the Middle South, Durrett set out to build a library that would include every book and pamphlet written about Kentucky or those by Kentucky authors. Soon his interests expanded to include neighboring states and finally they encompassed the entire Ohio Valley. In the process of building the library he became acquainted with other collectors and historians with similar interests. In 1884 these men organized under the name of the Filson Club and elected Durrett as their first president. The purpose of the organization was to provide members with a setting in which historical papers could be read and social amenities exchanged on a regular basis. The Durrett library was at the heart of the organization. One of the strengths of the library was in its long runs of early Kentucky newspapers and journals.

Around 1910 Professor William Dodd, of the History Department at the University of Chicago, became particularly eager to secure the Durrett library for his institution. After a number of offers and counteroffers, the University of Chicago authorized Walter Lichtenstein of the Northwestern University Library to go to Louisville and make a proper appraisal. In his careful eleven-page report Lichtenstein criticized the ''manuscript'' material as only transcription from original documents but identified the Kentuckiana and the early newspapers as genuinely important. The family agreed to accept the university offer of $22,000 and on April 10, 1913, after a last-minute local fund-raising effort failed, a freight car delivered the Durrett library at the Chicago Union Station. The books and papers in the Durrett collection now form an important part of the University of Chicago's holdings on Southern history.

Bibliography

B. *DAB* 5, 550; *NCAB* 2, 368; Cannon, 251–253; E. A. Henry, ''The Durrett Collection, Now in the University of Chicago,'' *PBSA*, 1914, 57–94; Robert Rosenthal, ''How the Durrett Collection Left Louisville and Came to Chicago'' (Paper read at a Meeting of the Filson Club, November 1, 1976).

DUYCKINCK, Evert A. (b. November 23, 1816, New York, N.Y.; d. August 13, 1878, New York, N.Y.). *Education*: A.B., Columbia University, 1835. *Collection Disposition*: New York Public Library; Bangs, March 23, 1874.

As early as 1700 the Duyckinck family had been closely associated with the cultural life of New York City. Since Duyckinck's father had been a printer and publisher it was natural that he should inherit a taste for all things literary. During the period just before the Civil War, Duyckinck edited *Arcturus* and *The Literary World*, two New York journals notable for their long lists of distinguished contributors. It was through his responsibilities with these journals and his editorial connections with the *Cyclopedia of American Literature* that he built up files of correspondence with such important literary figures as Melville, Poe, Lowell, Hawthorne, and Holmes. In addition to this manuscript archive, he also acquired first editions of American and English writers and long runs of American literary periodicals. In the spring of 1878 Duyckinck approached George Henry Moore, superintendent of the New York Lenox Library, with an inviting offer. Duyckinck wished to give the library the extensive family business papers along with 16,000 books. It was an easy offer to accept. The first installment arrived in May, with subsequent shipments following over the next four years. The Duyckinck library was one of the earliest and most significant gifts of American literature to come to the New York Public Library system.

Bibliography

B. *NCAB* 1, 431; Harry Lydenberg, *History of the New York Public Library* (New York, 1923), 101–102.

E

EAMES, Wilberforce (b. October 12, 1855, Newark, N.J.; d. December 6, 1937, New York, N.Y.). *Collection Disposition*: Anderson, May 17, 1905, March 8, November 26, December 13, 1906, April 11, 1907, April 26, 1910, January 30, 1911, March 31, 1913, April 5 and 6, 1915; New York Public Library; Library of Congress; Newberry Library; Case Memorial Library, Hartford, Connecticut.

Before he was twenty-five, Eames had worked in bookstores in Brooklyn and New York and started to absorb the bookish lore that was to make him one of the most respected bibliographers in the country. Through his bookstore connections he met Thomas W. Field*, compiler of the esteemed *Essay Towards an Indian Bibliography* (1873), and James Pilling, author of numerous studies of North American Indian languages. Eames worked closely with Pilling on bibliographic problems and contributed entire sections to his completed studies. In 1885 Eames was appointed personal assistant to the librarian at the Lenox Library in New York and began a forty-year association with the New York Public Library system.

From his earliest days Eames bought as many books as he could afford. Whenever he received a promotion the money went directly into books. His interests were diverse, but they centered on languages, history, and Americana. As an avid student of ancient languages and civilizations, he gathered books, manuscripts, tablets, and seals relating to Egypt, Sumer, and Babylonia. He also collected books on the Chinese and Japanese languages as well as those on the tribal dialects of Africa and India. He was interested in the organization of knowledge as represented by bibliography and book auction catalogs. Finally, and closest to his heart, were the collections of Americana. Here he amassed impressive holdings relating to American Indian languages, Indian captivities, colonial history, and early American printing. His growing expertise in all matters concerning Americana was demonstrated by his work on Joseph Sabin's *Dictionary of Books Relating to America*. Sabin died in 1881 with his great work done only to the letter *P*. Eames volunteered to carry the work forward in his spare time and got as far as "Smith" when administrative duties at the New York Public Library prohibited further efforts. He had been appointed Lenox librarian in 1893, and when the central New York Public Library building opened on Forty-second Street in 1911 he was placed in charge of the American history division.

By 1905 his Brooklyn residence began to buckle under the weight of some 20,000 books, pamphlets, and maps. He placed thousands of titles in literature, history, and linguistics up for sale in a series of auctions held at the Anderson Galleries between 1905 and 1915. In addition he sold large collections of his books directly to the Library of Congress, the Newberry Library, and the Case Memorial Library in Hartford, Connecticut. The materials on Indian captivity, African history, and Chinese linguistics went to the New York Public Library in a series of gifts and sales. Once all these transactions were completed, Eames set about building a new library focused on early American imprints. By 1923 his collection numbered over 12,000 pieces. This time he sold the books and pamphlets to the Rosenbach Company in Philadelphia and from there they went directly to Henry E. Huntington's* library. Eames became an international authority on all matters relating to American printing and American Indian materials. As such he was revered by a whole generation of American scholars. His biographers frequently speak of his love of learning and his generosity in sharing that learning. When he died his estate of books, portraits, and memorandums went to the New York Public Library, where a "Wilberforce Eames Americana Fund" was established. He was a bookman in the highest sense of the term, devoted to scholarly research not to enhance his own reputation but to improve the record.

Bibliography

A. "The Lenox Library and Its Founder," *Library Journal*, May 1899, 199–201. For complete bibliography, see Victor Paltsits, "Works and Contributions," in *Bibliographical Essays: A Tribute to Wilberforce Eames* (New York, 1924), 23–26.

B. *DAB*, Supp. 2, 162–163; *NCAB* 9, 275; Cannon, 348–358; *Grolier 75*, 75–77; *Dictionary of American Library Biography*, Bohdan Wynar, ed. (Littleton, Colo., 1978) 148–153; Harry Lydenberg, "Wilberforce Eames as I Recall Him," *PAAS*, October 1955, 213–236; Victor Paltsits, "Wilberforce Eames: A Bio-BibliographicalNarrative," in *Bibliographical Essays: A Tribute to Wilberforce Eames* (New York, 1924), 1–26; *Proceedings and Addresses at the Presentation of the New York Historical Society's Gold Medal to Dr. Wilberforce Eames* (New York, 1932); George Parker Winship, "Wilberforce Eames," *BNYPL*, January 1938, 2–9. Ruth S. Granniss, "Wilberforce Eames, American Scholar," *ABC*, 1932, 42–44.

EATON, J. Lloyd (b. July 8, 1902, Berkeley, Calif.; d. December 22, 1968, Berkeley, Calif.). *Education*: M.D., University of California Medical School, 1928. *Collection Disposition*: University of California at Riverside.

While he was still in high school Eaton had started to collect pulp adventure stories. By the time he was in medical school he had added detective stories and westerns, and after starting his professional practice he found himself attracted to fantasy and science fiction. At first he was satisfied with browsing in the bookshops in San Francisco, but as he became more sophisticated he widened his search to dealers in New York and London. He formed the bulk of his collection in the 1940s and early 1950s, when science fiction was still a somewhat unknown collecting area. One of Eaton's strongest interests was in pre–1920 materials, including "future war" and "lost race" genres with titles by John Polidori, Frank Aubrey, and Edgar Rice Burroughs. He also had complete or nearly complete coverage of such well-known twentieth-century writers as H. G. Wells, H. Rider Haggard, Arthur Conan Doyle, and H. P. Lovecraft. On the lighter side, he was first president of the "Elves, Gnomes, and Little Men Chowder and Marching Society," a group of science fiction enthusiasts organized in Berkeley, California. On Eaton's death his wife sold the complete library, 7,500 titles, to the University of California at Riverside. A curator was appointed, an impressive catalog was published, and an annual science-fiction conference was staged. Over a period of thirty years Eaton brought together a collection that now provides a scholarly resource for those interested in the history of science fiction.

Bibliography

A. *Dictionary Catalog of the J. Lloyd Eaton Collection of Science Fiction and Fantasy Literature* (Boston, 1982).

B. George Slusser, "Introduction," in *Dictionary Catalogue of the J. Lloyd Eaton Collection of Science Fiction and Fantasy Literature* (Boston, 1982), iii-v; Correspondence with Mrs. J. Lloyd Eaton, November 12, 1984.

EDELHEIM, Carl (b. 1844; d. September 28, 1899, Philadelphia, Pa.) *Collection Disposition*: American Art, March 7, 1900.

Although his financial resources were not equal to those of some of his friends in the Grolier Club of New York and the Philobiblon Club of Philadelphia, Edelheim gathered a very respectable library of fine printing. On his frequent trips to England he became acquainted with William Morris and acquired a nearly complete file of Kelmscott Press publications as well as numerous examples of the work of the Vale, Daniel, and Ergany presses. In *The Book Buyer* Ernest Dressel North praised Edelheim as a sophisticated collector. When his fine Kelmscott collection came up for auction in 1900, the prices broke all previous records. The *New York Times* referred to the sale as one of the most notable of the season.

Bibliography

B. Ernest Dressel North, "Notes of Rare Books," *The Book Buyer*, April 1900, 229; "Mr. Edelheim's Profits," *NYT*, March 17, 1900, 168; "Kelmscott Books," *NYT*, March 17, 1900, 170.

EDGAR, Herman L. (b. May 30, 1865, Newport, R.I.; d. September 5, 1938, Dobbs Ferry, N.Y.). *Education*: A.B., Harvard University, 1887. *Collection Disposition*: Anderson, November 22, 1920, January 24, 1921, January 30, 1924, April 18, 1944.

With profits made in the real estate business, Edgar bought first editions of nineteenth-century American and English literary classics. In an effort to concentrate on English writers, he sold the American side of his library at auction in late 1920. This was one of the first major sales after the death of the indomitable George D. Smith and it gave A. S. W. Rosenbach* an opportunity to assume Smith's mantle. For an investment of something over $21,000, Rosenbach secured Henry E. Huntington's* desiderata as well as his confidence. Four years later Edgar offered his small but choice English literature collection at auction. It contained the most distinguished selection of Thackeray to come on the market in many years. In addition to the Thackeray first editions, Edgar owned autographed copies of Conrad, Kipling, and Dickens and an assortment of Cruikshank illustrations and Ruskin letters. Edgar's collecting taste was verified by two successful auctions.

Bibliography

B. *NCAB* 29, 317; Cannon, 237.

ELKINS, William M. (b. September 3, 1882, Philadelphia, Pa.; d. June 5, 1947, Philadelphia, Pa.). *Education*: A.B., Harvard University, 1905. *Collection Disposition*: Free Library of Philadelphia.

After he completed his university education, Elkins entered the family banking business, an association he maintained throughout his professional life. As an avocation he collected books. Books and reading had been important to him from his earliest years and were passions he shared with his cousin Harry E. Widener*, who lived across the street. The boys traded pulp adventure stories by their favorite authors, G. A. Henty and Robert Louis Stevenson. At Harvard, Elkins began to invest in Dickens, Thackeray, and Shaw, with excursions into the Restoration dramatists Pinero and Congreve. For his first major author collection, Elkins chose Oliver Goldsmith and pursued that playwright with great diligence. He had first editions, letters, and manuscripts of all Goldsmith's works. At one time he considered doing a bibliography based on his collection, but the technicalities wore down his resolve. He simply grew tired, as he said, of holding one edition in his left hand and comparing it line by line with the edition in his right hand. His next collection, the works of Charles Dickens, was chosen more for fun than for bibliographic prestige. This collection got an impressive start with acquisitions from the so-called "Sentimental Library" of Harry B. Smith*. When the Smith library came on the market, Philadelphia bookseller A. S. W. Rosenbach* persuaded Elkins to put up the purchase price through his banking firm. Rosenbach allowed Elkins first choice on the rarities, and the collector acquired twenty-four Dickens presentation copies, among them a renowned

"Pickwick" inscribed by the author to his sister-in-law Mary Hogarth. Other purchases included Charles Lamb's personal copy of Drayton's works and an inscribed copy of Thackeray's *Vanity Fair*.

After focusing on British literature for a number of years, Elkins turned to Americana. Some of his most significant acquisitions came in 1928 from the Leconfield sale in London and later from the Herschel V. Jones* sale in New York. Elkins had used Jones' guide, *Adventures in Americana*, for a number of years and was delighted when the entire Jones library became available in 1939. Again, Elkins' banking firm helped Rosenbach finance the purchase, and again Elkins got the pick of the lot. Among the chief attractions were Hakluyt's "Voyages" with the rare Thorne map, nine Ptolemies, the DeBry "Voyages," and eighteen works by Cotton Mather. The record of this impressive purchase was carefully set down by Howell Heaney in a 1956 issue of *Papers of the Bibliographical Society of America*. Elkins also collected books and prints by the English children's author-illustrator Beatrix Potter. One of his last purchases was the original manuscript of Potter's *The Tailor of Gloucester*. Although Elkins considered selling his library, he changed his mind shortly before his death and instructed his heirs to give such items "as they would select" to the Free Library of Philadelphia. The family interpreted this recommendation liberally and presented the entire collection to the library along with Elkins' personal library furnishings. The William M. Elkins Room stands in the Free Library as a continuing tribute to a discriminating collector.

Bibliography

A. *Oliver Goldsmith, Bibliographically and Biographically Considered*, edited by Temple Scott and based on the collection of material in the library of William M. Elkins (New York, 1928).

B. Wolf and Fleming, passim; Howell Heaney, "The Americana Collection of William M. Elkins," *PBSA*, 2nd Q 1956, 130–168; Ellen Shaffer, "Portrait of a Philadelphia Collector: William McIntire Elkins 1882–1947," *PBSA*, 2nd Q 1956, 115–129.

ELLIS, Ralph (b. June 15, 1908, Jericho, N.Y.; d. December 17, 1945, Colusa, Calif.). *Collection Disposition*: University of Kansas.

The son of a wealthy New York family, Ellis was educated privately in South Carolina and California. At an early age he developed strong collecting interests in both ornithology and mammalogy. He went on numerous field trips in California with a scientific mentor and in 1931 participated in a Harvard zoological expedition to Australia. This trip, like so many other events in Ellis' brief life, ended in confusion and frustration—symptoms of a variety of illnesses that plagued him throughout his life. Ellis began to collect ornithology books while still a teenager. By 1926 he had gathered an impressive number of journals and proceedings of scientific societies, as well as a large collection of monographs on birds and mammals. He also began to collect the narratives of scientific voyages and explorations and related bibliographical works. Cost was always secondary to "need." He invested so heavily at the John Charles Phillips' auction in 1936 that his mother was forced to sell part of the family estate in order to pay the bills. His year and a half in England added even more titles to the rapidly growing library and included acquisition of a remarkable archive from the home of ornithologist John Gould. Even while he was confined to treatment centers in California during the early 1940s, Ellis managed to buy books and journals.

The final few months of his life were as hectic as the preceding years. Early in 1945, in an effort to move his library to a more hospitable environment, he had the 65,000 items packed and dispatched for New York in two boxcars. He ordered the shipment halted in Lawrence, Kansas, and there, under the supervision of an old friend, museum director Raymond Hall, the library found a permanent home. Ellis was given shelving, an office, and access to university laboratories. The arrangement seemed ideal. His death came suddenly that same year.

Bibliography

A. *A Catalog of an Exhibition of Landmarks in the Development of Ornithology from the Ralph Ellis Collection* (Lawrence, Kans., 1957); *A Catalogue of the Ellis Collection of Ornithological Books in the University of Kansas Libraries*, compiled by Robert Mengel, volume 1, A-B (Lawrence, Kans., 1972).

B. Robert Vosper, "A Pair of Bibliomanes for Kansas: Ralph Ellis and Thomas Jefferson Fitzpatrick," *PBSA*, 3rd Q 1961, 207–225; Adrey Borell, "Ralph Ellis Jr. 1908–1945," *Journal of Wildlife Management*, October 1947, 355–356.

ELLISON, Robert S. (b. November 6, 1875, Rushville, Ind.; d. 1945, Manitou Springs, Colo.). *Education*: A.B., Indiana University, 1900. *Collection Disposition*: Indiana University.

After practicing law for a number of years in Colorado, Ellison was appointed head of the Stanolind Pipe Line Company of Tulsa. Throughout his life he had been deeply interested in western history and North American Indian lore. His library, estimated at 3,000 books and 6,000 manuscripts, reflected both these topics. A particularly strong section of the library focused on overland travel and the settlement of the Pacific Northwest. This section contained pioneers' diaries and a large archive of books and pamphlets on Utah and the Mormons. One of the important manuscript files held in the library was the papers of Joseph Lane, first governor of the Oregon Territory. In 1946 Mrs. Ellison gave the books and manuscripts to Indiana University as a memorial to her husband. There the collection is housed in the "Ellison Room of Western Americana" of the Lilly Library. According to Robert A. Miller, former university librarian, the acquisition rounded out the university's coverage of western American history. It has provided an important research tool for serious students of the West.

Bibliography

B. *NCAB* F, 184; Oscar Winther, "The Robert S. Ellison Collection," *Indiana Quarterly for Bookmen*, January 1948, 7–19.

ELLSWORTH, James W. (b. October 13, 1849, Hudson, Ohio; d. June 3, 1925, Florence, Italy). *Collection Disposition*: Sold to A. S. W. Rosenbach, 1923.

Much of the Ellsworth fortune came from the coal fields of West Virginia and Ohio. As a gesture of gratitude he returned a substantial portion of his wealth to support various local cultural and educational activities. With the remainder of his money he built a large personal library. He was one of the regulars who clustered around the "Saints and Sinners" corner at McClurg's Bookstore in Chicago, swapping stories and books with Eugene Field* and his cohorts. His special interest ran to incunabula, with milder enthusiasms for Americana and Shakespeariana. In 1891 he bought the Gutenberg Bible at the Brayton Ives* sale for $14,000. Other high points in his collection included the four Shakespeare folios, the King-Hamy portolan map of 1502, a full set of the signers of the Declaration of Independence, Washington letters, and Lincoln manuscripts. It was the kind of library A. S. W. Rosenbach* could not resist. Rosenbach had customers waiting in the wings. Some 105 of the Ellsworth incunabula went to Henry E. Huntington*, the Bible to John H. Schiede*, and the four folios to Eldridge R. Johnson*. Rosenbach took full advantage of the Ellsworth collection to further one of his most successful negotiations of the 1920s.

Bibliography

B. *NCAB* 26, 176; Wolf and Fleming, 170, 186–187.

EMMETT, Burton (b. November 11, 1871, Lee, Ill.; d. May 6, 1935, Boggs Wharf, Melfa, Va.). *Collection Disposition*: University of North Carolina.

Emmett worked as a journalist and as a press agent before finding a permanent niche in the advertising business. With a keen understanding of the printing arts, he promoted the highest standards of book design through membership in the American Institute of Graphic Arts and editorship of *The Colophon*, a highly acclaimed book collector's quarterly. With his own collecting interests focused on the graphic arts, he built a notable library representing the work of the master printers and binders from the fifteenth to the twentieth century. He also had an extensive collection of books about books as well as first editions by Hemingway, Crane, Jeffers, and Sherwood Anderson. In 1951 his well-balanced and attractive library was purchased by the University of North Carolina.

Bibliography

B. *NCAB* 29, 432.

ENGEL, Solton (b. January 1, 1896, Hungary; d. August 29, 1961, Kennebunkport, Maine). *Education*: A.B., Columbia University, 1916; LL.B., New York University, 1918. *Collection Disposition*: Columbia University.

Aside from brief service in World War II, Engel devoted his entire career to insurance law and the various consulting appointments connected with that specialty. He made gifts to the Columbia University library over a long period of time under the modest designation "A member of the class of 1916." In 1958, however, he agreed to disclose his identity in connection with a large gift of Kipling material. He had gathered the books and letters over a considerable period of years chiefly through negotiations with New York bookseller James Drake. The Engel collection held American and British first editions, periodical publications, and contributions to anthologies. In addition to Kipling, Engel collected Clemens, Whitman, Lewis Carroll, and other well-known literary figures. Of particular interest was his inscribed edition of *Leaves of Grass* accompanied by a Whitman holograph. Engel's benefactions to Columbia were constant and significant. In a catalog listing the Engel gifts, former Director of Libraries Roland Baughman recalled an occasion when the collector discovered that the library lacked both the third and fourth Shakespeare folios. Immediately, he saw to it that these volumes were obtained. In 1967 the entire library came to Columbia, presented by Mrs. Engel as requested in her husband's will. In addition to the authors mentioned, Engel owned immaculate first editions of Gelett Burgess, George Ade, Longfellow, and Tarkington. This was no mere accumulation of prescribed high points but a gathering based on a highly individualistic personal taste. As a final act of generosity, Engel established an endowment to assure the continued growth of the collection.

Bibliography

A. *The Engel Collection*, edited by Kenneth Lohf (New York, 1967).
B. Correspondence with Mrs. Solton Engel, 1982.

EVANS, Herbert (b. September 23, 1882, Modesto, Calif.; d. March 6, 1971, Berkeley, Calif.). *Education*: B.S., University of California at Berkeley, 1904; M.D., Johns Hopkins, 1908. *Collection Disposition*: Sold to Jake Zeitlin of Los Angeles and John Howell of San Francisco, 1950–1965; Sale on March 31, 1975.

After beginning his career on the medical faculty of Johns Hopkins University, Evans moved to the University of California at Berkeley in 1915 and served as professor of anatomy at that institution until 1952. He was known for his studies in embryology and endocrinology and became internationally known as an authority on the function of the pituitary gland. He was a major participant in the isolation of Vitamin E. At Hopkins he came under the influence of the great medical bibliographer and collector Sir William Osler and Osler's pupil and avid collector Harvey Cushing*. It was not surprising that Evans turned to collecting landmarks in the history of science. To start his collection Evans wrote to the leaders in each scientific discipline asking them to identify the basic monographs in their own area. Building on this advice, he acquired the books and produced an exemplary catalog of 114 works entitled *Exhibition of First Editions of Epochal Achievements in the History of Science*. In his brief introduction Evans stated the case for collecting first editions. Evans said one needed these "first fruits" in order to understand subsequent achievements.

Between 1930 and 1965, Los Angeles bookdealer Jake Zeitlin estimated that Evans purchased no less than 20,000 volumes in the history of science. In addition, he formed two large collections of western Americana and a sizable general collection of poetry, art, and literature. Unfortunately his appetite for books was not backed by a large personal fortune. As bills accumulated, Evans would sell. Before the creditors were satisfied, however, he would start buying again. His first large science library went from Zeitlin to Lessing J. Rosenwald* and from Rosenwald to the Institute for Advanced Studies at Princeton. The second Evans library was divided between Bern Dibner and E. L. DeGolyer*, again through Zeitlin's efforts. Subsequent collections went to the Universities of Chicago, Texas, and Utah and to numerous private collectors. In most of these negotiations Evans was represented by Zeitlin in Los Angeles and Warren Howell in San Francisco. Evans was an energetic and knowledgeable bibliophile with a thorough understanding of the importance of first editions. His books now form the basis of some of the greatest history-of-science libraries in the United States.

Bibliography

A. *Exhibition of First Editions of Epochal Achievement in the History of Science* (Berkeley, Calif., 1934); *The Oregon Country and the Pacific Northwest*, as collected by Herbert Evans (San Francisco, 1958).

B. *NCAB* 57, 295; *CB*, 1959, 109-111; Jacob Zeitlin, "Eloge, Herbert Evans," *Isis*, December 1971, 507–509; Jake Zeitlin, "Herbert Evans," in *Books and the Imagination*, transcript of an Oral History (Los Angeles, 1980), passim; "Herbert Evans," *Biographical Memoir of the Fellows of the Royal Society of London* (1972), 83–186.

F

FABYAN, George (b. March 15, 1867, Boston, Mass.; d. May 17, 1936, Geneva, Ill.). *Collection Disposition*: Library of Congress.

During a professional career in the Riverbank Acoustics Laboratories in Illinois, Fabyan became interested in codes and ciphers. He gathered a large library on those subjects, some items dating back to the sixteenth century. His fascination with puzzles also extended into literature and included an intense study of the Shakespeare-Bacon controversy. He built an extensive holding of Bacon's works and the many critical examinations of those works. The entire Fabyan research collection was turned over to the Library of Congress in 1940.

Bibliography

B. *NCAB* 26, 93; *SCLC*, 103.

FALES, DeCoursey (b. June 1, 1888, Saranac Lake, N.Y.; d. June 19, 1966, New York, N.Y.). *Education*: A.B., Harvard University, 1911; LL.B., Columbia University, 1914. *Collection Disposition*: New York University; Pierpont Morgan Library; New York Public Library; Manhattan College.

After practicing law for a short time, Fales entered the banking business. He followed that career until his retirement in 1958. As a boy he was encouraged to collect by his father, Haliburton Fales, and it was in his father's name that Fales contributed a great library to New York University. Stimulated by Harvard Professor Bliss Perry, Fales began to collect the English novelist Sir Walter Scott. As his Scott collection grew he expanded his field of interest to a general coverage of eighteenth- and nineteenth-century American and English novelists. His ambitions went far beyond the traditional high-point books and included second and third editions, translations, association items, criticism, and biography. While Fales concentrated on Dickens, Scott, Thackeray, and Trollope, he also had extensive holdings of such minor authors as Amelia Opie, Henry Brooke, and the satiric Eliza Haywood. When Fales took up an author, he developed a complete archive on that person. In his Scott collection, for example, he acquired not only items by and about Scott but also pamphlets, speeches, broadsides, books, and articles by members of Scott's wide literary circle. Often these peripheral publications were harder to obtain than first editions of the author's own work. On another level, Fales gathered ephemera, letters, notes, manuscripts, and autographed materials. His Dickens collection was particularly rich in this regard, with more than 100 letters from the author to his various literary associates and illustrators. Fales also owned books from Dickens' personal library, playbills from his speaking engagements, texts of speeches themselves, and an extraordinary run of *The Gad's Hill Gazette*, edited and printed by Dickens' teenage son. The Thackeray material was equally notable, including many rare items from the Henry Van Duzer* library. One of the extremely choice items in the Fales library was entitled *The Proceedings of the Thirteenth Anniversary Festival of the Royal General Theatrical Fund* (1858) and included speeches by both Dickens and Thackeray.

In 1958 Fales presented his library to New York University and became, in his own terms, the "librarian in charge of acquisitions." Secondhand-book catalogs poured over his desk at the rate of ten or twelve a day, and each received his close attention. By virtue of this effort, his collection jumped from 8,000 books and 4,000 manuscripts to an astounding 50,000 books and 12,000 manuscripts in less than ten years. Fales reported that after he retired and started working for the university he pursued collecting with ten times the zeal he had devoted to it when buying books for himself. After having concentrated his attention almost entirely on the eighteenth and nineteenth centuries for twenty years, Fales widened his scope to include the significant, and not so significant, novelists of the twentieth century. He began with the Irish school, then went on to "the beats," detective fiction, and black authors. In addition to his major benefactions to New York University, he gave books and manuscripts to the Pierpont Morgan Library, the New York Public Library, and Manhattan College. It was Fales' goal to preserve the essence of an author by collecting his works in depth. Bibliographer Arthur Swann once observed that the Fales library contained not only the highways but also the byways. Fales was a discriminating and assiduous collector.

Bibliography

B. John T. Winterich, *The Fales Collection: An Appreciation* (New York, 1959); John T. Winterich, *The Fales Collection: A Record of Growth* (New York, 1963); J. W. Egerer, *Charles Dickens in the Fales Collection* (New York, 1965); J. W. Egerer, *De Coursey Fales 1888–1966* (New York, 1966).

FARQUHAR, Francis P. (b. December 31, 1887, Newton, Mass.; d. November 21, 1974, Berkeley, Calif.). *Education*: A.B., Harvard University, 1909. *Collection Disposition*: University of California at Los Angeles.

Professionally Farquhar was a certified public accountant, holding offices in the State Board of Accounting and the California Society of Certified Public Accountants. Outside of his business life he was an avid mountaineer, conservationist, bibliographer, historian, writer, and collector. In Farquhar all these interests flowed together in a productive harmony. He climbed mountains, loved the land, wrote articles and books about his favorite Sierras, edited the *Sierra Club Bulletin*, and in his spare time gathered one of the world's most impressive libraries on mountaineering and mountain travel. The broad scope of the Farquhar collection, some 2,000 volumes in total, was well displayed in the selected bibliography published by the University of California at Los Angeles. Starting with Conrad Gesner's *On the Admiration of Mountains* (1543), Farquhar's library ranged from classic works written in the late nineteenth century by Leslie Stephen, Edward Whymper, and A. F. Mummery to twentieth-century accounts of assaults on Everest and Kanchenjunga. Particular areas of strength in the collection described climbs in the White Mountains in New Hampshire, the Alaskan mountains, the Greek mountains, and the continental American ranges. Many of the copies in the library were inscribed to Farquhar from members of his wide circle of mountaineering friends.

In 1969 Farquhar and his wife made arrangements to have their books transferred to the University of California at Los Angeles. The transfer document stated that the library should be made "accessible to mountaineers, especially to young people desiring to climb mountains." An endowment fund provided by the Farquhars assured continued growth. The handsomely produced bibliography, published six years after Farquhar's death with photographs by Ansel Adams and Bradford Washburn, was an appropriate memorial to an important scholarly collector.

Bibliography

A. *Classics in the Literature of Mountaineering and Mountain Travel from the Francis P. Farquhar Collection of Mountaineering Literature: An Annotated Bibliography*, edited by James Cox (Los Angeles, 1980).

B. "Francis P. Farquhar," *PAAS*, April 1975, 27–31.

FEARING, Daniel B. (b. August 14, 1859, Newport, R.I.; d. May 26, 1918, Newport, R.I.). *Education*: A.B., Harvard University, 1882. *Collection Disposition*: Harvard University; Merwin, March 22, 1910, November 20, 1912.

The sketch of Fearing in the 1915 *Who's Who in America* identified him as a politician who served as mayor of Newport and a member of the Rhode Island State Inland Fish Commission. This last position was appropriate because it reflected Fearing's lifelong interest in the sport of fishing. He had been an avid fisherman from youth and at the age of thirty had prepared an extensive illustrated scrapbook on trout-fishing. This started him on a quest for books, pamphlets, drawings, sketches, reports, and manuscripts dealing with all aspects of the sport. First in priority were the various pieces of literature that treated fishing as a recreational sport. Within this group Fearing had extensive holdings of the

various editions of Izaak Walton's *The Compleat Angler*. He owned two copies
of the rare 1653 edition as well as multiple copies of the next four seventeenth-
century editions. In all, his library held 160 renderings of Walton's masterpiece.
Many of these were notable for their illustrations, inscriptions, and elaborate
bindings. As a supplement to the Walton collection, Fearing gathered angling
novels, travel books, and natural history, scientific treatises on fish culture,
reports of state fishery departments, and texts of fishing laws and regulations.
He attempted to be comprehensive, even including several manuscripts on fishing
and fifteen incunabula. He also owned a large number of books on whales and
whaling. Another section of the library included books on fish cookery, with
recipes for preparation of all kinds of fish dishes. The library was enriched by
thousands of prints, drawings, engravings, and postcards, all representing some
phase of angling or boating.

Fearing established an amiable relationship with the Harvard library officers
as early as 1910, when he gave them a number of rare editions of the works of
Persius in honor of classical philology professor Morris H. Morgan. It was on
this basis that his great collection on fish and fishing, some 12,000 items, went
to Harvard in 1915. The Fearing library was the second collection to be organized
in the magnificent new Widener Library building. After the books and pamphlets
were properly housed, Fearing decided to collect bookplates. His books and
bookplates were exhibited at the Grolier Club in New York and the Boston Club
of Odd Volumes. Fearing was known as a knowledgeable collector and a generous
donor.

Bibliography

A. *A Catalogue of an Exhibit of Angling Books Together with a Number of Manuscripts
. . . from the Collection of a Member of the Grolier Club* (New York, 1911); *The Making
of an Angling Library* (Santa Barbara, Calif., 1915); *A Catalogue of an Exhibition of
Angling Book Plates* (New York, 1918).

B. Mildred Gardner, "Literature of Angling," *Boston Transcript*, July 5, 1911, 1;
Goodspeed, 142–143; Alfred Potter, *The Library of Harvard University* (Cambridge,
Mass., 1934), 54–56; Will Wildwood, "Brief Memoir of Daniel B. Fearing," *American
Angler*, July 1918, 162; George Parker Winship, "The Daniel B. Fearing Collection,"
Harvard Alumni Bulletin, November 3, 1915, 22–24.

FEISS, Paul Louis (b. June 3, 1875, Cleveland, Ohio; d. January 20, 1952,
Cleveland, Ohio). *Collection Disposition*: Kent State University; Parke-Bernet,
December 15, 1953.

Although the family business demanded much of his time, Feiss was able to
form an impressive private library. He became interested in collecting at the age
of twenty, when he read the Arthurian legend. The acquisition of a secondhand
copy of Sir Thomas Malory's *Morte d'Arthur* led him to purchase other medieval
romances and histories. Because of the nature of his reading, Feiss soon developed

a taste for incunabula and fine printing, a taste he indulged by adding volumes from the presses of Anton Koberger, Christopher Plantin, and Jean Elzevir. Sample volumes from his English literature collection included first editions of Fielding, Goldsmith, Dickens, and Scott. In the broadest sense the Feiss books comprised what is often referred to as a "gentleman's library," an assortment of first editions and fine printing with a strong humanistic base. In 1952, Feiss' family gave the major portion of his library, 5,000 volumes, to Kent State University.

Bibliography

A. *The Sentiment of Book Collecting* (Cleveland, 1908).

B. *NCAB* D, 305; Julian Feiss, "The Paul Feiss Library; A Memoir," in *The Feiss Collection* (Kent, Ohio, 1975), vii-ix.

FIELD, Eugene (b. September 2, 1850, Saint Louis, Mo.; d. November 4, 1895, Chicago, Ill.). *Collection Disposition*: Anderson, December 18, 1923; Henkels, November 16, 1928; American Art—Anderson, October 25, 1933.

In 1883 Field moved to Chicago to write for the *Morning News*. For the next twelve years he contributed a steady diet of lively prose and poetry to Chicago readers in the form of a column entitled "Sharps and Flats." He wrote about politics, the theater, music, and books. Around 1888 Field began to concentrate more on books and collecting. In order to get his points across, Field created a mythical organization of book collectors called "Saints and Sinners" and located it in a musty corner of McClurg's Bookstore. Column after fanciful column described the bizarre behavior of the sinners who invested sizable portions of their time and money in book collecting. From his earliest days in Chicago, Field had found McClurg's, presided over by the sophisticated George M. Millard, a stimulating and diverting milieu. He was soon collecting English ballads and illustrated editions of King Arthur and Robin Hood. Field's serious collecting came later as he became more enamoured with bibliophilism and the kind of people it attracted. According to Slason Thompson, Field's biographer, it was sometimes difficult to separate the poet's genuine infatuation for collecting from cultivated affectation. In one corner of his library he brought together a large collection of the various editions of Horace, while in another he stored fine bindings, miniature books, and association copies. It was "a storeroom of books, inherited, purchased and presented." In his autobiographical essay *Auto-Analysis*, Field reported a personal fondness for every "quaint and curious line" in his collection of 3,500 volumes. During the last few months of his life, Field gave full play to his bookish fantasies in *The Love Affairs of a Bibliomaniac*, a series of essays on reading in bed, extra-illustration, and other bibliographic pleasures. It stands as an appropriate summary of his ironic and sentimental views.

Bibliography

A. *The Love Affairs of a Bibliomaniac* (New York, 1896); "Sharps and Flats," in *Writings in Prose and Verse of Eugene Field*, volume 12 (New York, 1907).

B. *DAB* 3, 362–363; *NCAB* 1, 158; Wallace Rice, "Eugene Field: Reader and Collector," *Reading and Collecting*, September 1937, 11–13; Slason Thompson, *Life of Eugene Field* (New York, 1927).

FIELD, Thomas W. (b. 1821, Onondaga Hill, N.Y.; d. November 25, 1881, Brooklyn, N.Y.). *Collection Disposition*: Bangs, May 24 and 29, 1875, May 22, 1882.

Any appraisal of Field's life must begin with a comment on the variety of professional careers he followed. He was trained as a teacher but after a short time in the classroom took jobs first as an engineer then as a florist. From 1849 to 1858 he served as principal of a Brooklyn high school, but he gave that up when his real estate investments began to yield high profits. In later years he was an assessor, superintendent of Brooklyn public schools, and an amateur historian and bibliographer.

Field's library was primarily a research tool used to support his varied writing activities. He wrote essays on pear culture, Brooklyn antiquities, and the Battle of Long Island. The largest portion of his library focused on the history and culture of the North American Indian. Field collected books, documents, and pamphlets on all aspects of aboriginal life within the United States. He included factual works as well as literary works that treated the Indian in a narrative or poetic form. A large portion of the library was given over to Indian languages, while other sections contained prayer books, local history, and biography. In 1873 Field issued a master list of his collection under the modest title *An Essay Toward an Indian Bibliography*. The list still stands as a useful work.

Field's fortunes declined in the mid–1880s and he was forced to sell his library at auction. Under careful management of master auctioneer Joseph Sabin, the books brought a fair return, although some items, like the handsome set of DeBry's "Voyages," yielded only a fraction of their market value. The importance of the Field library can not be overlooked in any analysis of American book auction history. It was the first time a significant collection of Indian materials was offered on the open market. It attracted William M. Darlington*, Samuel W. Pennypacker*, and Brayton Ives* and focused attention on an important area of American antiquities.

Bibliography

A. *An Essay Toward an Indian Bibliography* (New York, 1873).

B. *DAB* 6, 376; *NCAB* 24, 278; "The Thomas W. Field Library," *The American Bibliopolist*, June 1875, 145–150.

FIELD, William B. Osgood (b. 1870, Geneva, Switz.; d. October 6, 1949, Lake Monhegan, N.Y.). *Education*: M.E., Stevens Institute of Technology, 1894. *Collection Disposition*: Harvard University.

Engineer, sportsman, and bibliophile, Field collected in a number of diverse areas. He was interested in the American Revolutionary War and brought together an impressive library on that subject. His Rudyard Kipling collection, given to Harvard, formed an important addition to the Houghton holdings. Finally, his collections of drawings led to the publication of two impressive monographs, *Edward Lear on My Shelves* and *John Leach on My Shelves* (1930). Throughout his collecting career Field was closely associated with the Grolier Club of New York, serving as its president from 1924 to 1928.

Bibliography

B. "William Field, in Memoriam," *Grolier Yearbook*, 1950; *NYT*, October 7, 1949, 28.

FISKE, Daniel Willard (b. November 11, 1831, Ellisburg, N.Y.; d. September 17, 1904, Frankfurt am Main, Ger.). *Collection Disposition*: Cornell University; Icelandic National Library.

Although he never completed an academic degree, Fiske was recognized as an authority on Scandinavian languages and literature. After two years of study at universities in Copenhagen and Uppsala, he returned to New York and accepted a position in the Astor Library. In addition to providing him with a modest income, the New York location gave him an opportunity to pursue his two chief hobbies: book collecting and chess. During this period he joined Paul Morphy to launch *The American Chess Monthly* and to plan and organize the first American Chess Congress. In 1868 he accepted the post of librarian and professor of North European languages at the newly founded Cornell University. He served that institution for fifteen years, resigning in 1883 to take up permanent residence in Florence, Italy. As a collector, Fiske was ardent, meticulous, and scholarly. He began by gathering newspapers, journals, and reference books about Scandinavia and Iceland during his stay in those areas in the 1850s. Although his enthusiasms widened over the years, the Scandinavian collection remained an abiding interest. After he resigned from the Cornell faculty, he had more time to devote to bibliographical projects. Between 1886 and 1907 he published four so-called "Notices" enumerating his Icelandic holdings. After he died, some of these materials were given to the Icelandic National Library but the bulk of the collection went to Cornell.

The second great Fiske collection began in 1881 with the chance purchase of several works of Petrarch, the fourteenth-century Italian poet and humanist. Working with his usual vigor, Fiske was able to issue a small catalog within the next year enumerating some 1,200 choice Petrarch items. In a charming letter to the Cornell librarian, Fiske described the pleasure of roaming bookstores and sorting the mass of books that came to him from all over Italy. In his will Fiske presented the Petrarch collection to Cornell along with ample support funds to assure continuing development.

In the summer of 1891 Fiske took on another collecting area: books in the Rhaeto-Romanic language. He culled the shelves of bookdealers and shops in several small Austrian towns and in six weeks had gathered 1,300 titles. These were immediately shipped off to Cornell, where they formed a unique adjunct to the other language materials.

The last and perhaps greatest of all the Fiske collections, the Dante library, had its beginning in 1893. While searching for Petrarch material, Fiske accidently came on the Styagnini (1536) edition of the *Divine Comedy* and added it to his stock. He bought other Dante editions until, almost by chance, he became a Dante collector. In 1895 Fiske sent a letter to the Cornell Library with the first shipment of Dante books, stating his intention to develop a collection. In the "Introduction" to the Dante *Catalogue*, Fiske explained what he called "the charm of the chase" by saying he was a "happy slave" to bibliomania and could no more resist the bookstalls than the gambler could refrain from "testing the turn of cards or the roll of the dice." The task of building a Dante collection, however, was a challenge even for a determined and experienced addict like Fiske. It involved, necessarily, variant editions, bibliography, history, and translations. The text might appear in the form of musical compositions, articles, books, or proceedings of learned societies. In addition, the collection was not limited to materials by Dante but was to include commentary about the poet and his era. This task required time, money, and detailed bibliographic knowledge. Fortunately Fiske had all three. In the space of one year he forwarded 3,000 items to Cornell and by 1900 could report a total of over 7,000 sent. His success, as he pointed out, was chiefly due to helpful bookdealers. At the time of his death, librarians and bookdealers alike paid homage to his scholarly devotion and his collecting ardor. He was appropriately identified by Guido Biagi, the Laurentian librarian, as a truly munificent bibliographer.

Bibliography

A. *Catalogue of the Dante Collection*, compiled by Theodore Koch (Ithaca, N.Y., 1898–1900); *Catalogue of the Petrarch Collection*, compiled by Mary Fowler (Oxford, 1916); *Catalogue of the Rhaeto-Romanic Collection* (Ithaca, N.Y., 1894); *Catalogue of the Icelandic Collection* (Ithaca, N.Y., 1894).

B. *DAB* 4, 17; *NCAB* 25, 279; Cannon, 132–135; Wynne, 187–196; T. F. Crane, "Dante Collection," *Cornell Magazine*, May 1894; H. Hermannsson, "Fiske Icelandic Collection," *American Scandinavian Review*, May-June 1915; T. W. Koch, "The Growth and Importance of the Dante Collection," *Cornell Magazine*, June 1900; Horatio White, "A Sketch of the Life and Labors of Willard Fiske," *PBSA*, Willard Fiske Memorial Number, 3rd Q, 1918, 69–88; Horatio White, "The Book Collector and His Collections," in *Willard Fiske: Life and Correspondence* (Ithaca, N.Y., 1925), 114–148.

FITZPATRICK, Thomas Jefferson (b. April 2, 1868, Centerville, Iowa; d. March 28, 1952, Lincoln, Nebr.). *Education*: B.S., M.S., State University of Iowa, 1893, 1895. *Collection Disposition*: University of Kansas; Kansas City Public Library; Iowa Historical Society.

In 1895, after teaching in the Iowa public schools for a number of years, Fitzpatrick accepted a post as instructor of mathematics at Graceland College in

Lamoni, Iowa. Among his responsibilities was supervision of the library. It was during his eight years at Graceland and four years with the Iowa Historical Society as a "field collector" that his own collecting mania took root. By 1904 the trustees of the Historical Society reported that the Fitzpatrick collection, on loan to them, comprised some 6,000 volumes and over 5,000 pamphlets. It included, among other things, 100 volumes of the writings of Linnaeus, 30 rare volumes by eighteenth-century American naturalist C. S. Rafinesque, Iowa history, travel guides, geology, mathematics, and long runs of scientific serials. In addition, Fitzpatrick had started to assemble a remarkable collection of Mormon books and pamphlets. In 1913, when he was appointed a faculty member at the University of Nebraska, he owned 15,000 volumes. By 1927 he estimated the size of his library at 20,000 items, a figure that may have been far too modest. So rash was Fitzpatrick's buying that duplicates and triplicates frequently came to his shelves. Never a wealthy man, he used the sale of extra copies to augment his modest income. This seems to have done little, however, to decrease the total accumulation. In 1950 the city building inspector brought charges against Fitzpatrick for exceeding the allowable 40 pounds per square foot of floor load. The inspector found that the Fitzpatrick house carried an estimated 340 pounds per square foot with an overall total of 90 tons of printed material.

    After Fitzpatrick died, Kansas City bookseller Frank Glenn sifted through the contents of the book-laden thirteen-room house, an adjoining cottage, and a barn in Iowa City. Although the materials were in poor physical shape, their scope and number were impressive. The Linnaean collection numbered over 300 items, and Rafinesque was represented by 146 books and pamphlets, and sixteen manuscripts. These went to the University of Kansas along with the works of American botanists John Ray, John Torrey, Thomas Nuttall, and Asa Gray. The Americana and the Mormon collection went to the Kansas City Public Library. Fitzpatrick was a bibliomaniac in the fullest sense of the word, a blood brother of the great English accumulators Richard Heber and Sir Thomas Phillipps. Two Kansas libraries now offer scholars the riches of Fitzpatrick's collecting mania.

Bibliography

    B. F. B. Sylvester, "The Strange Treasure of Professor Fitzpatrick," *Town Journal*, February 1957; Malcolm Wyer, "Fitzpatrick as Collector," *Books and Libraries at the University of Kansas*, November 1953, 2–3; Robert Vosper, "A Pair of Bibliomanes for Kansas: Ralph Ellis and Thomas Jefferson Fitzpatrick," *PBSA*, 3rd Q 1961, 207–225.

FOLGER, Henry Clay (b. June 18, 1857, New York, N.Y.; d. June 11, 1930, Brooklyn, N.Y.). *Education*: A.B., Amherst College, 1879; LL.B., Columbia University, 1881; M.A., Amherst College, 1882. *Collection Disposition*: Henry Clay Folger Shakespeare Library.

    While he was a student at Amherst, Folger developed literary tastes that would lead him to form the largest Shakespeare library in the world. In his senior year he heard Ralph Waldo Emerson give one of his last public lectures, and that experience inspired him to read Emerson's essays on Shakespeare. After leaving college, one of his first purchases was the "Handy Volume Edition" of Shakespeare in thirteen volumes published in London by Routledge. In 1885 he married Emily Jordan, a Vassar graduate who shared his enthusiasm for Shakespeare and who spurred his desire to collect. Soon after his marriage, Folger bought a J. O. Halliwell-Phillipps facsimile of the 1623 First Folio, a purchase that Mrs. Folger identified as crucial to the development of the library. With the facsimile in hand, Folger began to study the printing variations in early texts. In 1889 he made his first rare book purchase and secured the Fourth Folio (1685) on thirty-day credit terms from Bangs auction rooms in New York.

Fortunately his financial means kept pace with his appetite for books. As a college graduate he had joined a subsidiary of Standard Oil and over the years kept moving up in the corporate structure. In 1911 he was appointed president of the Standard Oil Company of New York and in 1924 became chairman of the board. His collecting activities were carried on quietly but with great determination. In 1889, in a letter written to the Amherst class historian, he spoke of "a modest library." Ten years later he commented that it might develop into one of the finest in America or perhaps even the world. Nowhere was Folger's diligence better illustrated than through the series of events that led to his acquisition of the First Folio presented by William Jaggard to Augustine Vincent. The negotiations took four years and involved offers and broken agreements that would have exhausted the patience of most buyers. Folger persisted, however, and in the end obtained one of the most exciting of Shakespeare rarities. In 1907 he increased the stature of his collection by adding twenty-seven quartos from the library of Lord Howe and numerous texts and sources from Providence collector Marsden J. Perry*. Much of the Perry collection had a distinguished provenance, coming as it did from the shelves of British Shakespeare scholar J. O. Halliwell-Phillipps. In 1919, when Perry's holdings were brought to auction, Folger was again a major buyer. This time working through A. S. W. Rosenbach*, he was able to secure such prizes as the 1619 quarto, containing nine plays and reputed to be the first attempt to produce a collected edition of Shakespeare's works.

In many of his dealings Folger found himself in direct rivalry with the so-called dean of Shakespeare collectors William A. White* and the powerful Henry E. Huntington*. Most dealers knew, however, that while White and Huntington collected in many areas, Folger only wanted Shakespeare. They frequently made their first offers to him. As the collection continued to expand, Folger decided that it must be set aside permanently as a resource for scholars. He bought land in close proximity to the Library of Congress and proceeded quietly to work with architects on building plans. The cornerstone was laid on May 28, 1930, two weeks before the collector's death.

Folger's collection consisted of much more than Shakespeare's work. The collector understood the importance of related materials and brought together a panorama of Tudor and Stuart history. As it developed, the collection included manuscripts, sourcebooks, playbills, prints, promptbooks, histories, and biography. A particularly large section of the library was devoted to allusion books, texts that provide references to Shakespeare's work from contemporary and later authors. Another imporant portion deals with music and contains songbooks, vocal and instrumental renditions of the plays, and seventeenth-century instructional manuals. All this is augmented by background works treating the history and culture of the period before, during, and shortly after Shakespeare's career. Folger once stated that his purpose in gathering books was to provide scholars with a "kit of tools." The Memorial Library and its collections demonstrate how nobly that purpose was achieved.

Bibliography

A. *Catalog of the Manuscripts of the Folger Shakespeare Library* (Boston, 1971); *Catalog of Printed Books in the Folger Shakespeare Library* (Boston, 1970) and *Supplement* (Boston, 1976); "A Unique First Folio," *The Outlook*, November 23, 1907, 687–691.

B. *DAB* 6, 487–488; *NCAB* 23, 9–10; Cannon, 335–347; *Grolier 75*, 85–88; Wolf and Fleming, passim; John Schoenbaum, "The World's Finest Shakespeare Library Is This Side of the Atlantic," *Smithsonian Magazine*, April 1982, 119–126; Robert Smith, "The Pursuit of a First Folio," *The Colophon*, n.s., Winter 1938, 41–53; Louis B. Wright, *Of Books and Men* (Columbia, S.C., 1976), 119–125; Louis B. Wright, *The Folger Library: Two Decades of Growth* (Charlottesville, Va., 1968).

FOOTE, Charles B. (b. 1837, Bridgeport, Conn.; d. September 20, 1900, Oceanic, N.J.). *Collection Disposition*: Bangs, November 23, 1894; January 30, February 20, 1895.

Beginning in the 1880s Foote, a New York banker, set out to form a collection of American literature. As he stated in an interview in *The Critic*, he started the collection by sending out thousands of letters to friends and families of major New England authors asking for books and manuscripts that might be in their hands. He also placed advertisements in newspapers calling attention to his wants. The plan worked better than he had expected. He secured noteworthy Poe manuscript poems and letters, a large cache of Hawthorne's juvenile writing, and a number of Lowell, Whittier, and Longfellow rare first editions. Following another line, Foote acquired a large library of English literature representing the work of Dickens, Milton, Lamb, and Stevenson. According to Beverly Chew*, the highlight of Foote sales, held in 1894 and 1895, was the presence of modern American writers, many of whom had not been considered collectible before that time. In a number of cases the volumes were inscribed or enriched with autographed letters and manuscripts. In general the prices received were much above those Foote had originally given and made the sale, to quote the *Times*, "a triumph for bibliomania." According to the *New York Times*, William Benjamin acquired the original manuscript of Poe's "The Raven" for $75 on a bid made with "superlative nonchalance." All the books and manuscripts in the library were sold, with the exception of the Stevenson items, which Foote kept until his death. Eventually these came to rest in the Harvard Library as part of the bequest of Harry E. Widener*. Foote was admired by his fellow collectors and by bookdealers for his knowledge of books and his generosity. It was his custom to share duplicates with colleagues rather than to store them away. Chew paid Foote a handsome tribute in *The Bookman*, saying he was a discriminating buyer and "long recognized as one of our most intelligent collectors."

Bibliography

B. Cannon, 219–220; Beverly Chew, "Sale of the Foote Collection," *The Bookman*, February 1895, 61–62; "Sale of the Foote Collection of English Literature," *The Critic*, February 9, 1895, 101–107; "Searching for Rare Books," *The Critic*, March 2, 1895, 165–166. "The Foote Sale," *NYT*, November 24, 1894, 2; February 4, 1895, 3.

FORCE, Peter (b. November 26, 1790, Passaic Falls, N.J.; d. January 23, 1868, Washington, D.C.). *Collection Disposition*: Library of Congress.

After a number of years as a printing apprentice in New York, Force moved to Washington, D.C., to work on government contracts. He issued a highly successful annual statistical review, *The National Calendar*, and a daily newspaper, *The National Journal*. These publications involved him in Washington political life where, with the support of the Whig party, he campaigned successfully for the office of mayor. During his career Force collected printed and manuscript records of America's early history as they were available from historians, journalists, government officers, and booksellers. One of his most active suppliers, first as a copyist and later as a bookdealer, was the energetic Henry Stevens of Vermont. After graduation from Yale, Stevens combed New England for Force, securing materials of many kinds. Through these diversified efforts Force secured rare tracts, early newspapers, and the letters and papers of such important colonial leaders as Nathaniel Green, John Paul Jones, and John Fitch. Force's massive documentary history of the colonial period and the Revolutionary War, *The American Archives*, started to come out in 1836. By 1853, after nine of a projected twenty folio volumes had been issued, the Department of State suddenly withdrew its promised financial support, and with heavy outstanding bills and no assured income Force decided to put his library on the market. When the New York Public Library and the New York Historical Society failed to secure the required $100,000, Force turned to the Library of Congress. The chief librarian, Ainsworth Spofford, recognized the importance of the collection and recommended its purchase. Five weeks after his appeal, Congress voted funds to keep the material in Washington. By this farsighted act the Library of Congress acquired 22,000 printed volumes, 150,000 manuscript items, and 768 maps, making it the repository of one of the most distinguished collections of colonial history ever assembled.

Bibliography

B. *DAB* 3, 512–513; *SCLC*, 121–124; Frederick Goff, "Peter Force," *PBSA*, 1st Q 1950, 1–16; Ainsworth Spofford, "The Life and Labors of Peter Force, Mayor of Washington," in *Records of Columbia Historical Society of Washington, D.C.* (Washington,

D.C., 1899), 219–235; R. W. Stephenson, "Maps from the Peter Force Collection," *QJLC*, July 1973, 183–204; Henry Stevens, *Recollections of Mr. James Lenox* (London, 1886).

FORD, Gordon Lester (b. December 16, 1823, Lebanon, Conn.; d. November 14, 1891, Brooklyn, N.Y.). *Collection Disposition*: New York Public Library.

Ford was energetic and successful as a journalist, businessman, and politician. Before moving to Brooklyn in 1856 he had been president of a major New England railroad. Once established in the growing New York suburb, he became deeply involved in Republican politics. He was influential in the formation of the abolitionist newspaper *The Brooklyn Union*, held an editorial position on the *New York Times*, and ran successfully for city offices.

As part of his interest in politics, Ford built a large library of Americana, including books, manuscripts, maps, portraits, prints, and letters. Ford's library served as an admirable schoolroom for his eight children and became the center of much of the contemporary scholarly and literary life in Brooklyn. By 1899 the size of the collection consisted of 30,000 books and 70,000 pamphlets, maps, and prints. It was not a bibliophile's collection, but rather a working library gathered to support Ford's general interests in American history and economics. Some of the letters and manuscripts provided his sons with source materials they used in their publications. Eight years after Ford's death his sons Paul* and Worthington gave the entire historical archive to the New York Public Library. In a letter to the trustees, they estimated the size of the holdings at 100,000 items and declared it to be the largest collection on American history then in private hands.

Bibliography

B. *DAB* 6, 516–518; Cannon, 116–117; Paul Z. DuBois, *Paul Leicester Ford* (New York, 1977), passim; Harry M. Lydenberg, *The History of the New York Public Library* (New York, 1923), 378–380; Lindsay Swift, "Paul Leicester Ford at Home," *The Critic*, November 1898, 343–349.

FORD, Paul Leicester (b. March 23, 1865, Brooklyn, N.Y.; d. May 8, 1902, Brooklyn, N.Y.). *Collection Disposition*: New York Public Library; Yale University.

Like his older brother Worthington, Ford was greatly influenced by the bookish atmosphere in which he had been raised. Because of physical disabilities, he was not allowed to attend public schools and was educated at home by tutors. There he fell under the influence of the large library gathered by his father, Gordon Lester Ford*, and proceeded to print limited editions of family genealogy and history on a handpress. The Ford "Historical Printing Club" was praised by Adolf Growoll in his *American Book Clubs* as one of the most active in the country. Surely this was immoderate, but it did indicate the quality of the research Ford put into these juvenile ventures. Bibliographer-collector Wilberforce Eames* recalled seeing Ford at auctions as early as 1879 buying books with his father and brother. Ford's literary and historical output can only be described as voluminous. Between the years 1886 and 1893 he completed bibliographies of Hamilton and Franklin, edited Jefferson's writings, become co-editor of *The Library Journal*, and published articles in popular and scholarly journals. The multitalented Ford refused to confine himself to scholarly endeavors and in 1894 brought out *The Honorable Peter Stirling*, a novel of New York political life. The success of his first novel was overshadowed by the phenomenal popularity of his second, *Janice Meredith*, which came out in 1899. Over 200,000 copies were sold in ten months, making it an outstanding best-seller. In addition to these novels, Ford had time to write biographies of Washington and Franklin and to prepare a number of bibliographic studies. In 1894 he cataloged the rare book library of author-collector James L. Graham for the Century Corporation Association and on completion of that task paid tribute to Graham's good judgment in leaving the books to the club. Ford followed the same procedure and gave his father's books to the New York Public Library.

Recognized as a literary and historical scholar, Ford was chosen in 1902 by the officers of the Dodd, Mead publishing company to edit their new journal, *The Bibliographer*. This appointment coincided with the issue of two new books, full-length studies, one of the novelist James Fenimore Cooper and the other of colonial printer Hugh Gaine. All these projects came to an untimely end on May 8, 1902, when Ford was shot and killed by his brother Malcolm in a tragic family quarrel. Ford was deeply interested in books and backed his interest with a series of important bibliographies and historical studies. His manuscripts and correspondence, along with the books from his personal library, are to be found in the Beinecke Rare Book and Manuscript Library at Yale and at the New York Public Library.

Bibliography

B. *DAB* 6, 518–520; *NCAB* 13, 105; Cannon, 117; *Grolier 75*, 136–138; Paul DuBois, *Paul Leicester Ford* (New York, 1977); Wilberforce Eames, "Paul Leicester Ford," *The Bibliographer*, May 1902, 197; Victor Paltsits, "Paul Leicester Ford, Bibliographer and Historian," *The Bookman*, July 1902; Donald Gallup, "The Paul Leicester Ford Collection," *YLG*, October 1955, 70–73; Lindsay Swift, "Paul Leicester Ford at Home," *The Critic*, November 1898, 343–349.

FOWLER, Laurence H. (b. September 5, 1876, Baltimore, Md.; d. June 12, 1971, Baltimore, Md.). *Education*: A.B., Johns Hopkins University, 1898; B.S., Columbia University, 1902. *Collection Disposition*: Johns Hopkins University.

During the time of his work at Columbia, Fowler developed an appreciation for the history of architecture and the texts that illustrated that history. He was delighted by the rare editions of architectural classics he saw in the Samuel P. Avery* library and decided to begin a similar though more limited collection. At first he specialized in the works of the great Italian Renaissance draftsmen, but as his holdings multiplied he began to include classic works by French, English, and German architects. His buying began with a trip to Europe in 1902 and continued steadily until he retired forty years later. Never one to buy indiscriminately, he restricted himself to major historical works. Fowler's goal, like that of English collector Frederick Locker-Lampson, was to obtain quality not quantity. He enjoyed owning association copies from famous American architects of the eighteenth century. As a complement to the book collection, Fowler gathered an impressive archive of letters and portraits of prominent architects. In 1945, when he presented his library to Johns Hopkins University, it contained only 448 items, but all were important in the mosaic of architectural history. Fowler's catalog was printed in order to make the rich holdings more widely known. The collection stands as a scholarly archive on architectural history.

Bibliography

A. *The Fowler Architectural Collection of the Johns Hopkins University* (Baltimore, 1961).

FREDERICKSON, Charles, W. (b. 1823, Halifax, Can.; d. January 29, 1897, New York, N.Y.). *Collection Disposition*: Bangs, April 25, November 1, 1871, November 20, 1877, April 12, 1886, March 28, 1887, April 3, 1893, May 24 and 28, 1897.

During the Civil War, Frederickson became a cotton broker and acted as the chief purchasing agent for the Northern forces. He retired from business at age fifty-four to devote himself to book collecting. First he assembled a Shakespeare library, then, when he convinced himself that Shakespeare's writing had been done by others, he rid himself of all the "spurious" works and turned to Shelley, Keats, Lamb, Coleridge, and Cowper. Many of his books were of sentimental or association interest, and had letters and manuscript fragments bound in. The outstanding example of this genre was Frederickson's copy of Shelley's *Queen Mab* inscribed to his wife, Mary Wollstonecraft, "You see Mary, I have not forgotten you." Eventually this copy made its way to the collections in the Henry E. Huntington* Library and Museum in California.

Frederickson was one of the first Americans to concentrate on nineteenth-century English literature. His Shelley collection was the most impressive and included over 2,000 printed volumes and a large assortment of letters. Frederickson liked to own books that had once belonged to his favorite authors. He was able to secure a large number of volumes from Lamb's library, including a 1589 Chaucer and a presentation copy of Collier's *Poetical Decameron*. When the Frederickson library came up for sale in 1897, the Lamb books brought surprisingly high prices but the Shelley letters, according to Ernest Dressel North, went begging. Harry B. Smith*, later known for his own "Sentimental Library," was one of the principal buyers at the sale. Historian Clarence S. Brigham identified "Fred," with his long white beard, linen coat, and pockets stuffed with books and pamphlets, as one of the most familiar figures in late-nineteenth-century New York auction houses. With a talent for gathering important authors before they came into vogue and making them available to scholars, Frederickson was an ideal collector.

Bibliography

B. Clarence S. Brigham, "History of Book Auctions in America," in George McKay *American Book Auction Catalogues* (New York, 1937), 14; Cannon, 154–156; Ernest Dressel North, "Notes on Rare Books," *The Book Buyer*, March, June, July 1897; Harry B. Smith, "Gentleman of the Old School," *The Colophon*, September 1930, 583–584.

FRENCH, Frederick W. (b. September 10, 1842, Boston, Mass.; d. July 18, 1900, Boston, Mass.). *Collection Disposition*: Libbie, April 23, 1901.

French's professional life was spent in the family drug and paint firm in Boston. He was an early member of the Grolier Club of New York and similar organizations in Boston, Cleveland, and Chicago. His enthusiasm for the theater led him to gather plays and books relating to the history of the stage. This developed into a general interest in English literature, particularly late-nineteenth-century poetry. He cherished fine printing and owned, for example, one of the two vellum copies of the Grolier Club's first publication, *A Decree of Star Chamber*. French liked the work of William Morris' Kelmscott Press and managed to acquire an entire set of his publications. Added to all this was an extensive collection of the books illustrated by George Cruikshank. When the French library was brought to sale in 1901, enthusiastic buyers paid premium prices. It was a connoisseur's delight, with its emphasis on the elegant features of the nineteenth-century book arts.

Bibliography

B. Ernest Dressel North, "Notes on Rare Books," *The Book Buyer*, March 1901, 134; June 1901, 408.

FROST, Donald McKay (b. May 31, 1877, Charleston, S.C.; d. April 14, 1958, Boston, Mass.). *Education*: B.A., LL.B., Harvard University, 1899, 1902. *Collection Disposition*: American Antiquarian Society.

A lawyer by profession, Frost spent his leisure time collecting western Americana and following the trails of nineteenth-century frontier explorers. The most important part of his collection consisted of diaries and letters of the men and women who traveled west in search of gold, land, and adventure. His collection was small but choice. Along with Everett DeGolyer*, Everitt D. Graff*, Frederick W. Beinecke*, C. G. Littell*, and William Robertson Coe*, he was known as one of the most avid of western collectors. In addition to his professional and collecting activities, Frost took time to become involved in a number of bibliographic and historical societies. He was a faithful and active member of the Grolier Club, the Club of Odd Volumes, the Massachusetts

Historical Society, and the American Antiquarian Society. On his death the American Antiquarian Society received his western collection and a generous endowment for future purchases.

Bibliography

B. "Donald McKay Frost," *PAAS*, April 1958, 8–11.

FULTON, John F. (b. November 1, 1899, Saint Paul, Minn.; d. May 29, 1960, New Haven, Conn.). *Education*: B.S., Harvard University, 1921; B.A., Oxford University, 1923; M.D., Harvard University, 1927. *Collection Disposition*: Yale University.

Trained as a physiologist, Fulton spent the greater part of his professional life as a faculty member in the Department of Medicine at Yale. His research specialties in cerebral physiology, the physiology of the nervous system, and medical history resulted in the publication of over 500 articles and a score of books. Two remarkable biographies completed in the 1940s, one on chemistry professor Benjamin Silliman and the other of the renowned surgeon Harvey Cushing*, demonstrated Fulton's clear and agreeable writing skill.

It is possible to trace Fulton's interest in collecting back to 1919, when as a student at Harvard he bought a copy of Robert Boyle's *Sceptical Chymist*. His interest in Boyle continued through his years at Oxford and later in Edinburgh, where he had the good fortune to find an inexpensive cache of twenty rare items in a secondhand-book store. When Geoffrey Keynes' *Bibliography of Thomas Browne* came out in 1924, Fulton vowed to produce a similarly detailed work on Boyle. The result of his endeavors, a landmark of careful analytical scrutiny, was published by the Oxford University Press in 1930. Influenced by his exposure to Sir William Osler's library at Oxford and by close association with Cushing, Fulton developed a strong personal library on physiology, experimental medicine, and the history of medicine. In 1933 he was instrumental in convincing Cushing to return to Yale as a faculty member in the School of Medicine. A year later he joined Cushing and A. C. Klebs in what he called the "trinitarian plan" to turn their libraries over to Yale to form a medical-historical collection. In 1941 Yale officers and medical scholars from around the country participated in the dedication of the Cushing-Fulton-Klebs medical history collection. In spite of health problems during the last ten years of his life, Fulton continued to buy books on physiology and medical history for the Yale collections. According to colleagues, Fulton brought a remarkable memory for detail to his collecting activities. He could remember bibliographic minutiae and facts of provenance with ease long after he had handled a particular book or manuscript. He was respected both in England and in the United States as a careful bibliographer and a resourceful collector.

Bibliography

A. *Great Medical Bibliographers: A Study in Humanism* (Philadelphia, 1950); *A Bibliography of Robert Boyle* (Oxford, 1932); *Benjamin Silliman* (New Haven, 1947); *Harvey Cushing* (New Haven, 1946).

B. *DAB*, Supp. 6, 224; *NCAB* 53, 9; Geoffrey Keynes, "An Appreciation," *BC*, Autumn 1960, 262–264; William LeFanu, "John Fulton's Historical and Bibliographical Work," *JHMAS*, January 1962, 38–50; Arnold Muirhead, "John Farquhar Fulton," *BC*, Winter 1962, 427–436; Arnold Muirhead, "John Fulton, the Book Collector, Humanist, and Friend," *JHMAS*, January 1962, 2–15; "Bibliography of John Farquhar Fulton," *JHMAS*, January 1962, 51–71.

FURNESS, Horace H., Sr. (b. November 2, 1833, Philadelphia, Pa.; d. August 13, 1912, Philadelphia, Pa.). *Education*: A.B., Harvard University, 1854. *Collection Disposition*: University of Pennsylvania.

Events early in Furness' life directed him toward the scholarly editorial work on Shakespeare texts which would occupy him for nearly fifty years. As a boy growing up in Philadelphia he heard the actress Fanny Kemble give her richly executed Shakespeare readings. At Harvard he was influenced by classical scholar Francis James Child and charmed and inspired by visits with Ralph Waldo Emerson. After serving briefly in law offices and in municipal administration, he turned to the congenial study of Shakespeare. The result of his labors, the monumental *New Variorum Shakespeare*, was a detailed comparative study of the earliest versions of Shakespeare texts. In order to pursue his meticulous studies, Furness needed to surround himself with the books, journals, manuscripts, and ephemera of the Elizabethan age. His library, as it developed, was not a rare book collection but a working tool for a busy scholar. Folios and quartos were in the library, but its true distinction was in the vast amount of peripheral documentation that it contained on the works of Shakespeare's fellow dramatists and historical sources for the period. Furness was particularly interested in Shakespeare as a theatrical figure and acquired everything he could on Elizabethan stage history and the lives of the actors who performed in the plays. Since London was the center of the theatrical world, Furness also had a collection of books and pamphlets on that city and its history. Anything that was applicable to Shakespeare and his times was of interest to Furness.

In support of his early and abiding interest in the classics, Furness collected Horace in all the variant editions. In a letter written to his friend Duncan MacDonald in 1910, he referred to his Horatian library as including over 300 texts. This collection was established as a memorial to his only daughter, who had died of typhoid fever in 1909. Furness maintained personal friendships with novelist Owen Wister, poet Agnes Repplier, and Shakespeare scholars A. J. Rolfe, W. Aldis Wright, and Charles Eliot Norton. As the volumes of the *New Variorum* continued to be issued, Horace H. Furness Jr. joined his father in the scholarly editorial work. After Furness died his library continued to serve as an important resource. In 1915 Horace H. Furness Jr. presented the vast Shakespeare collection to the University of Pennsylvania along with a sizable trust fund in honor of his father. The university responded by adding an entire room to the university library for the 12,000 books and pamphlets. This well-appointed structure is an appropriate memorial to a graceful and productive scholar.

Bibliography

A. *The Letters of Horace Howard Furness* (Boston, 1922).

B. *NCAB* 8, 396; Agnes Repplier, "Horace Howard Furness," *Atlantic*, November 1912, 624–628; Felix Schelling, "The Horace Howard Furness Memorial," *Library Chronicle*, March 1933, 6–7; Mathew Black and William Miller, "Some Letters from Actors and Actresses to Dr. Horace Howard Furness," *Library Chronicle*, Spring 1963, 105–115.

G

GABLE, William F. (b. February 12, 1856, Upper Owachla, Pa.; d. 1921, Altoona, Pa.). *Collection Disposition*: American Art, November 5, December 3, 1923, February 13, March 10, November 24, 1924, January 8, March 3, April 16, 1925.

The story of Gable's rise to prominence had the characteristics of a Horatio Alger success novel. He worked in a grocery store as a teenager, opened his own store at the age of twenty-five, and at fifty owned one of the most prosperous business establishments in Pennsylvania. After hours Gable devoted himself to books and reading. He was a good customer of the antiquarian book trade. He bought frequently, paid his bills on time, and seldom argued about the price. According to bookseller Charles Everitt, Gable even bought books and pamphlets he did not want simply to help a dealer who needed money. Although his collecting tastes were eclectic, he favored association books, autographed manuscripts, and letters from important literary and historical figures. As a young man he wrote to authors for autographs and later, when he could afford it, purchased their first editions.

Among the many volumes in his library, Gable particularly enjoyed the poetry of Walt Whitman and the drawings of Kate Greenaway and George Cruikshank. Two years after Gable's death his library was listed for auction at the American Art Association in New York. Everitt called the auction a disaster since many of the fine items were sold for what he said were "waste-paper prices." Building a library had been Gable's chief pleasure. It would doubtless have pleased him to know a new generation of collectors had access to his treasures at reasonable prices. Gable was a gentlemanly collector, respected by members of the book trades and by his fellow bibliophiles.

Bibliography

B. *NCAB* 8, 358–359; Charles Everitt, *The Adventures of a Treasure Hunter* (Boston, 1951), 70–71; Robert Gable, "Introduction," *American Art Association Catalogue* (New York, 1923).

GALLATIN, Albert Eugene (b. July 23, 1881, Villanova, Pa.; d. June 15, 1952, New York, N.Y.). *Collection Disposition*: Princeton University; Harvard University.

By the end of the 1920s, Gallatin had become well known in New York art circles as a critic and painter. He had produced a number of monographic studies on contemporary artists and founded the Museum of Living Art based on his own avant-garde collection. His paintings were displayed in the permanent collections of some of the most prestigious museums in the country. In connection with his lifelong interest in the graphic arts, Gallatin brought together several important collections of prints and books. His holdings on the English artist Aubrey Beardsley included original drawings, books, manuscripts, page designs, posters, proofs, and letters. These materials formed the basis of a catalog published by the Grolier Club in 1945. Three years later he presented the impressive archive to the Princeton University Library. While working on Beardsley, Gallatin formed a complementary collection of books and manuscripts dealing with Beardsley's friend Sir Max Beerbohm. This gathering went to Harvard.

Bibliography

A. *Aubrey Beardsley: Catalogue of Drawings and Bibliography* (New York, 1945); *Sir Max Beerbohm: Bibliographical Notes* (New York, 1945); "Aubrey Beardsley," *PLC*, February 1949, 81–84; "A Bibliography of the Works of Sir Max Beerbohm," by A. E. Gallatin and L. M. Oliver, *HLB*, Winter, Spring, and Autumn 1951, 77–93, 221–241, 338–361; *The Gallatin Beardsley Collection in the Princeton University Library: A Catalogue*, compiled by A. E. Gallatin and Alexander Wainright (Princeton, 1952).
B. *NCAB* 42, 230–231.

GARRETT, John Work (b. May 19, 1872, Baltimore, Md.; d. June 26, 1942, Baltimore, Md.). *Education*: B.S., Princeton University, 1895. *Collection Disposition*: Johns Hopkins University.

Collecting came naturally to Garrett, as he explained in the autobiographical essay *A Library of Four Generations*. His great-grandfather, grandfather, and father had all been avid collectors and had left him with an impressive collection of Americana. To this base Garrett added treatises on exploration and discovery, English literature, ornithology, and above all Maryland history. One of the high points of his library was a collection of signatures of the members of the First Continental Congress. As a complement to his historical texts he had a number of rare maps and atlases, including the notable Wright-Molyneux atlas of 1599 and the Nicholas Visscher map, which provided the first delineation of the Pennsylvania-Maryland borders. As the American section of his library filled out, Garrett turned his attention to early European printing and to Elizabethan literature. His collection of incunabula, while not large, included such treasures as the 1465 Sweynheym and Pannartz printing of Lactantius' *Opera* and Caxton's 1480 *Chronicles of England*. The literary portion of the library included Shakespeare's first folios and first edition folios of the works of Jonson, Spenser, and Beaumont and Fletcher. It was the Maryland collection, however, that was preeminent. Dealers like A. S. W. Rosenbach* and Lathrop Harper considered Garrett their primary customer whenever Maryland items came into their hands. Although the collection included a generous sample of colonial imprints, its real strength came from the extensive holdings of promotional pamphlets printed in England. This section of the library was described in great detail in Elizabeth Baer's excellent bibliography *Seventeenth Century Maryland*. In addition to all these interests Garrett also enjoyed ornithology folios. He owned the Audubon elephant folios and the best editions of the works of John Gould and Mark Catesby.

In 1942 the family bequeathed the 35,000 item library along with the family residence, Evergreen House, to Johns Hopkins University. This facility has provided scholars with a unique resource for the study of early European printing, Elizabethan drama, and particularly the history of Maryland.

Bibliography

A. "A Library of Four Generations," in *John Work Garrett and His Library at Evergreen House* (Baltimore, 1944), 45–74; "Seventeenth Century Books Relating to Maryland," *Maryland Historical Magazine*, March 1939, 1–39.

B. *NCAB* A, 355; Wolf and Fleming, passim; Elizabeth Baer, *Seventeenth Century Maryland: A Bibliography* (Baltimore, 1949); B. Howell Griswold, "The Spirit of the Evergreen Library," in *John Work Garrett and His Library at Evergreen House* (Baltimore, 1944), 19–40.

GARRETT, Robert (b. June 24, 1875, Baltimore, Md.; d. April 25, 1961, Baltimore, Md.). *Education*: A.B., Princeton University, 1897. *Collection Disposition*: Princeton University.

Before attending college Garrett traveled extensively with his family, visiting Europe and the Near East. The year after his graduation he went to Syria as a member of the American Archaeology Expedition and was given the responsibility for drawing up the summary report for that project. Professionally, he was associated with the family banking firm in Baltimore.

During his travels abroad Garrett started to collect manuscripts. In an autobiographical comment he described how, as a teenager, he saw a fifteenth-century illuminated Book of Hours in an art shop in Rome and started his collection. Based on his study of J. B. Silvestre's *Universal Paleography*, he then began to buy a wide variety of classical scripts. He joined an expedition to Syria in 1896 and further focused his interest on eastern documents, a somewhat unknown field for American collectors at that time. In 1900 Garrett acquired an extensive collection of Arabic manuscripts and a large reference library from the estate of the Dutch orientalist M. T. Houtsma. This acquisition provided the base for the Princeton Department of Oriental Languages and Literature. At Garrett's instigation world renowned Near Eastern scholars, such as Enno Littmann and Philip Hitti, came to Princeton to teach and write. In 1905 Garrett made one of his more spectacular purchases and obtained an eleventh-century Kufic manuscript of the Koran written in gold on vellum sheets. Between 1925 and 1940 Garrett's collection of Muslim and Oriental manuscripts grew rapidly, and in 1940, with the addition of a collection of 4,000 Arabic manuscripts, it became recognized as one of the most distinguished in the country. As a final act of generosity Garrett provided Princeton's Institute of Advanced Study with an important collection of Maya texts translated into Latin. In an article written for the *Princeton Library Chronicle*, Garrett summarized his collecting career by saying it had been a "joy and an education" and that he hoped the materials gathered would be a source of perpetual value to the university.

Bibliography

A. *Catalogue of Turkish and Persian Manuscripts Belonging to Robert Garrett and Deposited in the Princeton University Library*, edited by Nicholas Martinovitch (Princeton, 1926); "Recollections of a Collector," *PLC*, April 1949, 103–116.

B. *NCAB* 48, 574; N. A. Faris, "The Garrett Collection of Arabic Manuscripts," *PLC*, April 1940, 19–25.

GAY, Ernest Lewis (b. 1874; d. November 26, 1916, Boston, Mass.). *Education*: A.B., LL.B., Harvard University, 1897, 1899. *Collection Disposition*: Harvard University.

Appropriately enough, Gay chose to gather the works of the eighteenth-century English poet and dramatist John Gay. Among the 900 items in his library, he had first editions, playbills, scores, portraits, and manuscripts. A particularly intriguing portion of the collection was devoted to works falsely attributed to Gay. In connection with his interest in the social setting of the eighteenth century, Gay collected a large number of pamphlets issued at that time. In 1927 the entire library was turned over to Harvard.

Bibliography

B. Alfred Potter, *The Library of Harvard University* (Cambridge, Mass., 1934), 78; *NYT*, November 28, 1916, 13.

GAY, H. Nelson (b. 1870, Newton, Mass.; d. August 14, 1932, Monte Carlo, Monaco). *Education*: A.B., Amherst College, 1891; A.M., Harvard University, 1896. *Collection Disposition*: Harvard University.

Shortly after graduating from Harvard, Gay accepted a fellowship that took him to Italy, where he remained most of his life. He was a prolific author, with interests in both American and Italian history. His published studies, which concentrated on diplomatic relations between Italy and the United States and the Italian Risorgimento (1815–1871), began to appear in Italian journals around the turn of the century. In order to have proper documentation on Italian history, Gay formed a large library of books, pamphlets, newspapers, and broadsides. He went beyond the usual published histories and also secured public documents, trial records, speeches, and commission reports. He was assiduous in gathering small-town newspapers and broadsides. He bought several thousand pamphlets at the Crispi sale of 1907. In addition to his studies of nineteenth-century Italian history, Gay produced a number of books, pamphlets, and reviews defending the fascist government of Benito Mussolini. Upon Gay's death these were offered to Mussolini for the Italian Centers for American Studies, but Harvard bought them first. In one stroke Harvard acquired an unrivaled gathering on Italian political and economic history.

Bibliography

B. Alfred Potter, *The Library of Harvard University* (Cambridge, Mass., 1934), 101–102; *Who Was Who Among North American Authors* (Chicago, 1976), 575.

GAYARRE, Charles E. A. (b. January 9, 1805, New Orleans, La.; d. February 11, 1895, New Orleans, La.). *Education*: A.B., College of Orleans, 1825. *Collection Disposition*: Louisiana State Library; Louisiana State University.

Throughout his life Gayarre was intimately involved with Louisiana history and politics. At the age of thirty he was elected to the United States Senate but because of ill health was unable to fulfill his term. He traveled to France for recuperation and there started to write his definitive *History of Louisiana*. He resumed his political career in 1844 and was appointed Louisiana secretary of state and superintendent of public education. In 1846 he acquired funds for the purchase of numerous foreign documents and with these as a base founded the state library. In order to support his own historical research, he collected pamphlets, documents, journals, and manuscripts on all aspects of Louisiana history. The third and fourth volumes of his state history reflected the depth of his personal library, as did his well-received biography *Philip II of Spain*. His efforts in collecting manuscripts and his writing have assured him a place in the circle of those prominent in strengthening the position of southern history.

Bibliography

A. "Autobiography of Charles Gayarre," *Louisiana Historical Quarterly*, January 1929, 5–32.

B. *DAB* 4, 196–197; *NCAB* 6, 253–254; Cannon, 243–244; *Louisiana Historical Society Publications*, Gayarre Memorial Number, March 1906.

GETZ, Estelle (b. June 14, 1880, Los Angeles, Calif.; d. June 2, 1943, Los Angeles, Calif.). *Collection Disposition*: American Art—Anderson, November 17 and 24, 1936.

Because of an accident sustained during childhood, Getz was confined to her home and educated by tutors. Lacking normal childhood companionships, she turned to books and reading. By the time she was thirty, Getz had become a confirmed collector with a wide range of interests. She was particularly drawn to literary rarities, fine printing, manuscripts, and elaborate examples of binding and illustration. At first she confined her purchases to the rare book section of the J. W. Robinson department store in Los Angeles but was soon doing business with Jake Zeitlin and Ernest Dawson. Zeitlin has said her regular purchases gave him his start in the book business. She was attracted to beautiful books production in many forms—fine bindings by Riviere, the delicate artistry of fore-edge paintings, the crisp vellum pages of a fifteenth-century Bible, sumptuously decorated extra-illustrated sets of Dickens, and handsomely illuminated medieval Books of Hours. She gathered an impressive group of incunabula, including a 1473 Peter Schoeffer printing of the *Decretales* and a 1495 second edition of the *Polychronicon*, printed by Wynkyn de Worde.

In another direction, Getz obtained several remarkable collections of literary manuscripts and letters. Her Ambrose Bierce archive, for example, was rich in the journalist's correspondence with William Randolph Hearst*, Gertrude Atherton, and Edwin Markham. Also included in her Bierce collection were notebooks, diaries, manuscripts, and autographed first editions. Letters were present from Darwin, Clemens, and Anglo-American novelist William McFee. The Kelmscott Press was well represented on her shelves, as was the work of distinguished California printer John Henry Nash. It was an impressive and lavish array. In 1936, when the depressed economy forced many collectors to sell, the Getz books and letters were distributed at auction. The two-volume sale catalogs reveal the collector's catholic tastes and her intelligent appreciation for the book arts.

Bibliography

B. Jake Zeitlin, *Books and the Imagination: Fifty Years of Rare Books*, interview with Joel Gardner (Los Angeles, 1980), passim; Correspondence with Robert E. Getz, May 1984, and Ellen Shaffer, librarian at the Silverado Museum, St. Helena, California, April 1984.

GILCREASE, Thomas (b. February 8, 1890, Robeline, La.; d. May 6, 1962, Tulsa, Okla.). *Collection Disposition*: Gilcrease Institute of American History and Art, Tulsa, Oklahoma.

As a young man, Gilcrease was able to claim 160 acres of government land in Oklahoma based on his mother's Creek Indian bloodline. The land turned out to be oil-rich, and he found he was a millionaire before he turned twenty-five. After establishing profitable connections in banking, farming, and real estate, Gilcrease began to spend a considerable amount of time in travel. He was deeply impressed with European museums and libraries and decided to establish the same kind of institution in Oklahoma. His interest in American history, particularly the part played by Native Americans in that history, led him to collect works of art and books and manuscripts on all phases of Indian culture. Because he wanted his library to have a broad representation of documents on American Indians, he purchased colonial history, frontier narratives describing the opening of the Mississippi Valley and the Southwest, Hispanic documents, tribal records, and manuscripts. He devoted a special place of importance to sources relating to the five civilized tribes: the Cherokees, Chickasaws, Choctaws, Creeks, and Seminoles. One of the outstanding archival holdings of the library consisted of the papers of John Ross, chief of the Cherokee tribes to 1866.

In his buying Gilcrease made intelligent use of the book trade. He was an established customer of Stevens and Robinson in London and of Charles Everitt, Hans P. Kraus, and A. S. W. Rosenbach*. Although Gilcrease's ambitions for his collection grew, oil revenues declined in the 1940s, leaving the collector heavily in debt to book and art dealers. By 1954 he owed so many bills that it appeared the books and artworks would be seized by creditors. In a dramatic affirmation for local history, the people of Tulsa voted a $2.5 million bond issue to pay off all financial obligations and keep the collections in place. In 1958 Gilcrease deeded the museum and contents to the city in recognition of its support. The Gilcrease Institute is an important center for the study of the North American Indian and stands as a tribute to its founder and to the people of Tulsa.

Bibliography

A. *The Gilcrease-Hargrett Catalogue of Imprints* (Norman, Okla., 1972); *A Guidebook to Manuscripts in the Library of the Thomas Gilcrease Institute* (Tulsa, Okla., 1969).

B. Wolf and Fleming, passim; Martin Wenger, "The Library," *American Scene*, 1963, 22–23; Aline Saarinen, "Thomas Gilcrease," in *The Proud Possessors* (New York, 1958), 307–325.

GIMBEL, Richard (b. July 26, 1898, Atlantic City, N.J.; d. May 27, 1970, Munich, Ger.). *Education*: A.B., Yale University, 1920. *Collection Disposition*: Yale University; U.S. Air Force Academy (Colorado Springs); Poe House, Philadelphia; American Philosophical Society.

For most of his professional life Gimbel was associated with the department store business, first in the family-owned organization in Philadelphia, later in Miami. As a hobby, shortly after he graduated from college, he began to collect the books and manuscripts of Edgar Allan Poe. This interest was intensified in 1934, when he was able to purchase Poe's Philadelphia residence, a site he promptly refurbished and turned over to the city as a museum. Gimbel included his extensive book and manuscript collection along with such delightful memorabilia as "Grip," a stuffed raven said to have been the inspiration for Poe's best-known poem. In 1969 Gimbel was able to crown all his previous gifts by presenting the museum with the original manuscript of Poe's *Murders in the Rue Morgue*.

While Poe continued to interest Gimbel over the years, he gradually took on a number of other collecting areas. He built an impressive archive of books and manuscripts by both Charles Dickens and Thomas Hardy, a collection of the works by American patriot Thomas Paine, and finally a library of materials relating to the history of flight. This last collection started almost by chance. While serving in the Air Force in World War II, Gimbel visited a bombed-out bookshop in London hoping to buy something from the hardy owner. There was no literature to be had, but in the basement he was shown a trunk of books and pamphlets on aeronautics. He bought the contents and started what became one of the most distinguished aeronautical collections in the country. Once launched on a project, Gimbel gave it his full attention. In addition to books and pamphlets, he was soon acquiring stamps, sheet music, posters, dinner plates, watches, and valentines with flight motifs. With the traditional tales of airplane flights he acquired accounts of ballooning, parachute drops, and rocket travel. One large portion of the library was devoted to imaginary flights and included everything from Greek myths to the comic-strip adventures of Buck Rogers.

In 1953 Gimbel retired from the Air Force and was given the title of Curator of Aeronautical Literature at the Yale University Library. In that capacity he arranged exhibitions, published bibliographies, and generally made his materials available to the Yale scholarly community. After his death the entire aeronautics archive, 20,000 items, was bequeathed to the United States Air Force Academy in Colorado. A separate area was set aside in the academy library to house the collection and to serve as a research center for the study of aeronautical history. The splendid Dickens library remained at Yale, while the Thomas Paine materials went appropriately to the American Antiquarian Society. Gimbel was a determined and intelligent collector. The fruits of his labors are now available to researchers in a number of public scholarly institutions.

Bibliography

A. *Dickens and Dickensiana: A Catalogue of the Richard Gimbel Collection in the Yale University Library*, compiled by John Podeschi (New Haven, 1980); *Thomas Paine: A Bibliographical Checklist of Common Sense with an Account of Its Publication* (New Haven, 1956); "Quoth the Raven: An Exhibition of the Works of Edgar Allan Poe . . . from the Collections of H. Bradley Martin and Colonel Richard Gimbel," *YLG*, April 1959, 138–189.

B. Howell Heaney, "The Raven, Revisited," *Manuscripts*, Spring 1973, 87–95; James Mooney, "Richard Gimbel," *PAAS* October 1970, 245–247; J. Navarro, "AFA Keeps Man's Flight Memories," *Denver Gazette Telegraph*, August 21, 1977, 31; "New Haven Gimbel," *The New Yorker*, June 7, 1958, 24–26.

GOELET, Ogden (b. 1846, New York, N.Y.; d. August 27, 1897, on board his yacht off Cowes, Isle of Wight). *Collection Disposition*: American Art— Anderson, January 3 and 24, 1935, January 13 and 20, 1937, November 23, 1954.

The son of an old and wealthy New York family, Goelet devoted himself to the management of his estate, yachting, and collecting. The Goelet Cup, which he established, was the chief prize offered by the New York Yacht Club at the turn of the century. His collecting enthusiasms included Americana and nineteenth-century English literature. The foundations of the Goelet library were laid with the materials he secured in the 1870s from the Almon Griswold*, William Menzies*, and George Brinley* sales. This was the period in which Joseph Sabin was the principal figure in New York bookselling, and through his expert hands Goelet acquired an impressive collection of books and manuscripts. Sabin's bids established Goelet as one of the leading private buyers at the Brinley auction in 1878. Again, during the 1880s, Goelet made significant purchases of Americana, this time from the sale of the libraries of Henry C. Murphy* and Samuel L. M. Barlow*. Around 1885 Goelet's interests expanded to include the manuscripts, letters, and printed works of Dickens and Thackeray. In the case of Dickens he was able to secure several notable collections of letters as well as an array of first editions of the novels. The books remained in the hands of the family for over thirty years after Goelet died. It was not until 1935 that the Americana items, once the possessions of Brinley, Barlow, and Murphy, came again into the market. Although the Goelet set of the "Jesuit Relations" brought $10,400, most of the Americana went at a sacrifice. Goelet was not a bibliographer by training, but he had two great advantages: immense wealth and the counsel of Joseph Sabin. With backing of that kind he was able to form one of the showpiece collections of the nineteenth century.

Bibliography

B. William Reese, "George Brinley and His Library," *Gazette of the Grolier Club*, 1980, 24–39; "Death of Ogden Goelet," *NYT*, August 28, 1897, 7; "Foreword," in *American Art Association—Anderson Catalogue: The Library of the Late Ogden Goelet* (New York, 1935).

GOLDSTONE, Adrian H. (b. May 23, 1897, San Francisco, Calif.; d. June 10, 1977, San Francisco, Calif.). *Collection Disposition*: University of Texas at Austin; Stanford University; Steinbeck Library, Salinas; San Jose State University; California Book Auction Galleries, December 1981.

As a young man Goldstone worked as a salesman and, as he put it, "knew every rut and chuckhole in the Salinas Valley." Almost incidentally he became a collector, dropping into local bookshops to relieve the boredom of long weekends on the road. As his business prospered he became a familiar figure in some of the more sophisticated shops in Los Angeles, Chicago, and Washington, D.C. In Chicago he met Ben Abramson, energetic owner of the Argus Book Shop, and it was there that he was introduced to the work of John Steinbeck. Abramson had known Steinbeck personally, carried all his books, and acted as a one-man Chicago publicity agent for the California novelist. Goldstone recognized Steinbeck's talents immediately. Through Abramson and other dealers he began to buy first editions, translations, journal publications, anthologies, and manuscripts. As his Steinbeck materials accumulated, Goldstone decided to diversify and began to collect Hemingway, Machen, and Sinclair Lewis. It was the Machen books that led Goldstone to do a bibliography. In 1965, with the help of Wesley Sweetser, he published a carefully constructed examination of Machen's works. Ten years later he produced an ambitious Steinbeck bibliography, built largely from examples in his own private library. While the Machen and Steinbeck collections reflected Goldstone's literary interests, his detective fiction showed a taste for lighter reading. This large collection, made up of landmark authors from the nineteenth and twentieth centuries, was sold at auction in 1981. His attitude toward collecting was nicely summarized by a comment he made after his Steinbeck books were sold to Texas. He considered starting all over again, he said, but changed his mind because "all it would take was money." For Goldstone, collecting meant more than that.

Bibliography

A. *Bibliography of Arthur Machen*, by Adrian Goldstone and Wesley Sweetser (Austin, Tex., 1965); *John Steinbeck: A Bibliographical Catalogue*, by Adrian Goldstone and John Payne (Austin, Tex., 1974); "Book Collecting and Steinbeck," *San Jose Studies*, November 1975, 129–135.

B. "Adrian H. Goldstone 1897–1977" and "Introduction," in *California Book Auction Galleries Catalog*, December 9, 1981; Maurice Dunbar, *Books and Collectors* (Los Altos, Calif., 1980), 73–74.

GOODHART, Howard L. (b. February 5, 1884, New York, N.Y.; d. August 10, 1951, New York, N.Y.). *Education*: A.B., Yale University, 1905. *Collection Disposition*: Bryn Mawr College; Yale University; Phyllis Goodhart Gordon.

From 1906 to 1922 Goodhart worked in the family banking business in New York. At the age of forty he retired in order to pursue his research interests and collecting. His fascination with early printing stemmed from the acquisition of a sixteenth-century text by Leonardo Bruni needed by his daughter for her undergraduate studies at Bryn Mawr. That purchase started Goodhart on a quest for incunabula and led to the formation of a library of over 1,400 examples. He was intensely interested in education, and many of his books represented the subject matter of the *trivium* and the *quadrivium*. In addition to the grammatical, rhetorical, and mathematical works, his library was rich in the writing of the major fourteenth-century Italian humanists Dante, Petrarch, and Boccaccio. He also had the best editions of Cicero, Justinius, Ovid, Livy, Caesar, and Suetonius. An impressive section of the library was made up of translations from Greek by the fourteenth-century scholar Poggio Bracciolini. Many of these came from the distinguished printing shops of Sweynheym and Pannartz of Rome and Nicolas Jenson and Aldus Manutius of Venice. Although Goodhart acquired his rarities from all over the world, his chief suppliers were A. S. W. Rosenbach* in New York and E. P. Goldschmidt and Maggs Brothers in London. John Fleming and Edwin Wolf II belittled some of Goodhart's purchases in their biography of Rosenbach as "dull theology," but few would argue with the importance of the

1470 Fust and Schoeffer *Epistolae* of Saint Jerome, the Holford copy of Higden's *Polychronicon* (1495) or the Sweynheym and Pannartz *Lactantius* (1468).

The manuscripts in the Goodhart library were few but choice. Often they complemented the incunabula. In the case of Philo Judaeus, a first-century Jewish philosopher, the collection of manuscripts and incunabula was almost exhaustive. The bibliography in Erwin Goodenough's *The Politics of Philo Judaeus* came entirely from the Goodhart library. In the preface to that volume, Goodhart revealed both his generosity and sense of humor by offering scholars the loan of "any but a few" of the books listed. Since Goodhart's collecting interests had been stimulated by his daughter's studies, it was fitting that on his death the library was divided between Bryn Mawr and her personal library. Her well-executed catalog of the collection was an appropriate tribute to a distinguished collector.

Bibliography

A. *Fifteenth Century Books in the Library of Howard Lehman Goodhart*, compiled by Phyllis Goodhart Gordon (Stamford, Conn., 1955); "Foreword," in *The Politics of Philo Judaeus*, by Erwin Goodenough (New Haven, 1939).

B. *Grolier 75*, 218–220; Wolf and Fleming, passim; Phyllis Goodhart Gordon, "To Hold the Renaissance in Our Hands," *Bodleian Library Record*, December 1974, 137–155; Millicent Sowerby, *Rare People and Rare Books* (London, 1967), passim.

GRAFF, Everett D. (b. August 7, 1885, Clarinda, Iowa; d. March 11, 1964, Rome, Italy). *Education*: A.B., Lake Forest College, 1906. *Collection Disposition*: Newberry Library; Lake Forest College.

Immediately after graduating from college, Graff began his career in the steel business. He joined the Joseph Ryerson Company of Chicago and rose Horatio Alger fashion from mail clerk to president. In civic affairs Graff was active in the Chicago Art Institute and in the Newberry Library, serving as president of both organizations. From 1924 until his death, Graff collected books, manuscripts, maps, broadsides, and pamphlets describing the development of the Trans-Mississippi West. In much of his buying he was aided by the knowledgeable Chicago bookdealer and bibliographer Wright Howes. Between 1924 and 1945 Graff bought background studies and secondary sources, but during the late 1940s and 1950s he began to concentrate on primary records. According to his bibliographer, Colton Storm, Graff's library was notable for its carefully arranged inner groupings. Each book, document, or map fit into an overall plan. Often the plan emphasized the "civilization" of the West, including railroading, the pony express, cattle drives, business history, military life, church history, and education. As the library developed, Graff became more and more concerned with his plan. Each new piece had to meet stringent standards for inclusion. He made significant additions to his library at the auctions of C. G. Littell* in 1945 and of Herschel V. Jones* in 1947. As the Graff collection grew its fame became known beyond Chicago. In 1946 the University of Michigan displayed a group of Graff's Texas books and issued a handsome catalog prepared by Colton Storm. This began a mutually satisfactory working relationship between the two men with Storm designated as compiler of the Graff catalog. This list of over 4,800 items enriched by lengthy notes by Graff and detailed bibliographic descriptions by Storm has long been recognized as a major bibliographic contribution to the study of the West.

On Graff's death, the 10,000-item library went to the Newberry, along with a fund of $100,000 for ongoing purchases. Graff specifically authorized the Newberry to sell duplicates whenever the library held a better copy. Although the sale failed to live up to expectations, the Graff collection made an important contribution to the library's Americana holdings. Graff's books, when combined with those already donated by Edward E. Ayer*, helped establish the Newberry as one of the premier institutions in the country for the scholarly study of the American West.

Bibliography

A. *A Catalogue of the Everett D. Graff Collection of Western Americana*, compiled by Colton Storm (Chicago, 1968).

B. *DAB*, Supp. 7, 294; *NCAB* 50, 721; Lawrence Towner, "Every Silver Lining Has a Cloud: The Recent Shaping of the Newberry Library's Collections," in *The Flow of Books and Manuscripts* (Los Angeles, 1968), 35–50; Lawrence Towner, ed., *An Uncommon Collection of Uncommon Collections: The Newberry Library*, 2nd edition (Chicago, 1976), 23–24.

GREENE, Albert Gorton (b. February 10, 1802, Providence, R.I.; d. January 3, 1868, Cleveland, Ohio). *Education*: A.B., Brown University, 1820. *Collection Disposition*: Bangs, March 29, 1869.

A lawyer by profession, Greene took up collecting to support his literary interests. He wrote light verse for the Providence newspapers and had a wide range of literary friends, including Ralph Waldo Emerson, Margaret Fuller, and Julia Ward Howe. Through these associations and by assiduous personal searching he acquired a large personal library on American history and letters. Musty pamphlets, sermons, broadsides, and well-thumbed hymnals were all grist for Greene's eclectic tastes. John Russell Bartlett, the Providence bibliographer, remembered Greene as a hardworking bibliophile often found rummaging through shelves of secondhand-book shops for obscure Americana. In addition to these personal forays, Greene followed the New York auctions with care and became a good customer of both Joseph Sabin and William Gowans. The Rufus W. Griswold sale in 1859 gave Greene the opportunity to obtain a particularly fine assortment of American literature. These books added luster to the somewhat drab holdings already in the Greene collection. But buyers were unenthusiastic when the Greene library itself was brought to auction in the spring of 1869. Caleb Fiske Harris*, a Providence collector who was just starting to develop his distinguished collection of American poetry, did make a number of significant purchases. Since the Harris library eventually went to Brown University, it can be claimed that Greene influenced the formation of one of the chief collections of early American poetry in this country.

Bibliography

B. *DAB* 4, 561–562; *NCAB* 9, 501; John Russell Bartlett, "Senator Anthony's Gifts to Brown University," *Providence Journal*, September 24, 1884; William Gowans, *Catalogue of American Books for Sale* (New York, 1869), 26; Roger Stoddard, "C. Fiske Harris, Collector of American Poetry and Plays," *PBSA*, 1st Q 1963, 14–32.

GRIBBEL, John (b. March 29, 1858, Hudson City, N.J.; d. August 25, 1936, Camden, Maine). *Collection Disposition*: Parke-Bernet, October 30, 1940, January 22, 1941, April 16, May 7, November 19, 1945, January 28, December 8, 1947.

As a Philadelphian interested in books, Gribbel quite naturally formed a business relationship with bookdealer A. S. W. Rosenbach*. Gribbel was attracted to the poetry of Robert Burns, the whimsey of Lewis Carroll, and the letters of Lincoln, Jefferson Davis, and John Paul Jones. Rosenbach, working in Philadelphia, and Maggs in London knew how to satisfy Gribbel's desires. Rosenbach provided Burns manuscripts, while Maggs supplied Carroll letters and first editions. Avid as he was, Gribbel had a sense of fair play. When an important set of Burns manuscripts came to him almost accidentally, he generously turned them back to the people of Scotland. At the Gribbel sales, strong prices prevailed. Gribbel was a shrewd collector and one who pursued his favorites with singleness of purpose. The Parke-Bernet catalogs provide ample testimony to his intelligent determination.

Bibliography

B. *NCAB* 27, 68; Wolf and Fleming, passim; "Foreword," in *Parke-Bernet Catalog* (New York, 1940).

GRISWOLD, Almon W. (b. 1833, Johnstown, Vt.; d. November 27, 1890, New York, N.Y.). *Education*: Harvard University. *Collection Disposition*: Bangs, May 14, 1868, February 28, April 19, 1876; Leavitt, January 9, February 8, 1878, June 1, December 6, 1880.

A lawyer by profession, Griswold collected American history, bibliography, English literature, and the classics. Bibliographer Joseph Sabin used the Griswold books in the construction of his *Dictionary of Books Relating to America*. Among the Griswold treasures were the 1624 folio edition of John Smith's *General History of Virginia* and the extra-illustrated copy of H. E. Ludewig's *Literature of American Local History*. The literature division of his library contained rare Shakespeariana as well as first editions of Ben Jonson, Beaumont and Fletcher, and John Milton. Because Griswold disposed of some of the finest of these materials privately, no records are available. The public sale catalogs, covering the years 1868–1880, represent the efforts of the Bangs and Leavitt auction houses. The Leavitt catalogs carried the charming designation "Gems from the Library of a Bibliomaniac." Apparently the device worked, as Robert Hoe III*, Henry E. Huntington*, and Ogden Goelet* made sizable purchases from the stock. In 1860 Wynne estimated the size of the Griswold library to be 7,000 items, all in excellent condition. It was one of the richest pre–Civil War collections and its sale provided the basic materials for several other distinguished libraries.

Bibliography

B. Cannon, 319; Wynne, 245–256; *NYT*, March 19, 1898, 178; *NYT*, November 28, 1890, 5.

GUNST, Morgan (b. March 9, 1887, San Francisco, Calif.; d. August 3, 1958, San Francisco, Calif.). *Collection Disposition*: Stanford University; Grolier Club.

In 1906, when the San Francisco fire destroyed the family tobacco business, Gunst dropped out of Stanford University to help his father. Although he never earned a degree, Gunst became one of Stanford's most active supporters. He was an original member of the Stanford Associates and led fund-raising activities for more than twenty years. One of his special projects was the development of the library's rare book department. In his personal collecting Gunst concentrated on the work of fine presses and craft binderies. He gathered the best work of previous centuries and commissioned leading European binders to create fine pieces of contemporary work for his shelves. Not content merely to collect, he took an active part in many bibliographic clubs and societies, arranging exhibits and promoting the cause of fine printing. The Book Club of California was his particular favorite. Over a period of twenty-five years he served on all its committees and in 1946 was elected president. The 4,000-volume Gunst collection, now housed in the Stanford Library, includes remarkable examples of book design, printing, and illumination. The university has appropriately chosen to identify the gift as the "Morgan A. and Aline D. Gunst Memorial Library of the Book Arts and the History of the Book."

Bibliography

B. Paul Bennett, *Some Notes on the Engaging By-paths and Enduring Pleasures of Fine Bookmaking*, A Keepsake Commemorating the Dedication of the Morgan A. and the Aline D. Gunst Library of the Book Arts and the History of the Book (San Francisco, 1963); *Essays in Memory of Morgan A. Gunst*, Written by Members of the Book Club of California, the Grolier Club of New York, the Roxburghe Club of San Francisco, the Société de la Reliure Originale, and the Board of Directors of the Leland Stanford University (Stanford, Calif., 1962).

GUYMON, E. T. "Ned" (b. June 8, 1900, Liberal, Kans.; d. February 23, 1983, San Diego, Calif.). *Education*: A.B., Occidental College, 1922. *Collection Disposition*: Occidental College.

After graduating from Occidental, Guymon built a successful real estate business in San Diego. In the late 1920s he read A. Edward Newton's* *This Book*

Collecting Game and set out to collect first editions of American and English literature. When he discovered a multitude of affluent collectors already ahead of him, he switched to detective and mystery fiction, an open area with little competition. First he acquired standard works by Edgar Allan Poe and A. Conan Doyle, then he broadened his approach to include Agatha Christie, Dashiell Hammett, and Dorothy Sayers. His books came from musty bookshops, secondhand-book stores, estate sales, and household auctions. According to Guymon, he built his library by crawling through the back rooms of every bookshop between San Diego and Vancouver. As the collection grew, he secured autographed first editions from Erle Stanley Gardner, Raymond Chandler, and Frederic Dannay. The Dannay-Guymon correspondence spanned over thirty years and was a veritable history of the development of the American detective novel. As Guymon continued to buy books and magazines, storage space became a problem. In 1962 he gave the entire 15,000-volume library to Occidental College for its Special Collections Department. The Guymon collection has been incorporated into many areas of the teaching program and is judged to be an important college resource. It is one of the finest detective fiction collections in the country.

Bibliography

A. "Why Do We Read This Stuff?" in *The Mystery Story*, edited by John Ball (San Diego, 1976).

B. Joyce Caulfield, "The First Edition: A Mysterious Attraction," *San Diego Union*, October 14, 1981; Tyrus Harmsen, "E. T. Guymon Jr., Book Collector," *Occidentaliana*, April 1983; Steve Frank, "E. T. Guymon Jr." *Seacoast*, February 1981, 15–16.

H

HAGEN, Winston (b. September 14, 1859, Cincinnati, Ohio; d. February 1, 1918, New York, N.Y.). *Education*: A.B., Amherst College, 1879. *Collection Disposition*: Anderson, May 13, 1918.

After graduating from college, Hagen studied the law and practiced in New York for thirty-five years. He was well known in book circles at the turn of the century as a collector of English literature. Originally Hagen planned to form a small library of landmark books which would illuminate the progress of literature from Chaucer to Swinburne. In this respect he modeled his library after the Rowfant Library of English collector Frederick Locker-Lampson. In this "cabinet library" two small cases held first editions of the most important volumes in English literature. When Dwight Church* brought the Rowfant Library to the United States, Hagen was one of the most enthusiastic customers. As other tempting opportunities arose, Hagen found it difficult to stay with his modest' plan. Ultimately he bought English literature in a more ambitious way. He seized the opportunity to enrich his Dryden and Milton holdings at the Marshall Lefferts* sale of 1902 and added John Donne from the Henry Poor* sale in 1909. Hagan's Milton holdings included an amazing run of the editions of *Paradise Lost*. According to Beverly Chew*, who wrote the foreword to the sale catalog, the Hagen library was one of the best ever submitted to the public at auction. Buyers responded enthusiastically, providing the estate with a very satisfying return. Hagen was a reader and a book lover rather than just an accumulator. His library reflected a highly developed intelligent connoisseurship.

Bibliography

B. *NCAB* 25, 373; Cannon, 225–226; Beverly Chew, "Foreword," in *Catalogue of the Library of the Late Winston H. Hagen* (New York, 1918).

HALSEY, Frederick R. (b. 1847, Ithaca, N.Y.; d. September 29, 1918, New York, N.Y.). *Education*: A.B., Harvard University, LL.D., Columbia University. *Collection Disposition*: Sold to Henry E. Huntington, 1915; Anderson, February 17, 1919; American Art, April 20, 1921.

A prominent New York lawyer and collector, Halsey found a congenial circle of friends in the Grolier Club. He was on close terms with such Grolier regulars as Edwin B. Holden*, Beverly Chew*, William Loring Andrews*, and Robert Hoe III*. Over a period of thirty-five years, Halsey formed a library of some 20,000 volumes of English, American, and continental literature. He had the first, third, and fourth Shakespeare folios and long runs of rarities by Dickens, Stevenson, Milton, Shelley, and Meredith. Undoubtedly Halsey's eminence as a collector stemmed from his acquisition of works by Poe. In *Yankee Bookseller* Charles Goodspeed told how Halsey obtained not one but two copies of *Tamerlane*, that rarist of all Poe items. In 1915 both went to Huntington, but as the California collector sold unwanted duplicates, *Tamerlane* came on the market again and Halsey, ever the enthusiast, bought it back. Halsey continued to add books to his library up to the time of his death. In both his print and book collections Halsey showed taste and intelligence. It is a tribute to his judgment that books he owned are now shelved with those of Robert Hoe III*, Elihu Dwight Church*, and Henry Huth in the remarkable Henry E. Huntington Library.

Bibliography

B. Cannon, 150–151; Goodspeed, 199–200.

HAMILTON, Sinclair (b. October 17, 1884, New York, N.Y.; d. August 28, 1978, Martha's Vineyard, Mass.). *Education*: A.B., Princeton University, 1906; LL.B., Columbia University, 1909. *Collection Disposition*: Princeton University.

At first Hamilton was drawn to collect such standard English and American nineteenth-century novelists as Brontë, Trollope, and Hawthorne. After a time, however, his interests changed and he began to concentrate on European woodcuts and wood engravings as they appeared in fifteenth- and sixteenth-century books and pamphlets. Because these examples were expensive in a highly competitive market, Hamilton began to look for a similar field he could enjoy on a more reasonable financial level. Since no one seemed to be interested in American woodcuts, Hamilton decided to take that on as his specialty. He started with the woodcuts of Winslow Homer, done at the end of the nineteenth century, and worked backward to the earliest colonial examples he could find. The eighteenth-century almanacs and chapbooks included woodcuts, but the artists were seldom identified. Alexander Anderson, an early nineteenth-century craftsman, was one of the first artists whose name was carried in print with his work. He and his numerous pupils pioneered the styles that Frank Bellew, Felix Darley, Augustus Hoppin, and Thomas Nast would popularize later in the century. All these illustrators were prominent on the Hamilton shelves. In 1945 Hamilton gave the first portion of his library to Princeton, a gift he continued to supplement until shortly before his death. In recognition of this generosity, Princeton awarded Hamilton an honorary degree of Doctor of Humane Letters, with a citation that referred to his taste, persistence, and zeal. These were the qualities that had endeared him to the university community and made him a successful collector.

Bibliography

A. "Early American Book Illustration," *PLC*, April 1945, 101–126; "Early American Book Illustration," in *Early American Book Illustrators and Wood Engravers 1670–1870* (reprinted with revisions from *PLC*, April 1945; Princeton, 1958; Supp. 1968), xxiii–xlviii; "A Talk," *PLC*, Winter 1979, 183–185.

B. Frank Mather, "A Collection of Early American Illustrated Books," *PLC*, April 1945, 99–100; A. Hyatt Mayor, "Sinclair Hamilton," *PLC*, Winter 1979, 185–186; "Sinclair Hamilton," *PAAS*, October 1978, 173–181.

HANLEY, Thomas E. (b. August 6, 1893, Bradford, Pa.; d. April 9, 1969, Bradford, Pa.). *Education*: A.B., Harvard University, 1912. *Collection Disposition*: University of Arizona; University of Texas; Saint Bonaventure University; Bradford Public Library; Harvard University.

While he was still a student at Harvard, Hanley began to collect rare first editions of Shaw, Whitman, and Thackeray. After he had filled in most of the important titles by those authors, he began to add books and manuscripts by Joyce, D. H. Lawrence, T. E. Lawrence, Pound, and many other twentieth-century luminaries. At the same time, he acquired many standard works in history, art, and the humanities.

While Hanley was visiting Tucson, Arizona, in the 1930s he met former Bostonian Arthur Olaf Anderson, dean of fine arts at the University of Arizona. Anderson convinced his wealthy visitor that the one thing Arizona needed was a substantial library, and soon large shipments of books on art, music, theater, dance, photography, and literature began to pour into Tucson. By 1959 Hanley had given an estimated 35,000 items to the western university. About this time his attention was turned to the University of Texas at Austin. Harry H. Ransome, dean of the College of Arts and Sciences, wrote to Hanley and suggested that parts of his library might be appropriately placed in Texas. Ransome began by inquiring about the D. H. Lawrence collection but eventually negotiated for the entire Hanley library. The bulk of the collection went to Austin by purchase in 1958, with a second portion, consisting chiefly of manuscripts, following six years later. In addition to these purchases, Hanley made numerous gifts of books and art to the University of Texas, Saint Bonaventure University, Harvard, and the Bradford Public Library in his hometown in Pennsylvania. Hanley also gave Harvard an impressive collection of the manuscripts and letters by the poet Alan Seager and an endowment for the Houghton Rare Book Library. He believed in providing students with a wide range of humanistic reading and research material and made this belief manifest by giving large collections to several major American academic libraries.

Bibliography

B. *NCAB* 55, 286; Tullah Hanley, *The Love of Art and the Art of Love* (Blue Earth, Minn., 1975); Harry H. Ransome, "The Hanley Library," *The Library Chronicle*, Spring 1959, 33–35.

HARDING, George L. (b. 1893, Indianapolis, Ind.; d. August 30, 1976, Berkeley, Calif.). *Education*: A.B., Indiana University, 1915; M.B.A., Harvard University, 1917. *Collection Disposition*: California Historical Society—Kemble Collections; Harvard University; Indiana University; Bancroft Library at the University of California at Berkeley.

During his early student days Harding developed a strong interest in printing. He took classes from typographical authority Daniel Berkeley Updike and got to know Frederick Goudy and W. A. Dwiggins. Although he himself never printed, he was deeply interested in the process from the historical point of view. One of his early collecting passions was for the books, pamphlets, and ephemera from Updike's Merrymount Press. With the master typographer's help, Harding built this collection into the second largest in the country, giving place only to the Huntington Library. Shortly after moving to the West Coast, Harding bought the William Loy typographical library, a record of early nineteenth-century California printing. Loy had been a typefounder and had collected a large library of early trade catalogs and ephemera. All these materials fit Harding's varied research interests. In 1933 he issued a bibliography of nineteenth-century California-Spanish imprints, and followed it the next year with a biography of Augustin Zamorano, California's first printer.

Secondhand-book dealers knew Harding as an excellent customer. He bought important items, even when the prices seemed high, with the belief that one only regrets the books one does not buy. Of the many learned associations to which he belonged, Harding was most active in the California Historical Society. He held all the major offices in that organization, including that of president. In 1963 Harding donated his printing archive to the California Historical Society in the name of California's pioneer printer-editor Edward C. Kemble. During the last years of his life, Harding served as honorary curator of the Kemble Collections, devoting a large amount of his time to augmenting the already strong holdings. Harding insisted on the plural "collections" because his gift, he claimed, consisted of four separate libraries: the Loy holdings, the archive of the San Francisco printing firm of Taylor and Taylor, the trade journals of Haywood Hunt, and his own vast personal collection. In his enthusiasm for gathering California printing history, Harding had no rivals. The Kemble Collections are the product of his energetic and informed interest.

Bibliography

A. *Census of California-Spanish Imprints 1833–1845* (San Francisco, 1933); *Don Augustin V. Zamorano: Statesman, Soldier, Craftsman, and California's First Printer* (Los Angeles, 1934); *Charles Murdock: Printer and Citizen of San Francisco* (Berkeley, Calif., 1973).

B. Dean Anderson, James Elliott, Roger Levenson, Albert Shumate, and Roby Wentz, "Our Memories of George Laban Harding, 1893–1976," *The Kemble Occasional*, December 1976; Bruce Johnson, "The Kemble Collections," *California History*, Summer 1981, 188–193; Oscar Lewis, "In Memoriam," *California Historical Quarterly*, Winter 1976–1977, 376–377.

HARKNESS, Edward S. (b. January 22, 1874, Cleveland, Ohio; d. January 29, 1940, New York, N.Y.). *Education*: A.B., Yale University, 1897. *Collection Disposition*: New York Public Library; Yale University; Library of Congress.

In the affluent years following World War I, Harkness was known for his wide-ranging philanthropy. With a fortune made in Standard Oil, Harkness built hospitals, endowed museums, established loan funds, and bought books and manuscripts. Not a collector in the usual sense, he figured significantly in the distribution of many important research materials. Some of his enthusiasm for collecting can be attributed to his wife, Mary S. Harkness*, who bought manuscripts and rare books in the early 1920s and induced him to do the same. In 1926, acting with his wife, Harkness commissioned A. S. W. Rosenbach* to buy the "Melk Copy" of the Gutenberg Bible. Harkness suggested a bid limit of $75,000 for this first book produced from movable type, but Rosenbach had to go to $106,000 before the prize was his. The ultimate winner in this high-stakes contest was the Yale University Library, where the great Bible came to rest, a magnificent tribute to the Harknesses' generosity. In subsequent negotiations with Rosenbach, Harkness bought a massive collection of early Peruvian and Mexican documents for the manuscript section of the Library of Congress. Later Rosenbach was able to convey Calvin Coolidge's personal thanks to Harkness for what the President, in an unusual burst of enthusiasm, called a great gift to the nation. Other notable gifts went regularly to the New York Public Library and to Yale. Ten years after Harkness died his remaining books and literary and historical manuscripts went by bequest to the New York Public Library. Harkness was more interested in supporting humanistic research than in building an impressive personal library. He achieved that purpose by making significant gifts to major institutional collections.

Bibliography

A. *The Harkness Collection in the Library of Congress: Calender of Spanish Manuscripts Concerning Peru, 1531–1651* (Washington, D.C., 1932); *The Harkness Collection in the Library of Congress: Documents from Early Peru: The Pizarros and the Almagros, 1531–1578* (Washington, D.C., 1936); *The Harkness Collection in the Library of Congress: Manuscript Concerning Mexico, A Guide* (Washington, D.C., 1974).

B. *DAB*, Supp. 2, 283–285; Wolf and Fleming, passim; Robert Hill and Lewis Stark, "The Edward Harkness Collection," *BNYPL*, December 1950, 585–594; *Guide to the Research Collections of the New York Public Library* (Chicago, 1975), passim; *SCLC*, 156–157.

HARKNESS, Mary S. (b. July 4, 1874, Brooklyn, N.Y.; d. June 6, 1950, New York, N.Y.). *Collection Disposition*: New York Public Library; Yale University; Library of Congress.

Working with rare bookdealers in both the United States and England, Harkness formed several notable collections. In some cases she bought Americana as a gift for her husband, Edward S. Harkness*, and in others she invested in literature to please herself. She owned the first four Shakespeare folios as well as strong representations of the work of Dickens, Thackeray, and Conrad. Original literary manuscripts in her library included those of Poe, Whittier, and Thoreau, while historical documents and letters carried the signatures of Franklin and Jefferson. Among the many illustrated books in the Harkness library, the works of Rackham and Cruikshank predominated. In 1926 Mrs. Harkness and her husband purchased the "Melk Copy" of the Gutenberg Bible through A. S. W. Rosenbach* for Yale at a cost of $106,000. Although Mrs. Harkness never narrowed her collection to one specific area, she was enthusiastic about books of beauty and literary importance. In 1951 she bequeathed her collection of books, manuscripts, and prints to the New York Public Library.

Bibliography

B. Wolf and Fleming, passim; Lewis Stark and Robert Hill, "The Bequest of Mary S. Harkness," *BNYPL*, May 1951, 213–224; *Guide to the Research Collections of the New York Public Library* (Chicago, 1975), passim.

HARRIS, Caleb Fiske (b. March 9, 1818, Warwick, R.I.; d. October 2, 1881, Moosehead Lake, Maine). *Collection Disposition*: Brown University; Providence Public Library; Leavitt, April 30, 1883, April 22, 1884, January 24, 1888.

By the time he was forty, Harris had made enough money in the commission business in New York to allow him to retire and pursue his collecting interests. He returned to his native Rhode Island, married, and built a large house on the edge of the Brown University campus. His taste in books ran to English drama, the literature of slavery and the Civil War, and American poetry. In all these areas he built distinguished collections. In addition to the Shakespeare folios, he owned important printings of the work of most of the masters of English drama from the seventeenth through the eighteenth centuries. His poetry collection included first editions of Donne, Carew, Milton, and Burns along with long runs of the works of Byron, Coleridge, and Gray. Harris retained this group of books until his death, but after 1869 he shifted his interest to American history and letters. He was fascinated with the literature of slavery and the Civil War and set out to develop a research collection of primary sources. In addition to books, he gathered broadsides, pamphlets, sermons, music, newspapers, and documents representing both the Northern and Southern points of view. The section of the library dealing with the war itself was particularly strong, including regimental histories, biography, campaign descriptions, letters, poetry, drama, and fiction. After Harris' death this archive of some 8,300 pieces went to the Providence

Public Library. Harris' most important collection covered American poetry and drama. He began to acquire poetry as early as 1860, but his first substantial purchases occurred in 1869 at the Albert Greene* sale. Of the 1,850 lots offered, Harris carried away 1,350—more than 75 percent of the total. The Greene library was not distinguished but did provide a multitude of pamphlets, songsters, hymnals, and other ephemera that illustrated the literary efforts of colonial America. With these purchases as a base, and with the assistance of New York bookdealers William Gowans and Joseph Sabin, Harris began to build an important poetry library. He was also aided by knowledgeable Providence bibliographer John Russell Bartlett and London bookdealer Bernard Quaritch.

In all his book-trade negotiations, Harris was a tough and unyielding customer, turning back unsatisfactory copies and complaining bitterly when his commissions were exceeded. At one point he threatened to withdraw his business from Sabin if the New York agent failed to follow explicit directions. In 1873 Harris secured one of his greatest treasures, an inscribed copy of the 1845 edition of Poe's *The Raven*. By the following year, with Bartlett's aid, Harris issued an *Index to American Poetry and Plays*, a carefully prepared catalog of the 4,000 pieces in his collection. It came as a revelation to Harris' contemporaries that so much creative literature had been produced so early by American hands. In addition to the descriptions of the work of Longfellow, Lowell, and Bryant, Harris' catalog provided an approach to the writing of hundreds of minor authors. During the next five years Harris added another 1,000 items to his library, with a number of distinguished items coming from the first sessions of the George Brinley* sale.

After Harris' death the collection was dispersed at a number of sales through Providence bookseller Sidney Rider. The enterprising Rider sold the *Bay Psalm Book* to Mrs. John Carter Brown, then attempted to sell the poetry. After lengthy negotiations Harris' cousin Henry B. Anthony purchased the entire collection. Brown University received the books in 1884 as one of the bequests in Anthony's will. The Harris Collection has grown to be one of the most important of its kind in the United States. It stands as a tribute not only to Harris but also to Greene, who assembled the material, and to Anthony, who provided the bequest.

Bibliography

A. *Index to American Poetry and Plays in the Collection of C. Fiske Harris* (Providence, R.I., 1874); *Dictionary Catalog of the Harris Collection of American Poetry and Plays* (Boston, 1972).

B. *DAB* 5, 304; *NCAB* 22, 457; John Russell Bartlett, "Senator Anthony's Gift to Brown University," *The Providence Journal*, September 24, 1884; J. R. T. Ettlinger, "A Harris Letter Book," *Books at Brown*, 1958, 129–131; Horatio Rogers, *Private Libraries of Providence* (Providence, R.I., 1878), 181–202; Roger E. Stoddard, "C. Fiske Harris, Collector of American Poetry and Plays," *PBSA*, 1st Q 1963, 14–32.

HARRISSE, Henry (b. March 24, 1829?, Paris, France; d. May 13, 1910, Paris, France). *Collection Disposition*: Library of Congress; Bibliothèque Nationale; Charles Chadenat (sale), 1912; Hotel Drouot (sale), 1911.

After unsuccessful attempts at teaching and legal practice, Harrisse found his true vocation in historical research. His chief interest was Americana and his principal resource was the extensive private library of New York collector Samuel L. M. Barlow*. He advised Barlow on purchases, compiled a bibliography of his library, and wrote a lengthy introduction to his 1890 auction catalog. It was Barlow's collection and his financial support that provided the base for two of Harrisse's major publications, *Notes on Columbus* and the much respected *Bibliotheca Americana Vetustissima*. From 1870 until the time of his death, Harrisse lived in Paris, where he practiced law, bought books for Barlow, and published a series of bibliographies and articles relating to American history. His outspoken publications on Columbus challenged the traditional historical assumptions and involved Harrisse in a never-ending round of scholarly charges and countercharges. Although Harrisse thought of himself more as a bibliographer than a collector, he formed an impressive private library. His papers and maps on the exploration of America went to the Library of Congress, while his books on art and literature went to the Bibliothèque Nationale. He is remembered for his contributions to American historical scholarship.

Bibliography

A. *Biblioteca Barlowiana* (New York, 1864); *Bibliotheca Americana Vetustissima* (New York, 1866); *Notes on Columbus* (Cambridge, Mass., 1866); "Samuel Latham Mitchill Barlow," in *Catalogue of the American Library of S. L. M. Barlow* (New York, 1889).

B. *NCAB* 17, 37–38; Cannon, 103–106; *SCLC* 158; Randolph Adams, "Henry Harrisse, Bibliographer," in *Three Americanists* (Philadelphia, 1939), 1–33; Frederick R. Goff, "Henry Harrisse, Americanist," *Inter-American Review of Bibliography*, January-April 1953, 3–10; Adolf Growoll, *Henry Harrisse* (New York, 1889); Henry Vignaud, *Henry Harrisse, Étude Biographique et Morale* (Paris, 1912); Joseph Rosenblum, "Two Americanists: Samuel L. M. Barlow and Henry Harrisse," *ABC* March/April 1985, 14–25.

HAWKINS, Rush C. (b. September 14, 1831, Pomfret, Vt.; d. October 25, 1920, New York, N.Y.). *Collection Disposition*: Brown University; University of Vermont; Leavitt, March 21, 1887; Merwin, February 14, 1906.

After serving in the military for many years, Hawkins knew how to fight for what he wanted. By the time he was thirty-five he had served in the Mexican War, studied law, formed his own brigade of Northern volunteers, and at the end of the Civil War had achieved the rank of brigadier general. Wherever Hawkins went controversy seemed to follow. After a stormy term in the New York state legislature, he resigned to devote himself to travel and collecting.

In an essay written in 1910, Hawkins remembered his early enthusiasms for novels of adventure and pirate sagas. As he matured, his tastes turned from these melodramatic tales to Americana and to early European printing. On a trip to

England in 1878 he came under the influence of Henry Bradshaw, a Cambridge University librarian who was developing a new approach to the study of incunabula based on its place of origin. Following Bradshaw's guidelines, Hawkins set out to gather the first books produced in the European towns where printing originated. In order to achieve his goal, Hawkins took advantage of the expertise of such well-known dealers as Bernard Quaritch, Richard Garnett, and Albert Cohn. Through their hands came examples from 141 of the 238 towns where fifteenth-century printing was known to have existed. For many years Hawkins and his wife, Annmary Brown, daughter of a distinguished Rhode Island family, planned to build a Gutenberg memorial to house their treasures. When she died in 1903 the general decided to dedicate it as the Annmary Brown Memorial Library. The building, as planned, also served as a mausoleum for his wife and himself. As he remarked to his librarian, Margaret Stillwell, his body would serve as "an anchor," since he believed that anyone wanting to move the books would think twice before they moved the books and him. Hawkins provided his books with first-class accommodations not only physically but also bibliographically. In 1909 he employed noted English bibliographer Alfred W. Pollard to prepare a catalog. This was a handsome job and did much to publicize the library's holdings. Hawkins' own thoughts about collecting were direct and forceful. In a short essay appended to his 1910 catalogue, he wrote: "The highest type of collector is the man endowed for his work by natural inclination and trained by observation and study, who enters the chosen field with a well defined object in view." No better statement could be made as a summary of Hawkins' own collecting style.

Bibliography

A. "Some Late Statements About Early Printing," *The Bibliographer*, February 1902, 61–68; *Catalogue of Books Mostly from Presses of the First Printers*, cataloged by A. W. Pollard (Oxford, 1910).

B. *DAB* 4, 415–416; *NCAB* 5, 238; Cannon, 188–191; *Grolier 75*, 8–10; A. W. Pollard, "General Rush Hawkins," *The Library*, December 1920, 171–178; Margaret Stillwell, "General Hawkins as He Revealed Himself to This Librarian," *PBSA*, 1st Q 1923, 69–97; Margaret Stillwell, *The Annmary Brown Memorial* (Providence, R.I., 1925); Margaret Stillwell, *Librarians Are Human* (Boston, 1973).

HEARST, William Randolph (b. April 29, 1863, San Francisco, Calif.; d. August 14, 1951, Beverly Hills, Calif.). *Collection Disposition*: Parke-Bernet, November 16, 17, and 30, December 1, 1938, January 11 and 12, November 21 and 22, 1939, April 16, 1963.

With an inherited fortune and a profitable newspaper empire at his command, Hearst could buy anything he wanted. In order to decorate his palatial estate at San Simeon, California, and his townhouses in New York, he bought by the roomful. His collecting appetites were prodigious, encompassing medieval castles, tapestries, statuary, armor, silver, majolica plates, guns, furniture, ship figureheads, books, and manuscripts. In building his library, Hearst used the same eclectic gathering process he employed to obtain his paintings, tapestries, and porcelain vases. When he saw something he liked, he bought it, regardless of the price. His wide-ranging collection included a variety of documents from the Revolutionary War period, Lincoln letters, expensively bound sets of Conrad, Byron, and Dickens, Eugene Field manuscripts, illuminated manuscripts, Rackham illustrations, and inscribed Jack London first editions—a potpourri of the beautiful, the expensive, and the nondescript. The depression sapped Hearst's fortunes, to the point that he was forced to sell many of his choice possessions. In a series of sales held in New York between 1938 and 1939 a substantial portion of the Hearst library was liquidated. The three libraries at the Hearst castle at San Simeon remained untouched, however, and in 1970 Sotheby Parke Bernet valued them at about $100,000. As measured by the foot, the Hearst libraries were impressive, as were some of the items within the libraries. Hearst, however, was an accumulator rather than a collector.

Bibliography

B. *DAB*, Supp. 5, 283–388; *NCAB* 39, 7–9; Edmond Coblentz, *William Randolph Hearst: A Portrait in His Own Words* (New York, 1952); Geoffrey Hellman, "Monastery for Sale," *The New Yorker*, February 1, 1941, 33–39; W. A. Swanberg, *Citizen Hearst* (New York, 1961); John Tebbel, *The Life and Good Times of William Randolph Hearst* (New York, 1952); Anne M. McGrath, "Bookman Looks at the Great Sales," *AB*, April 23, 1984, 3118.

HECKSCHER, John G. (b. 1835?; d. July 4, 1908, New York, N.Y.). *Collection Disposition*: Merwin, April 25, 1906, February 2 and 15, March 2, 1909.

As a sophisticated turn-of-the-century New York clubman, Heckscher owned racehorses, took an interest in yachting, and formed a large library of sporting books. He specialized in works on fishing, particularly those with engraved plates and watercolors. He owned all four early editions of Walton's *Compleat Angler*, a nearly complete collection of the sporting classics by English novelists Robert Surtees and Pierce Egan, Audubon's *Birds of America*, and a large assortment of dueling literature. A small portion of his library was dispersed at Merwins in 1906, but the major part did not come on the market until after his death. The sale of the first edition of *The Compleat Angler* to Daniel B. Fearing* brought the estate $3,900, the highest price paid during the season for a single volume. Although Heckscher's private life was somewhat chaotic, as reported in the *New York Times* in October 1905, he was known as a gentleman and a connoisseur. Heckscher's sporting library was one of his chief ornaments.

Bibliography

B. "News for Bibliophiles," *The Nation*, February 25, 1909, 191; "J. G. Heckscher at 70 Weds a Young Widow," *NYT*, October 20, 1905; "A Record Year for Book Sales," *NYT*, April 10, 1909, 236.

HEINEMAN, Dannie N. (b. November 23, 1872, Charlotte, N.C.; d. January 31, 1962, New York, N.Y.). *Education*: Technische Hochschule, Hanover, Ger., 1895. *Collection Disposition*: Morgan Library; Heineman Foundation.

Although Heineman was born in the United States he spent most of his professional life in Europe, where he served for forty years as director of the Belgian Public Utilities Management Company. As a collector, Heineman specialized in music manuscripts, eighteenth- and nineteenth-century European literature, and books and manuscripts on science and philosophy. Although the most active period in his collecting career fell between 1920 and 1940, while he was still living in Europe, he continued to add important items after he moved to the United States. The library was small but choice, consisting of some 1,500 printed books and 1,700 manuscripts and letters. The assortment of music manuscripts, built on Heineman's deep interest in music, was unusually rich and included samples of the work of Bach, Franz Schubert, Chopin, Richard Wagner, and Mozart. The material in science and philosophy was equally distinguished, with autographed contributions by Leibniz, Kepler, Schopenhauer, Darwin, and others. Beyond these archives the major portion of the library consisted of literary materials. The section of German literature included many first editions and manuscripts by Goethe and Heine. In each case hundreds of letters were present, along with poems in draft and proof states. As Herbert Cahoon of the Pierpont Morgan Library has pointed out, French literature made up the bulk of the collection with a galaxy composed of Voltaire, Ronsard, Stendahl, Balzac, Zola, and de Maupassant. In each case letters and manuscripts complemented each other in a stunning array. In 1977, after Mrs. Heineman's death, the family gave the collection to the Pierpont Morgan Library in New York. There the material has been kept together in the Heineman Room and forms an appropriate addition to the library's collection of humanistic treasures.

Bibliography

B. Herbert Cahoon, "The Dannie and Hettie Heineman Collection," in the *Pierpont Morgan Library Report to the Fellows 1975–1977*, 21–43; Herbert Cahoon, "Dannie and Hettie Heineman," *BC*, Winter 1980, 497–520; Edward N. Waters, "The Music Collection of the Heineman Foundation," *Music Library Association Notes*, 1949–1950, 181–216; "Library's Library," *The New Yorker*, March 31, 1973, 30–31.

HELLMAN, George S. (b. November 14, 1878, New York, N.Y.; d. July 17, 1958, New York, N.Y.). *Education*: A.B., A.M., Columbia University, 1899, 1900. *Collection Disposition*: New York Public Library; Anderson, November 25, 1919.

As a poet, critic, essayist, editor, and bookdealer, Hellman was involved in a myriad of literary activities over a period of nearly fifty years. During the early part of his career, from 1900 to 1910, he worked for the rare book and art dealer Arthur H. Harlow and counted John Pierpont Morgan* and William K. Bixby* among his favored customers. He was imaginative in securing manuscripts from the friends and families of notable nineteenth-century New England authors and with these in hand wrote a stream of critical essays and monographs. His interest in Washington Irving led him to form a large personal collection of books and manuscripts, which he presented to the New York Public Library in 1929. This gift included a portion of the original manuscript of *Wolfert's Roost* and inscribed copies of several one-act plays. Hellman's autobiography, *Lanes of Memory*, is a readable account of the life of a perceptive bookdealer/author/collector.

Bibliography

A. *Lanes of Memory* (New York, 1927).

B. *NCAB* A, 149–150; R. W. G. Vail, "The Hellman Collection of Irvingiana," *BNYPL*, April 1929, 207–219.

HENDERSON, Jennie Crocker (b. 1887, San Francisco, Calif.; d. January 2, 1974, Hillsborough, Calif.). *Collection Disposition*: University of California at Berkeley.

As a member of a family where book collecting was recognized as a serious hobby, Henderson started to form a personal library while she was in high school. After trying to collect Rudyard Kipling, Henderson followed the lead of her older brother Templeton Crocker* and turned to Californiana. During a twelve-year stay in New York, she increased her holdings considerably with purchases at auction and through direct negotiations with bookdealers Edward Eberstadt, George D. Smith, and A. S. W. Rosenbach*. One of the more important items she acquired during that time was the 1835 *Manifesto* of Mexican governor José Figueroa printed in California by Augustin Zamorano. In the aftermath of heated bidding, Henderson found that her offer for the *Manifesto* had left her brother the underbidder. Over a long period of years Henderson gathered an impressive collection of Bret Harte manuscripts and books. Perhaps the best known of these was the handwritten copy of "Tennessee's Partner," presented by Harte to Ina Coolbrith, the "Poet Laureate of California." In 1923 Henderson bought the manuscript from Coolbrith and placed it in her collection beside "A Bride of the Sierras" and "Flip." In addition to these manuscripts, Henderson had many documents on the founding of San Francisco and a wide range of early newspapers. In his 1979 sale catalog Warren Howell identified the Henderson library as "the last of the great collections of California."

Bibliography

B. Warren Howell, "Jennie Crocker Henderson," in *California*,Catalogue 50 (San Francisco, 1979); Warren Unna, "Some Highlights of the Henderson Collection," *QNLBCC*, Winter 1951, 3–9.

HERSHOLT, Jean (b. July 12, 1866, Copenhagen, Den.; d. June 2, 1956, Los Angeles, Calif.). *Collection Disposition*: Library of Congress; University of California at Los Angeles; Andersen Museum in Odense, Denmark; Parke-Bernet, March 23, 1954.

By the time he was twenty, Hersholt had acted in Copenhagen theaters and played a minor part in the first motion picture produced in Denmark. In 1931 he came to the United States to act in Hollywood productions, launching a career that lasted for more than thirty years. He is chiefly remembered for his 1935 movie portrayal of Allan Defoe, the doctor who delivered the Dionne quintuplets, and his "Dr. Christian" radio and motion picture series.

As a collector, Hersholt gathered Californiana and theater books, along with a handful of his favorite authors—Dickens, Walpole, and preeminently Hans Christian Andersen. In his introduction to the 1942 Limited Editions Club's *Hans Christian Andersen, Maker of Fairy Tales*, Hersholt commented that he viewed book collecting as the greatest of all indoor sports. The lure of collecting Andersen, a fellow Dane, drew Hersholt into the intriguing world of rare editions, proof states, manuscripts, and letters. Andersen was difficult, as Hersholt explained in an article in *The Colophon*, because of the large number of adaptations and translations and the lack of any good bibliography. In 1951, when Hersholt's collection was presented to the Library of Congress, it was evaluated as the best record of Andersen's work outside Denmark. Two of the highlights of his library were the pseudonymous *Ungdoms Forsog* (Youthful Attempts), Andersen's first appearance in print, and six pamphlets issued in Copenhagen between 1835 and 1842 containing his fairy tales. One of the unique sections of the Hersholt collection consisted of Andersen's letters. Among these his exchanges with American editor Horace Scudder and his British publisher Richard Bentley are most revealing. In 1954 the entire Andersen collection was fully described in a handsome Library of Congress catalog.

While Andersen was the principal object of Hersholt's zeal, he developed several other author and subject collections. His friendship with novelists Sinclair Lewis and Hugh Walpole led to extensive holdings of presentation copies that also went to the Library of Congress. Later he gave a sizable collection of Danish history and literature to the University of California at Los Angeles. In 1954 Parke-Bernet offered the remainder of the library—early California books and a sampling of American and English literature. The first 150 items all concerned the early history of California and the settlement of the West. Following these came extensive sections of Clemens, Dickens, and Galsworthy. In many ways Hersholt was an ideal collector, avid in his interests, discriminating in his purchases, and generous in the disposal of his holdings.

Bibliography

A. "An American Andersen Collection," *American Scandinavian Review*, June 1944, 143–150; "Hans Christian Andersen's Fairy Tales, Published First in America," *The Colophon*, February 1940, 5–12; "Introduction," in *Hans Christian Andersen, Maker of Fairy Tales* (New York, 1942); *Catalog of the Jean Hersholt Collection of Hans Christian Andersen: Original Manuscripts, Letters, First Editions, Presentation Copies, and Related Materials* (Washington, D.C., 1954).

B. *NCAB* F, 93; *SCLC*, 167–168; *Current Biography*, 1944, 288–291; Frederick Goff,

"The Hersholt Collection of Anderseniana," *QJLC*, May 1952, 123–127; Frederick Goff, "The Hersholt Gift of Works of Hugh Walpole and Sinclair Lewis," *QJLC*, August 1954, 195–198.

HESS, George H. (b. 1873, Dubuque, Iowa; d. 1954, Saint Paul, Minn.). *Collection Disposition*: University of Minnesota.

Hess began collecting dime novels, he once said, to try to find those he had read and inscribed as a boy. That goal escaped him, but in the process of searching he accumulated 80,000 separate publications. His strongest gathering was perhaps the novels issued by the Beadle Publishing Company of New York. The small sextodecimo books printed on cheap paper featured western heroes, detectives, and poor boys who rose almost predictably from rags to riches. Hess also acquired volumes from the famous "Lakeside Library" issued by Donnelly, Loyd, and Company of Chicago and the copies of that series put out by other publishers such as the "Home Library," the "Riverside Library," and the "Fireside Library." Another part of his library featured the boys' and girls' series books distributed in decorated cloth bindings in the early decades of the twentieth century—"The Bobbsey Twins," "Nancy Drew," and "Tom Swift" in all their many versions. In 1954 the entire collection was given to the University of Minnesota Library as Hess had requested. This archive provided scholars with a comprehensive record of nineteenth-century popular culture as well as a unique look at young people's reading tastes.

Bibliography

B. Randolph Cox, "On the Track of Popular Culture: The Story of the Hess Collection of Dime Novels, Story Papers, and Newsstand Literature," *Dime Novel Roundup*, December 15, 1973, 134–141; Austin McLean, "The Hess Collection of Dime Novels, Story Papers, etc. at the University of Minnesota," *ABC*, January-February, 1975, 25–29.

HOE, Robert III (b. March 10, 1839, New York, N.Y.; d. September 22, 1909, London, Eng.). *Collection Disposition*: Anderson, April 24, May 1, 1911, January 8 and 15, April 15 and 22, November 11, 18, and 25, 1912, February 10, 1913.

From 1803, when the first family member arrived from England, the Hoe name became firmly attached to developments in the printing industry. After serving in numerous apprenticeship positions, Robert Hoe III took over management of the business in 1886. His personal fortunes grew along with the company's successful expansion in all phases of graphic arts reproduction. This provided him with the resources to develop one of the most extraordinary libraries ever formed in America. He acquired manuscripts, incunabula, Books of Hours, Aldines, Elzevirs, fine bindings, early French and English literature, and Americana. In his introduction to *A Catalogue of Books by English Authors Who*

Lived Before the Year 1700, Hoe provided an explanation of his own catholic goals: "Having commenced collecting when quite young, and with no definite plan, my purchases have been such as only a progressive or artistic taste and knowledge suggested." In many ways Hoe lived at the right time. The period of his most active interest in collection development, 1880–1908, corresponded with the time when numerous great collections were broken up and brought to auction. The sumptuous "Pembroke Hours," came from the Brayton Ives* sale while Malory's *Morte d'Arthur*, printed by Caxton in 1485, came from Abbie Pope's* auction. He obtained other priceless rarities from the Charles Kalbfleisch* and Almon Griswold* sales in America and the Beckford and Ashburnham sales in England. London dealers Benjamin Quaritch and Ernest Maggs kept Hoe in mind whenever choice books appeared in their shops. Hoe not only bought books and manuscripts but also documented his holdings with a series of sixteen bibliographic catalogs issued between 1903 and 1909. These volumes, compiled by James Wright and Caroline Shipman, furnished a meticulous index to the Hoe library. Infected by book collecting, Hoe determined to surround himself with others of like mind. In 1884 he and eight other bibliophiles formed the Grolier Club of New York, an organization devoted to the study and promotion of the book arts. At an early meeting Hoe was elected the club's first president. It was also Hoe who formed and subsidized the Club Bindery, a clique within the Grolier Club devoted to fine craft binding. Although the Club Bindery existed only for a short time, it produced some remarkable books.

In the matter of the disposition of his library, Hoe formed a careful plan. He was appalled at the condition of some of the institutional libraries he had seen in Europe and determined that his own books should not meet that fate. Arrangements leading up to the auction at the Anderson Auction Company in New York were elaborate. The annotated catalogs were done by talented bibliographer Arthur Swann and carried a special foreword by Hoe's friend and notable collector Beverly Chew*. The lavish offerings attracted Ludwig Baer from Frankfurt, Théophile Belin of Paris, and Maggs and Quaritch from London. The record-breaking prices paid by the glamorous bidders were reported as news events in the daily press. George D. Smith seized top honors buying for Henry E. Huntington*. He obtained the Gutenberg Bible on vellum for $50,000, the "tall copy" of the first Shakespeare folio for $13,000, and the "Book of St. Albans" for $13,000. John Pierpont Morgan* was able to get *Morte d'Arthur* for $42,800, and Quaritch bought the paper copy of the Gutenberg Bible for $27,500. Smith topped all buyers with an investment of better than $1 million. Surprisingly, the Americans outbid their European rivals. When the last session was over in November 1912, the sale total reached an unprecedented $1,932,000, a record that held until the Thomas W. Streeter* sale of 1966. Hoe's importance as a collector can be explained in terms of his broad approach to fine printing and literature. His resourcefulness produced a library that, according to Chew, was "the finest the country has ever contained."

Bibliography

A. *Bookbinding as a Fine Art* (New York, 1886); *A Short History of the Printing Press* (New York, 1902).

B. *DAB* 5, 105; *NCAB* 45, 422; Cannon, 157–169; *Grolier 75*, 24–26; O. A. Bierstadt, *The Library of Robert Hoe* (New York, 1895); Gelett Burgess, "The Battle of the Books," *Collier's*, February 10, 1912, 17; G. W. Cole, "Book Collectors as Benefactors of Public Libraries," *PBSA*, 1st Q 1915, 47–110; Frederick King, "The Complete Collector," *The Bookman*, January 1913, 510–523; Wesley Towner, *The Elegant Auctioneers* (New York, 1970), 258–280; "Robert Hoe's Great Library," *NYT*, April 2, 1911, 192.

HOFER, Philip (b. March 14, 1898, Cincinnati, Ohio; d. November 9, 1984, Cambridge, Mass.). *Education*: A.B., A.M., Harvard University, 1921, 1929. *Collection Disposition*: Harvard University; New York Public Library.

By 1938, when Hofer accepted a position at the Harvard Library in order to establish a Department of Printing and Graphic Arts, he had already served a distinguished apprenticeship. From 1929 to 1934 he had been curator of the Spencer Collection in the New York Public Library and for the next three years had served as the assistant to Belle da Costa Greene in the Pierpont Morgan Library. During those early years he had focused his personal collecting interests on materials that would illuminate the study of the graphic arts. He acquired items that illustrated the highest achievements of typographers, artists, binders, and calligraphers from earliest times to the twentieth century. While his original emphasis was on European examples, he broadened his scope in the late 1950s and began to acquire manuscripts and printed works from the Middle East and the Orient. According to Harvard bibliographer William A. Jackson, Hofer's collections of illuminated manuscripts and incunabula were small but select. Writing in 1960, Jackson could refer to some 500 choice manuscript items in the Hofer library. While Hofer was interested in these early periods, he gave his more serious attention to the sixteenth and seventeenth centuries. The impressive catalogs of his French and Italian books compiled by Ruth Mortimer attest to his devotion to that era. His own *Baroque Book Illustration* covers the seventeenth century. Never one to limit his collection to merely antiquarian examples, Hofer acquired a wide range of books from the nineteenth and twentieth centuries, showing the work of such artists as Derain, Dufy, Matisse, Picasso, Grosz, and Rouault. While many of his books were models of fine binding and excellent typography, Hofer was more interested in the illustrative matter contained in woodcuts, engravings, and etchings. In addition to books themselves, he acquired woodblocks, type, paper, printing and binding tools, and an impressive gathering of prints, engravings, etchings, and calligraphy samples.

In all cases Hofer's bywords were quality and selectivity. In the book world his catholic tastes and discerning eye were legendary. In 1968 he retired from full-time curatorial duties, having presented his collection to Harvard the previous year. He continued to support the growth of the collection up to the time of his death. In the *London Times*, critic and editor Nicolas Barker wrote, "Hofer created a monument to the art of the book that no other could have conceived."

Bibliography

A. *Baroque Book Illustration* (Cambridge, Mass., 1951); *French 16th Century Books*, compiled by Ruth Mortimer (Cambridge, Mass., 1964); *Italian 16th Century Books*, compiled by Ruth Mortimer (Cambridge, Mass., 1974); "The Graphic Arts Department: An Experiment in Specialization," *HLB*, Spring 1947, 252–253; "The Artist and the Book, 1860–1960," in *The Artist and the Book 1860–1960* (Boston, 1961); "The Early Illustrated Book: Highlights from a Lecture," *QJLC*, April 1978, 77–91; *Eighteenth Century Book Illustration* (Los Angeles, 1956).

B. Nicolas Barker, "Philip Hofer," *London Times*, November 22, 1984, 14; David P. Becker, "Philip Hofer, Scholar," *ABC*, January/February 1985, 6–7; August Heckscher, "Prince of Rat-Packers," *ABC*, January/February 1985, 8–9; Con Howe, "Philip Hofer, A Personal Recollection," *ABC*, January/February 1985, 3–6; William A. Jackson, "Philip Hofer: Book Collector," *BC*, Summer 1960, 151–164; Autumn 1960, 292–300; James E. Walsh, "Notes on the Philip Hofer Reference Collection," *BC*, Summer 1969, 159–169; Peter Wick, "Philip Hofer, Scholar-Collector," *HLB*, July 1968, 301–303.

HOGAN, C. Beecher (b. September 6, 1906 St. Albans, Vt.; d. 1983). *Education*: A.B., M.A., Yale University, 1928, 1933. *Collection Disposition*: Yale University.

During the years he taught English at Yale, Hogan developed several extensive personal book collections. His interests were catholic and included E. A. Robinson, Jane Austin, L. Frank Baum, Robinson Jeffers, and Edgar Rice Burroughs. According to the tribute written by Herman W. Liebert in the *Yale Library Gazette*, Hogan was an "unflagging and idiosyncratic collector" who ranged widely over American and English literature. Hogan's talent for bibliography was demonstrated in a meticulous work on E. A. Robinson. This useful compilation was based almost entirely on materials from Hogan's own library. In his article "If You Must Write a Bibliography" he explained how the Robinson index developed and in the process provided readers of *The Colophon* with an unusually sane and intelligent approach to an arcane field. In a typical gesture of generosity, Hogan gave his various collections to the Yale Library.

Bibliography

A. *Bibliography of E. A. Robinson* (New Haven, 1936); "If You Must Write a Bibliography," *The Colophon*, February 1937, 165–175.

B. Herman W. Liebert, "Charles Beecher Hogan," *YLG*, October 1983, 6–8.

HOGAN, Frank J. (b. January 12, 1877, Brooklyn, N.Y.; d. May 15, 1944, Washington, D.C.). *Education*: LL.B., Georgetown University, 1902. *Collection Disposition*: Library of Congress; Parke-Bernet, January 23, April 24, 1945, April 23 and 24, 1946.

Few lawyers in the 1920s and 1930s could match Hogan's list of distinguished clients or his record of courtroom successes. He represented Andrew W. Mellon, General Electric, and Armour and Company and in his best-known case won acquittal for E. L. Doheny. As a collector, Hogan worked with all the energy and enthusiasm that contributed to his success in the legal profession. Around 1930 he began to acquire solid holdings of contemporary American authors based on the listings provided in Merle Johnson's *High Spots of American Literature*. In this endeavor he entered into a friendly rivalry with Estelle Doheny*, who was herself starting to form an impressive library. Hogan expanded his interests when Millicent Sowerby, bibliographer of the A. S. W. Rosenbach firm, turned his attention to the Elizabethans and to the titles included in the Grolier Club list *One Hundred Books Famous in English Literature* (1902). Accounts of Hogan's buying as set down by Sowerby, David Randall, and Wolf and Fleming indicate his great enthusiasm for association and inscribed copies. He had, for example, Keats' *Poems* (1817) inscribed to William Wordsworth, Upton Sinclair's *The Jungle* inscribed to Mark Twain, and Ellen Terry's *Story of My Life* with copious and savage annotations by George Bernard Shaw. Among the treasured manuscripts in his collection were Longfellow's "The Village Blacksmith" and Burns' "Auld Lang Syne." Hogan was fortunate in his negotiations with Rosenbach and Randall and doubly fortunate to be buying when prices were low. His dozen Shakespeare quartos, from the J. T. Adams sale in London, came to him at remarkably low figures. The famous Earl of Roseberry First Folio, on the other hand, cost him $80,000, a substantial amount in any era.

With his flair for the dramatic, Hogan loved to exhibit his books and talk about them. He was a frequent and favored guest at meetings of the Grolier Club in New York and the Zamorano Club in Los Angeles. His collecting came to an end suddenly when he was stricken with Parkinson's disease. In 1941 he gave the Library of Congress a choice collection of rare children's books, but the bulk of his collection remained intact. After weighing all the options, Hogan decided that the library should be enjoyed by other collectors instead of going to an institution. The books, as he put it, "should be the intimates of others, whose loving hands will fill the place left vacant by my passing." The sales, which took place from January 1945 to April 1946, brought disappointing returns. His First Folio, for example, went for a $30,000 sacrifice, and his splendid copy of Spenser's *Faerie Queene*, with verses in the author's own hand, brought an unbelievably low $6,000. Even the determined loyalty of such old friends as Rosenbach and Randall could not bolster prices. Hogan's approach to collecting may have been impetuous, but he obtained the books he wanted and he enjoyed the process. His library was an appealing and highly personal selection of literary treasures.

Bibliography

A. "Introduction," in *Fifty Famous Novels by English and American Authors 1719–1922* (Washington, D.C., 1935); "Foreword," in *The Romantics: An Exhibition of Books and Autographed Letters from the Collection of Frank J. Hogan* (Los Angeles, 1938).

B. *NCAB* 33, 132–133; Wolf and Fleming, passim; *Grolier 75*, 200–202; Millicent Sowerby, *Rare People and Rare Books* (London, 1967).

HOLDEN, Edwin B. (b. June 8, 1861; d. 1906, New York, N.Y.). *Education*: A.B., Columbia College, 1885. *Collection Disposition*: American Art, April 21, 1910; Anderson, November 9, 1910, January 9, 1912; American Art, April 28, 1920.

Although poor eyesight prevented him from pursuing his chosen profession of architecture, Holden developed a keen eye for prints and rare books. He found complete support for his enthusiasms within the membership of the Grolier Club of New York, an organization he joined in 1888. Since the club had only been organized for four years, Holden found himself on intimate terms with many of the early members: Beverly Chew*, Walter Gilliss, William Loring Andrews*, E. G. Kennedy, and others. This was an active affiliation that Holden continued until his death. Like many of his Grolier colleagues, Holden took particular pleasure in the physical aspects of a well-made book—the binding, the paper, and the quality of the illustrations. In 1895 he took a leading role in the formation of two groups within the Grolier Club: the Club Bindery and the Society of Iconophiles. The purpose of the Club Bindery, with Holden as first president, was to bring to America the same high production standards then known only in Europe. A number of French binders came to America under the auspices of the Grolier Club and set up shop. Although the idealistic goals of the founders were never quite realized, some remarkable work was done. The members of the Society of Iconophiles set out to gather prints and views of New York and to commission new engravings and etchings in order to preserve a graphic record of the cultural heritage of the city. Such artists as Joseph Pennell and Sidney L. Smith contributed to the production of a number of significant volumes.

Holden's personal library consisted of first editions of British and American literature, French illustrated books, fine bindings, and early American printing. He had the second and fourth Shakespeare folios, the first folio of Spenser's *Faerie Queene*, and numerous first editions of Donne, Herrick, and Thackeray. He also owned examples from the Doves, Vale, and Daniel presses, as well as complete runs of volumes issued by the Grolier, Caxton, and Rowfant clubs. Although the Holden print collection was sold shortly after his death, the major portion of the library did not appear on the auction market until 1920. The sale prices were satisfactory, with Rosenbach, Drake, Hill, and Wells competing for the fine bindings and first editions. Holden's place in the history of American book collecting is closely associated with the Grolier Club. Through that organization he promoted high standards in the graphic arts.

Bibliography

B. *Grolier 75*, 111–114; Arthur Holden, "Recollections of the Grolier Club," *Grolier Gazette*, 1977, 58–71; E. A. Thompson, "The Club Bindery," *Book Collector's Packet*, January 1946, 8–9.

HOLDEN, Miriam Y. (b. April 12, 1893, Boston, Mass.; d. January 7, 1977, New York, N.Y.). *Collection Disposition*: Princeton University.

In a brief autobiographical note in *AB Bookman's Weekly*, Holden described her collecting career as accidental. When she moved to New York in 1917 she became interested in the problems of the urban Negro and started to buy books in order to inform herself on the roots of social discrimination. Her reading led her to consideration of discrimination against women. In order to verify the historical record of women's achievements, she began to build a collection of books, periodicals, pamphlets, pictures, clippings, speeches, and cartoons. She did not seek rare books as such, but only items that would serve to document the significant role of women in Western society. The collection included nineteenth-century periodicals, proceedings and papers of women's congresses, tracts issued by women's associations, and early works on birth control and obstetrics. In the fall of 1979 her family presented the archive of some 6,000 items to Princeton, where it was dedicated as the Miriam Y. Holden Collection on the History of Women.

Bibliography

A. *AB*, November 27, 1961, 1967–1969.

B. Jean Aroeste, "The Miriam Holden Collection," *PLC*, Winter 1980, 163–164; Gerda Lerner, "Miriam Holden, in Remembrance and Friendship," *PLC*, Winter 1980, 164–168.

HOLLIDAY, William J. (b. October 30, 1895, Indianapolis, Ind.; d. April 18, 1977, Tucson, Ariz.). *Education*: A.B., Yale University, 1917. *Collection Disposition*: Arizona Historical Society; Yale University; Parke-Bernet, April 20, 1954.

Immediately after graduating from Yale, Holliday began to work for the family steel business in Indianapolis. He built a home in Tucson in 1935 and spent winters there until his death. According to those who knew him best, he was a compulsive collector. He started with stamps, turned to firearms and books, and finally developed a large collection of post-impressionist painting. His book-collecting interests focused on western Americana, and naturally his guide was Henry Wagner's* bibliography *The Plains and the Rockies*. Although he had an outstanding collection of materials relating to the history and development of the Southwest, his shelves included works on all areas of western expansion. He had books and pamphlets on the California gold rush as well as on Mexican history. He owned numerous immigrant's guides, narratives of overland travel, and tales of the early colonizers of the western region. Perhaps the star items in his library were the 1834 journal of William Anderson's six-month trek from Saint Louis to the Rocky Mountains and William Sublette's 1833 notebook on his dealings with the Rocky Mountain Fur Company. These sources were crucial in tracing the history of the development of the West. Holliday also made it his business to own standard state and local histories and biographies. His most active collecting period, from 1935 to 1950, was supported by such notable bookdealers as Glen Dawson of Los Angeles, David Magee in San Francisco, and Edward Eberstadt in New York. Toward the end of that period, he gave some 7,000 volumes of his southwestern lore to the Arizona Historical Society in Tucson. In 1954 Holliday sold the family steel interests, remarried, and placed his library up for sale at auction. He owned a dazzling gathering of western Americana, one of the best to come on the market in many years.

Bibliography

B. David Magee, "The W. J. Holliday Sale of Western Americana," *QNLBCC*, Summer 1954, 60–64; Correspondence file in the Arizona Historical Society (Tucson).

HORNER, Harlan H. (b. May 4, 1878, Moravia, Iowa; d. 1965). *Education*: A.B., University of Illinois, 1901; A.M., State Teachers College at Albany, N.Y., 1915. *Collection Disposition*: University of Illinois.

The year after he graduated from the University of Illinois, Horner accepted a post with the New York Education Commission. He continued that affiliation until 1939, when he retired as associate commissioner of New York State education. As an avocation, Horner collected books and pamphlets about Abraham Lincoln. In addition to the material bearing directly on Lincoln, he gathered biographies of the Civil War cabinet members, Union generals, and the President's political friends and foes. He also bought children's books, foreign-language material, newspaper scrapbooks, and bibliographies. Horner used many of these publications in writing a series of lively articles and pamphlets touching on all phases of Lincoln's life and achievements. In 1951 Horner turned over his collection to the University of Illinois Library, where it has provided the foundation for a Lincoln Room. He continued to add material to the collection up to the time of his death.

Bibliography

B. *Collections Acquired by the University of Illinois Library 1897–1974* (Urbana, Ill., 1974), 23; Leslie Dunlap, *Lincoln Room* (Urbana, Ill., 1953).

HOUDINI, Harry (b. April 16, 1874, Appleton, Wis.; d. October 31, 1926, Detroit, Mich.). *Collection Disposition*: Library of Congress; University of Texas.

Collecting books about magic and spiritualism came naturally to Houdini, who was often identified as the greatest magician and escape artist in the world. In speaking to the members of the Club of Odd Volumes of Boston, he said bibliographic research had been a part of his life from his earliest years. At the age of twenty-four he published a promotional pamphlet entitled *Magic Made Easy* with a short bibliography of his favorite conjuring literature. On tours he visited bookshops, studied in libraries, and talked with magic collectors. In England he met Henry Evanion, a retired magician who had collected handbills, lithographs, and memorabilia for over fifty years. Eventually this collection became part of Houdini's growing archive.

As Houdini's reputation grew in the theatrical world, he was asked to duplicate the acts of the popular spirit mediums. He devoted a great amount of time to a study of spiritualism and in the process gathered a library on the subject. In *A*

Magician Among the Spirits, his exposé of spiritualism, Houdini described his library as the product of thirty years of searching. With an ever-increasing schedule of travel and public appearances, Houdini found he had less and less time to devote to books. During the last years of his life he was assisted in selecting and arranging his materials by Alfred Becks, a librarian who had formerly worked at Harvard. With Becks' help, duplicates were eliminated and essential titles were found and collated. In 1924 Houdini decided to give the magic and spiritualism collection to the Library of Congress. The annual report of the librarian for 1927 said the collection contained over 5,000 books, pamphlets, and journals. A separate collection of playbills, posters, and theater memorabilia went to the University of Texas.

Bibliography

A. *A Magician Among the Spirits* (New York, 1924).

B. *DAB* 5, 248–249; *NCAB* 22, 79; *SCLC*,180; L. N. Beck, "Things Magical in the Collections of the Rare Book Division," *QJLC*, October 1974, 209–234; Milbourne Christopher, *Houdini: The Untold Story* (New York, 1969); *ARLC*, 1927, 29–31.

HOWE, Parkman Dexter (b. September 20, 1889, Brooklyn, N.Y.; d. 1980, Boston, Mass.). *Education*: A.B., Harvard University, 1911. *Collection Disposition*: Harvard University; University of Florida.

In a brief essay published in *The Book Collector*, Howe attributed his original interest in collecting to his father's influence. The elder Howe had been a determined collector and had gathered an impressive library of American history and literature. On his father's death, Howe received as a bequest a number of rarities by the nineteenth-century New England poets and novelists. Chief among these was a selection of first editions of the writings of Whittier, who had been a classmate of Howe's grandfather and a friend of his father. With Whittier as a starting point Howe moved quickly to Longfellow, Holmes, Hawthorne, Emerson, and Thoreau. In all cases he concentrated on "first books" and inscribed association copies. For example, he was able to obtain the copy of *Two Years Before the Mast* that Dana had presented to Dr. George Shattuck, the physician who had advised him to take a sea trip. Also on the Howe shelves was Longfellow's first book, embellished with an inscription to his mother, Thoreau's own copy of *A Week on the Concord and Merrimack Rivers*, and Henry Adams' *Memoirs of Marau Taaroa, Last Queen of Tahiti*, with the queen's penciled corrections in the margins. According to Howe, the decade of the 1930s was a good time to collect, since many valuable books came on the market at reasonable prices. Parts of the Stephen Wakeman* library were still to be found in Boston bookshops, as were volumes from private family libraries, like that of James Russell Lowell. Howe took advantage of this situation and with the help of Boston bookdealer Charles E. Goodspeed and New York dealers David Randall and John S. Van E. Kohn bought some remarkable rarities. Early in his career Howe decided to avoid collecting letters and manuscripts, although later he modified that policy in order to admit at least one manuscript by each of his favorites. In the case of Thoreau, for example, Howe owned the text from which the poet read his Harvard commencement address of 1837.

In many of his collecting ventures Howe found himself in friendly competition with Carroll A. Wilson*. The older collector acted as a mentor, guide, and friend. When Wilson died he bequeathed five of his Whittier rarities to Howe. The choice of specific titles was left entirely to Howe. After Howe obtained most of the nineteenth-century items on his want list he shifted to the earlier periods. According to Goodspeed, when Howe turned to the seventeenth century he became a "high spot" collector. He bought representative first editions by Anne Bradstreet, Cotton Mather, and Noah Webster. These authors furnished an appropriate background for the nineteenth-century figures he already held in such depth.

By the mid–1960s Howe became concerned about the disposition of his books. Although he had given some items to Harvard, he believed another institution might profit more from his New England authors. Harvard, he believed, already had most of what he had. Howe's will left the decision to the family. After considering a number of alternatives, they chose to sell the library intact to the University of Florida. The handsome descriptive catalog of the Howe library issued by the university is a permanent tribute to a sophisticated and enthusiastic collector.

Bibliography

A. *The Parkman Dexter Howe Library*, edited by Sidney Ives (Gainesville, Fla., 1985); "New England Authors," *BC*, Winter 1963, 467–475.

B. George T. Goodspeed, "The Book Collector Afield"; Sidney Ives, "Preface"; and Charles A. Rheault, "The Book Collector at Home," all in *The Parkman Dexter Howe Library*, Part I edited by Sidney Ives (Gainesville, Fla., 1985).

HOWE, William T. H. (b. 1874, Boston, Mass.; d. August 19, 1939, New York, N.Y.). *Education*: A.B., Yale University, 1893. *Collection Disposition*: Sold to Dr. Albert Berg.

In 1931, after serving in almost every capacity from salesman to auditor, Howe was appointed president of the American Book Company. His business connections provided him with a rare opportunity to acquire a large personal library. On trips abroad he formed friendships with Galsworthy, Yeats, and James Stephens and later entertained them at his Kentucky estate. Through these friendships he developed outstanding collections of manuscripts and inscribed first editions. He was also a well-known customer in secondhand-book shops and an active bidder at auction sales. The Henry Van Duzer*, George McCutcheon*, and John Clawson* sales all yielded important items for his shelves. His holdings of nineteenth-century American authors were particularly strong, with full runs of first editions of Whitman, Thoreau, Cooper, and Poe. Although the collection was not as widely known as some others, fellow bibliophiles recognized Howe's eminence. Carroll A. Wilson* spoke of Howe as the greatest collector of American literature of his time, and Richard Curle dedicated *Collecting American First Editions* (1930) to him as "good friend and wise collector." The high points in the Howe library included Poe's *Tamerlane*, Keats' *Endymion* presented to Leigh Hunt, Dickens' reading copies of *David Copperfield* and *Nicholas Nickleby*, and rich manuscript files of Whitman, Clemens, Lamb, and others. On Howe's death the collection came to the attention of Albert A. Berg*, a benefactor of the New York Public Library. Berg moved quickly and secured the entire archive. New York Public Library officers were delighted to acquire one of the most important private collections of American letters ever gathered.

Bibliography

B. Cannon, 237–241; Alfred Goldsmith, "William T. H. Howe: An Appreciation," *PW*, September 16, 1939, 1101–1102; John Gordan, "A Doctor's Benefaction," *PBSA*, 4th Q 1954, 303–314; Frederick M. Hopkins, "The W. T. H. Howe Collection Goes to the New York Public Library," *PW*, September 28, 1940, 362–363.

HUNT, Rachel McMasters Miller (b. June 30, 1882, Turtle Creek, Pa.; d. February 22, 1963, Pittsburgh, Pa.). *Collection Disposition*: Carnegie Institute of Technology.

As a young girl growing up on her grandmother's estate in western Pennsylvania, Hunt spent many hours observing the birds and flowers. She came to know the Latin names for all the species of plants and began to gather books on nature and gardening. At the same time, she became interested in the craft of hand bookbinding. She was attracted to the work of the English master binder T. J. Cobden-Sanderson and studied with one of his pupils in Pittsburgh. When Cobden-Sanderson visited the United States in 1902, he met Hunt, admired her work, and invited her to study with him in London. On her return to Pittsburgh in 1903 she set up her own bindery and produced some ninety handcrafted works for family and friends. This interest in beautiful bindings led her to collect. At first she centered her attention on incunabula and herbals but later included medical botany, early agriculture, colorplate books from the seventeenth through nineteenth centuries, voyages and travels, and even landscape gardening. Added to this was her extensive collection of portraits of botanists, and botanical illustrators accompanied by samples of their manuscripts and letters. In the area of botanical illustration the collection was particularly strong, with 3,000 watercolors, 2,400 prints, and more than 400 black-and-white drawings. The heart of the library consisted of books and manuscripts covering the botanical advances made during the eighteenth century. During this period Linnaeus contributed original research and organization to the field, while explorers were beginning to show concern for plants and animals. The records of these expeditions, which often included detailed renderings of local flora and fauna, became an important part of the Hunt library.

In the 1920s and 1930s Hunt traveled widely and established close connections with bookdealers in Europe and in England. She had particularly good luck in the shops in France and the Netherlands, where botanical rarities were regularly saved for her inspection. The Hunt library was built book by book, without aid of an agent or any massive *en bloc* purchases. According to George H. M. Lawrence, director of the Hunt Library, Hunt made many of the purchases on the basis of her personal examination of secondhand-book catalogs. In the decades following World War II, Hunt was active in behalf of her collecting interests, giving talks, mounting exhibitions, and publishing articles in botanical journals. Many scholarly institutions were interested in the disposition of her library. In 1958 the Hunts initiated talks with the officers of the Carnegie Institute of Technology with regard to the housing of the botanical collections. Three years later the Hunt Library and the Rachel McMasters Miller Hunt Botanical Library were dedicated in an impressive October ceremony. Her collection of some 3,000 botanical books, supplemented by prints, manuscripts, and letters, formed the basis of a separate penthouse research facility. With a generous endowment from the estate, the Hunt Library has extended its scholarly services through publication, symposiums, and exhibitions. At the 1961 dedication, California bookman Lawrence Clark Powell identified Hunt as the "perfect collector," knowledgeable about her books and prudent in provision for their use. It was an appropriate tribute for a great collector.

Bibliography

A. *The Catalogue of Botanical Books in the Collection of Rachel McMasters Miller Hunt*, volume 1, compiled by Jane Quinby (Pittsburgh, 1958); volume 2, compiled by Allan H. Stevenson (Pittsburgh, 1961).

B. George H. M. Lawrence, "Rachel McMasters Miller Hunt 1882–1963," *Huntia*, 1964, 5–15; George H. M. Lawrence, *The Hunt Botanical Library: A Decennial Report* (Pittsburgh, 1970); Lawrence Clark Powell, "Building with Books," in *Dedication Exercises: The Hunt Library* (Pittsburgh, 1961), 4–16.

HUNTINGTON, Henry E. (b. February 27, 1850, Oneonta, N.Y.; d. May 23, 1927, Philadelphia, Pa.). *Collection Disposition*: Henry E. Huntington Library and Art Gallery; Anderson, March 29, November 21, 1916, January 24, February 26, December 10, 1917, February 4, April 24, November 1, 1918, March 6 and 10, 1919, January 28, March 11, 1920, January 8, 1923, December 2, 1924.

By the time he was forty, Huntington had worked successfully in a number of railway management positions in the East under the direction of his uncle Collis Huntington. In 1882 he moved to San Francisco to share in the management of the emerging Southern Pacific Lines. When Collis died in 1900, responsibilities for the entire West Coast rail system, real estate holdings, and shipping lines fell to "H. E.," as Huntington was called. By 1911, with the sale of some of his business interests, Huntington was able to spend more time on philanthropy and collecting.

One of Huntington's earliest book transactions was carried on in 1904 through bookdealer Isaac Mendoza, who supplied him with an assortment of volumes illustrated by Cruikshank as well as a number of Kelmscott Press books. By 1908 Huntington had formed strong affiliations with bookdealers George D. Smith of New York and Charles Sessler of Philadelphia. Through the redoubtable Smith he was able to secure a large number of fine bindings and incunabula from the Henry Poor* sale. In 1911, again working with Smith, he captured the fine American and English literature collection from the sale of the library of Elihu Dwight Church*.

By this time Huntington had fixed the basic goal of his collecting efforts, that of building a library to reflect Anglo-Saxon culture in its broadest sense. His wide-ranging purchases at both the Robert Hoe III* sales in New York and the Henry Huth sales in London went far to further that goal. At the Hoe sale Huntington invested over $1 million and secured some of the world's leading rarities, including a Gutenberg Bible on vellum. Before the sale was concluded, Huntington astounded the book world again with the news of the purchase of the Beverly Chew* library of English literature. In 1915 he added the 20,000-volume Frederick Halsey* library of American and English literature, and from the other side of the Atlantic he secured important portions of the libraries of the Earl of Pembroke and the Duke of Devonshire as well as the Bridgewater House collection formed by Sir Thomas Egerton. In this last transaction Huntington secured the famed "Ellesmere Chaucer," along with rare editions of Marlowe, Spenser, and Ben Jonson. From the Britwell Court library formed by William Henry Miller, he obtained thirteen incunabula and a wide selection of Americana. In the ten years between the Bridgewater House purchase and his death, Huntington continued to buy rarities, with a growing emphasis on incunabula and American historical manuscripts. His acquisition of fifteenth-century imprints from the James Ellsworth* library and from Otto Vollbehr placed the Huntington collection on an equal footing with major libraries of the world. In his search for Americana, Huntington bought the papers of Robert Morris, banker of the Revolutionary War, and those of British General James Abercromby, as well as the Grenville Kane* collection of George Washington letters and manuscripts. These documents were supported by a growing collection of works on the Civil War, the Spanish-American War, Native American culture, westward expansion, and Californiana. The California materials came chiefly from the libraries of Augustin MacDonald and Henry R. Wagner*.

After George Smith died in 1920, A. S. W. Rosenbach* took over most of the Huntington commissions. It was through his efforts that the collector secured the Americana from the library of Wilberforce Eames* and the incunabula of Sir Thomas Phillipps. Considering the frantic pace of Huntington's buying, it is amazing that space in his New York townhouse lasted as long as it did. By 1920 a major move to the San Marino estate seemed the best possible solution. With the arrival of the books, manuscripts, and paintings at the California site, the Henry E. Huntington Library and Art Gallery became recognized as one of the preeminent humanistic research centers in the world. In Huntington's own words, it represented "the reward of all the work I have ever done and the realization of much happiness."

Bibliography

B. *DAB* 5, 414–416; *NCAB* 15, 17–19; Cannon, 302–317; *Grolier 75*, 57–60; Wolf and Fleming, passim; Robert Schad, "Henry Edwards Huntington, the Founder and the Library," *HuLB*, May 1931, 3–32; Robert Schad, "A Quarter Century at the Huntington Library," *QNLBCC*, Fall 1952, 75–80; George Sherburn, "Huntington Library Collections," *HuLB*, May 1931, 33–104; James Thorpe, "The Founder and His Library," *HuLB*, August 1969, 291–308; Louis Wright, *Of Books and Men* (Columbia, S.C., 1976), 64–68.

HURST, John F. (b. August 17, 1834, Salem, Md.; d. May 4, 1903, Washington, D.C.). *Education*: A.B., Dickinson College, 1854. *Collection Disposition*: Bangs, May 19, 1896; Anderson, May 2, November 28, December 12, 1904, March 20, 1905.

After teaching Latin and Greek in New York for two years, Hurst turned to a career in the ministry. He preached in several cities in New Jersey before going abroad for further study. In 1871 he accepted a teaching position at Drew Theological Seminary and two years later was appointed president of that institution. The last twenty years of his life were spent in administrative work as bishop of the Methodist Church. In addition to teaching and preaching, Hurst established a scholarly reputation with a stream of books, articles, and reviews. His *History of the Christian Church*, for example, was considered a masterpiece of facile writing and careful research. In many cases Hurst was able to document his writing from volumes in his personal library. As might be expected, he had an excellent holding of the theological classics, but unexpectedly he owned a superb library of Americana too. His holdings of sixteenth-century Mexican imprints, colonial pamphlets, early German printing in America, and Indian language texts were outstanding. He also had books from George Washington's own library and an extensive collection of books by Cotton and Increase Mather*. His Benjamin Franklin library, perhaps the largest collection of the nineteenth century, held books, pamphlets, broadsides, and letters. Hurst worked closely with secondhand-book dealers and was known to be an avid and intelligent customer. This reputation brought a continuing stream of books, pamphlets, and maps to his already crowded shelves. The situation finally became so critical that he sold some of the secondary items at auction in 1896. The most important portions of his library however were not dispersed until after his death. The Hurst sales were landmark events for buyers of Americana.

Bibliography

B. *DAB* 5, 427; *NCAB* 9, 122; Albert Osborn, *John Fletcher Hurst* (New York, 1905).

174   HYDE, DONALD F.

HYDE, Donald F. (b. April 17, 1909, Chilliocothe, Ohio; d. February 5, 1966,
New York, N.Y.). *Education*: A.B., Ohio State University, 1929; J.D., Harvard
University, 1932. *Collection Disposition*: Four Oaks Farm, Somerville, N.J.

Trained in the law, Hyde combined a highly successful professional practice
with an avid interest in books and collecting. In 1940 he and his wife, Mary,
an equally zealous collector, moved to New York and began to buy in earnest.
With his enthusiasm for the eighteenth century, Hyde concentrated on Samuel
Johnson and his circle. Fortunately Johnson material was at hand. At the second
A. Edward Newton* sale, Hyde was able to purchase a number of significant
manuscripts and letters at bargain prices. He even bought the good doctor's
elaborate silver teapot, an artifact that figured importantly in a post-Newton-sale
celebration. Over the next few years, Hyde employed bookdealers A. S. W.
Rosenbach* in Philadelphia, Gabriel Wells in New York, and William Robinson
in London to further his Johnson quest. In the mid–1940s, he met Ralph H.
Isham*, the man responsible for securing the Boswell papers for Yale. In the
process of working with Isham, Hyde obtained a number of important Johnson
items for his own collection. It was Hyde who provided the financial and legal
help that enabled Isham to straighten out the tangled web of the Boswell papers.
While still involved in the Boswell negotiations, Hyde swept aside the competition,
bought the Robert Adam* library of Johnson materials, and brought the books
and manuscripts to his New Jersey estate, Four Oaks Farm, to join the Newton
and Isham archives already in place. The resulting library of Johnson material
was formidable—one-third of all known Johnson letters, the only known
manuscript page of the *Dictionary*, diaries, second and third drafts of *The Plan*,
and many limited and inscribed editions. Along with all this material Hyde had
notable letters and documents connected with Boswell, Mrs. Thrale, Dr. Dodd,
and others whose lives touched Johnson's. He also had what he called ''a
respectable'' Henry Fielding collection and the largest gathering of Oscar Wilde
books and manuscripts in private hands. In 1960 he started to collect Japanese
manuscripts.

Not satisfied to merely collect, he took an active part in the major book and
bibliographic societies in this country. He served as president of both the Grolier
Club of New York and the Bibliographical Society of America. In 1965 he was
elected to the prestigious Roxborough Club, London's oldest book-collecting
group, the fourth American ever to be so honored. With a deep intellectual
interest in literary source materials, Hyde created a library of research value that
will continue to stimulate scholarship on Johnson and his century.

Bibliography

A. ''The Hyde Collection,'' *BC*, Autumn 1955, 208–216; *Four Oaks Library*, edited
by Gabriel Austin (Somerville, N.J., 1967).

B. Wolf and Fleming, passim; Gabriel Austin, ''Donald Hyde: A Memoir,'' in *Eighteenth Century Studies in Honor of Donald Hyde*, edited by W. H. Bond (New York,
1970), ix-xiii; David Buchanan, *The Treasure of Auchinleck* (New York, 1974); Mary

Hyde, "Remarks" on the Presentation of the Sixth Donald Hyde Award, *PLC*, Spring 1973, 199–204; Lawrence Thompson, "Donald Hyde," *ABC*, March 1966, 10–11; "Donald Frizell Hyde," *PBSA*, 1st Q 1966, 101.

I

IRWIN, Theodore (b. May 25, 1827, Sodus, N.Y.; d. December 25, 1902, Oswego, N.Y.). *Collection Disposition*: Sold to John Pierpont Morgan.

With money from his various banking and railroad interests, Irwin invested in books and prints. He owned a number of distinguished manuscripts and incunabula as well as several monuments of sixteenth-century English literature. His most important manuscript was undoubtedly the "Golden Gospels," an eighth-century vellum folio produced by Pope Leo X as a tribute to King Henry VIII for his defense of the Sacraments. Another outstanding manuscript in the Irwin library was the illuminated "Apocalypse of St. John," with its eighty-five full-page paintings. He owned a Gutenberg Bible and incunabula printed by Jensen, Sweynheym and Pannartz, and Caxton. In 1881 he bought the Edward Asay* library, famous for its many Shakespearean rarities. Eventually he owned the first four folios, many quartos, and a wide range of the literature and history of Shakespeare's day. Not lacking in Americana, he had Eliot's "Indian Bible" and the rare large-paper copy of the 1624 printing of Smith's *History of Virginia*.In 1887 Irwin issued a cataog with descriptions of all his books and prints. Thirteen years later this became a sales list as he disposed of his library to John Pierpont Morgan* for an estimated $200,000. In 1900, when news of the sale was made public, many city dealers were astounded that such a library could have existed in Oswego, New York. Irwin's catalog showed that living in a small city need not handicap a determined and affluent collector.

Bibliography

A. *Catalogue of the Library . . . Belonging to Theodore Irwin* (New York, 1887).

B. *NCAB* 26, 164–165; Ernest Dressel North, "Notes on Rare Books," *The Book Buyer*, June 1900, 387–388.

ISHAM, Ralph H. (b. July 2, 1890, New York, N.Y.; d. June 13, 1955, New York, N.Y.). *Collection Disposition*: Yale University; American Art, January 7, 1927; Sotheby (London), June 16, 1930; American Art—Anderson, May 4, 1933.

The son of a wealthy New York family, Isham traveled abroad widely, attended Cornell and Yale, and did some desultory journalistic work while he was still in his twenties. When he was at Yale he became interested in the eighteenth century, particularly the literary efforts of Samuel Johnson and his biographer James Boswell. Partly by circumstance and partly by design, this interest led to a lifetime in pursuit of the Boswell manuscripts.

As early as 1924 there were rumors that a collection of Boswell papers existed at Malahide Castle outuside Dublin, the residence of Lord Talbot de Malahide, a descendant of Boswell. When Yale professor Chauncey Brewster Tinker* failed to get access to the papers, Isham took over the quest. After a preliminary visit in 1926, he knew that he had come upon a resource of extraordinary scholarly value. He made his first substantial purchase the next year, paying £13,000 for letters and assorted manuscripts, including sixteen leaves of the *Life of Johnson*. Along with the texts, Isham secured publication rights from the Talbots, launching him on a complicated search for an editor and publisher. After heavy investments of his own money, publishing arrangements were finally concluded with Viking in New York and Heinemann in London. In the meantime more manuscripts were discovered at Malahide, and Isham purchased them. All this placed such a severe drain on his finances that he was forced to sell his personal library. Unfortunately, buyers for rare books in 1933 were scarce and the sales, according to the indefatigable collector-writer A. Edward Newton*, were nothing less than a slaughter. In a further money-making venture, Isham sold a number of pages of the *Life of Johnson* to A. S. W. Rosenbach*, but the proceeds barely covered immediate expenses. In 1936 more Boswell papers were found at Fettercairn House, and in 1940 still more turned up at Malahide. Long court battles ensued, with invaluable legal and financial aid coming from New York lawyer and Johnson enthusiast Donald F. Hyde*. From the first the Boswell papers had been of great interest to Yale University. In 1949, with $450,000 secured largely from the Old Dominion Fund and McGraw-Hill, Yale made the purchase. The *Boswell Papers*, privately printed by Isham and edited first by Geoffrey Scott and then by Frederick Pottle, are a unique tribute to Isham's determination and his sophisticated collecting skills.

Bibliography

B. *DAB*, Supp. 5, 349; *Grolier 75*, 233–236; Wolf and Fleming, passim; William H. Bond, "Glimpses of the Colonel," *Harvard Magazine*, April 1976, 51–56; David Buchanan, *The Treasure of Auchinleck: The Story of the Boswell Papers* (New York, 1974); Frederick Pottle, *Pride and Negligence* (New York, 1982); *NYT*, November 8, 1948, 1; Gabriel Austin, *Four Oaks Library*, edited by Gabriel Austin (Somerville, N.J., 1967).

IVES, Brayton (b. August 23, 1840, Farmington, Conn.; d. October 22, 1914, Ossining, N.Y.). *Education*: A.B., Yale University, 1861. *Collection Disposition*: American Art, March 5, 1891, April 6, 1915.

Immediately after graduating from Yale, Ives enlisted in the Union Army. After a series of important assignments, he was commissioned by General Philip Sheridan as a brevet brigadier general. After the war he became active on Wall Street and in 1877 was elected president of the New York Stock Exchange. In his first collecting ventures, Ives was guided by prominent New York bookseller Joseph Sabin. In Sabin's shop at 64 Nassau Street, Ives was able to examine, to his delight, local histories, Indian narratives, accounts of Spanish and French exploration, and sermons of the colonial divines. The introduction to his 1891 sales catalog includes a charming account of his browsing at the Sabin shop. A large part of the Ives collection came directly from the shelves of like-minded collectors. He took advantage of the opportunities offered in the George Brinley*, William Menzies*, and Samuel L. M. Barlow* sales in this country and, more notably, in the Sunderland, Beckford, Syston Park, and Hamilton Palace sales in England. In many cases his interests were represented at these sales by distinguished London auctioneer and bookdealer Bernard Quaritch. As Ives' collecting interests broadened he took more pleasure in adding works that represented first things: early printing, voyages and discovery, first folios, and important first editions of classic works in literature and history. He owned a Gutenberg Bible, first printings from Italy, France, and England, Columbus letters in both Spanish and Latin, and original classical codices. These works, as he remarked in the 1891 catalog, "would hold the esteem of intelligent men and women forever." As for manuscripts, his library included, among many distinguished pieces, the "Pembroke Hours," one of the most beautiful examples of fifteenth-century English illumination ever produced. The area of Americana was also well developed with a copy of Eliot's 1663 translation of the Bible into Algonquin and examples of the works of the major explorers from Vespucius to Champlain. In the category of English literature, Ives began with Caxton and Wynkyn de Worde and ranged through Shakespeare and Shelley, with fine editions throughout. It was a surprise to fellow collectors in 1891 when Ives put substantial portions of his library up for sale at auction. Apparently the timing was wrong, since the gems in the library brought only a fraction of what he had paid. For example, the "Pembroke Hours," for which Ives had given $12,000, went to Robert Hoe III* for a mere $5,900, while the Gutenberg Bible brought only $14,800, less than Ives had paid Hamilton Cole*. The library that had cost Ives $165,000 returned only $124,375. After the sale, Ives continued to collect, but with a major emphasis turned to literary classics by Shelley, Browning, Poe, Hawthorne, Tennyson, Thackeray, Byron, and Dickens. At the 1911 Hoe sale, with the help of New York bookdealer George D. Smith, he bought back some of the items Hoe had previously purchased from him.

After his death the works of the nineteenth-century authors in their fine bindings by Zaehnsdorf and Bedford were placed up for sale at auction but did little better than the first Ives collection. The war in Europe had taken the attention of collectors away from the rare book market. In spite of the poor returns at his sales, Ives is remembered as one of the dominant figures in collecting at the turn of the century, one of the original members of the Grolier Club of New York, and an ardent patron of the book arts.

Bibliography

A. "Introduction," *Catalogue of the Library of Brayton Ives* (New York, 1891).

B. Cannon, 147–150; *Grolier 75*, 27–30; Randolph Adams, *The Case of the Columbus Letter* (New York, 1939); J. B. Thacher, "A Bibliographical Romance," *The Bibliographer*, October 1902, 269–284; Joseph Rosenblum, "The Two Collections of Brayton Ives," *ABC*, September-October 1984, 3–13; Wesley Towner, *The Elegant Auctioneers* (New York, 1970), passim.

J

JEFFERSON, Thomas (b. April 2, 1743, Goochland County, Va.; d. July 4, 1826, Monticello, Va.). *Education*: William and Mary College, 1762. *Collection Disposition*: Library of Congress; Poor Auction House, February 27, 1829; Leavitt, November 5, 1873.

The facts of Jefferson's active life have been recorded in many biographical and critical works. From these texts and his own letters it is clear that his interests in reading and book collecting played an important part in shaping his intellectual development. An early training in the classics gave him a love for Latin and Greek, while later legal studies provided him with an analytical approach to learning. References to the pleasures of reading and the importance of owning a large personal library permeate his extensive correspondence. According to Dumas Malone, his chief biographer, Jefferson's books were acquired for very practical purposes. Simply put, he wanted to have at hand the tools for learning about religion, politics, philosophy, history, science, and the arts. Rare books, fine bindings, and special editions, as such, had no place in his library.

Influenced by his professors at William and Mary College, Jefferson started a personal library of texts and law books while he was still a student. In 1770 this collection was burned in the fire that destroyed the family estate at Shadwell. Undaunted, Jefferson started rebuilding immediately, and by 1773 he could boast some 1,200 volumes, a figure he doubled over the next ten years. His interests were diverse and included history, law, political science, religion, achitecture, and the sciences. Among his greatest pleasures, after he was dispatched as minister to France in 1784, was the opportunity to select books directly from the continental dealers. At last he was able to take advantage of the book riches of the Old World. Years later, in a frequently quoted letter to newspaper editor Samuel Harrison Smith, Jefferson remembered afternoons spent in Paris examining the contents of bookstores. He also had standing orders with dealers in Amsterdam,

Frankfurt, Madrid, and London for books he cound not find in Paris. When Jefferson returned to the United States in 1790, fifteen packing cases of books were included in the cargo. Although the next two decades were filled with political responsibilities, Jefferson continued to add to his library as he could. At the time of his retirement from the presidency, he estimated his collection to be 8,000 volumes. Notable holdings included early colonial newspapers, classics of philosophy and science, tales of exploration and discovery, sets of early laws of Virginia, and the records of the Virginia Company. This was the collection that Jefferson offered to sell to Congress in 1814 after the British burned the original library to the ground. In describing his library, Jefferson emphasized its unique character, saying it had taken fifty years of diligent effort to bring it together. After some heated debate, Congress agreed to the purchase for what seems a remarkably reasonable price: $23,950. As soon as the transaction was completed, Jefferson started to buy books again. Although his financial situation was precarious, he could not live without books, as he pointed out charmingly in a letter to John Adams*. This last collection was intended both as a solace for his old age and a nucleus for the library of the new University of Virginia. Sadly, financial reverses made an auction necessary, and in 1829 the books were dispersed. Jefferson was a true bibliophile, endowed with taste and energy and a consuming belief in the importance of the printed word.

Bibliography

A. *Catalogue of the Library of Thomas Jefferson*, compiled by E. Millicent Sowerby (Washington, D.C., 1952–1959).

B. *DAB* 5, 17–35; *NCAB* 3, 1–5; Cannon, 38–49; Randolph Adams, "Thomas Jefferson, Librarian," in *Three Americanists* (Philadelphia, 1939), 69–96; A. D. Ladenson, "I Cannot Live Without Books," *Wilson Library Bulletin*, April, 1978, 624–631; William Peden, "Some Notes Concerning Thomas Jefferson's Libraries," *William and Mary Quarterly*, 3rd Series, July 1944, 265–272; Charles Sanford, *Thomas Jefferson and His Library* (Hamden, Conn., 1977).

JOHNSON, Eldridge R. (b. February 6, 1867, Wilmington, Del.; d. November 14, 1945, Morristown, N.J.). *Education*: A.Ed., University of Pennsylvania, 1928. *Collection Disposition*: Parke-Bernet, April 3, May 8, October 29, 1946.

As president of the Victor Talking Machine Company, Johnson amassed a sizable fortune. Later, when the Radio Corporation of America bought out his interests, that fortune grew to extraordinary proportions. Johnson was an enthusiastic if somewhat erratic print collector who made occasional side trips into book buying. He purchased many prints and books through A. S. W. Rosenbach*. In 1923 he boosted morale in Rosenbach's shop by buying the four Shakespeare folios that the Philadelphia dealer had just obtained from the James Ellsworth* sale. Five years later he made headlines by buying the original manuscript of Lewis Carroll's *Alice in Wonderland* and two 1865 presentation copies. Johnson paid $149,882.29 for these rarities and immediately became known as the owner of one of the world's most treasured original documents. Although he bought many other Carroll first editions and several decorated fifteenth-century Books of Hours, he was always referred to as the owner of "Alice." When the Johnson library came to auction in 1946, Rosenbach bought back the precious manuscript and through arrangements with the Library of Congress had it returned to its appropriate home in the British Museum Library. Johnson's whirlwind buying career merits attention in any consideration of American book collecting.

Bibliography

B. Wolf and Fleming, passim.

JOLINE, Adrian H. (b. June 30, 1850, Ossining, N.Y.; d. October 15, 1912, New York, N.Y.). *Education*: A.B., Princeton University, 1870; LL.B., Columbia University, 1872. *Collection Disposition*: American Art, December 15, 1914, January 18, February 23, March 22, April 28, May 17, October 19, November 22, 1915, February 23, 1916.

In addition to pursuing a successful career as a corporation lawyer, Joline formed a large library of autographs and books. He specialized in letters and manuscripts from distinguished literary and political figures. For example, he had a complete set of autographs from the signers of the Declaration of Independence, the Presidents and Vice-Presidents of the United States, and the members of the Continental Congress. His literary archive included letters from Poe, Wordsworth, Shelley, Keats, Lamb, and Byron and books autographed by these men. In *Meditations of an Autograph Collector*, Joline described how his autographed books often impressed those who turned "dull, lackluster eyes" on individual letters and manuscript pages. He could always get an enthusiastic response, he said, when he showed visitors his English edition of Poe's *Poems* dedicated by the author to "Miss Elizabeth Barrett, of England" or his books autographed by Lamb. Joline reflected his joy in collecting in a number of pleasant monographs published around the turn of the century. His collections were sold at auction shortly after his death.

Bibliography

A. *Meditations of an Autograph Collector* (New York, 1902); *Diversions of a Book Lover* (New York, 1903); *At the Library Table* (New York, 1910).
B. *DAB* 5, 155–156; *NCAB* 15, 392.

JONES, Herschel V. (b. August 30, 1861, Jefferson, N.Y.; d. May 24, 1928, Minneapolis, Minn.). *Collection Disposition*: Merwin, April 5, 1906; Anderson, December 2, 1918, January 29, March 4, 1919, January 23, 1923; Rosenbach Company, 1939.

From an early age Jones knew he wanted to be a journalist. After working on a hometown paper for a short time, he moved to Minneapolis and took a job as a reporter on the *Journal*. He became an expert on agricultural prices and eventually bought a weekly trade paper called *Commercial West*. With the profits, he and his brother purchased control of the *Minneapolis Journal* in 1908.

Among the terms that might be applied to Jones' style as a book collector, one might choose eclectic, energetic, or even meandering. He was all these and more. Jones probably sold more books than any of his contemporaries. The assorted authors that constituted his first purchases were sold at Merwin's in 1906. For the next ten years he collected a broad spectrum of American and English literature, fifteenth-century printing, fine bindings, and manuscripts. As his enthusiasm for the Elizabethans grew, his interest in the other periods paled. He arranged for a second sale in 1916. Now he was ready to collect in earnest. First came the mighty Shakespeare folios and quartos, the dedication copy of Milton's *Comus*, and the Sweynheym and Pannartz printing of Augustine's *City of God* (1467), followed by first editions of Robert Greene, Caxton's *Chronicle of England*, and other literary jewels. A. Edward Newton*, J. P. Morgan Jr.*, and John L. Clawson* were some of the chief buyers when these books came to the auction block. Once the dust had settled, Jones set out to gather the Elizabethans again, but this time a more select list. He sold these in 1923 for $137,000. With English literature finally out of his system, Jones turned to Americana, a subject that had interested him for some time. Through A. S. W. Rosenbach* he purchased Columbus letters, George Washington's *Journal* of 1754, rare Spanish Southwest titles, travel accounts, and a wide range of colonial tracts. In a period of seven years, John Fleming and Edwin Wolf II estimated that he spent $1 million and brought together an extraordinary library of Americana. This library was described in detail in a handsome catalog entitled *Adventures in Americana* issued just before Jones' death. When the family faced the task of settling the estate, Rosenbach's name was prominent among the possible buyers. In a special arrangement with Carl, the collector's son, Rosenbach bought the entire Americana library for $225,000, a bargain by any standards. The books sold themselves. The Jones library was well known to such avid western collectors as Everitt DeGolyer*, Everett D. Graff*, Thomas W. Streeter*, and Herbert S. Auerbach*, and almost overnight they became Rosenbach customers. Jones was a knowledgeable and irrepressible bookman. His trail included a series of exciting auctions and a magnificent catalog of Americana. The introduction to *Adventures in Americana* described him as imbued with good judgment and courage. If the editors had added ''a spirit of adventure'' they would have captured Jones' essence.

Bibliography

A. *Adventures in Americana 1492–1897, Being a Selection of Books from the Library of Herschel V. Jones* (New York, 1928); *Americana Collection of Herschel V. Jones*, prepared by W. Eames (New York, 1938).

B. Cannon, 218–219, 269–270; *Grolier 75*, 115–117; Wolf and Fleming, passim.

JONES, Matt B. (b. May 15, 1871, Waitsfield, Vt.; d. July 1, 1940, Newton Center, Mass.). *Education*: A.B., Dartmouth College, 1894; LL.B., Harvard University, 1897. *Collection Disposition*: Sold to Goodspeed's Bookshop; Vermont Historical Society; American Antiquarian Society.

After practicing law in Boston, Jones accepted the position of chief counsel for the New England Telephone and Telegraph Company. In 1919 he was made president of that company, serving until his retirement in 1936. By avocation he was an antiquarian and a collector, with a primary interest in Vermont. He was active in the New England Historic Genealogical Society, the American Antiquarian Society, the Massachusetts Historical Society, and the Colonial Society of Massachusetts. In 1908 he published a history of his birthplace, Waitsfield, Vermont, and in 1939 a general state history, *Vermont in the Making 1750–1777*. After he had obtained a complete Vermont library he turned his attention to Americana before 1800. Michael Walsh of Goodspeed's Bookshop in Boston estimated that in a twelve-year period Jones spent $100,000 developing this section of his library. At the time of Jones' death, Walsh was named to advise the heirs on the disposal of the library. With their agreement, he bought the entire contents for Goodspeed's.

Bibliography

B. "Matt B. Jones," *PAAS*, October 1940, 171–174; Michael Walsh, "Adventures in Americana," in *Four Talks to Bibliophiles* (Philadelphia, 1958), 85–86.

K

KALBFLEISCH, Charles H. (b.?—nineteenth century; d.?). *Collection Disposition*: New York Public Library.

Although little is known of Kalbfleisch's background, there is ample reason to believe that he inherited an interest in books from his father. According to Harry Lydenberg, the elder Kalbfleisch was a linguist and an enthusiastic collector of Americana. After his father's death in 1873, Kalbfleisch added to the family library along already established lines. He bought books at the William Menzies* sale of 1876 and was one of the chief buyers at the first and second George Brinley* sales three years later. In several instances Kalbfleisch found himself pitted against the powerful James Lenox*. It must have been an occasion for rejoicing when he was able to beat Lenox's bid and carry off the rare New England travel narratives. The focus of the Kalbfleisch library was on the literature of exploration and travel with representative titles from the hands of such well-known chroniclers as Petrus Apianus and Cortés. As a supplement to his books, Kalbfleisch owned a number of sixteenth-century maps and charts as well as the standard works on the settlement of New England and the South. It is not clear why the library was sent to London in 1898, nor under what circumstances it was returned to New York. Bookdealer J. O. Wright showed the books to Robert Hoe III*, Marshall Lefferts*, and Wilberforce Eames*. All made purchases, with Eames getting a *Bay Psalm Book* (1651) for the New York Public Library. The remainder of the library was purchased by Alexander Maitland, Lenox's nephew, and presented to the New York Public Library.

Bibliography

B. Cannon, 112–113; "Early Books, Mostly Relating to America," *BNYPL*, January 1899, 9–22; Harry Lydenberg, *History of the New York Public Library* (New York, 1923), 186.

KANE, Grenville (b. June 12, 1854, New Rochelle, N.Y.; d. July 17, 1943, Tuxedo Park, N.Y.). *Education*: A.B., Trinity College, 1875; LL.B., Columbia University, 1878. *Collection Disposition*: Princeton University; Parke-Bernet, December 4, 1945.

Although trained as a lawyer, Kane decided to enter banking. He was a world traveler, a yachtsman, and an avid rare book collector. His enthusiasms can be divided into three major categories: manuscripts, incunabula, and Americana. Fortunately the breakup of several older libraries during the period between 1878 and 1930 offered numerous opportunities to enhance his holdings. He bought heavily at the George Brinley*, Robert Hoe III*, and Wilberforce Eames* sales in this country and at the Sir John Thorold (Syston Park) and Henry Huth sales in England. Kane was much more interested in building a historically significant collection than in amassing a great number of titles. He insisted that incunabula be dated and that they be in pristine physical condition. His manuscripts were acquired to match or complement the printed texts. The best known of these was the fifteenth-century *Vitae Duodecim Caesarum* of Suetonius, with its striking miniatures of the Caesars. Kane's 105 incunabula represented the work of Europe's finest printers—Ratdolt, Jenson, Fust and Schoeffer, and de Spira, among others. Because of Kane's meticulous method of selecting examples, his incunabula tell the story of the rapid spread of printing throughout fifteenth-century Europe.

The Americana portion of the library, some 600 items, began with an impressive collection of Ptolemy's atlases, progressed through the narratives of the French and Spanish explorers, and closed with the tracts of the colonial and revolutionary periods. Kane had the standard works on exploration and navigation, including the Rome and Basel versions of the "Columbus Letter," an impressive set of Hulsius' "Voyages," and a long run of de las Casas tracts. For the colonial period, Kane had variant editions of John Smith's *History of Virginia*, tracts on the Arnold-André affair, and a large collection of George Washington letters. The depth of the Americana in the Kane library prompted Grolier Club librarian Ruth Granniss to identify it as the finest collection in private hands. After Kane's death, A.S.W. Rosenbach* was named collection appraiser. When Rosenbach's work was done and the $450,000 pricetag was established, the heirs looked for an institution that would keep the books together. At the urging of librarian Julian Boyd, Princeton University rose to the occasion and bought the entire library. This decision has provided Princeton scholars with one of the strongest Americana collections in the country.

Bibliography

B. *NCAB* 32, 29–30; *Grolier 75*, 71–74; Wolf and Fleming, passim; "Grenville Kane," *PAAS*, October 1943, 127–129; Curt Buhler, "Incunabula of the Grenville Kane Collection," Henry Lydenberg, "Grenville Kane"; Dorothy Miner, "Manuscripts in the Grenville Kane Collection"; and Boies Penrose, "The Grenville Kane Americana," all in *PLC*, "Grenville Kane Memorial Issue," Autumn 1949, 1–48.

KELLER, Carl Tilden (b. August 26, 1872, Fort Kearney, Nebr.; d. May 13, 1955). *Education*: A.B., Harvard University, 1894. *Collection Disposition*: Harvard University.

The Keller collection consisted of nearly all of the editions of Cervantes' *Don Quijote* published before 1900. In addition to full coverage of editions in Spanish, Keller had versions in all the European languages. Keller supported the publication of works in Icelandic, Manchu, and Sanskrit where translations did not exist. A selection of the works in the collection was displayed at the Harvard College Library in 1947 to commemorate the four-hundredth anniversary of Cervantes' birth. At that time Keller's library included 750 variant editions and over 2,000 individual volumes. Although the collection focused on editions of *Don Quijote*, Keller obtained an impressive assortment of commentaries and imitations. In all, the Keller collection has provided a distinguished resource for Harvard's Spanish literary scholars.

Bibliography

A. *Bibliografía Crítica de Editiones de Quijote impressas 1605 hast 1917* (Cambridge, Mass., 1939).

B. William Jackson, "The Carl T. Keller Collection of Don Quijote," *HLB*, Autumn 1947, 306–310.

KERLAN, Irvin (b. September 18, 1912, Saint Cloud, Minn.; d. December 28, 1963, Washington, D.C.). *Education*: B.S., M.S., M.D., University of Minnesota, 1931, 1933, 1934. *Collection Disposition*: University of Minnesota.

Trained as a physician, Kerlan began practicing in rural Minnesota, moved on to Kentucky, and finally established himself in Washington, D.C., as a research investigator in the Food and Drug Administration. For recreation Kerlan turned to book collecting. His first venture, an attempt to gather rare illustrated books, was, he found, too expensive for his modest income. Another interest emerged when a friend gave him a handsome illustrated copy of *Johnny Cottontail*. The text and the illustrations in this children's classic seemed to flow together in a mood of spontaneous gaiety. Kerlan had found the antidote he needed for his professional research activities. He began by buying the early editions of British and American children's classics—John Newbery's publications, hornbooks, and colonial primers—but again he found the cost of building a significant collection beyond his reach. As a result he turned more and more to the work of contemporary children's authors, an area where he soon established a preeminent reputation. He directed his initial efforts toward obtaining the first editions of the books that had received the American Library Association's Newbery and Caldecott awards. By 1949 he was able to document the success of this venture with a detailed bibliography. Although award books always interested him, he began to focus his attention on the working materials of contemporary children's authors and illustrators. This meant the development of a unique archive of manuscripts, proofs, layouts, color separations, and trial drawings, the essential ingredients of children's book publishing in the twentieth century. Over a period of years Kerlan convinced many prominent authors and illustrators to contribute their working papers and drawings to his collection, which he based at the University of Minnesota. For example, Marguerite Henry, author of Newbery winner *King of the Wind* (1948), gave her typescripts, manuscripts, galleys, and preliminary dummies to provide what was a complete history of the making of a children's classic. Prominent illustrators such as Roger Duvoisin and Helen Sewell placed their sketches and finished drawings with Kerlan as contributions to his growing historical archive. Much of the credit for the breadth of the collection can be attributed to Harold Kittleson, of the book department of the Power's Department Store in Minneapolis, as assiduous a gatherer as the doctor himself.

In addition to a demanding professional life and his own buying activities, Kerlan mounted exhibits, loaned books to libraries, spoke to educational groups, and contributed articles and bibliographies to learned journals. In 1949 the first volumes from the Kerlan collection arrived at the University of Minnesota, and for the next fourteen years the shipments arrived regularly. At the university a special room was devoted to the Kerlan collection, and a curator was appointed to manage the ongoing affairs of acquisitions, cataloging, and reference. An ambitious program of awards and publications was launched. Students of children's literature from all over the world have used the collection for their research needs. Kerlan proved that it was possible to set out on a somewhat uncharted collecting path and make a significant contribution.

Bibliography

A. "Collecting Leads On," *AB*, January 5, 1952, 24–25; "Collecting Children's Books," *Private Library*, January 1964, 1–4; "Collecting Contemporary Books for Children," in *Bibliophile in the Nursery* (New York, 1957), 457–467; *Newbery and Caldecott Awards: A Bibliography of First Editions* (Minneapolis, 1949).

B. *NCAB* 52, 534–535; Karen Hoyle, "The Kerlan Collection," *The Children's Literature Newsletter*, Spring-Summer 1978, 13; Karen Nelson, "The Kerlan Collection," *Top of the News*, no. 2, 1968, 181–186; Norine Odland, "The Kerlan Collection of Children's Literature in the University of Minnesota Library," *Elementary English*, November 1967, 749–752; Peggy Sullivan, "A Tale of Washington's Irvin," *Horn Book*, June 1961, 288–289; *A Brief Guide to the Manuscripts, Original Art, and Letters from Authors and Artists in the Kerlan Collection of Children's Literature*(Minneapolis, 1963).

KERN, Jerome (b. January 27, 1885, New York, N.Y.; d. November 22, 1945, New York, N.Y.). *Collection Disposition*: Anderson, November 2, 1927, January 7 and 21, 1929.

In addition to being one of the most important popular composers of the early decades of the twentieth century, Kern was also an avid book collector. Kern always did things in a big way. His shows were extravaganzas, his life-style flamboyant, and his library treasure-laden. At first he was attracted to autographs of composers, but shortly he found himself caught up in the heady domain of rare books and manuscripts. Some of his early buying was influenced by his long association with a songwriting partner, Harry B. Smith*, a notable collector of inscribed "sentimental" copies. Following Smith's lead, Kern began to purchase books and letters that had personal associations with leading literary figures of the eighteenth and nineteenth centuries. His knowledge of editions and values grew under the direction of such sophisticated bookdealers as Quaritch, A.S.W. Rosenbach*, and Gabriel Wells. Soon he became an expert in the niceties of bibliographic points and binding variants. His collections of Dickens, Thackeray, Lamb, Jonson, and Goldsmith were based on the amiable principles of association proclaimed by A. Edward Newton* in *The Amenities of Book Collecting*. Handwritten dedications, like the one from Stevenson to his nurse Cummy in *A Child's Garden of Verses*, were common in the Kern books. He gathered Dickens first issues in parts along with letters, manuscripts, and memorabilia. He had the famous letter from Elizabeth Browning to Edgar Allan Poe commenting on "The Raven" and Shelley's own copy of *Queen Mab* with revisions in the author's hand. The library was spectacular by any standard.

Almost as quickly as Kern entered the rare book world he decided to withdraw. The reasons given for this sudden shift were various, some saying he had grown tired of the responsibility of ownership, others contending that he wanted to invest in other lines. In any case, the Kern sale was heralded as one of the most important events in the history of twentieth-century bookselling. At the Anderson Galleries, under the direction of the ubiquitous Mitchell Kennerley, preparations went forward for *the* event of the 1927 auction season. A well-printed catalog displayed the fruits of Kern's enthusiasms. On the first day of the sale, in what could only be described as a circus atmosphere, prices rose higher and higher. Browning's first book, *The Battle of Marathon*, which Kern had purchased for $1,650, brought a resounding $17,500 from Rosenbach. The manuscript of Conrad's *Victory*, purchased in the John Quinn* sale for $800, brought $4,000, while the *Pickwick Papers*, in parts, bought in 1920 for $3,500, went for $28,000. As the *New York Times* reported, it was "a bull market for rare books and manuscripts." Total receipts came to over $1,700,000, the largest amount ever realized at a book auction up to that time. The collection was attractive, the marketing was handled skillfully, and the mood of the country was extremely optimistic. Furthermore, it was thought to be a mark of distinction to own a book with a Kern plate. Those who wanted that privilege paid the price.

Bibliography

B. *DAB*, Supp. 3, 417–418; *NCAB* 34, 15; Cannon, 213–214; Wolf and Fleming, passim; Robert Benchley, "Do I Hear Twenty Thousand?" *The Bookman*, March 1929, 14–17; David Ewen, *The World of Jerome Kern* (New York, 1960); Michael Freedland, *Jerome Kern* (London, 1978); Wesley Towner, *The Elegant Auctioneers* (New York, 1970), 446–450.

KERR, Lowell (b. January 10, 1901; d. August 12, 1980, New York, N.Y.). *Education*: A.B., University of Michigan, 1923. *Collection Disposition*: University of Michigan.

From 1936 until 1966 Kerr was actively engaged in the production of *The Exporters Encyclopedia* and other affiliated trade publications. His lifelong collecting interest was the nineteenth-century Pre-Raphaelite poet Algernon Charles Swinburne. In addition to books by and about Swinburne, Kerr collected manuscripts, photographs, drawings, and letters, a diverse mixture of the author's best creative efforts. In 1935 the demands of Kerr's business life were such that he decided to give a portion of his library to the University of Michigan. This process culmunated in the presentation of the bulk of the collection in 1966. Few points of Swinburne bibliographic scholarship escaped Kerr's notice. He gathered first and subsequent editions, binding variants, and copies inscribed by Swinburne to his friends. The research value of the collection, however, was in its manuscript holdings, some seventy in the author's own hand. Many of the letters trace Swinburne's relationship with his publishers and critics. The books and manuscripts are cherished at the University of Michigan as one of its important author collections.

Bibliography

B. Correspondence with Mrs. Helen Butz, Department of Rare Books, University of Michigan.

KILGOUR, Bayard L. (b. February 27, 1904, Cincinnati, Ohio; d. July 21, 1984, Cincinnati, Ohio). *Education*: B.S., Harvard University, 1927; *Collection Disposition*: Harvard University.

Kilgour developed two outstanding book collections while he pursued an active business career as President of Cincinnati Bell Telephone. His interest in the eighteenth-century English adventurer and author T. E. Lawrence led him to develop a comprehensive collection of Lawrence's books, letters, and manuscripts. When the materials were turned over to Harvard they were said to have been the finest collection in private hands. Even more important was the Kilgour collection of Russian materials. As an undergraduate he had enjoyed Russian literature and started to build a personal library. He was particularly interested in the poets and novelists of the nineteenth century and began to develop outstanding holdings of the works of such well-known figures as Pushkin and Turgenev. Between 1950 and the time of his death he presented over two thousand choice volumes to the Harvard University Library. During his later years he became interested in early printing and gave Harvard many examples of the work of the first Russian presses. In recognition of this generosity, Harvard appointed him Honorary Curator of the Slavic Collection. Kilgour's intelligent and discriminating taste are amply displayed in the 1959 catalog of his Russian literature collection.

Bibliography

A. *The Kilgour Collection of Russian Literature 1750–1920* (Cambridge, 1959).

B. "Bayard L. Kilgour, Jr. 1904–1984," *Harvard Library Bulletin*, Spring 1984, 192–193.

KREISLER, Fritz (b. February 2, 1875, Vienna, Austria; d. January 29, 1962, New York, N.Y.). *Collection Disposition*: Parke-Bernet, January 27, 1949; Library of Congress.

Known internationally as a violin virtuoso and composer, Kreisler was also an ardent book collector. During his concert travels he accumulated a notable library of illuminated manuscripts, incunabula, and fine bindings. He once estimated that during his professional career he spent over half his personal money on books and manuscripts. Although the Kreisler library was not large, it included samples of the work of most master printers and binders of the fifteenth and sixteenth centuries. Among the distinguished craftsmen represented in his collection were Johann Bamler, Anton Sorg, Anton Koberger, and Peter Schoeffer. In 1949 he disposed of his library, 174 rarities, at auction for the benefit of two New York City charities, the Golden Rule Foundation and Lenox Hill Hospital. In a separate transaction he presented the manuscripts of Brahms' "Concerto for Violin and Orchestra, Opus 77" and Chausson's "Poeme" to the Library of Congress.

Bibliography

B. *CB*, 1944, 358–361; Louis Lochner, *Fritz Kreisler* (New York, 1950), 384–392.

KURRELMEYER, William (b. January 17, 1874, Osnabrück, Ger.; d. 1957, Baltimore, Md.). *Education*: A.B., Ph.D., Johns Hopkins University, 1896, 1899. *Collection Disposition*: Johns Hopkins University.

From 1900 to 1947 Kurrelmeyer served as a faculty member in the German Department at Johns Hopkins University. The personal library he built served to augment the meager holdings of the newly established university. In commenting on Kurrelmeyer's book-buying, William McClain, a teaching colleague, said few could compete with him in knowledge of German books or in tenacity in obtaining them at reasonable prices. One of Kurrelmeyer's early scholarly projects was the editing of the first German Bible. This was a large undertaking and involved the collation of all existing pre-Lutheran texts. Over the early years of the century Kurrelmeyer accumulated an impressive Bible collection, including, for a time, a *Mentelbibel* (1466), named for its Strassburg printer Johann Mentelin. Since Kurrelmeyer did not collect rare books, he sold it to a German scholar who needed the text for his own research. In another line of research, Kurrelmeyer developed a bibliographic and literary interest in a group of publications that came to be known as "Doppeldrucke." These were unauthorized issues of the works of well-known eighteenth-century authors brought out after the original edition had been exhausted. By careful analysis of texts, Kurrelmeyer found that this practice was followed by legitimate publishing firms in the case of Christoph Wieland, Schiller, and other well-known writers of that time. In many cases, the unauthorized texts contained errors and were the source of literary misinterpretation. Again, in order to complete his research, Kurrelmeyer built up a large collection of the variant renderings of the works of these authors. He also collected lexicography, an undertaking that fit with his role as editor of *Modern Language Notes*.

When the Kurrelmeyer collection was presented to Johns Hopkins in 1957 it consisted of 25,000 volumes, with representation of all the major and minor German authors from the seventeenth century to the early twentieth century. Not satisfied with books alone, Kurrelmeyer gathered a collection of over 1,600 manuscript items. A particularly useful archive includes a long series of letters from writers Karl Gutzkow, Friedrich Gerstäcker, and Paul Keyse to their publisher, Hermann Costenoble. These letters provide many insights into the social and literary history of the late nineteenth century. Kurrelmeyer's careful textual work could not have been done without his library. His collection provides continued research potential for scholars at Johns Hopkins.

Bibliography

A. "Bibliography of William Kurrelmeyer," *Modern Language Notes*, May 1953, 291–299.

B. William McClain, "William Kurrelmeyer, German American, 1874–1957," *The Report: A Journal of German-American History*, 1978, 8–18.

L

LADA-MOCARSKI, Valerian (b. 1898; d. June 8, 1971, New York, N.Y.). *Education*: M.A., Columbia University, 1954. *Collection Disposition*: Yale University.

Known as an active personality in the book world, Lada-Mocarski developed three important collections for the Yale Library. These included the printed works of Lenin, early descriptions of and travels in Russia, and materials on the Russian settlement and the administration of Alaska. His *Bibliography of Books on Alaska Published Before 1868* became the standard source for the period. As a result of his knowledge of Slavic materials, Lada-Mocarski was appointed adviser to the Yale Russian Collections. During his tenure he made regular and significant contributions to that section of the library.

Bibliography

A. *Bibliography of Books on Alaska Published Before 1868* (New Haven, 1969); "Modern French Book Art," *Craft Horizons*, January 1964, 36–41.

B. *Who's Who in America*, 1970, 411.

LAMBERT, Samuel W. (b. June 8, 1859, New York, N.Y.; d. February 9, 1942, New York, N.Y.). *Education*: A.B., Ph.B., Yale University, 1880, 1882; M.D., College of Physicians and Surgeons, Columbia University, 1885. *Collection Disposition*: Yale University; New York Academy of Medicine.

As a practicing physician, teacher, and administrator, Lambert was one of the most respected members of the New York medical profession in the early twentieth century. He was described by one biographer as a thorough humanist, an assessment that surely fit a man who was not only a distinguished scientist but also a graceful Latinist and a follower of Izaak Walton. Lambert's two chief avocations were fishing and collecting books about fishing. From an early age Lambert decided to support his enthusiasm for fishing with a book collection devoted to Walton, the patron saint of all fishermen. He gathered all editions of Walton's *Lives* and *The Compleat Angler* as well as the variant editions of the works of Walton's closest friend, Charles Cotton. It was Cotton who contributed a treatise on fly-fishing to the fifth edition of the *Angler*, and it was his verses that appeared in the 1675 edition of *Lives*. When Cotton built a fishing house on the banks of the Dove in 1674, his initials were intertwined with Walton's on a stone over the door. Wood from this fishing house went into the binding of the covers of the 1808 edition, a copy of which was in the Lambert library. The Walton bibliographer, Peter Oliver, commented that nearly all the editions of any importance from the seventeenth century to the middle of the twentieth century could be found in the Lambert collection.

Lambert's professional library was built with the same attention to detail that went into the development of the Walton collection. In one instance Lambert wanted to reproduce some Vesalius woodblock cuts for a new edition of the *Atlas of Anatomy*, but the officers of the University of Munich, who owned the book, were reluctant to help. Lambert's persistence paid off when a search of a basement archive produced the long-lost blocks. During his term as president of the New York Academy of Medicine, Lambert devoted much time to the library. It was largely through his efforts that money was obtained to purchase the notable medical collection of Edward C. Streeter*. Lambert applied the same energy that made him a successful physician to the development of the rare book facilities at the Academy of Medicine and to the formation of a fine Walton library for Yale.

Bibliography

A. *When Mr. Pickwick Went Fishing* (New York, 1924).

B. *NCAB* 37, 281–282; *Grolier* 75, 92–94; Tucker Brooke, "The Lambert-Cotton-Walton Collection," *YLG*, April 1943, 61–65; P. Van Ingen, "Samuel W. Lambert," *Bulletin of the New York Academy of Medicine*, April 1942, 294–296.

LAMBERT, William Harrison (b. March 9, 1842, Reading, Pa.; d. June 1, 1912, Philadelphia, Pa.). *Collection Disposition*: Metropolitan, January 14, February 11 and 25, March 9, April 1, 1914.

As a young man, Lambert served with distinction in the Union Army, rising from private to major in three years. When the war was over he entered the insurance business and became head of the Philadelphia office of New York Mutual Life. He collected books about Abraham Lincoln and books by the English novelist William Makepeace Thackeray. He began his Lincoln collection immediately after the end of the war, stimulated by his own military experiences and a deep admiration for the martyred President. Among the many rarities in his collection were books from Lincoln's own library, letters, playbills from the Ford Theatre, where Lincoln was shot, funeral sermons, and autographed copies of official government proclamations. An extraordinary letter in the Lambert collection recorded Lincoln's proposal of marriage to Mary Owens and her refusal. In addition to books and letters, Lambert also acquired Lincoln's office furniture, his cane, and what was reputed to be a piece of his hair. In 1914, at the Lambert auctions, many of these treasures were secured for the Henry E. Huntington* library by the redoubtable bookdealer George D. Smith.

In forming his Thackeray library, Lambert followed the same pattern he had used with the Lincoln material, adding not only books but also sketches, drawings, and watercolors. Among the 130 Thackeray letters in the Lambert library, the most unusual were those written to Mrs. Brookfield, a series deemed so intimate that they had been omitted from the official published volumes based on John Pierpont Morgan's* holdings. Lambert liked to say that Morgan had the Thackeray letters that everybody had read but that he had the ones no one had read. The collection also included manuscripts, periodical contributions, translations, and Thackeray ephemera of all kinds. Perhaps the greatest of Lambert's treasures was the manuscript of *The Rose and the Ring*, which the collector had obtained directly from Thackeray's daughter Lady Richmond Ritchie. The sale of the Thackeray materials in 1914 was an event of considerable importance, and it attracted not only American dealers but also representatives of the most important London houses as well. The high point of the sale came with the offering of *The Rose and the Ring*. The bidding started at $10,000 and increased rapidly, until Smith drove out the competition with an unbeatable $25,000. Although Lambert was not a wealthy man, he was able to form two outstanding personal collections. His enthusiasm and industry were justified by the high prices dealers paid for his books.

Bibliography

B. *NCAB* 10, 457; Mark Neely, "Fun and Fellowship: The Amenities of Early Lincoln Collecting," *ABC*, November/Dececmber 1983, 2–8; Ernest Dressel North, "Notes on Rare Books," *The Book Buyer*, May 1900, 311–312; "Major W. H. Lambert," *The Booklovers Quarterly*, December 1912, 12–14; "Lincoln Materials," *NYT*, January 4, 1914, Section V, 1.

LAPHAM, Edwin N. (b. 1850; d.?). *Collection Disposition*: Anderson, December 1, 1908.

For a short time during the early part of the twentieth century, Lapham was president of the Merwin-Clayton Book Sales and Auction Company. This appointment ended in 1912, the last year in which the company conducted sales. His personal collection, obtained largely through Chicago bookdealer Walter Hill, featured Browning, Dickens, Keats, Wordsworth, and Coleridge, the classic nineteenth-century British literary giants. He had immaculate copies of Dickens' *Pickwick Papers*, Coleridge's *Sibylline Leaves*, and Rossetti's manuscript translation of Burgess' *Lenore*. His W. S. Landor collection, highlighted by the proof sheets of *Imaginary Conversations*, was described in the sale catalog as "second to none." Many of the volumes in the library displayed the elegant binding styles of Bedford and Sangorski. In the introduction to his sale catalog, Lapham praised Walter Hill's diligence in obtaining fine and "correct" copies. By 1934, when Carter and Pollard published their famous *Enquiry into the Nature of Certain Nineteenth Century Pamphlets*, it turned out that the Lapham library had been larded with forgeries created by the infamous Thomas J. Wise. At the Lapham sale the forgeries, including the 1847 "Reading edition" of Elizabeth Barrett Browning's *Sonnets*, brought the estate a handsome $1,766. Lapham's library was a typical and, as it turned out, somewhat naive gathering of English literary monuments.

Bibliography

B. *NYT*, December 3, 1908, 3.

LEA, Henry Charles (b. September 19, 1825, Philadelphia, Pa.; d. October 24, 1909, Philadelphia, Pa.). *Education*: Private tutors. *Collection Disposition*: University of Pennsylvania.

The stimulation of a highly intellectual home life had a powerful influence on Lea as he grew into manhood. His father was an important Philadelphia publisher, while his mother, daughter of journalist Mathew Carey, had strong literary interests. At the age of twenty Lea had published a number of articles on fossil shells and on classical mythology. In 1843 he joined the family publishing firm and quickly rose to management responsibilities. Although burdened by poor health, Lea managed to produce a prodigious amount of original writing. Beginning in 1847 and lasting until 1858, he was forced to pursue what he called a period of "intellectual leisure," away from the family business. During this time he began to read Froissart and other major chroniclers of medieval history. Since this area of study called for materials not available in the United States, he set out to build his own archive. He sent to France and Germany for a wide range of history and biography. Scholarly copyists combed the major European archives and libraries with instructions to select any and all documents in the area of religious history. Lea was an extraordinary linguist and insisted that the documents be provided in full text and in their original languages.

In 1866 Lea published his first major treatise, *Superstition and Force*, which he followed in 1867 with *An Historical Sketch of the Sacerdotal Celibacy*. These books, with their extensive documentation, established Lea's scholarly reputation. Between 1887 and 1888 he produced his major work, *A History of the Inquisition of the Middle Ages*. Over the next twenty years Lea issued a half-dozen more books and a series of scholarly articles, all focused on religious and intellectual history. In 1878, in answer to a question from an editor, he estimated his personal library to be 15,000 volumes, with very full sections on the inquisition, ecclesiastical courts, celibacy, and witchcraft. The comprehensive nature of his witchcraft library was well illustrated by an incident related by historian W. W. Keen. While Keen was traveling in Italy he sent Lea an antiquarian book catalog offering rare works on witchcraft. Of the eighty titles given, Lea had every one.

Through avid collecting Lea had in some cases nearly exhausted European resources. After his death, Lea's heirs presented the books and manuscripts to the University of Pennsylvania as the "Henry Charles Lea Memorial Library." With its varied riches the Lea collection became a major resource for scholarly research on the history of medieval Christianity.

Bibliography

B. *DAB* 11, 67–69; *NCAB* 23, 117; E. S. Bradley, *Henry Charles Lea* (Philadelphia, 1931); E. P. Cheyney, "The Henry C. Lea Library," *Pennsylvania Library Chronicle*, March 1933, 4–5; "Henry Charles Lea," *PAPS*, 1911, iii–xli.

LEFFERTS, Marshall C. (b. November 28, 1848, New York, N.Y.; d. April 30, 1928, New York, N.Y.). *Collection Disposition*: Bangs, April 21, 1902; Sotheby's (London), June 9, 1902; Anderson, March 14 and 16, 1927; Harvard University.

Throughout most of his professional life, Lefferts was associated with the Celluloid Manufacturing Company of New York. His collecting interests—English and American literature—matched those of contemporaries John H. Wrenn*, Herschel V. Jones*, Winston Hagen*, and Frederic R. Halsey*. In the later years of the nineteenth century, Lefferts concentrated on the works of Pope, with the idea of compiling a definitive bibliography of that literary giant. His interests in this regard were well known to bibliographers and bookdealers in America and in England. Bibliographer Thomas J. Wise occasionally supplied him with notes on Pope rarities, but there is no record that Lefferts bought books from the master of manufactured first editions. By 1910 Lefferts had given up the idea of a bibliography and sold his massive collection to Dodd, Mead & Company in New York. They commissioned Luther Livingston to prepare a handsome catalog and subsequently sold the entire collection to Harvard. Ten years earlier the major portion of the Lefferts library had been sold to bookdealer George Richmond, who promptly divided it into two portions, one for American literature and one for English. Trying for the best possible market, Richmond sold the American books in London and the English books in New York. In both cases the results were disappointing. The American titles took a particularly severe beating at Sotheby's. A mixed sale of the remaining books took place in New York a year before Leffert's death. An active Grolier Club member with interests in American and English letters, Lefferts was a typical affluent collector of the turn of the century.

Bibliography

B. *NCAB* 10, 243; Cannon, 152–154.

LEHMANN, Frederick W. (b. February 28, 1853, Prussia; d. September 12, 1931, Saint Louis, Mo.). *Education*: A.B., Tabor College, 1873. *Collection Disposition*: American Art—Anderson, December 2, 1930.

When Lehmann's library was brought to auction in 1930, collectors expected to see a rich variety of Dickens material. In this they were not disappointed, since Lehmann owned one of the five signed copies of *The Great International Walking Match* and numerous rare broadsides, burlettas, and sketches. The surprise for many was the solid representation of American letters starting with Poe and proceeding through Clemens, Emerson, Harte, and Longfellow. For example, Lehmann had Poe's own copy of volume one of *The Broadway Journal*, a periodical that held several of the author's early contributions. In many cases the works in the Lehmann library represented the first published appearance of notable American authors. In addition to these standard collectable works, Lehmann specialized in such elaborations as extra-illustrated sets, fore-edge paintings, and embroidered bindings. Finally, he had a remarkably full run of the publications of collector-author William Loring Andrews*. Because of the depressed economic situation in the late 1930s, the Lehmann books were sold for bargain prices.

Bibliography

B. Cannon, 235–236; *NYT*, September 13, 1931, 28.

LEITER, Levi Z. (b. November 2, 1834, Leiterberg, Md.; d. June 9, 1904, Washington, D.C.). *Collection Disposition*: American Art—Anderson, February 15, December 15, 1933.

Throughout his life, Leiter was best known as an early partner of Chicago department store tycoon Marshall Field. After he left the Field organization he turned to banking and real estate. Toward the end of the 1880s he retired from most of his business affiliations in order to devote himself to travel, collecting, and civic interests. He was one of the early supporters of the Chicago Historical Society and became the second president of the Art Institute.

As a collector, Leiter concentrated on Americana, much of which he obtained in 1876 at the William Menzies* sale and in 1879 at the George Brinley* sale. He was also a regular customer of bookdealer Joseph Sabin in New York and Bernard Quaritch in London. Starting with the chief works of exploration and discovery, the Leiter library progressed through the colonial and revolutionary periods and stopped at the time of the reconstruction following the Civil War. His collection of Confederate documents and newspapers was said to have been second only to that held in the Library of Congress. Although the Leiter library was not noted for its manuscript holdings, it did contain the David Hartley papers relating to the signing of the Treaty of Ghent. These documents came to Leiter from the Edward Assay* sale and eventually passed into the William L. Clements* library in Ann Arbor, Michigan. The literary holdings in the Leiter library included long runs of first editions of Robert Browning, Dickens, Spenser, and Shakespeare. Quaritch is reported to have identified the Leiter first folio as the only one he had ever seen in the original binding. When an annotated catalog was issued in 1907, bibliophiles had their first close look at the collection. Leiter's Americana was rated then as one of the strongest holdings in the country.

Bibliography

A. *Catalogue of the Books and Manuscripts and Maps Relating Principally to America Collected by Levi Leiter* (Washington, D.C., 1907).

B. *DAB* 6, 157–158, *NCAB* 12, 472; "Levi Zeigler Leiter," in *Chicago and Its Makers* (Chicago, 1929), 735; "Levi Leiter," *Chicago Tribune*, June 10, 1904, 5.

LEMPERLY, Paul (b. 1858, Cleveland, Ohio; d. May 4, 1939, Cleveland, Ohio). *Collection Disposition*: Parke-Bernet, January 4, 1940.

Lemperly grew up in Cleveland, where he followed a career in the wholesale drug business. As a young man he became interested in contemporary English and American fiction. He bought new editions and sent them to the authors for an autograph or inscription. In this way he built up an impressive collection of presentation first editions from Hardy, Crane, Housman, Conrad, and Kipling. Of these personalized copies, none were more precious to Lemperly than his Hardy collection. He owned one of the twenty-five copies of the 1903 edition of *The Dynasts*, as well as a copy of *Wessex Tales* inscribed by Hardy to Robert Browning. Perhaps the choicest item in the entire Hardy group was a copy of the author's tribute to George Moore, *G. M.: A Reminiscence*. Lemperly's copy was mailed to him by Mrs. Hardy just a few days before Hardy's death and included her signed card. Since Lemperly had little money to spend on prescribed rarities, he wisely concentrated on books that came directly from the authors themselves. This kind of collecting produced some remarkable items and, as Lemperly claimed, only cost him postal charges. Occasionally he bought items in the second hand trade, but as more and more collectors moved into the field of contemporary literature he found the prices of first editions beyond his means. For most of his secondhand purchases Lemply did business with Percy Lawler at the Dodd, Mead firm in New York. When Lawler moved to the Rosenbach Company in 1916, Lemperly wrote that although he regretted the dissolution of a friendship with Lawler the prices charged by the Philadelphia firm would be more than he could pay.

Lemperly was one of the small group of bookmen who gathered in Cleveland in 1892 to form the Rowfant Club. The club's name—his suggestion—was used to honor the memory of the splendid "Rowfant" library gathered in England at the turn of the century by Frederick Locker-Lampson. In two anecdotal talks, later printed as *Among My Books* and *Books and I*, Lemperly described the pleasures and pitfalls of gathering what he was pleased to call his "poor man's library." In the course of collecting, Lemperly gathered a large number of autographed bookplates. In 1930 he presented these to the Flora Mather College of Western Reserve University as a memorial to his daughter. Lemperly collected enthusiastically throughout the depression. Seven months after his death the collection of 5,000 volumes was sold at auction. Lemperly is remembered as a thoughtful collector who developed a uniquely satisfying personal library.

Bibliography

A. *Among My Books* (Cleveland, 1929); *Books and I* (Cleveland, 1939).

B. N. L. Lewis, "Foreword," in *Parke-Bernet Catalog*, January 1940; *The Rowfant Club Yearbook 1938*, 34–35.

LENOX, James (b. August 19, 1800, New York, N.Y.; d. February 17, 1880, New York, N.Y.). *Education*: A.B., Columbia University, 1918. *Collection Disposition*: New York Public Library.

As the only son of a wealthy New York merchant, Lenox had both the time and the means to indulge his collecting tastes. He was engaged in the family business until 1845, when he retired to devote himself entirely to books and travel. About that time he began what was to be a long and close business relationship with London bookdealer Henry Stevens. Stevens, who had been raised in New England, was just starting his business, and the Lenox orders were exactly the kind of support he needed. When Lenox began to buy from Stevens his orders were largely for Bibles and Testaments, but gradually they came to include incunabula, Americana, and the Elizabethan authors. In 1847 Stevens helped Lenox obtain a Gutenberg Bible at the Wilkes sale in London for £500, a price the local papers referred to as "mad." The years 1854 and 1855 were particularly busy for Lenox, with Stevens sending him more than $50,000 worth of books. In 1854 Lenox spent £860 for Bibles and Testaments at the William Pickering sale, then the following year added Shakespeare folios and quartos at the James Baker sale. In many of his business negotiations with Stevens, Lenox found himself in direct competition with John Carter Brown* of Providence, Rhode Island. A particularly dramatic confrontation came about with the sale of the 1493 Basle "Columbus Letter." Brown secured the book with a bid of 25 guineas over the Lenox bid of £25, but that hardly settled the matter. Lenox threatened Stevens with legal action based on what he claimed were his "rights." Finally Brown sent the book to Lenox in a rare gesture of bibliographic peacemaking. During the Civil War, Lenox cut back his buying considerably, with instructions to Stevens to send only Vespucci, DeBry, Hulsius, or the "Jesuit Relations." It was during this period that he refused a number of very important Americana items proposed to him by the indefatigable Stevens, among them the large paper copy of Smith's *Virginia* and John Brereton's *A Brief and True Relation . . . of the Voyage of Gosnold's to New England in 1602*. Lenox came to regret many of these decisions and at the George Brinley* sale bought the items he had once turned down.

During the late 1860s Lenox became more and more concerned about the proper maintenance of his library. The organization and listing of the flood of books, pamphlets, and maps had simply gotten out of hand. After a period of negotiation he offered the entire library to the City of New York to be administered under a board of trustees. In March 1870 Lenox gave the city his property between Seventieth and Seventy-first Streets on Fifth Avenue and funds for a building. The collection was moved in and the building was opened for public inspection seven years later. Harry Lydenberg has supplied an excellent description of the library's services and continued growth in the nineteenth century. In 1895 the Lenox Library was incorporated with the Astor and Tilden collections to form what became the basis for the New York Public Library system. According to those who knew him best—and they were few—Lenox was an energetic and intelligent collector but a somewhat dour and unapproachable individual. His library was one of the finest ever brought together in nineteenth-century America.

Bibliography

A. "Curiosities of American Literature: Smith's General History of Virginia, New England, and the Summer Islands," *Norton's Literary Register* 1854 (signed "L").

B. *DAB* 6, 172–173; *NCAB* 3, 413; Cannon, 72–77; Wilberforce Eames, "The Lenox Library and Its Founder," *Library Journal*, May 1899, 199–201; Harry Lydenberg, *History of the New York Public Library* (New York, 1923), 95–128; Wyman Parker, *Henry Stevens of Vermont* (Amsterdam, The Netherlands, 1963), passim; Henry Stevens, *Recollections of Mr. James Lenox* (London, 1886), passim.

LEWIS, John Frederick (b. September 10, 1860, Philadelphia, Pa.; d. December 24, 1932, Philadelphia, Pa.). *Collection Disposition*: Free Library of Philadelphia; Moore Institute.

An admiralty lawyer by profession, Lewis found an enriching avocation in the study of history and art. In connection with these enthusiasms he made regular and significant contributions to all the important cultural institutions in his native city of Philadelphia. At various times he was president of the Mercantile Library, the Academy of Music, and the Academy of Fine Arts, and over a long period of years he was a trustee of the Free Library. By the time he was thirty-five he had turned his general interest in the graphic arts into a serious study of the art of engraving. As a matter of course he acquired a large personal reference library. As his enthusiasm for the print arts deepened, he began to buy examples of man's earliest "written" records—the tablets and cylinders of the Sumerians and Babylonians. Over a period of thirty years he secured more than 2,800 examples of cuneiform writing, a remarkable record of the daily lives of ancient peoples. Moving to the medieval period, Lewis began to collect illuminated European manuscripts and incunabula. At the Robert Hoe III* sale in 1911 he was able to acquire four Books of Hours, a thirteenth-century French psalter, and a sixteenth-century German missal. Along with these complete manuscripts, Lewis wisely gathered single leaves and fragments to fill out the record of the work of the medieval scribes. Ellen Shaffer estimated that this collection of fragments numbered over 2,000 items and ranged in time from the sixth to the eighteenth century. As the prices of Western manuscripts rose alarmingly in the 1920s, Lewis began to focus on the less popular but equally beautiful products of Eastern cultures. As a connoisseur of the graphic arts, he was attracted to the splendid calligraphy and subtle coloring of Eastern works. Soon that collection rivaled his European holdings. As an avid collector, Lewis delighted in sharing his treasures with others. Friends were frequently treated to "lectures" on block books or the history of engraving accompanied by a display of splendid illustrative examples taken from his own well-stocked shelves.

When Lewis died he willed his treasures to Philadelphia institutions—books on costume design went to the Moore Institute and the collections of European and Oriental manuscripts to the Free Library. These gifts have enriched the lives of countless students and casual visitors. They furnish a striking record of the development of communication through the graphic arts.

Bibliography

A. *A Descriptive Catalogue of the John Frederick Lewis Collection of European Manuscripts in the Free Library of Philadelphia*, compiled by Edwin Wolf II (Philadelphia, 1937); *Oriental Manuscripts of the John Frederick Lewis Collection in the Free Library of Philadelphia*, compiled by M. A. Simsar (Philadelphia, 1937).

B. Ellen Shaffer, "John Frederick Lewis 1860–1932," *Manuscripts*, Winter 1963, 42–46.

LEWIS, Wilmarth S. (b. November 14, 1895, Alameda, Calif.; d. October 7, 1979, Hartford, Conn.). *Education*: A.B., Yale University, 1920. *Collection Disposition*: Yale University.

From his earliest years Lewis was intensely interested in literature and collecting. At Yale he was attracted to one of the most magnetic members of the English faculty, the great teacher and collector Chauncey Brewster Tinker*. Under Tinker's guidance he contributed stories and essays to the "Yale Lit" and eventually became a member of the editorial board. Following World War I he worked on the staff of Yale University Press and then briefly for the Alfred A. Knopf publishing firm in New York. Because he had a comfortable inheritance he was able to devote most of his time to collecting and writing. While he was still a student, Lewis started to collect John Masefield's works and had the good fortune to meet the poet on an Atlantic crossing. Masefield introduced Lewis to Horace Walpole's letters and suggested that the Gothic novelist might make an interesting figure for further study. In addition to writing *The Castle of Otranto* and several historical works, Walpole chronicled contemporary events in a flood of gossipy letters exchanged with a wide variety of notable correspondents.He had also established his own press at his Strawberry Hill estate and printed limited editions of authors that pleased him. It was this man, a keen observer of the eighteenth century, who attracted Lewis' interest and held it for more than fifty years. Through Elkin Mathews and other British dealers, Lewis began to receive letters and association volumes. As the trickle mounted to a flood, Lewis found himself a self-made Walpole authority. In 1926 he published *A Selection of the Letters of Horace Walpole* and six years later *Horace Walpole's Fugitive Verses*.

Lewis saw it as his goal not only to collect Walpole letters and books but also to recreate a part of the eighteenth century by securing the works of Walpole's contemporaries, publications of the Strawberry Hill Press, portraits, drawings, architectural designs, and even artifacts of the Walpole household such as tableware, lamps, and jewelry. He had the ability to cajole treasures out of the hands of the owners with an awesome combination of finesse and determination. The twelfth Earl of Waldegrave, writing to his wife, admitted that although he could not remember all the details, he guessed he had promised certain manuscripts to Lewis and he supposed he would hand them over in due course. Ten years later the earl's servants packed ten zinc-lined cases of precious Walpoliana into the Lewis Daimler and marked them for delivery to Farmington, Connecticut. Sometimes the chase became overpowering. At the 1939 John Spoor* sale, where a fine Walpole collection was offered, Lewis became so excited when it appeared that he might lose a copy of *Mysterious Mother* that he overbid his own agent and became the buyer and underbuyer at one stroke. So avid was Lewis' search and so far-flung was his net that by 1940 Farmington had become synonymous in the book trade with Walpole. The British Museum simply gave up any competitive efforts and referred all questions and price quotations to Lewis. Eventually Lewis was able to claim ownership of 2,500 original Walpole letters, a little over one-third of all the novelist had written. Beyond this he had copies of 3,500 more that he had seen in libraries or in private collections. In 1933 Lewis convinced the trustees of Yale to sponsor a new edition of Walpole's letters based on his own collection. When the first two volumes came out in 1937, reviewers heralded the event as a major scholarly achievement. The meticulous standards of the subsequent volumes of the Yale Edition of *Horace Walpole's Correspondence* justified this initial enthusiasm and have provided scholars with a unique literary and historical commentary.

Out of the "Walpole factory," as it has been called, have come biographies, bibliographies, and memoirs that have turned a new light not only on Walpole but on the entire literary world of the eighteenth century. From the beginning Lewis had built the collection for Yale. It was to complement other great holdings, such as the Boswell-Johnson archive built so lovingly by Tinker and Ralph H. Isham*. The Walpole library stands today in Farmington as an oasis for grateful Walpole scholars. Lewis often said, "Collecting preserves interest in living." His own busy and productive life was the best possible testimony to the truth of that statement.

Bibliography

A. *Collector's Progress* (New York, 1951); *One Man's Education* (New York, 1967); *Horace Walpole's Library*, Sandars Lecture (Cambridge, Mass., 1958); "Horace Walpole, Collector," *PMHS*, 1980, 45–51.

B. *CB*, 1973, 254–257; John Carter, "Wilmarth S. Lewis," *The Times Literary Supplement*, May 9, 1952; Geoffrey Hellman, "The Steward of Strawberry Hill," *The New Yorker*, August 6, 1949, 26–37, and August 13, 31–41; Herman W. Liebert, "Wilmarth Sheldon Lewis," *YLG*, April 1980, 198–200; Mary Maldegrave, "Lefty Wilmarth Sheldon Lewis," *BC*, Summer 1980, 239–250.

LEWISOHN, Adolph (b. May 27, 1849, Hamburg, Ger.; d. August 17, 1938, Saranac Lake, N.Y.). *Collection Disposition*: City College of New York; Parke-Bernet, January 25, February 28, 1940.

Born in Germany, Lewisohn came to the United States at the age of eighteen to work with his brothers in the feather and wool business. The family expanded their interests rapidly and soon had holdings in copper mines throughout the West. In addition to his business interests, Lewisohn devoted a great deal of time to various charities and social causes. He was one of the chief advocates for prison reform and wrote a number of articles on the subject for the popular press. As he grew in stature in the business world, he began to surround himself with the traditional hallmarks of the wealthy—large estates, a retinue of servants and an impressive art and book collection. The library included a second Shakespearean folio, a number of sixteenth-century Persian manuscripts, sumptuous editions of Dryden, and elaborate examples of the binder's art. A variety of inscribed dedication copies rounded out this elaborate collection. It was said that the Lewisohn art gallery and library at 881 Fifth Avenue was one of the showplaces of New York in the 1920s. Always interested in German culture, Lewisohn donated a large personal library of German literary texts to the City College in 1910. The German ambassador and Andrew Carnegie were on hand to accept the gift. The remainder of the library was disposed of at auction in 1940, but low prices were the order of the times.

Bibliography

A. *Catalogue of the Private Library of Mr. Adolph Lewisohn* (New York, 1923).

B. DAB, Supp. 2, 383; *NCAB* 33, 428; "Adolph Lewisohn," *City College Alumnus*, 1938, 89; *NYT*, August 18, 1938, 1.

LILLY, Josiah K. (b. September 25, 1893, Indianapolis, Ind.; d. May 5, 1966, Indianapolis, Ind.). *Education*: Pharmacy Certificate, University of Michigan, 1914. *Collection Disposition*: Indiana University.

Throughout his life, Lilly was associated with the family pharmaceutical business in Indiana. In 1948 he rose to president of the company and served in that capacity until 1953, when he moved on to the board of trustees. According to his librarian, David Randall, he began to collect books around 1926 with the purchase of an undistinguished Clemens title from the James Drake firm in New York. In 1929 the book-collecting fuse had smoldered enough to encourage him to participate in the Jerome Kern* sale. As Randall tells it, the New York potentates monopolized the first several sales with unprecedented high bids, but Lilly came into his own with some important purchases in the later sessions. He liked to work from such lists as the Grolier Club's *One Hundred Books Famous in English Literature* and Asa Don Dickinson's *One Thousand Best Books*. This was not for any lack of imagination but rather as a way to organize his buying. After he had American and English literature under good control, he turned to continental authors. His runs of Dostoyevsky, Turgenev, Heine, and Montaigne, for example, were complete and in fine physical condition. In all his buying, Lilly insisted on original bindings or, at the very least, appropriate contemporary binding. His collection of continental literature with uncut pages and in original wrappers was unique. Turning to his home state, Lilly gathered large collections of the books and manuscripts of Hoosier authors Lew Wallace and James Whitcomb Riley. The Riley collection was particularly distinguished because it combined Lilly's interest in local writing with his affection for juvenile literature.

In an important bibliographic venture, Lilly supplied the capital for Jacob Blanck to work on his massive *Bibliography of American Literature*. This reference source continues to serve as a monument to Lilly's generosity. Since he had business interests in scientific fields, it is not surprising that Lilly began to gather influential medical and scientific texts. He obtained first editions of Copernicus, Kepler, Bacon, Darwin, Freud, Osler, and Vesalius as well as twentieth-century accounts of the discovery of atomic power. But in *Dukedom Large Enough*, Randall argued that Lilly's first loves were the classic fifteenth-century travel accounts of America, the narratives of colonial settlement, and the tracts of the Revolutionary War. He also owned many works dealing with western expansion, the Civil War, and reconstruction. His copy of General Order No. 9, the Confederate surrender document, was autographed by Robert E. Lee. As for literature, Lilly concentrated on writers he liked. His Poe holdings were particularly distinguished and included *Tamerlane and Other Poems* (1827), a presentation copy of *Tales* (1845), manuscripts of *Eulalie* and *To Margaret*, and the love letters Poe sent to Sarah Whitman.

Lilly was a resourceful and energetic collector, working for the fun of the chase more than from any wish for personal prestige. After the Kern sale he seldom bought at auction, preferring to work with individual dealers like Randall, whom he trusted. In 1956 the books and manuscripts were turned over to Indiana University, and four years later the handsome Lilly Library building was dedicated on the Bloomington campus. By this time Lilly had turned away from books to concentrate on other collecting areas. Although he continued to support the library, he bought no books after 1956. By this time, however, he had formed one of the most remarkable scholarly private libraries ever assembled in the United States.

Bibliography

B. *NCAB* 53, 237; David Randall, "Josiah Kirby Lilly," *BC*, Autumn 1957, 263–277; David Randall, "J. K. Lilly, America's Quiet Collector," *AB*, June 27, 1966; David Randall, *Dukedom Large Enough* (New York, 1969), 339–354.

LITTELL, C. G. (b. 1882, Cairo, Ill.; d. October 2, 1958, Oconomowoc, Wis.). *Education*: A.B., Indiana University, 1901. *Collection Disposition*: Parke-Bernet, February 5, March 5, November 5, 1945.

When Littell started working for the R. R. Donnelley Printing Company in 1903 he was a bill collector. His ability led to promotions and eventually to appointment as president of the company. While he served as executive officer, Donnelley was issuing the "Lakeside Classics," a series of carefully edited reprints of important historical studies. Littell had always been interested in American history and now with improved financial means began to form a library of rare Americana. Since his chief interest was the opening of the West, he used the Henry R. Wagner* *Plains and the Rockies* and the Herschel V. Jones* *Adventures in Americana* as buying guides. Although he favored books on California, Colorado, and the Northwest, he also bought books and maps dealing with the American Revolution, the Southern colonies, the Civil War, and railroading. His collection of pamphlets on the California gold rush was particularly notable. Littell retired from Donnelley in 1945 and disposed of his library in a series of three New York sales that same year.

Bibliography

B. "President C. G. Littell Retires," *The Lakeside News*, May 1945, 132–134; "C. G. Littell," *Chicago Tribune*, October 3, 1958.

LIVERMORE, George (b. July 10, 1809, Cambridge, Mass.; d. August 30, 1865, Cambridge, Mass.). *Collection Disposition*: Libbie, November 20, 1894.

Although he never completed a university degree, Livermore was recognized as a serious and capable historian. He wrote in a variety of fields, but always with a historical perspective. His book defending the use of Negro troops in the Civil War, for example, rested its argument on the success of the same practice in the Revolutionary War. At heart, Livermore was an antiquarian. He owned the 1642 New Testament, a Michael Servetus Bible of 1542, and rare editions of Eliot's "Indian Bible." He had several manuscript Bibles and a rare *Biblia Pauperum* block book believed to be dated around 1440. Along with several other Cambridge collectors, he gave money for the purchase of 300 volumes from George Washington's library in order to keep them from going to the British Museum. He was an active member of several antiquarian societies and a close friend of such notable collectors as Edward A. Crowninshield* and Charles Deane*. After Livermore's death his books were held in trust at Harvard but after a number of years were sold at auction at Libbie's in Boston.

Bibliography

B. *DAB* 11, 305–306; *NCAB* 6, 139; Farnham, 62–67; Charles Deane, "Memoir of George Livermore," *PMHS*, 1869, 415–468.

LOCKE, Robinson (b. March 15, 1856, Plymouth, Ohio; d. April 20, 1920, Toledo, Ohio). *Collection Disposition*: New York Public Library; American Art Association, November 9, 1921.

The son of a famous journalist who used the pen name "Petroleum V. Nasby," Locke quite naturally turned to newspaper work. He assumed editorship of the *Toledo Blade* in 1888 and continued in that office until his death. As a collector,

Locke gathered early printing, Americana, first editions of American and English authors, theater memorabilia, and private press books. The theater material was perhaps the most significant. Beginning in 1890, when he was writing the drama criticism for the *Blade*, Locke started to save programs, clippings, playbills, photographs, and critical reviews bearing on performances and performers. ''The Archive,'' as he liked to call it, expanded into a multitude of files and cabinets, and the hobby soon became serious. Friends and family added more to the growing collection. In a memoir written in 1925, Mrs. Locke described how she once gave her husband 1,700 programs and playbills from early Boston performances, while her mother added an assortment of theater posters.

Around 1918 Locke wisely decided to give the theater and cinema collection to the New York Public Library in order to ensure its preservation. In all, the gift came to some 800 bound volumes and 2,500 portfolios of clippings, pictures, and programs. The biographical portion of the archive was particularly strong, with contemporary records on Mary Pickford, Douglas Fairbanks, Charlie Chaplin, and other stage and screen notables. When the remainder of the library was brought to auction in 1921, the chief buyers were Gabriel Wells, Charles Sessler, and Ernest Dawson. Books illustrated by George Cruikshank sold between $15 and $25, while books with Bewick's engravings went for $10 more. Locke is chiefly remembered for his contribution to the New York Public Library.

Bibliography

B. *NCAB* 13, 165; John Harrison, *The Man Who Made Nasby* (Durham, N.C., 1969), passim; ''The Robinson Locke Dramatic Collection,'' *BNYPL*, May 1925, 307–322.

LOCKWOOD, Thomas (b. February 7, 1873, Buffalo, N.Y.; d. August 19, 1947, Buffalo, N.Y.). *Education*: A.B., Yale University, 1895; LL.B., Cornell University, 1897. *Collection Disposition*: University of Buffalo.

Successful in several careers—politics, banking, and law—Lockwood was a well-known civic figure in his home city of Buffalo in the early twentieth century. His urge to collect began at Yale and continued unabated for more than forty years. In a memorial volume published at the time of the opening of the Lockwood Library Building at Buffalo, he paid tribute to the assistance of George D. Smith, A.S.W. Rosenbach*, Mitchell Kennerley, and Barnet Beyer, four knowledgeable bookdealers who, he said, had guided his collecting activities. Lockwood was chiefly interested in American and English literature but sometimes extended those boundaries to include fine printing, autographs, and selected titles in history and philosophy. The distinctive portion of the library lay in its finely bound first editions of English literature. Perhaps most notable among these were the volumes of Shakespeare, Milton, and Spenser. Lockwood owned the first four folios, as well as the first issue of the first edition of Books I, II, and III of the *Faerie Queen* (1590) and the 1667 edition with the first state of the title page of *Paradise Lost*. Many of his books were bound in the sumptuous styles of leading British craftsmen of the nineteenth century. Shelley's *Prometheus Unbound* (1820), for example, was done in blue levant morocco from the workshop of Thomas Cobden-Sanderson. Other rarities displayed the expertise of Rivière and Bedford. The selection of American first editions, while not as imposing as the English array, offered a number of outstanding items. His nineteenth-century section was complete, with Emerson, Melville, Longfellow, Thoreau, and Whitman all in pristine first editions. The Hawthorne firsts were particularly impressive, beginning with *Fanshawe* (1828) and proceeding to *Doctor Grimshawe's Secret* (1882), the latter represented in a splendid uncut copy. Manuscripts were not plentiful in Lockwood's collection, but they were distinguished. He held, for example, a series of Robert Lewis Stevenson's letters to his mother and father covering a period of over twenty-five years.

Although Lockwood was not a bibliographer, he appreciated the beauty of a finely printed page and enjoyed the sense of association in an autographed presentation copy. In 1935 he gave his books to the University of Buffalo library with a certain sense of nostalgia. Each book was special, as he told a reporter, and each brought back memories of the years of searching and the excitement of the unexpected finds. All of them, he said, were "old friends."

Bibliography

A. *A Selection of Books and Manuscripts in the Lockwood Memorial Library of the University of Buffalo*, with an "Appreciation" by Thomas B. Lockwood (New York, 1935).

B. "Thomas B. Lockwood, Donor of Library, Dies at 74," *Buffalo Evening Post*, August 19, 1947.

LOGAN, James (b. October 20, 1674, Lurgan, Ireland; d. October 31, 1751, Germantown, Pa.). *Collection Disposition*: Free Library of Philadelphia.

After coming to America in 1699 as secretary to William Penn, Logan became an important colonial officer. He was at once a politician, fur trader, land speculator, judge, and self-taught scholar. In his youth Logan had been exposed to an intensive classical education by his father, a learned clergyman. In order to understand science and languages better Logan began to collect books. By the time he was twenty he had 700 or 800 volumes, an amazing gathering for someone of his age. Within the next five years, however, he had to sell his books in order to raise money for a business venture. When that failed he accepted Penn's invitation to travel to America.

Of all the early American bibliophiles, Logan was the most avid. At the time of his death his library held some 3,000 volumes, with particular strengths in the classics, science, history, and linguistics. The task of forming such a library in colonial America was formidable, but as revealed in Edwin Wolf's *Library of James Logan of Philadelphia*, Logan possessed the required energy and determination. He sought out intellectuals wherever he could and entered into lengthy exchanges with them on book lore and other scholarly topics. He carried on such correspondence with Governor Robert Hunter of New York, Dr.

Cadwallader Colden, Johann Fabricius, Benjamin Franklin, and Swedish botanist Carl Linnaeus. In recognition of Logan's studies on the pollination of corn, Linnaeus named a shrub *Logania* in his honor. While the Quaker politician might have been considered merely attentive in his correspondence with other scholars, he was assiduous in his contacts with bookdealers. His letters to London agents John Whiston, Josiah Martin, Thomas Osborn, and William Innys reveal a cantankerous and thoroughly meticulous bibliophile in search of accuracy and economy. He quibbled about prices, excoriated "sham editions," criticized binders, and waspishly withdrew his business when his standards failed to be met. On trips to London he prowled the bookshops and left long lists of desiderata in the hands of dealers and librarians.

In 1730 Logan moved from the city to his newly built country estate of "Stenton" near Germantown and began the most active period of his book-buying career. In addition to his official responsibilities, he was at this time pursuing an active journalistic career, issuing scientific studies relating to his botanical and mathematical interests and providing translations of the classics. His work on Cicero's *Cato Major*, printed by Franklin in 1744, was considered excellent. Throughout the 1730s Logan's book-buying never slackened, nor did his acerbity toward dealers who he believed were out to cheat him. In February 1740 he suffered a stroke and as a result slackened his buying somewhat. In any case, it was a good time to examine the library that he had accumulated over the past forty years and to think about its eventual disposition. In a letter written in 1742 Logan revealed to bookdealer Josiah Martin that he planned to leave his Latin, Greek, Oriental, and scientific books to the city of Philadelphia for "the public good." Once that decision was made, he turned again to active buying, as if to make sure the gift would be worthwhile. At about the same time, Logan decided to produce some form of organized catalog. In 1743 and 1744, with the help of his scholarly son-in-law, Logan prepared a detailed annotated listing of the major portion of the library. The only thing lacking was a proper library building. During the last years of his life Logan put an enormous amount of effort and thought into the design of an ideal structure to hold his collection. Because of legal complications, the building was not completed during his lifetime, but nine years after his death, in 1760, the Logan Library was opened to the public. By 1792, with a desire to make the books more available, the heirs asked the Free Library of Philadelphia to take custodianship of the library, a request the city was quick to affirm. The finest private library of colonial times was thus provided a permanent and appropriate home.

Bibliography

B. *DAB* 11, 360–362; *NCAB* 2, 278–279; Cannon, 27–37; Marie Corey, "Three Early Philadelphia Book Collectors," *ABC*, November/December 1981, 2–13; Frederick Tolles, *James Logan and the Culture of Provincial America* (Boston, 1957); Edwin Wolf II, *James Logan 1674–1751, Bookman Extraordinary: An Exhibition of Books and Manuscripts* . . . (Philadelphia, 1971); Edwin Wolf II, *The Library of James Logan of Philadelphia 1674–1751* (Philadelphia, 1974).

LORING, Rosamond Bowditch (b. May 2, 1889, Boston, Mass.; d. September 17, 1950, Boston, Mass.). *Collection Disposition*: Harvard University.

While learning the techniques of craft bookbinding, Loring became more and more interested in decorated book papers. She found it difficult to buy good quality papers, however, and impossible to locate adequate collections of samples for comparative examination. In order to cope with these barriers, she began to make her own papers and to collect examples of the best work of other craftsmen. Since no bibliographies existed to indicate the presence of decorated papers, Loring simply had to work her way through the shelves of secondhand-book shops item by item. The papers she wanted were as likely to be found in a copy of Benjamin Franklin's *Cato Major* as in a French children's book or a Lutheran hymnal. Over the years she formed what the renowned printer and historian Dard Hunter called "the most comprehensive and intelligently gathered collection of its kind in America." She secured examples of hand- and machine-made marbled papers from all over the world, adding, as time and opportunity allowed, paste papers, woodblock prints, and European gilt papers. The entire collection was presented to Harvard University, where it forms an integral and valued part of the Graphic Arts Collection in the Houghton Library.

Bibliography

A. *Marbled Papers* (Boston, 1933); *Decorated Book Papers*, 2nd edition (Cambridge, Mass., 1952).

B. Dard Hunter, "Rosamond Loring's Place in the Study and Making of Decorated Papers," and Walter Muir Whitehill, "Rosamond Bowditch Loring," both in *Decorated Book Papers*, 2nd edition (Cambridge, Mass., 1952).

LOWELL, Amy (b. February 9, 1874, Brookline, Mass.; d. May 12, 1925, Brookline, Mass.). *Collection Disposition*: Harvard University.

In 1902 Lowell decided to concentrate her talents on writing poetry and devoted the next ten years to study and travel as preparation for that career. Her literary reputation was founded on a series of volumes of Imagist poetry and prose criticism that began to appear in 1912. According to the Foster Damon biography, she began to collect books at the age of six with *Rollo Learning to Read*. From that beginning she amassed a literary library of 12,000 volumes. Her energy and decisiveness in book collecting were characteristic of her general approach to life. She did not hesitate to take the field with vigor against even the most prestigious competition when she wanted a certain volume or manuscript. Such was the case when A.S.W. Rosenbach* found himself her agent in the quest for a highly desirable copy of Keats' *Lamia* (1820) inscribed to Fanny Brawne. The book was from the Henry Buxton Forman collection and was scheduled for sale in New York in early 1920. Lowell told Rosenbach to get it at any price, even if the amount would keep her out of the book market for years. When the bidding was over, Lowell had her Keats for $4,050, a price she considered eminently just. The precious *Lamia* was only one of the jewels in her extensive Keats collection. Over the years Lowell gathered a remarkable number of early editions and manuscripts, including such dazzling items as the original holograph of "The Eve of St. Agnes." All this material she put to use in the development of her Keats biography. Far from limiting her business to the Rosenbach firm, Lowell was a good customer of Charles Goodspeed in Boston, Gabriel Wells in New York, and Quaritch in London. In addition to Keats holdings, her library included inscribed and rare works of Hardy, Austin, Brontë, and Ben Jonson, among other figures of the eighteenth and nineteenth centuries. In many cases her collecting tastes ran parallel to those of the bibliophilic writer A. Edward Newton*, and this bond supplied the basis for a pleasant exchange of letters and a firm literary friendship.

According to Lowell's will, her entire library was to go to the trustees of Harvard University and in the event that they turned it down to the Boston Public Library. The trustees happily accepted the terms of the will, which included a large bequest and funds for an Amy Lowell Poetry Room. The Poetry Room remains, and the collection is one of the treasures of the Houghton Library.

Bibliography

B. *DAB* 6, 453–455; *NCAB* 19, 407–408; Fleming and Wolf, passim; F. C. Flint, "Amy Lowell," in *American Writers*, volume 2 (New York, 1974), 511–533; S. Foster Damon, *Amy Lowell* (Boston, 1935); Maxwell Luria, "Miss Lowell and Mr. Newton: The Record of a Literary Friendship," *HLB*, January 1981, 5–34.

M

MACKALL, Leonard L. (b. January 29, 1879, Baltimore, Md.; d. May 19, 1937, Fredericksburg, Va.). *Education*: A.B., Johns Hopkins University, 1900. *Collection Disposition*: Johns Hopkins University; New York Academy of Medicine; William Welch Medical Library of Johns Hopkins; Grolier Club; Savannah Public Library; Georgia Historical Society; Yale University.

While Mackall was an undergraduate at Johns Hopkins he developed scholarly interests in both German literature and medical history. The first interest led to the second. When the great medical historian Sir William Osler needed biographical background on an obscure eighteenth-century German physiognomist, Mackall was able to help because he knew the person in question to have been a correspondent of Goethe. From then on, Mackall and Osler were bibliographic friends. Mackall edited the historian's notable Yale lectures and assisted with much of the final work on *Bibliotheca Osleriana* (1929). Mackall himself became deeply interested in the bibliographic problems connected with the publications of the eighteenth-century theologian and surgeon Michael Servetus. This led him to form what was called the greatest Servetus library in the world, a collection he willed to the Medical Library at Johns Hopkins. Mackall's Goethe scholarship was even more impressive than his work on Servetus. During a six-year stay in Germany he produced a number of articles and books based on Goethe's correspondence. In order to do this research, Mackall built up an extensive personal library on German literature. When he returned from Germany his reputation as a bibliographer was such that he was appointed librarian at the famous Wymberley DeRenne* library. He served in that position from 1916 to 1919, completing a thorough three-volume catalog of the collection. During this period he became active in the Bibliographical Society of America, the Grolier Club, and the American Antiquarian Society. When the editors of the *New York Herald Tribune* began to look for a knowledgeable person to write a new column on book collecting, Mackall was the obvious choice. The column, "Talks for Bibliophiles," begun in 1924, gave Mackall a chance to air his lively views on collectors, values, and auctions. He was forthright in his condemnation of what he called "fad prices" built up to take advantage of unwary private collectors. He was equally emphatic in his belief that books should be placed where they would be most appreciated and used. He provided the best possible example of this philosophy by his own generous giving. Although some of his books went to institutions, many went to individual collectors. One story described how he sent a rare first edition of Edward Gibbon's *Decline and Fall* as a gift to a complete stranger, Professor John Bury of Cambridge University, because he knew Bury to be the world's leading Gibbon scholar. The Grolier Club and the New York Academy of Medicine also benefited from his generosity, as did many other society and public libraries. The bulk of his library, some 10,000 volumes of Germanic studies, and the bibliographic materials were willed to Johns Hopkins. During the last year of his life he was elected to the presidency of both the Georgia Historical Society and the Bibliographical Society of America, fitting tributes to one who contributed so fully to the art and science of bibliography.

Bibliography

A. "Sir William Osler," *PBSA*, 1st Q 1920, 20–32; "Servetus Notes," in *Contributions to Medical and Biological Research*, dedicated to Sir William Osler (New York, 1919), 767–777; "Six Books," *Bulletin of Johns Hopkins Hospital*, January 1930, 83–90. "Talks for Bibliophiles," *New York Herald Tribune*, September 21, 1924 to 1937.

B. John Fulton, "Humanism in Bibliography: an Appreciation of Leonard Mackall," *Special Libraries*, October 1937, 279–283; Archibald Malloch, "Death of Mr. Leonard Mackall," *Bulletin of the New York Academy of Medicine*, July 1937; Lawrence C. Wroth, "Leonard Mackall," *New York Herald Tribune Books*, May 30, 1937, 13; "The Mackall Library," in Johns Hopkins University Library, *Ex Libris*, November 1937; "In Memoriam," *Georgia Historical Quarterly*, March 1938, 32–40.

MACKENZIE, William (b. July 30, 1758, Philadelphia, Pa.; d. July 23, 1828, Philadelphia, Pa.). *Collection Disposition*: Library Company of Philadelphia; Loganian Library of Philadelphia.

Although Mackenzie was known as a leading colonial merchant, few details of his early life are available. Reports indicate that he came into a considerable inheritance while still a young man and was able to retire at the age of thirty. For a young merchant in the unsophisticated territory of Pennsylvania, he had an extraordinary taste for rare and beautiful books. As Marie Corey has stated, he seems to have been the first American to take an interest in collecting rare books as such. He must have had extensive business relationships with European bookdealers, but unlike James Logan* and Isaac Norris*, who kept detailed records, no evidence of his transactions is available. From published catalogs we know he bought incunabula, French literature, and Americana. Among early printers represented in his library were Anton Koberger, Sweynheym and Pannartz, Nicolas Jenson, and William Caxton. These were not odd volumes but often represented the finest examples of the printer's craft. Mackenzie had a fondness for French books, and his library featured the works of such fifteenth-century craftsman printers as Guillaume Le Roy and Antoine Verard. Instead of acquiring the traditional austere theological and philosophical tracts favored by other colonial collectors, Mackenzie favored the finely made showpieces. Far from restricting himself to incunabula, he bought numerous eighteenth-century color-plate books, Dibdin's bibliographical contributions, and the works of the contemporary English literary stylists. Nor was Americana forgotten. The records of the library show numerous pamphlets from the revolutionary period, many of them from the collections of William Byrd* and Benjamin Franklin. On Mackenzie's death the books were divided between the Library Company of Philadelphia and the Loganian Library, thus furnishing both Philadelphia institutions with unique and distinguished holdings.

Bibliography

A. *Catalogue of the Loganian Library*, volume 2 (Philadelphia, 1829); *Catalogue of the Library Company*, volume 2, Eighth Supplement (Philadelphia, 1829).

B. *DAB* 6, 97–98; Marie Corey, "Three Early Philadelphia Book Collectors," *ABC*, November-December 1981, 8–9; Edwin Wolf II, "American Book Collectors Before 1800," *Gazette of the Grolier Club*, 1971, 23–24.

MACLURE, William (b. 1763, Ayr, Scotland; d. March 23, 1840, San Angel, Mexico). *Collection Disposition*: Academy of Natural Sciences of Philadelphia, transferred to Historical Society of Pennsylvania then to University of Pennsylvania; American Geological Society.

After considerable success in the American mercantile trade, Maclure gave up his Scottish citizenship and adopted the United States as his home. In 1803 President Jefferson recognized his abilities in international affairs by appointing him to a commission directed to settle American claims incurred against France in the naval war of 1798–1799. Maclure was able to combine official duties with travel in connection with his avocational interest in geology. As a self-taught scientist he gathered samples of rock throughout France, Germany, and the low countries. At the same time, he began to collect books and pamphlets on the natural sciences and on European culture. Back in the United States, he continued his geologic investigations and published the results with the newly formed Academy of Natural Sciences at Philadelphia. Over the next few years he traveled widely, adding to his growing library at every opportunity. He was a reformer and imbued with the philosophy of the worth of the common man as expressed in the writing of Rousseau and his followers. He set out to build a comprehensive library of this elusive literature. In the decade between 1810 and 1820, Parisian bookdealers still had the broadsides, pamphlets, and newspapers from the Time of Terror. Maclure accumulated over 25,000 separate items, a great archive on the revolutionary period. It was the kind of collection that any large library would have been proud to own. From Maclure's point of view, the Academy of Natural

Sciences, to which he had just been elected president, seemed the ideal repository. The European books would provide a certain amount of prestige for the new institution, and incidentally, the materials would be convenient for Maclure's own use. By 1819 most of the "European Library" had been transferred to the Academy.

Ever restless in his pursuit of reform, Maclure and a few other learned Philadelphians joined Robert Owen in establishing the New Harmony, Indiana, community in 1826. Maclure started several schools on the model developed by J. H. Pestalozzi, as well as a Workingman's Institute and a community library. Three years later, when the New Harmony experiment began to lose its bright promise, Maclure moved to Mexico and shortly thereafter ordered his library transferred to the Academy of Natural Sciences in Philadelphia. While his generosity was chiefly directed to the Academy, other gifts went to the American Geological Society and the American Philosophical Association. Maclure's major collection, the French revolutionary materials, had a somewhat checkered history. In 1861 the Historical Society of Pennsylvania bought the entire set of volumes from the Academy for the modest amount of $500. They languished in the Historical Society rooms until 1949, when the University of Pennsylvania Library agreed to take them on and to provide a much needed index. This task was finally completed in 1966 with the issue of the *Catalogue of the Maclure Collection*. In an introductory essay the editor raised a question about the formation of the collection, casting doubt on Maclure as the original owner and proposing instead the name of a French journalist, Marc Antoine Jullien de Paris. It was certainly Maclure, however, who owned the collection, brought it to the United States, and established it in a safe and scholarly setting. He is to be remembered as a significant figure in nineteenth-century book collecting.

Bibliography

A. *The Catalogue of the Maclure Collection of French Revolutionary Materials* (Philadelphia, 1966).

B. John Jensen, "Seven Volumes from the Maclure Collection: A Catalogue," *Pennsylvania Library Chronicle*, Spring 1960, 83–102; John Jensen and James Hardy, "Maclure Collection Serials," *Pennsylvania Library Chronicle*, Winter 1963, 30–42; John Jensen, "Collector and Collection: A Note," in *The Catalogue of the Maclure Collection of French Revolutionary Materials* (Philadelphia, 1966), xvii–xxiii; S. G. Morton, *A Memoir of William Maclure* (Philadelphia, 1841).

MAIER, Frank (b.?—nineteenth century; d.?) *Collection Disposition*: Anderson, October 21, 1902; November 16, 22, and 30, 1909.

Along with his friends William H. Arnold* and Jacob C. Chamberlain*, Maier was deeply interested in American literature. His collection was somewhat more diverse than theirs, however, since in addition to the standard fare of Emerson, Lowell, and Holmes, he included the more popular Thomas Bailey Aldrich, Eugene Field, and Bret Harte. In the case of Aldrich, for example, he had first editions, presentation copies, and letters from the author to his publisher. At the heart of the Maier library was a small but rich Poe collection. Of particular interest was a presentation copy of *Al Aaraaf, Tamerlane, and Minor Poems* (1829) with a publication date changed by hand to read "1820." Chamberlain claimed that Poe himself made the change, but this was never proven. Stephen H. Wakeman* paid $2,903 for this Poe rarity at the Maier sale in 1909. If that figure shocked the conservative members of the book world, the $3,800 paid by John Pierpont Morgan* for *Murders in the Rue Morgue* (1845) must have sent them into an apoplectic state. It was, as the *New York Times* reported in a November 25, 1909, headline, the highest price ever paid for a single American printed work and just the kind of triumph Morgan loved. Another unique feature of the Maier collection was the inclusion of journal publications. In the case of Lowell, Holmes, Emerson, and others, the sale catalog correctly identified journals as containing "rare first appearances" of specific poems and essays. For those who wanted to form a "complete" collection of a specific author, this raised a new and troublesome dimension. Maier is remembered as a prominent and pioneering collector of American literature.

Bibliography

B. Cannon, 178–179; "News for Bibliophiles," *The Nation*, November 11, 1909, 455; November 18, 1909, 482–483; December 2, 1909, 536; "Maier Sale," *NYT*, November 25, 1909, 1.

MASON, William Smith (b. December 8, 1866, Lake County, Ill.; d. January 11, 1961, Evanston, Ill.). *Education*: A.B., Yale University, 1888. *Collection Disposition*: Pomona College; Yale University.

With the profits from a real estate fortune amassed at the turn of the century, Mason collected Americana in the form of books, maps, and manuscripts. Many of the rarities in the collection dealt with the early exploration and settlement of the West Coast. His copy of *Estracto de Noticias del Puerto de Monterey* (1770), for example, was a prime document in California history and thought to be one of the two copies in American libraries. A special portion of Mason's library was devoted to books and pamphlets on the "Days of '49," that period of history when California ceased to be a part of Mexico. In 1915 Mason gave his entire collection of books, maps, and documents relating to the history of California and the West to the Pomona College Library. The initial gift was backed by an annual grant of $500 for the purchase of additional items of California interest.

Mason was also an avid collector of materials by and about Benjamin Franklin. In 1935, when the Franklin collection was presented to Yale, the university librarian, Andrew Keogh, called it the single most significant gift ever made to that institution. The importance of the collection was its unity and scope. It included not only Franklin's own books, manuscripts, and letters but also those of his contemporaries. In this one collection, historians had available a unique index to the social and political events of eighteenth-century America, France, and England. The library included 11,000 books, 850 pamphlets, 400 broadsides, and more than 1,300 periodical volumes. Among the great rarities are a complete run of the six numbers of the *General Magazine and Historical Chronicle* (1741), fourteen of the "bagatelles" printed at Franklin's private press at Passy, and a variety of pamplets on the American Revolution. There is a nearly complete collection of the issues of *Poor Richard's Almanac,* the *Pocket Almanacs,* and more than 140 English editions of the *Autobiography.* The letters and manuscripts are of great scholarly interest and have served as the principal source for the Yale edition of *The Papers of Benjamin Franklin* started in 1959. Mason was no mere accumulator of prescribed rare books but a shrewd, self-taught expert. He knew the Franklin literature and he used his knowledge to develop a well-balanced collection of books and documents. Thanks to his efforts, Yale stands at the top of the list of institutions able to support Franklin research.

Bibliography

B. *NCAB* 50, 260; Dorothy Bridgwater, "The Mason-Franklin Collection," *YLG,* July 1940, 16–19; George Eddy, "A Ramble Through the Mason-Franklin Collection," *YLG,* April 1936, 65–90; Victor Marriott, "The Mason Collection," *Pomona Quarterly Magazine,* January 1915, 59–63.

MASSEY, Linton R. (b. January 27, 1900, Marietta, Ga.; d. November 9, 1974, Charlottesville, Va.). *Education*: A.B., University of Pennsylvania, 1922. *Collection Disposition*: University of Virginia.

Born in Georgia, Massey became one of America's most important collectors of Southern literature. After a successful business career he retired to his estate in Keswick, Virginia, where he could pursue his hobby of book collecting. In the 1920s Massey wrote short stories for *The Smart Set* and became interested in other young creative writers of the time. In that connection he began to collect the works of Aldous Huxley, Sinclair Lewis, Sherwood Anderson, and a number of other rising talents. By 1930 his interest in creative writing led him to William Faulkner. Over the years his Faulkner collection became a consuming passion. Massey bought manuscripts, first editions, letters, clippings, memorabilia, and works of criticism in all languages. For over thirty-five years he bought from almost all the dealers in modern literature in the United States and Europe. His longest and closest affiliation was with Mrs. Louis Henry Cohn of the New York House of Books. Through her he kept track of all new works about Faulkner as well as older editions that appeared at auctions. Massey met Faulkner for the first time in 1957 and the two established an immediate and warm friendship. This led to the formation of the Faulkner Foundation and eventually to the deposit of Faulkner's manuscripts and papers at the University of Virginia Library. The Massey collection was deposited in the Rare Book Room of the university in 1959 and established Virginia as *the* institution to consult for Faulkner research materials. During the same year Massey mounted a large book and manuscript exhibition in the library which he and Faulkner entitled "Man Working 1919–1962." Ten years later a handsome catalog of the entire Massey collection was printed at the University Press. Throughout his lifetime Massey continued to add to the collection and by bequest provided for its continued growth. In addition to collecting, Massey was active in a wide circle of bibliographic societies. He is properly remembered as "The Faulkner Collector."

Bibliography

A. *"Man Working," 1919–1962, William Faulkner: A Catalogue of the William Faulkner Collections at the University of Virginia* (Charlottesville, Va., 1968).

B. Fredson Bowers, "Linton Reynolds Massey," in *Chapter and Verse—3*, Report to the Associates of the University of Virginia Library (Charlottesville, Va., 1975), 5–8; Joan St. C. Crane, "A Memorial to Linton Massey: William Faulkner's 'Marionettes,' " in *Chapter and Verse—3* (Charlottesville, Va., 1975), 9–10; John Cook Wyllie, "Introduction," in *"Man Working," 1919–1962, William Faulkner: A Catalogue* (Charlottesville, Va., 1968), xv; Correspondence with Joan St. C. Crane, Curator of American Literature, University of Virginia Library, August 1982.

MATHER family: Richard (b. 1596, London, Eng.; d. April 22, 1669, Windsor, Conn.). **Increase** (b. June 21, 1639, Dorchester, Mass.; d. August 23, 1723, Boston, Mass.). *Education*: A.B., Harvard College, 1656; M.A., Trinity University, Dublin, 1658). **Cotton** (b. February 12, 1662, Boston, Mass.; d. February 13, 1727, Boston, Mass.). *Education*: A.B., Harvard College, 1678. *Collection Disposition*: American Antiquarian Society; Massachusetts Historical Society.

The Mather library was by many accounts the largest and finest collection of its time in America. Its growth took place over a period of 100 years and involved four generations of the Mather family. Richard, the first member of the Mather family to settle in America, brought books with him when he arrived in 1635, but nothing specific is known about his library. It is likely that it included the usual treatises on religion and philosophy commonly owned by ministers of that day. He is remembered as one of the three men selected to translate the psalms from Hebrew, a task that resulted in publication of the *Bay Psalm Book* (1640). When he died his books were divided among his sons, with Increase, the youngest, receiving a small portion of the whole. On this base Increase built a large library, a virtual necessity in view of his offices as pastor of the important North Church of Boston and president of Harvard University. When fire gutted the Mather home in 1676, Increase reported in his diary that only 100 volumes were damaged out of several thousand in the library. Subsequent diary entries reveal Increase's frustration at the time required to dry out the books and build new shelves.

When Increase died in 1723, his eldest son, Cotton, inherited the largest portion of the library, with small allotments going to the other children. Long before this time, Cotton had been active in building the collection for use in connection with his writing and clerical responsibilities. It was Cotton who brought the library to its full maturity of 7,000 to 8,000 volumes. He was a man of wide learning, an accomplished linguist, and a prolific author. The library was his workshop. John Duston, an English bookdealer who visited in Boston in 1686, referred to the Mather library as "the glory of New England and of all America." The history of the great Mather library after Cotton's death is somewhat clouded. Although a property inventory drawn in 1728 made no mention of books, it seems clear that many of them went to Cotton's oldest son, Samuel, then to his heirs, and eventually to the Massachusetts Historical Society and the American Antiquarian Society. A list published in the 1910 *Proceedings* of the Antiquarian Society provides the best index of the Mather holdings. One is impressed with the scholarly nature of the library, made up of tracts, books of psalms, Bibles, and histories. The Mather library was an important working tool for its owners and an unequaled representation of the colonial intellectual vigor.

Bibliography

B. *DAB* 6, 386–395; *NCAB* 4, 232; 6, 412; 5, 143; Granniss, 301–302; Julius H. Tuttle, "The Libraries of the Mathers," *PAAS*, 1910, 269–356.

MAYFIELD, John S. (b. December 3, 1904, Meridan, Tex.; d. April 26, 1983, Bethesda, Md.). *Education*: B.A., University of Texas, 1930; M.A., Southern Methodist University, 1932. *Collection Disposition*: Syracuse University; Georgetown University.

By the time Mayfield entered the University of Texas he was already a confirmed collector. He started with bird's eggs at age ten, progressed to cigar bands, moved on to stamps, and finally came to books. At the University of Texas he came under the influence of good teachers, observed with interest the exhibitions in the library, and began to collect works by Byron. This collection consisted of books, letters, manuscripts, binding variants, and critical materials. He was later to lavish similar meticulous devotion on other literary figures, chiefly the nineteenth-century English poet Algernon Charles Swinburne. For more than fifty years Mayfield pursued Swinburneiana, as he called it, both in America and abroad. He made a particular effort to secure all the available copies of the first edition of *Atalanta in Calydon*, originally issued by Edward Moxon in 1865. Although standard bibliographies agreed that only 100 copies of the book had been issued, Mayfield obtained 101 copies personally and located some 65 others in libraries. It was the kind of literary one-upmanship that pleased him enormously. From 1961 to 1971 he was curator of manuscripts and rare books at Syracuse University and contributed numerous short essays on Swinburne to *The Courier*, a quarterly he edited for the Library Associates. In November 1965 Mr. and Mrs. Mayfield presented a part of their collection of 50,000 books, manuscripts, and letters to the Syracuse University Library, a gift prompted by their deep affection for the faculty and students. The Yale edition of Swinburne's letters, edited by Cecil Lang, took its substance from the Mayfield Syracuse collection.

In addition to Swinburne, Mayfield collected books and manuscripts from numerous other literary figures he liked. He was a friend and correspondent with American poets Robinson Jeffers, Edwin Markham, Vachel Lindsay, and Robert Frost and from them obtained an assortment of presentation copies and letters. His personal prerequisite for collecting was that the material collected must be good reading, intelligible, and have a personal appeal. Furthermore, he believed that to collect for investment was not only idiotic but sinful. In his later years Mayfield was a popular speaker and the recipient of many awards, among which was the Sir Thomas More Medal presented annually by the Gleeson Library Associates of the University of San Francisco. After leaving Syracuse, Mayfield returned to his home in Maryland and began a fruitful association with the Georgetown University Library, also taking up duties as librarian of the Army and Navy Club in Washington. His impressive list of publications and his great generosity highlighted a long and active career.

Bibliography

A. *Notes About the Mayfield Library* (Syracuse, N.Y., 1966); *Swinburneiana: A Gallimaufry of Bits and Pieces About Algernon Charles Swinburne* (Gaithersburg, Md., 1974); "All's Fair in Love and Book Collecting," *AB*, April 16, 1979, 2872; "A Swinburne Collector in Calydon," *QJLC*, Winter 1980, 25–34; "A Swinburne Puzzle," *BC*, Spring 1955, 74–78.

B. Austin Paulnack, "John Mayfield," in *Notes About the Mayfield Library* (Syracuse, N.Y., 1966); "John S. Mayfield," *AB*, May 23, 1983, 3990–3991; James Marren, "Caught for a Lifetime in a World of Books," *Syracuse Record*, October 19, 1978, 8; Correspondence with Mrs. John (Edith S.) Mayfield, June 1984.

McCLUNG, Calvin M. (b. May 12, 1855, Saint Louis, Mo.; d. March 12, 1919, Knoxville, Tenn.). *Education*: A.B., East Tennessee University, 1874; Ph.B., Yale University, 1876; A.M., Tennessee University, 1877. *Collection Disposition*: Lawson McGhee Library (Knoxville, Tenn.).

While pursuing a business career in Knoxville, McClung built up an impressive collection of materials on Tennessee history. This included books, documents, newspapers, autographs, and maps of eastern Tennessee and the adjoining areas. He was a keen student of genealogy, and many of the books in his library related to the history of the state's first families. As a trustee of the Lawson McGhee Library, he was responsible for the appointment of its first librarian, the distinguished Mary Rothrock. Because of Rothrock's interest in local history, Mrs. McClung gave the books and papers to the McGhee Library. The collection was dedicated in 1921.

Bibliography

A. *Calvin Morgan McClung Historical Collection . . .* , presented to Lawson McGhee Library by Mrs. Calvin M. McClung (Knoxville, Tenn., 1921).

B. *NCAB* 20, 382; *Calvin M. McClung Historical Collection, Lawson McGhee Library* (Knoxville, Tenn., 1971); "Calvin M. McClung," *Tennessee Historical Quarterly* 2, 59.

McCORMICK, CYRUS H. (b. May 16, 1859, Washington, D.C.; d. June 2, 1936, Lake Forest, Ill.). *Collection Disposition*: Princeton University.

After his father retired from the Harvester Company in 1884, McCormick took over as president. For the next thirty-five years his career was tied to the expansion and development of Harvester products. The modest book collection he began as a student eventually grew to a select but impressive library of Americana and English and American literature. Many of his finest books came from the auctions held during the early twentieth century. Starting with the Robert Hoe III* sale of 1911 and continuing through the disposal of John L. Clawson's* library in 1926, McCormick bought carefully and well. His Americana section of some 140 books was marked by such obvious rarities as the second edition of the 1493 "Columbus Letter," early travel narratives, and scarce pamphlets from the colonial and revolutionary periods. His Virginia holdings were particularly notable, founded as they were on the promotional tracts distributed by the Virginia Company in England to attract settlers. He also owned seventy Jefferson letters, an archive that revealed the statesman's intimate views on politics, architecture, slavery, and gardening. In 1948 historian Louis B. Wright explored the diversity of this collection in a laudatory article in the *Princeton Library Chronicle*.

The literary section of the library, like its Americana counterpart, was small but choice. It included the Hoe copy of Homer's works (1488) in five volumes, the first issue of Spenser's *Faerie Queen* (1590), and Shakespeare's *Poems* (1640) with both title pages. He also had American first editions by Poe, Emerson, Longfellow, Whitman, and Lowell. The question of the disposition of the library after McCormick's death was settled without debate. He had served for years on the Princeton board of trustees and provided financial support for numerous scholarships and buildings. The gift of his books was simply another mark of his deep affection for the university.

Bibliography

B. *DAB*, Supp. 2, 402–404; *NCAB* D, 286; Robert Garrett, "Cyrus H. McCormick"; James Thorpe, "English and American Literature in the McCormick Collection"; Alexander Wainwright, "From Columbus to J. C. Adams: Notable Americana in the McCormick Collection"; and Louis B. Wright, "Materials for the Study of the Civilization of Virginia," all in *PLC*, November 1948.

McCUTCHEON, George Barr (b. July 26, 1866, Lafayette, Ind.; d. October 23, 1928, New York, N.Y.). *Collection Disposition*: American Art, April 20, 1925, April 21, 1926; Chicago Book and Art Auctions, April 26, 1934.

At his home in Indiana, where books were part of the furniture, McCutcheon grew up on Dickens, Thackeray, Scott, and Cooper. His literary interests led to a career in writing, first as a journalist and then as a successful popular novelist. The release of *Graustark* in 1901 followed by *Brewster's Millions* the next year launched McCutcheon on a full-time writing career. In 1900 he resigned from newspaper work and moved to Chicago to write fifty more novels. As McCutcheon's income increased he began to buy sets of standard authors bound in green-cloth, gilt-edged volumes. In Chicago, where he was exposed to the splendid wares of McClurg's rare book room, his tastes began to form along more sophisticated lines. He was further drawn toward bibliomania on trips to New York, where he visited Dodd, Mead's book rooms and became acquainted with the knowledgeable bibliographer Luther Livingston. Since Dickens had been a boyhood favorite, McCutcheon started to build sets of the early issues of *Nicholas Nickleby* and the *Pickwick Papers*. This was not as easy as it first appeared. By trading and trading again he eventually secured one of the finest "Pickwick" sets in existence. Soon his interests spread to Kipling, Stevenson, Thackeray, and Ainsworth. First editions and limited autographed sets soon began to crowd his library shelves. It was at this point, according to his charming essay *Books Once Were Men*, that McCutcheon discovered one of the great truths of collecting, as he put it, "One cannot have everything unless one has everything." Lacking the money and inclination to get *everything*, he decided to concentrate on a few favorites. He traded away the miscellaneous sets of Reade, Marryat, and Ainsworth in favor of Hardy, Kipling, Stevenson, Thackeray, and Dickens. At one point he gave up an entire collection of George Meredith in order to get *To the Thompson Class* (1883), one of the rarest of Stevenson's pamphlets. Whenever possible McCutcheon obtained autographed letters and had them bound into the appropriate first editions he already owned. They added what he called an "intimate spice" to his library. In 1925 McCutcheon reduced his collection further by selling off the Hardy, Stevenson, and Kipling items and the following year disposed of Dickens and Thackeray. Buyers responded enthusiastically to both the McCutcheon sales with prices reaching well above the expectations of the owner. At the 1926 sale the perfect copy of "Pickwick" went for a record-breaking $7,000.

McCutcheon was an astute and sensitive collector. He understood the importance of working with reputable dealers and the fallacy of trying to collect for profit. Furthermore, he concentrated on authors he liked rather than following fashions set by others. His candid thoughts on collecting are happily preserved for modern-day book lovers in his autobiographical *Books Once Were Men*.

Bibliography

A. *Books Once Were Men* (New York, 1925).

B. *DAB* 12, 12; *NCAB* 14, 264; Cannon, 230–232; "Getting into Six Figures," *The Bookman*, May 1925, 332–335; "Brothers Under the Pen," *Collier's*, April 11, 1927, 14.

McGREGOR, Tracy W. (b. April 14, 1869, Berlin Heights, Ohio; d. May 6, 1936, Washington, D.C.). *Collection Disposition*: University of Virginia.

In a biographical sketch published at the University of Virginia in 1963, librarian William Runge described McGregor as a humanist. The characterization was accurate and richly deserved. In 1891 McGregor took over the management of the Detroit Mission for the Destitute, a family-supported charity that provided funds for farm relief and training for the feebleminded. In 1925 he and his wife set up the McGregor Fund, a philanthropic foundation, to carry out their various charitable projects. At the same time, working with the American Historical Association, he sponsored the so-called "McGregor Plan," under which college libraries could obtain matching funds for the purchase of Americana.

Not until his move to Washington, D.C., in 1932 was McGregor able to indulge his long-standing personal interest in book collecting. Already enthusiastic about Americana and somewhat knowledgeable about bibliography through his friendship with the Clements Library curator Randolph Adams, McGregor started to collect in earnest. His chief support in this process came from New York bookdealers Lathrop Harper and Gabriel Wells. Harper took the responsibility for the Americana while Wells advised on literature. The McGregor library was built in an incredibly brief four years. Particular pockets of strength developed around exploration and travel, southeastern and New England colonial history, the Revolutionary War period, and the writings of Increase and Cotton Mather. Among the many high points were the "Columbus Letter" printed in Florence in 1493, an exceptional set of Hakluyt's "Principal Navigations," Jefferson's own annotated copy of *Notes on the State of Virginia*, a copy of the *Federalist Papers* owned by Alexander Hamilton's son, and a set of documents from the first fourteen congresses. In 1930 McGregor purchased the extensive Mather collection of some 2,000 items owned by William Gwinn Mather of Cleveland. Because of the influential position of the Mathers, this collection offered a wealth of information on colonial social history. The Civil War period was also well represented, with over 1,000 Confederate imprints, a volume of General Philip Sheridan's privately printed war reports, and a complete set of the Confederate *Index*. Although the literature section of the McGregor library was not as distinguished as that taken up by Americana, it did include, for example, Shakespearean folios and first editions of Gray's *Elegy* and Fielding's *Tristram Shandy*. Just before his death, McGregor visited Charlottesville, Virginia, to discuss moving his collection to the University of Virginia campus. The trustees of the McGregor Fund formalized that wish and presented the library to the university in April 1939. The original gift of 8,000 volumes has grown steadily and today is provided with expert curatorial supervision in the "Tracy McGregor Room." Because of his many benefactions to the University of Virginia, McGregor is remembered as a philanthropist as well as a collector.

Bibliography

B. *NCAB* 34, 67; *Grolier 75*, 172–174; William Runge, "The Tracy McGregor Library and Its Founder," *University of Virginia News Letter*, July 15, 1963, 41–44.

McKEE, Thomas Jefferson (b. 1840; d. July 16, 1899). *Collection Disposition*: Anderson, November 22, 1900, January 28, April 29, December 2, 1901, February 17, May 12, 1902, April 27, 1903, February 20, 1905, April 19, 1906.

McKee practiced law in New York from shortly after the Civil War until the time of his death. His avocation was the theater, an interest that led him to gather an extensive library of books, journals, photographs, and playbills—in fact, everything he could find related to the British and American stage. As the theater collection became well established McKee expanded his interests to include English and American poetry and American history. In contrast to some collectors who concentrated on a narrow list of prominent authors, McKee took on the entire range of English and American literature. His sales catalogs read like pages from the *Cambridge Bibliography of English Literature*, with volumes by Drayton, Hooke, Lovelace, Spenser, Goldsmith, Heywood, and others. In the case of Elizabethan titles, many came from the library of McKee's friend Charles W. Frederickson*. At one time Frederickson had collected in this period, but then he became convinced that Shakespeare was a hoax and decided to sell all his holdings. Like Frederickson, McKee collected Shelley. The high point in his collection was undoubtedly the autographed copy of *Adonais* (1821) that was inscribed to Leigh Hunt. In the American literature portion of the library, McKee had important holdings of most of the nineteenth-century New England poets and novelists. His Poe collection was particularly strong. What collector would not be pleased to see the 1827 *Tamerlane and Other Poems* standing next to the 1829 *Al Aaraaf, Tamerlane, and Minor Poems*? The McKee library was most distinguished, however, in the department of the theater. The editor of *The Athenaeum* claimed that the collection included some 520 quarto plays printed before 1700 and almost everything of consequence from the Robert Lowe *Bibliographical Account of English Theatrical Literature* (1888). In addition to printed books, the collection was strong in the ephemera of the theatre—playbills, drawings, photographs, programs, and clippings.

After McKee's death an announcement in the *New York Times* claimed that the library would not be sold, but arrangements for a sale were soon under way. The newly established Anderson Auction Company issued a handsome catalog and announced the first sales for November 1900 and January 1901. In an article in *The Book Buyer*, Ernest Dressel North warned potential buyers to examine the physical condition of the books with particular care. North claimed that the auction house had not been as scrupulous about exact descriptions of bindings and facsimile pages as an expert would wish. Regardless of those cautions, the McKee sale was a great financial success. One commentator remarked that books that might have sold for only ten cents reached forty or fifty cents in the atmosphere of spirited auction-room bidding. Not surprisingly, Poe's *Tamerlane* commanded the highest price of the sale, a record-breaking $2,050. In subsequent sessions the English and American literature brought continued high returns, as did the small but choice gathering of Americana. The formation of the McKee library illustrated what could be done in the late nineteenth century with a blend of determination and enthusiasm.

Bibliography

B. Cannon, 323–326; Ernest Dressel North, "The McKee Sale," *The Book Buyer*, August 1899, 46; October 1900, 212–213; January 1901, 576–577; June 1901, 469; June 1902, 408–409; Robert Roden, "The Sixth McKee Sale," *The Bibliographer*, June 1902, 236–245; "The McKee Sale," *NYT*, August 26, 1899, 562; "The McKee Sale," *Literary Collector*, October 1902.

McPHERSON, William (b. July 16, 1885, Orange, Calif.; d. September 8, 1964, Garden Grove, Calif.). *Education*: A.B., University of California at Berkeley, 1914. *Collection Disposition*: Pomona College.

Over a period of fifty years McPherson followed a number of careers: public school teacher, rancher, and amateur historian. After graduating from the University of California he began teaching in San Juan Capistrano, but his unpopular pro-German views made it impossible for him to hold a job. In 1918 he returned to the family home in Orange, where he worked as a fruit grower for the rest of his life. McPherson became interested in book collecting while he was a student at Berkeley, and when he had any spare money he purchased California history and literature from the San Francisco shops of Charles Newbegin and John Saddler. By 1923, when he read his first paper to the members of the Orange County Historical Society, he could boast a library of 2,000 volumes, mostly state and local history. He became a regular customer of Ernest Dawson in Los Angeles and bought whatever Dawson could supply from Robert E. Cowan's* *Bibliography of the History of California*. Eventually McPherson's interests became known to such sophisticated California bookmen as Arthur Ellis, Gregg Layne, and Cowan himself. These men helped him develop his collection and sharpen his knowledge of bibliography. When McPherson discovered an unknown pre–Civil War diary, Ellis agreed to print it on his handpress, a job that took almost four years to complete. The result was a creditable piece of historical editing and a handsome example of hand printing. By 1929 McPherson's library had grown to the point where he had to build a separate facility just to house journals and newspapers. Hard times came in the 1930s, however, and McPherson was forced to sell back parts of the collection to Dawson and to friends in the Orange County Historical Society. At the same time, McPherson's own health began to deteriorate to the point where he was unable to give attention to either the ranch or the books. By the end of the 1940s the library, which had held some 10,000 items, lay in disrepair. Water had leaked in and dirt covered the piles of books and journals. On McPherson's death the bank took over the estate, including the remaining parts of the library. At first the sorting job looked hopeless, but with the aid of students under the direction of Don Meadows, an old family friend, damaged items were discarded while others were cleaned and organized. There were no heirs. By McPherson's will the library, still rich in California history, went to Pomona College.

Bibliography

B. Don Meadows, *A California Paisano: The Life of William McPherson* (Claremont, Calif., 1972).

MEEK, Frederick M. (b. May 28, 1902, Staffordshire, Eng.; d. September 7, 1979). *Education*: A.B., Mt. Allison University, 1924; B.D., Yale University, 1929. *Collection Disposition*: Whittier College.

In 1946, after serving as minister in a number of smaller churches, Meek was appointed to the Old South Church of Boston. Book collecting was his chief hobby throughout the thirty-five years of his active ministry and his retirement. He developed strong collections of Thoreau, Hawthorne, and Longfellow, but his first and most enduring interest was Whittier. He haunted Boston bookshops for years in order to obtain Whittier's books in all their variant issues. He also gathered Whittier letters, manuscripts, portraits, and personal memorabilia. In a letter dated October 8, 1984, Mrs. Meek stated that her husband's chief interests had been in "Whittier the man, the astute politician and militant Quaker." At the time of Meek's death the collection totaled 6,200 items and was, according to Jacob Blanck, editor of the *Bibliography of American Literature*, the most complete in private hands. In 1980, following her husband's wishes, Mrs. Meek presented the library to Whittier College in California. In that appropriate setting the Meek Library furnishes students and faculty with a research archive on one of America's most fervent abolitionists and best-known poets.

Bibliography

B. Correspondence with Mrs. Frederick Meek, October 8, 1984.

MEINE, Franklin J. (b. May 18, 1896, Chicago, Ill.; d. December 27, 1968, Washington, D.C.). *Education*: Ph.B., University of Chicago, 1917; M.A., Carnegie Institute of Technology, 1919. *Collection Disposition*: University of Illinois.

Throughout his life, Meine was closely associated with writing and publishing. He worked as an editor for Consolidated Book Publishers in Chicago and then from 1948 to 1956 was editor-in-chief of the *American People's Encyclopedia*. His private area of interest was American folklore and humor. His first book, *Tall Tales of the Southwest* (1930), was followed by a series of similar studies devoted to Mike Fink, Davy Crockett, and other legendary American heroes. In order to support his writing and as an avocation, he collected joke books, ballads, cartoons, comic almanacs, reminiscences of comedians, and humor magazines. He was also interested in Samuel Clemens and formed a large library based on his first editions, foreign translations, manuscripts, memorabilia, and magazine contributions. In 1955 he sold the humor and folklore materials, some 8,500 volumes, to the University of Illinois. The Clemens collection followed by bequest in 1968.

Bibliography

B. Norman Cram, "The Caxton Club of Chicago," *QNLBCC*, Spring 1956; *Collections Acquired by the University of Illinois Library 1897–1974* (Urbana, Ill., 1974), 34–35; *Chicago Tribune*, December 28, 1968.

MENNEN, William E. (b. December 20, 1884, Newark, N.J.; d. February 18, 1968, Morristown, N.J.). *Education*: B.E., Cornell University, 1908. *Collection Disposition*: Cornell University.

In 1953 Mennen gave Cornell the four Shakespeare folios, followed in 1954 by first editions of Dickens. He also provided funds for the purchase of the manuscripts of Ford Madox Ford and Ezra Pound. The report by the director of the Cornell libraries for 1956 included a notice of Mennen's backing in the purchase of a large collection of James Joyce's letters. Throughout his life Mennen cherished fine and beautiful books and donated them generously to the Cornell libraries.

Bibliography

B. Cornell University Library, *Reports of the Director, 1950–1965*; *NYT*, February 19, 1968, 39.

MENZIES, William (b. 1810; d. February 21, 1896, Brattleboro, Vt.?). *Collection Disposition*: Bangs, February 15, 1865; Leavitt, November 13, 1876.

Aside from a few scattered notices, little is known of Menzies' early life. In his chronicle of nineteenth-century bookselling, William Brotherhead remembered Menzies as a modest and generous Scotsman who had risen to wealth from the ranks of labor. However that may be, Menzies was a diligent collector of early European and American printing, Americana, Scottish literature, and extra-illustrated books. By 1860 James Wynne could report that the Menzies library contained some 4,000 volumes, most of which related to American history. Menzies was one of the first to collect examples of early American printings of William Bradford and Benjamin Franklin. By the time his collection came up for sale, he owned more than fifty Bradford titles and twenty by Franklin. In addition to the materials on American printing, he bought a number of important early European examples. He owned books printed by Gutenberg, Fust and Schoeffer, Caxton, and Wynkyn de Worde, a distinguished quartet. Of the books relating to America, he possessed early travel narratives, colonial history, Revolutionary War tracts, and a strong section on George Washington. The star of the lot was undoubtedly Washington Irving's *Life of Washington*, which Menzies had expanded with portraits and letters to ten volumes. Early American poetry was represented in the library by first editions of the work of Anne Bradstreet, Philip Freneau, and Phillis Wheatley. Menzies' affection for Scottish literature was displayed by copies of the famous Kilmarnock edition of the works of Robert Burns and subsequent Edinburgh and New York editions. Throughout, the books were notable for their pristine condition. In the sale catalog Joseph

Sabin stated that the physical quality of the Menzies books surpassed that of any other collection handled by him during his entire career. This was high praise indeed, considering Sabin's lofty position in the nineteenth-century American book world. In 1876 a writer in the *American Bibliopolist* could describe the Menzies sale as the "bibliographical event of the season." Presided over by Sabin, the sale underlined for the first time the importance of American printing and American authors. The long runs of Bradford printing and the George Washington materials caught the fancy of both private and institutional buyers. Joseph W. Drexel* paid $4,080 for the elaborate *Life of Washington*, while Edward G. Asay*, Brayton Ives*, and Joseph Cooke* took the early European printings. Menzies' collecting career is well documented in the carefully produced catalog of his extraordinary library.

Bibliography

B. Cannon, 352–353; Wynne, 313–334; William Brotherhead, *Forty Years Among the Old Booksellers of Philadelphia* (Philadelphia, 1891), 8–11; Frederick Goff, *Joseph Sabin, Bibliographer* (Amsterdam, The Netherlands, 1963), 22–25; "The Menzies Library," *The American Bibliopolist*, December 1876, 128–133; *NYT*, November 21, 1876, 1.

MILLER, DeWitt (b. March 1, 1857, Cross River, N.Y.; d. July 29, 1911, Boise, Idaho). *Collection Disposition*: The Cassedy School in Forest Glen, Maryland.

After trying his hand at a number of careers—teaching, journalism, and the ministry—Miller settled down to the one that suited him best: traveling lecturer. He spoke to Chautauqua assemblies, business groups, church societies, and literary guilds from one end of the country to the other. Wherever he stopped for the night he looked for books. This habit, formed over the years, led him into musty secondhand-bookshops from Baltimore to Seattle. Miller's aim, as suggested by his biographer, Leon Vincent, was simply to build a good general library. In the fulfillment of that aim, however, Miller became more expert than Vincent's modest assessment would indicate. By reading catalogs and talking with bookdealers, he became knowledgeable about printing and binding. He enjoyed owning the attractive volumes issued by John Baskerville and William Pickering. He was fond of association copies, books with presentation notes or corrections in the author's hand, or books that had once been in the library of a famous person. He had shelves of titles by Johnson, Thackeray, and Trollope, along with the works of the diarists and letter writers Pepys, Gibbon, Walpole, and Chesterfield. Toward the end of his life he moved his books to a two-story library built for him by a friend on the grounds of a girls' school in Maryland. There among the oak trees Miller's gentleman's library found an appropriate resting place.

Bibliography

B. Leon Vincent, *DeWitt Miller: A Biographical Sketch* (Cambridge, Mass., 1912).

MILLER, Winlock (b. July 21, 1906, Seattle, Wash.; d. July 14, 1939, Seattle, Wash.). *Education*: A.B., LL.B., Yale University, 1928, 1931. *Collection Disposition*: Yale University.

The Yale University Library's collection of western Americana was given an enormous boost in the 1940s by substantial gifts from William Robertson Coe* and Winlock Miller. Miller had grown up in Washington, and his family had long been involved in the political destiny of that state. From his grandfather he had inherited a number of important manuscript collections that dealt with the Indian wars of 1856 and the administration of Territorial Governor Isaac Stevens. Another archive consisted of the thirty scrapbooks of clippings and notes kept by nineteenth-century West Coast historian Elwood Evans. In addition to these sources Miller had long runs of early newspapers and journals and a wide selection of pamphlets and books on all topics that concerned the development of the states of Washington and Oregon. In accordance with his wishes the collection was presented to Yale in 1950. Along with the Coe materials and other contributions by Henry R. Wagner* and Frederick W. Beinecke*, it goes to form one of the country's strongest gatherings of western American history.

Bibliography

B. Paul Winkler, "The Pacific Northwest Collection of Winlock Miller, Jr.," *YLG*, October 1951, 44–52.

MOORLAND, Jesse E. (b. September 10, 1863, Coldwater, Ohio; d. April 30, 1940, New York, N.Y.). *Education*: A.B., Howard University, 1891. *Collection Disposition*: Howard University.

For over twenty-five years Moorland worked in various administrative posts in the International Young Men's Christian Association (YMCA). He was particularly effective in seeking funds for construction of YMCA buildings for Negroes throughout the United States. During the course of his duties, he built up an extensive personal library on Negro history. In 1914 Kelly Miller, professor of mathematics and sociology at Howard University, persuaded Moorland to donate his 3,000-volume library to the university in order to start an academic program on Negro life. At that time the Moorland collection was heralded as the largest and most complete in the country. He added to the collection regularly, and as a trustee of the university saw to it that adequate space was set aside for his books when the new library building opened in 1939. In 1946 Arthur Spingarn's* collection was added to the Moorland books to form what is designated as the "Moorland-Spingarn Research Center."

Bibliography

B. *DANB*, 448–452; Michael Winston, ''Moorland-Spingarn Research Center: A Past Revisited, a Present Reclaimed,'' *New Directions: The Howard University Magazine*, Summer 1974, 1–6.

MORGAN, John Pierpont (b. April 17, 1837, Hartford, Conn.; d. March 31, 1913, Rome, Italy). *Collection Disposition*: Pierpont Morgan Library.

John Pierpont Morgan was born into a wealthy New York family with interests in hotels, insurance, and international banking. His early school years, spent in Switzerland, were followed by advanced study at the University of Göttingen in Germany. Morgan was introduced to the pleasures of collecting by his father, a connoisseur of painting, silver, and autographs. According to one account, Morgan's original urge to collect came as a response to a gift from his father, the original manuscript of Sir Walter Scott's *Guy Mannering*.

After the death of his father in 1890, Morgan came into a large inheritance, which he began to invest lavishly in books, manuscripts, and artwork. In order to make sure he got what he wanted, Morgan found it easier to buy entire libraries than to select in the traditional way, item by item. Bernard Quaritch in London and George Richmond in New York, among others, were constantly looking for significant and tempting collections to move from their shops to the Thirty-sixth Street mansion. It was his appetite for large, ready-made libraries that gave Morgan his reputation as an accumulator rather than a collector. In 1891 he bought the important Sir Charles Fenn collection of European autographs. Within the next ten years he acquired a Gutenberg Bible, a Mainz psalter, the James Toovey collection of early English printed books, and the Theodore Irwin* rare books and manuscripts. The Irwin library was particularly rich in early illuminated manuscripts, of which the most famous was the eighth-century Hamilton Palace Golden Gospels, printed on purple vellum and orginally given to King Henry VIII by Pope Leo X. At the turn of the century, in a major coup, Morgan acquired part of the medieval library of English printer-designer William Morris. The 700 volumes obtained included 100 illuminated manuscripts and the works of all the early sixteenth-century printers, with an extraordinary assemblage of 32 books from the shop of England's first printer, William Caxton. Next Morgan added three substantial collections of French literature: Edward Ker's *Chansons de Geste*, George Burchard's medieval romances, and George De Forest's library of literary tales and sagas. In many of his decisions Morgan relied heavily on the advice of his cousin, Junius S. Morgan*, a knowledgeable bibliophile and collector.

As the library holdings grew in size and sophistication, the need for improved physical facilities became apparent. In 1906, after four years of planning, an architectural jewel in Italian Renaissance style designed by Charles F. McKim rose on Morgan's Murray Hill property. No expense was spared to make the library an appropriate setting for the great treasures within. In another stroke of good judgment, Morgan employed Belle da Costa Greene as his first librarian.

Greene, who had worked in the Princeton library, was as determined and knowledgeable as her employer, and together they made a formidable team. In 1908, when Lord Amherst announced the sale of his Caxton collection, Greene was able to talk the family into a private arrangement, thereby snatching the rarities from under the noses of the London bookdealers. Morgan's last major purchases came in 1911 at the Robert Hoe III* sale in New York and at the Henry Huth sale in London. His bid of $42,800 at the Hoe sale carried away the superb copy of Caxton's printing of Malory's *Morte d'Arthur* over the spirited bidding of Henry E. Huntington*.

In 1924 John Pierpont Morgan Jr.* turned the library over to a board of trustees and to the state of New York as an educational institution. Since that time, exhibitions, handsome catalogs, and scholarly seminars have brought the Morgan treasures to national and international attention. The building and the collection stand as one of the great monuments to private collecting and to the cultural inheritance as represented in paintings, manuscripts, coins, books, prints, and drawings. The Morgan Library is a library devoted to the entire range of humanistic expression.

Bibliography

B. *DAB* 7, 175–180; *NCAB* 14, 66; Cannon, 277–291, *Grolier 75*, 18–20; Frederick B. Adams, *An Introduction to the Pierpont Morgan Library* (New York, 1964); Frederick Lewis Allen, *The Great Pierpont Morgan* (New York, 1949); Gardner Teal, "An American Medici, J. Pierpont Morgan and His Various Collections," *Putnam's Magazine*, November 1909, 130–143; "Mr. Morgan's Great Library," *NYT*, December 4, 1908; "Memoir," *London Times*, April 1, 1913, 6–7.

MORGAN, John Pierpont, Jr. (b. September 7, 1867, Irvington-on-Hudson, N.Y.; d. March 13, 1943, Boca Grande, Fla.). *Education*: A.B., Harvard University, 1889. *Collection Disposition*: Pierpont Morgan Library.

When Morgan inherited his father's collection of rarities in 1913, it included 19,175 volumes, 1,305 manuscripts, and 1,098 prints. With the assistance of his knowledgeable and energetic librarian, Belle da Costa Greene, Morgan continued to enlarge these collections, particularly in holdings of medieval manuscripts and early printed books. He added such distinguished items as the eighth-century collection of sermons in Anglo-Saxon known as the "Blickling Homilies," a choice *Lancelot du Lac* written and illuminated in France in the early fourteenth century, several works by William Caxton, England's first printer, and a fine Ptolemy *Cosmographia* printed in Bologna in 1477. Although the magnitude of Morgan's acquisitions was not as great as that achieved by his father, he did add important manuscripts, books, autographed letters, bindings, and prints.

In February 1924 Morgan turned the building and collections over to the public under the administration of a board of trustees. In an interview granted to the *New York Times* he estimated the value of the collections to be in the neighborhood of $8.5 million, a figure that specialists considered far too modest. In 1928 Morgan commissioned the construction of an annex to the library in order to accommodate more books and to provide reading-room space for scholarly research. He not only augmented the library's collections but with the careful management of Greene made them more accessible to users. His single purpose, as he stated in a 1924 letter to the trustees, was to increase "the value of the whole for educational purposes."

Bibliography

A. *The Pierpont Morgan Library: Review of the Activities and Acquisitions of the Library from 1936 Through 1940* (New York, 1941); *The First Quarter Century of the Pierpont Morgan Library*, a Retrospective Exhibition in Honor of Belle da Costa Greene. (New York, 1949).

B. *DAB*, Supp. 3, 537–538; *NCAB* 15, 181–182; Cannon, 288–291; Wolf and Fleming, passim; Frederick B. Adams, *An Introduction to the Pierpont Morgan Library* (New York, 1964); John Forbes, *J. P. Morgan Jr. 1867–1943* (New York, 1981); John Winkler, "Mighty Dealer in Dollars," *The New Yorker*, February 2 and 9, 1929, 23–26, 27–36; "J. P. Morgan Gives Library to the Public," *NYT*, February 17, 1924, 1; "J. P. Morgan Dies," *NYT*, March 13, 1943, 1.

MORGAN, Junius S. (b. June 5, 1867, Irvington-on-Hudson, N.Y.; d. August 18, 1932, Valmont, Switz.). *Education*: A.B., A.M., Princeton University, 1896. *Collection Disposition*: Princeton University.

Morgan's early years were strongly influenced by his exposure to the faculty and library facilities at Princeton. After he graduated and served a few years in the family business, he returned to his alma mater and took a position as associate librarian. In addition to his library responsibilities, Morgan acted as chief adviser to his uncle, John Pierpont Morgan*, who was then building one of the world's greatest collections of early manuscripts, incunabula, and fine printing. Morgan's personal interests were in bibliography, philosophy, and Greek and Roman classical literature. In the area of the classics he was particularly successful in obtaining an outstanding collection of early editions of Virgil. This was an interest that had been stimulated during his undergraduate days by the lively teaching of Dean West, Giger Professor of Latin. In a tribute written in 1932, Philip Rollins* stated that Morgan had entered West's class with a liking for Latin and came out with a love for the language and an urge to collect Virgil. By the time he graduated he owned several important editions. Eventually the depth of his Virgil holdings was said to be unequaled in any library in America and only exceeded by one or two European institutions. Chronologically the collection began with the Sweynheym and Pannartz edition of 1469 and progressed through all the important versions up to the end of the eighteenth century. The showpiece in the collection was the 1541 Aldine edition bound for Jean Grolier. In all cases, condition and binding were given close attention, with the result that the Morgan books represented the finest in the bookmaker's art. In later years Morgan lived in Paris and bought heavily from auction sales throughout Europe. During this period he built a large collection of color-plate books and Elzevir editions. According to a French bookdealer who worked with Morgan over a long period of years, content and condition were always more important than price. The results of Morgan's collecting efforts now provide Princeton scholars with a remarkable Virgilian gathering.

Bibliography

B. *NCAB* 30, 19; *Grolier 75*, 156–159; Philip Rollins, "Junius Spencer Morgan," *Biblia*, November 1932; "A Gift to Princeton," *The Book Buyer*, January 1897, 953.

MORSE, Willard S. (b. June 12, 1856, Ware, Mass.; d. October 4, 1935, Santa Monica, Calif.). *Collection Disposition*: Wilmington, Delaware, Society of Fine Arts; Denver Public Library; William and Mary College; University of Southern California.

Morse started his working career as foreman of a small smelting plant in Denver and eventually rose to become general manager of the entire Guggenheim mining operation in Mexico. In several of his business assignments Morse found himself closely allied with the avid book collector Henry R. Wagner*. When Morse retired in 1922 and moved to California, he saw Wagner more frequently and began to collect more actively. While he was still working for the Guggenheims he had started modest collections of the works of the poet Eugene Field and of sample drawings and books of the distinguished American illustrator Howard Pyle. To these he added books by Clemens, London, Bierce, and Joaquin Miller. He got to know the widows of both Miller and London and was able to secure from them a number of notable manuscripts and first editions. He also obtained files of early newspapers and journals with contributions by Clemens and London. After he had satisfied his initial interests in these authors, he turned to Sinclair Lewis, Howells, Harte, and Lafcaido Hearn. In each case he kept meticulous notes on price, binding variants, and provenance. The range of his interests was extraordinary. Before he died in 1935 he had formed respectable collections of all these writers.

In the disposition of the library, Mrs. Morse sold the bulk of materials to Dawson's Book Shop in Los Angeles, retaining only the Eugene Field materials, which she sold at a bargain price to the Denver Public Library. This amiable gesture was prompted by happy memories of the days in Denver when Field and Morse had been close friends. Elmer Belt* bought the S. Weir Mitchell and Upton Sinclair books from Dawson's, while the College of William and Mary secured the Cabell books and letters. The University of Southern California bought the largest portion of the Morse library, including sizable collections of Bierce, Lewis, and Howells. The Howells library was perhaps the most distinguished, with over 160 printed works as well as numerous letters and manuscripts. The outstanding Clemens collection eventually went to Yale.

Although Morse only bought and collected seriously for ten years, his achievements were remarkable. As a result of his interests, several academic institutions now hold significant collections of American authors.

Bibliography

A. *Howard Pyle, a Record of His Illustrations and Writings*, compiled by Willard Morse and Gertrude Brinckle (Wilmington, Del., 1921).

B. *NCAB* 26, 481–482; Henry R. Wagner, *Willard Samuel Morse, a Great Collector* (Los Angeles, 1939).

MUNK, Joseph A. (b. November 9, 1847, North Georgetown, Ohio; d. December 4, 1927, Los Angeles, Calif.). *Education*: Certificate, Eclectic Medical Institute of Cincinnati, 1869. *Collection Disposition*: Southwest Museum, Los Angeles.

According to his autobiography, Munk became interested in the West as a young man growing up on a farm in rural Ohio. He was fascinated by the books he read about hunting and Indian warfare in the small town library. It was an interest that remained throughout his life and led to the formation of what came to be one of the country's leading libraries on Arizona and the West. After Munk completed his medical studies he moved to Topeka, Kansas, where he established his professional practice. It was from Topeka in 1884 that Munk made his first trip to Arizona. This was a turning point in his life, as it fixed his interest on collecting printed materials on the raw new territory. Back in Topeka he read whatever he could find on the West, starting with *Hinton's Handbook to Arizona* (1878) and Peter's *Life of Kit Carson* (1873). As far as Munk was concerned, the task of building an Arizona library meant acquiring everything that mentioned the territory, its people, or its landscape. This included books, newspapers, documents, maps, government surveys, and ephemera. Munk felt these "scraps," as he put it, would collectively be useful to future scholars. He was not concerned with the niceties of binding, edition, or even physicial condition as long as he got what he wanted. Rare books as such had no place in his library.

In 1892 Munk moved to Los Angeles, a relocation that recommended itself for both professional and avocational reasons. Certainly his professional career could only prosper in the growing city, and of course he would be closer to Arizoniana. Shortly after moving to Los Angeles, Munk became acquainted with Robert E. Cowan* and Charles F. Lummis, two literary figures who would have considerable influence on the development of the library. Cowan was a knowledgeable San Francisco bookdealer and bibliographer who supplied Munk with many important items. In the case of Lummis—author, librarian, and Southwest promoter extraordinary—the tie was even closer. Lummis advised Munk on choice books, made him a member of the Southwest Museum board, and eventually gave Munk's Arizona library a permanent home. As the collection grew from 200 volumes in 1894 to over 1,000 in 1901, Munk consulted Cowan and other friends about the eventual disposition of the books. Of course he would like them to go to Arizona, but no suitable fireproof building was available either in Phoenix or in Tucson. It was the right moment for Lummis. If the Arizona materials were deposited in Lummis' new Southwest Museum, they would be well cared for, available to the donor at all times, and convenient for scholars in the area. The agreement was drawn and the Munk library, grown to 8,000 volumes, was officially conveyed to the museum in 1910. Four years later, when the new building was constructed, Munk's collection, now increased to 16,000 volumes, was given a room of its own. Although Munk had disagreements with the museum officers over the next ten years, and even started proceedings once to move the library to the University of Arizona, relationships in general were amiable. Munk continued to support the library with gifts as long as he lived, and in his will he provided a $10,000 bequest for additional purchases. The materials Munk collected form a significant and useful research collection on Southwest history.

Bibliography

A. *Activities of a Lifetime* (Los Angeles, 1924); *Features of an Arizona Library* (Los Angeles, 1926); *Story of the Munk Library of Arizoniana* (Los Angeles, 1927); "Rapid Growth of the Munk Library of Arizoniana in the Southwest Museum," *Masterkey*, January 1928, 19; *Bibliography of Arizona*, edited by Hector Alliot (Los Angeles, 1914).

B. Glenna Schroeder, "It May Do Somebody Some Good After I Am Gone," *Journal of Arizona History*, Summer 1984, 111–128.

MURPHY, Henry Cruse (b. July 5, 1810, Brooklyn, N.Y.; d. December 1, 1882, Brooklyn, N.Y.). *Education*: A.B., Columbia University, 1830. *Collection Disposition*: Leavitt, March 3, 1884.

As a lawyer, then as a politician in Brooklyn city government Murphy was eminently successful in the early part of the nineteenth century. His appointment as city attorney was a stepping-stone to his election as mayor at the age of thirty-two. Subsequent opportunities placed him in the New York state legislature and later in The Hague as the United States' chief diplomatic minister to the Netherlands. Throughout his distinguished political career he wrote articles and texts that focused on his scholarly interest in the Dutch settlement of the New World. In order to carry on the research that his writing required, he built an extensive scholarly library. The most important part of that library reflected his deep interest in the period of exploration and in those men who were first to record their impressions. Among these texts were the "Jesuit Relations" and the great works of DeBry, Hakluyt, Hudson, and Champlain, to name only a few. As a complement to the texts on early discovery, Murphy had twenty-six early editions of Ptolemy's *Cosmographia* ranging in date from 1462 to 1600. In another section of the library Murphy gathered a large number of books and tracts on American Indian languages, customs, and beliefs. Both Wynne and Cannon note his extensive holdings of rare Indian Bibles. While he did not have the first edition of the Eliot "Indian Bible," he did have the equally rare second edition (1685) with a dedication to Governor Robert Boyle. His library held excellent documentation on the settlement of New England and the southern states, with particularly strong holdings of early statutes and constitutional conventions, proceedings of historical societies, journals, and newspapers. Books from the presses of William Bradford, Peter Zenger, and Benjamin Franklin were prominent in many of these holdings.

When the Murphy library came on the market in 1884, the *New York Times* optimistically suggested it would set new price standards for Americana. Buyers resisted this prediction, however, and offered only "careful" bids. Robert Calep's *More Wonders of the Invisible World*, for example, brought only $75, half the figure it sold for at the William Menzies* sale eight years earlier. The price of the second edition of the Eliot Bible also went far below expectations. Among those to profit from this bargain-basement event were John Carter Brown*, the Lenox Library of New York, the Pennsylvania Historical Society, and the American Geographical Society. Some of the blame for the poor showing of the Murphy books was attributed to bibliographer John Russell Bartlett, who prepared what was said to have been a superficial catalog. Murphy was a knowledgeable bibliophile, an energetic collector, and a competent historian. His library was one of the outstanding collections assembled in the late nineteenth century.

Bibliography

B. *DAB* 7, 350–352; *NCAB* 10, 33; Cannon, 107; Wynne, 335–346; Henry Stiles, "Henry Cruse Murphy," *Record of the New York Genealogical and Biographical Society*, January 1883; "The Sale of Henry C. Murphy's Library," *NYT*, March 4, 1884, 2; "The Late Hon. Henry C. Murphy and His Library" (Preface), in *Catalogue of the Magnificent Library of the Late Hon. Henry C. Murphy* (New York, 1884), v–viii.

N

NEWTON, A. Edward (b. August 26, 1864, Philadelphia, Pa.; d. September 29, 1940, Philadelphia, Pa.). *Collection Disposition*: Bangs, May 18, 1896; Anderson, November 29, 1926; Parke-Bernet, April 16, May 14, October 29, 1941; Free Library of Philadelphia.

After working for a short time as a stationery salesman in a Philadelphia bookstore, Newton turned to the more profitable line of manufacturing. He converted a bankrupt electrical company into a profitable enterprise and in the transaction gave himself the freedom he wanted to follow a second and more enjoyable career as a writer and book collector. Newton was one of those rare individuals who could claim with some justice to have been a collector for life. In *This Book Collecting Game* he told how, as a small boy, he gathered some twenty or thirty volumes about Napoleon, then turned quickly to the English literary giants Dickens, Scott, and Johnson. By the time he was thirty, Newton's library had grown to a considerable size and included a number of first editions. In 1896, however, the collection had to be sacrificed in order to bring in enough money for the down payment on a house. Once that was taken care of, Newton was again ready to enter the world of book auctions and bookshops. He became, as he put it in *This Book Collecting Game*, an "ex officio member of the Johnson circle," a status that incidentally led to lifelong enthusiasms for Goldsmith, Trollope, Blake, and Lamb. Since Newton made it his business to know most of the major bookdealers in the United States and England, tempting catalogs came to him from all directions. Francis Edwards and Ernest Maggs had regular dealings with him from their London shops, as did Walter Hill, Gabriel Wells, and A. S. W. Rosenbach* in the United States. It was Rosenbach to whom Newton was most deeply attached, and it was from him that Newton bought the substantial portion of his library.

Beginning in 1915 Newton began to share his enthusiasms for books and collecting with the public in a series of articles that appeared in the *Atlantic Monthly*. These pieces, entitled "The Amenities of Book Collecting," carried the Newton message that reading could be fun and that book collecting was the most stimulating of all indoor hobbies. Over the next twenty years Newton repeated that theme in a series of popular articles and books, to the delight of a wide range of armchair collectors. Thoroughly imbued with the importance of books and reading, Newton was at the center of literary activities in Philadelphia in the 1920s and 1930s. He was a friend of poets Amy Lowell* and Agnes Repplier, both of whom he entertained at Oak Knoll, his lavish country home. A classic photograph reproduced in *End Papers* shows Miss Repplier pouring tea from Dr. Johnson's silver teapot while Yale Professor Charles Osgood and the Newtons look on with rapture.

In 1936 Newton was nominated A.S.W. Rosenbach Lecturer at the University of Pennsylvania and delivered a series of talks entitled "Bibliography and Pseudo-Bibliography." While the content was not scholarly, it glowed under Newton's touch, complete with personal references and nostalgic asides. Newton became less active in the book-collecting game after that and spent his last days in declining health in Philadelphia. The library, by his express wish, was distributed at auction. In honor of the man who had devoted his life to books, the sale was planned with great care. Parke-Bernet outdid itself by printing an elaborate catalog with introductions by Professors Osgood and Frederick Pottle and a special separate brochure replete with tributes from Rosenbach, Wells, and others. All the trappings were arranged for a memorable event. As the sale progressed, however, prices fell below expectations as bidders discovered that many volumes in the Newton library were in less than fine condition. However, Rosenbach's steady customers were delighted to pick up Hardys, Blakes, and Johnsons for bargain prices. The anticipated firecracker of a sale fizzled badly in the fall of 1941, with disappointing returns for the heirs. Newton's reputation easily survived the disaster, however, and his name still conjures up an aura of hearty and optimistic bibliomania.

Bibliography

A. *The Amenities of Book Collecting* (Boston, 1922); *This Book Collecting Game* (Boston, 1928); *End Papers* (Boston, 1933).

B. *NCAB* 31, 191–192; *Grolier 75*, 131–132; Wolf and Fleming, passim; Charles Osgood, "Introduction"; Swift Newton, "A Final Word"; William Winterrowd, "Edwin Newton"; and Frederick Pottle, "Introduction," all in *Rare Books Collected by A. Edward Newton* (New York, 1941); Maxwell Luria, "Miss Lowell and Mr. Newton: The Record of a Literary Friendship," *HLB*, January 1981, 5–34; A.S.W. Rosenbach, "The Age of Newton"; Randolph Adams, "An American Book Collector"; Gabriel Wells, "A Tribute"; Arthur Swann, "No Bunching Please"; and Margaret Williamson, "King of Bibliophiles," all in *The Rare Books and Manuscripts Collected by the Late A. Edward Newton* (New York, 1941); Chauncey Brewster Tinker, "The Caliph of Books: A.E.N.," *Atlantic Monthly*, December 1943, 102–106.

NICHOLS, Charles Lemuel (b. May 29, 1851, Worcester, Mass.; d. February 19, 1929, Worcester, Mass.). *Education*: A.B., Brown University, 1872; M.D., Harvard University, 1875. *Collection Disposition*: American Antiquarian Society; Massachusetts Historical Society.

In addition to his professional career as a physician, Nichols was a tireless collector and author. He was interested in colonial printing in general and in Isaiah Thomas' work in Worcester in particular. He produced a number of well-researched bibliographies and biographies based on materials in his extensive personal library. All these interests came together in his long-standing affiliations with the American Antiquarian Society, the Massachusetts Historical Society, and the Boston Club of Odd Volumes. He served as an officer in all these organizations, wrote articles for their journals, and gave books and manuscripts generously to their libraries. He is remembered as an enthusiastic collector and a careful bibliographer.

Bibliography

B. *DAB* 7, 490; *NCAB* 24, 423; "Charles Lemuel Nichols," *PAAS*, 1929; Lawrence C. Wroth, "Dr. Nichols of Worcester," *Brown Alumni Magazine*, May 1929.

NORRIS, Isaac (b. October 23, 1701, Philadelphia, Pa.; d. July 13, 1766, Philadelphia, Pa.). *Collection Disposition*: Dickinson College.

Norris came to book collecting naturally since his father had been interested in learning and had owned a sizable library. The elder Norris had been a friend of the eminent Philadelphia bibliophile James Logan* and through him had established connections with London bookdealers. In addition, Norris had married Logan's daughter and struck up an immediate bibliographic friendship with his father-in-law. Edwin Wolf II has written that since none of Logan's own children was interested in the library, Norris assumed the role of intellectual heir. This came to an end when Norris' wife died and a disagreement arose over details of the inheritance. Cut off from the Logan influence, Norris set out to build his own career both as a politician and a book collector. Happily, both careers prospered. Norris became Speaker in the Pennsylvania Assembly and was elected and reelected to that office over a period of fourteen years. At about the same time, Norris began to invest heavily in books. He ordered collections through Benjamin Franklin in America and from Thomas Osborn in London. His interests were broad, including theology, philosophy, medicine, the sciences, history, and travel. In addition to buying books in bulk, Norris also selected individual volumes as they fit his needs. Through Franklin he bought the Baskerville Press Virgil and later subscribed to that press' distinguished rendering of Milton. He bought Estienne editions of the classics and long runs of historical and bibliographic journals. Beginning in 1757 Norris attempted to make a comprehensive catalog of his library but five years later had to report to Franklin that the job was still in progress.

On Norris' death his books went to his daughter Mary, wife of statesman John

Dickinson. For many years they were stored in a small building on the Dickinson estate given over for that purpose. John Adams* saw the library in 1774 and declared it "very grand." After the war Dickinson and his wife presented a large portion of the library to the new college bearing his name. Wolf commented that the 1,900 titles chosen were somewhat inappropriate because few were in English and others were in inferior and outdated editions. The scientific studies were so specialized that neither students nor faculty would have found them useful. Euclid was available in eight different editions, none of them in English. The arguments of alchemists and the French religious theoreticians of the seventh century were far removed from the interests of the Dickinson students. Although the Norris books did little for the colonial students, they are of interest as a sample of an early American collection.

Bibliography

B. *DAB* 7, 554–555; *NCAB* 5, 88; Marie Korey, *The Books of Isaac Norris at Dickinson College* (Carlisle, Pa., 1976), with an introduction by Edwin Wolf, 1–14; Frederick Tolles, *Meeting House and Counting House: The Quaker Merchants of Colonial Philadelphia* (Chapel Hill, N.C., 1948), 161–204.

O

OOST, Stewart Irvin (b. May 20, 1921, Grand Rapids, Mich.; d. June 11, 1981, Chicago, Ill.). *Education*: B.A., M.A., Ph.D., University of Chicago, 1941, 1947, 1950. *Collection Disposition*: Southern Methodist University.

In addition to a teaching career that spanned thirty years, Oost had an impressive publication record. First at Southern Methodist University and then at the University of Chicago he produced a long list of articles and reviews on Roman imperialism, Greek political institutions, and the later Roman Empire. Many of these appeared in *Classical Philology*, a journal he edited for over twenty years. He was an omniverous reader with catholic tastes. As a consequence his private library was sizable and included ancient history, classical philology, and allied subjects. In 1978 he inherited the large classical library of his Chicago colleague Bernard Einarson. On Oost's death his entire library, said to be one of the largest private collections of the classics in the United States, went to Southern Methodist University. His will generously provided for future purchases in the classical field.

Bibliography

B. Edward Bassett, "Stewart Irving Oost," *Classical Philology*, April 1982, 93–96.

OPPENHEIMER, Edgar S. (b. June 12, 1885, Blieskastel, Ger.; d. April 29, 1959, New York, N.Y.). *Collection Disposition*: Yale University; Hauswedell, November 23, 1956; Sotheby's (London), July 1, October 21, 1974, October 16, 1975, October 21, 1976, April 21, October 13, 1977, June 2, 1982. Sotheby Parke Bernet, January 26, 1971.

Up until 1941, when he emigrated to the United States, Oppenheimer had been primarily interested in contemporary German book arts. In the early 1940s, however, he switched his collecting emphasis entirely to children's books. With the help of such dealers as Walter Schatzki and Michael Papantonio* of New York, P. H. Muir of Elkin Mathews of London, and Ernst Hauswedell of Hamburg, he built one of the largest private libraries of children's books in the world. Among the rarities in his collection were one of the five existing copies of the 1844 first edition of *Little Goody Two-Shoes*, and the manuscript of William Roscoe's *The Butterfly's Ball*. In 1949 Oppenheimer secured the F. R. Russell collection of children's books, which had provided the substance for a major exhibition at the National Book League in London. That acquisition, according to Percy Muir, placed the Oppenheimer collection of children's books in a preeminent position. In 1954, when the Pierpont Morgan Library staged a large exhibition of children's books, Oppenheimer provided 100 rare volumes. By the time he died in 1959, the collection had reached an astounding total of 7,000 volumes. Mrs. Oppenheimer kept the books for a time but eventually had them sold at auctions in England and in the United States.

Bibliography

B. Walter Schatzke, "Children's Books Exhibition at the Pierpont Morgan Library," *BC*, Spring 1955, 43–44; Correspondence with Laura Gabriel, Assistant to Mr. Oppenheimer, June 1984; Correspondence with Herbert Cahoon, Curator of Autographed Manuscripts, Pierpont Morgan Library, April 1983.

OSBORN, James M. (b. April 22, 1906, Cleveland, Ohio; d. October 17, 1976, New Haven, Conn.). *Education*: B.A., Wesleyan University, 1928; M.A. Columbia University, 1934; B.Litt., Oxford University, 1937. *Collection Disposition*: Yale; Bodleian Library; Pierpont Morgan Library.

The pattern of Osborn's collecting seems to have been established from his academic experiences at Columbia and Oxford. He became acquainted with the workings of the rare book market while a student at Columbia and made a few modest purchases at New York auctions. This was only a harbinger of events to come. Once at Oxford, Osborn became aware of the riches available in the manuscript holdings of the Bodleian Library. He was particularly drawn to the extensive manuscript collection built by eighteenth-century Shakespeare scholar Edmond Malone. It had been Malone's careful practice to gather manuscripts and rare printed editions as a base for his scholarly writings on Shakespeare and Dryden. Osborn decided to follow the same system, collecting with the left hand and turning out scholarly monographs with the right. As it happened, the 1930s were a good time to acquire seventeenth- and eighteenth-century literary and historical documents. Osborn liked to refer to these as having "evidential value." In 1937 he was fortunate to be able to purchase a large stock of Restoration manuscripts from London dealer Percy Dobell. Shortly after this he bought the important collection of the papers of Joseph Spence, intimate of Alexander Pope.

While the original emphasis of the Osborn library was on verse, it soon broadened to include literature in general and historical documents. Among many original source materials, Osborn secured diplomatic papers from seventeenth-century ambassadors and envoys, petitions to the Privy Council, speeches made in Parliament, letters concerning the Civil War, and contemporary accounts of the formation of the Armada. Probably the materials on the eighteenth century bulked the largest, with extensive holdings of manuscripts and printed texts representing the work of playwright Richard Brinsley Sheridan, statesman Edmund Burke, and musicologist Dr. Charles Burney. The Burke letters, now at Yale, are the largest holding in America, while the Sheridan correspondence is the largest anywhere. Burney was a close friend of Samuel Johnson, and many items in the vast 4,000-item holdings tie in nicely with the Yale Johnson archive. In addition, the Burney collection includes over 100 unpublished letters addressed to the musician's daughter, novelist Fanny Burney. While Osborn's first love was manuscripts, he added printed volumes as they applied to his research activities. In 1955 Laurence Witten was able to report that there were 5,000 volumes in the library, many of which had "evidential value," with canceled title-pages and annotations jotted in an author's hand. Frequently the books had unusual association interest, like the one-volume Milton from the library of A. E. Housman. As Osborn stated, the collections were gathered not just for present needs but also for research paths to be followed in the future.

As the manuscripts and books developed into substantial units they were turned over to the Yale Library, given first on deposit and later as permanent gifts. In several cases where it seemed particularly appropriate, materials were given to the Bodleian Library. In this way the scholars of Oxford received the manuscript autobiography of sixteenth-century musician Thomas Whythorne and an extensive literary archive of novelist Joyce Carey. In a talk written for delivery at the University of California at Los Angeles, Osborn identified scholar-collectors as those dedicated bibliophiles who enrich learning by bringing together books and manuscripts. He referred to Henry E. Huntington*, John Pierpont Morgan*, Henry Clay Folger*, and William A. Clark*, but surely his own name stands with these in equal prominence.

Bibliography

A. "The Osborn Collection, 1934–1974," *YLG*, October 1974, 154–170; "The Osborn Collection 1934–1974: A Catalogue of Manuscripts Exhibited in the Beinecke Rare Book and Manuscript Library, October 1974–February 1975," *YLG*, October 1974, 171–211; "Some Experiences of a Scholar-Collector," in *Building Book Collections* (Los Angeles, 1977), 3–16. "Neo-Philobiblon," *Texas Library Chronicle*, September 1972, 15–29.

B. Stephen Parks, "The Osborn Collection," in *The Beinecke Rare Book and Manuscript Library* (New Haven, 1974), 101–107; Stephen Parks, "The Osborn Collection: A Biennial Progress Report," *YLG*, January 1970, 114–138; Stephen Parks, "The Osborn Collection: A Second Biennial Progress Report," *YLG*, January 1972, 1–25; "A Third Biennial Report," *YLG*, January 1974, 145–162; "A Fourth Biennial Report," *YLG*, January 1976, 164–186; "A Fifth Biennial Report," *YLG*, January 1978, 103–121; Laurence Witten, "James Marshall Osborn," *BC*, Winter 1959, 383–396.

P

PALMER, George Herbert (b. March 19, 1842, Boston, Mass.; d. May 7, 1933, Boston, Mass.). *Education*: A.B., Harvard University, 1864; B.D., Andover Theological Seminary, 1870. *Collection Disposition*: Wellesley College; Harvard University.

After completing his undergraduate studies, Palmer traveled to Europe for advanced work in philosophy and the classics. Because of poor physical health he was never able to complete a program, but gained much in the experience through travel and exposure to languages. In 1870 he accepted an offer from President Charles Eliot of Harvard to tutor Greek studies. After two years he moved to the Department of Philosophy, where he served with great distinction until his retirement in 1913. Along with such colleagues as Henry James, Josiah Royce, George Santayana, and Hugo Münsterberg, Palmer brought Harvard students a level of teaching and scholarship unequaled in any institution in America.

In addition to his professional volumes, Palmer gathered an outstanding collection of the works by and about the seventeenth-century metaphysical poet George Herbert. Since Palmer's given names had been taken from the English poet, the collection had a sentimental connection. In addition to Herbert's works, the collection included manuscripts, criticism, and biography relating to the author's family and friends. Palmer presented the entire philosophy library and the Herbert collection to Harvard in 1912. Palmer's other important collecting interest, shared with his wife, was nineteenth-century English poetry. In 1887 Palmer married Alice Freeman, president of Wellesley College, and together they set out to form a private library of English poetry. First in priority were the works of the Brownings, followed by those of Tennyson and Ruskin. In February 1911 Palmer presented part of the Browning collection to Wellesley as a memorial to his wife, who had died nine years earlier. The gift included first editions, anthologies, and collateral material. At the commencement exercises of 1918 Palmer presented Wellesley with his Tennyson collection and a few years later the entire library of English literature. In a final and crowning donation Palmer gave Wellesley his magnificent series of Elizabeth Barrett Browning holograph letters bound in eleven morocco volumes. These letters, many of which were unpublished at that time, included important exchanges between Browning and her family, critics, and friends. Palmer's will provided continued support for the collection through income received as royalties from the sale of several of his books. Throughout his life Palmer steadfastly refused to have his name attached to any of the collections. In 1936, however, the trustees appropriately voted to identify the endowment he had given as the George Herbert Palmer Fund.

Bibliography

A. *A Herbert Bibliography* (Cambridge, Mass., 1911); *Life of Alice Freeman Palmer* (Boston, 1908); *The Autobiography of a Philosopher* (New York, 1930); *Notes on a Collection of English Poetry Intended for Wellesley College* (Cambridge, Mass., 1915).

B. *DAB* 8, 180–182; *NCAB* 6, 427–428; A. Edward Newton, *This Book Collecting Game* (Boston, 1928), 26–31; Ethel Roberts, *A Brief History of the Wellesley College Library* (Wellesley, Mass., 1936), 11–13.

PAPANTONIO, Michael (b. February 25, 1907, Union City, N.J.; d. August 20, 1978, New York, N.Y.). *Collection Disposition*: American Antiquarian Society.

For over thirty years, Papantonio, a New York antiquarian bookdealer, and John S. Van E. Kohn, were co-proprietors of the Seven Gables Bookshop. Around 1935 Papantonio started a personal collection of early American bindings, an area of the book arts that had failed to attract the attention of other collectors. After a desultory beginning the collection got its start in 1948 when Papantonio acquired a copy of the *New York Mirror and Ladies' Literary Gazette*, a handsome example of early-nineteenth-century craftsmanship bound in tan calf with gilt and blind-tooled border decorations. Over the next thirty years Papantonio obtained almost 1,000 bindings representing the best work of American craftsmen from the seventeenth through the nineteenth centuries. Among these were samples of cathedral bindings, embossed morocco and polished calf bindings, gold tooling, doublures, and marbled and colored endpapers. Papantonio's special interest was in ticketed volumes in which the name of the binder was identified. In 1972 a group of librarians encouraged Papantonio to arrange a selection of his bindings for a traveling exhibition. It was the first time such a display had been made available to the public since Papantonio had mounted a small exhibit at the Grolier Club in 1962. Crowds attended the showings at Cornell, the American Antiquarian Society, the University of Virginia, the Pierpont Morgan Library, and finally at Princeton, where a binding seminar concluded the year-long tour.

About three years before his death, Papantonio began to turn over his collection to the American Antiquarian Society in Worcester, Massachusetts, thereby furnishing scholars with a unique and artistic record of American bookmaking.

Bibliography

A. *Early American Bookbindings from the Collection of Michael Papantonio* (New York, 1972); "A Bookseller's View of the Collector," *PLC*, Winter-Spring 1977, 87–96.

B. Hannah D. French, "Early American Bookbindings in the Library of Michael Papantonio," *ABC*, July-August 1974, 24–26; Marcus McCorison, "Early American Bookbindings from the Collection of Michael Papantonio," *PAAS*,October 1983, 381–414; "Michael Papantonio," *PAAS*, October 1978, 181–184.

PARRISH, Morris L. (b. 1867, Philadelphia, Pa.; d. July 10, 1944, Philadelphia, Pa.). *Collection Disposition*: Princeton University; Parke-Bernet, March 3, 1938.

Parrish grew up in a socially prominent Philadelphia family where books and reading were a part of the household. He was initiated into the fine points of book collecting when he had a set of Dickens in parts rebound, thereby destroying their "issue condition." From then on he insisted on original state, and in so doing established "Parrish condition" as a standard that has meant perfection to all succeeding bookdealers and collectors. He collected the novelists he liked, chiefly the Victorians—Thackeray, Kingsley, Hardy, Trollope, Meredith, Stevenson, and many others. The twin characteristics of his author collections, as David Randall has pointed out, were condition and completeness. Once Parrish decided to gather an author's works he wanted everything—books, pamphlets, binding variants, broadsides, and in the case of novels adapted to the theater, playbills, programs, and scripts. He was not particularly interested in association copies or manuscripts, although he had some distinguished samples of both. His Lewis Carroll mathematics manuscripts, for example, were particularly notable. For a time he collected some American authors, but when it seemed impossible to secure full runs he sold the complete lot in New York in 1938. Using his library as a base, Parrish contributed a number of highly useful author bibliographies to the literature. Among these were treatments of Carroll, Kingsley, Trollope, Collins, and Reade. In his bibliographic work Parrish described with care but did not pontificate. Among all his author collections, perhaps the Trollope section was supreme. In 1928 he purchased the impressive collection of Victorian bibliographer Michael Sadleir. Although many of the Sadleir copies were in good or fine state, Parrish weeded and traded sometimes five or six times in order to bring the level of the whole to near perfection. After a fire at his home in New Jersey, which fortunately spared the books, Parrish turned to his Princeton friends for advice. He wanted a home for his library that would be safe and supportive. In addition, he wanted a replica of his own library room built to house the books. When the Firestone Library was planned, the university administrators saw to it that his wishes were carried out. Since that time the collection has been augmented regularly by sizable gifts from collectors who knew Parrish and respected his collecting goals. Parrish is remembered as an intelligent and fastidious collector.

Bibliography

B. *Grolier 75*, 160–163; John Carter, "The Library at Dormy House," *The Colophon* 3, June 1939, 25–36; Glenn Christensen, "The Thomas Hardy Library"; Sarah Dickson, "The Bulwer Lytton Library"; Gordon Gerould, "The Dickens Collection"; Thomas Parrott, "Morris L. Parrish and the Dormy House Library"; David Randall, "Some Observations upon the Morris L. Parrish Collection"; Michael Sadleir, "An English Memory"; Robert Taylor, "The Trollope Library"; and Margaret Thorp, "The Kingsley Collection," all in *PLC*, November 1946; David Randall, *Dukedom Large Enough* (New York, 1969), 317–321.

PARSONS, Edward Alexander (b. March 28, 1878, New Orleans, La.; d. February 19, 1962, New Orleans, La.). *Education*: A.B., College of Immaculate Conception; LL.B., Loyola University. *Collection Disposition*: University of Texas.

Long before Parsons became a prominent New Orleans attorney he was an avid book collector. In his autobiography, *The Wonder and the Glory*, he described how as a teenager he set aside bus money to buy books until he had several cases packed to capacity. Friends and relatives provided additional titles on birthdays and at Christmas, and soon he had the beginnings of an admirable collection. At first he favored the studies of early Greek, Egyptian, Mesopotamian, and Roman civilizations, with their large panoramic illustrations of the Parthenon, the Pyramids, and St. Peter's Church in Rome. History led him to literature, literature led him to art, and art led him back to history, geography, and travel. Later he acquired a number of notable narratives of discovery and travel and also a fine library of Louisiana history. Throughout the 1920s and 1930s Parsons traveled widely and obtained books and manuscripts from the chief bookdealers of England and Europe. He was as familiar a customer at Sotheby's auction rooms in London as he was at the Anderson Galleries in New York.

As Parsons collected books and manuscripts on the ancient world, he began to write a number of well-received historical studies. In 1921 he issued *The Latin City*, followed the next year by *Stones of Reims* and two years later by *Dante Alighieri*. In 1952 he published his major work, *The Alexandrian Library, Glory of the Hellenic World*, a book that enabled him to bring together all his humanistic ideals. For Parsons the Alexandrian Library and its staff of scholarly attendants epitomized the best in ancient culture. It was natural, then, that as he considered the disposition of his own library he would look for a similar setting. Librarians at the University of Texas had been aware of the existence of the Bibliotheca Parsoniana from 1938, when Frank Glenn, a Kansas City bookdealer, distributed a leaflet announcing the collection's availability. Although Parsons visited Austin and several of the Texas librarians went to see the books at Number 5 Rosa Park in New Orleans, funding remained a problem. Between 1954 and 1958 Harry H. Ransom, then dean of the College of Arts and Sciences, mounted a massive campaign to secure the books. With the help of several major private donors, Ransom saw his efforts rewarded in 1958, when the Texas Board of Regents authorized the purchase. When three sealed vans containing the 750 book cartons arrived in Austin, the university found it had obtained a library of classic dimensions, one that would contribute to the study of the ancient and oriental worlds, the book arts, English and French literature, and American history. This was not merely a collection of 48,000 books and manuscripts; it was a unified humanistic library.

Bibliography

A. *The Alexandrian Library, Glory of the Hellenic World* (New York, 1952); *The Wonder and the Glory: Confessions of a Southern Bibliophile* (New York, 1962).

B. "The Parsons Collection: A Library for Texas," in *A Guide to the Humanities Research Center* (Austin, forthcoming).

PAULLIN, George W. (b. July 17, 1864, Philadelphia, Pa.; d. November 18, 1933, Evanston, Ill.). *Education*: LL.B., Wake Forest University, 1893. *Collection Disposition*: American Art, April 1 and 29, 1929.

All Paullin's professional interests seemed to have led him to collecting. As a young man he worked for an ethnologist and collected Indian materials. When he entered the fur trade he began to obtain accounts of the early western trappers. Later as a trustee of the Chicago Sanitary District he gathered materials on canals and railroads. Finally, as a politician and loyal citizen of Illinois, he formed an impressive collection on Lincoln and the Civil War. In addition to the areas already mentioned, Paullin collected rare pre–Chicago fire imprints and early Illinois printing. All these interests complemented each other. Historian Carl Cannon observed that Paullin's Indian captivity materials were the strongest items in the library. The eighty-eight rare titles assembled in the sale catalog seem to provide testimony to Cannon's claim. The Paullin sale was one of the first to bring a substantial collection of midwestern materials to the attention of eastern buyers.

Bibliography

B. *NCAB* 25, 161; Cannon, 262–263.

PEARSON, Norman Holmes (b. April 13, 1909, Gardner, Mass.; d. November 5, 1975, New Haven, Conn.). *Education*: A.B., Yale University, 1932; M.A., Oxford University, 1941; Ph.D., Yale University, 1941. *Collection Disposition*: Yale University.

Almost all Pearson's professional life was spent at Yale. He received his academic degrees from that institution and served on the English faculty for more than twenty years. His extensive publication record included *Poets of the*

English Language, with W. H. Auden, and the *Oxford Anthology of American Literature*, with William Rose Benét. Pearson's collecting interests were diverse and took in many of the poets and novelists of the second half of the century. He was particularly enthusiastic about modern American poetry and formed notable collections of the works of Hilda Doolittle, Ezra Pound, Robert McAlmon, William Carlos Williams, and John Gould Fletcher. He also owned long files of literary journals, nineteenth-century English juveniles, and drawings and sketches by well-known writers. When he "took up" an author he tried to be as comprehensive as possible. In the case of Fletcher, for example, he had first editions of books, musical scores, issues of journals, anthologies, leaflets, broadsides, photographs, clippings, and manuscripts. Almost as soon as a collection was organized Pearson would turn it over to the Yale Library. An examination of the issues of the *Yale Library Gazette* for the years 1950–1975 would reveal a steady stream of gifts. In a 1970 issue the editor reported that although Professor Pearson was on leave in Japan he had sent the library several McAlmon first editions, a run of literary journals, and some new Pound manuscripts. Pearson was a productive scholar and a generous friend to the Yale libraries.

Bibliography

A. "The Gertrude Stein Collection," *YLG*, January 1942, 45–47; "The John Gould Fletcher Collection," *YLG*, January 1956, 120–125.

PECK, Clara S. (b. February 16, 1896, Brooklyn, N.Y.; d. April 20, 1983, New York, N.Y.). *Collection Disposition*: Princeton University; Pierpont Morgan Library; Transylvania University; Rockwell Museum of Corning, New York.

As a teenager, Peck developed a love for horses. In a note written to her father in 1909 she declared her satisfaction with everything that he gave her for Christmas but reminded him that she still wanted a "live horse." Soon that wish was granted. By 1930 Peck had become a connoisseur of saddle horses and the owner of a large stable in Fayette County, Kentucky. Along with her interest in breeding and raising horses, she developed an equal enthusiasm for sporting books and manuscripts. In the early 1930s, she made significant purchases from A.S.W. Rosenbach* and H. P. Kraus. In *Rosenbach: A Biography*, Fleming and Wolf identify her as part of the doctor's "royal flush"—ace, Arthur Houghton; king, Lessing J. Rosenwald*; queen, Peck; jack, Frank J. Hogan*; and ten, John H. Scheide*. In 1935 Rosenbach sold Peck the cornerstone of her collection, the famed Earl of Pembroke's copy of the "Book of St. Albans" (1486), the first example of color printing done in England and the first book of its kind to be written by a woman. She backed up this treasure by obtaining the first five editions of Izaak Walton's *Compleat Angler*, a long run of novels by Robert Surtees, and a handsomely illustrated set of the *Collections of British Field Sports* (1807) by Edward Orme. Two other high points in her collection were the magnificent 1387 manuscript *Livre de la Chasse*, now in the Pierpont Morgan

Library, and a sixteenth-century Persian manuscript of the *Shah Nameh*, given to Princeton. When Peck left Kentucky in 1958 she presented many of her sporting books, including the "Book of St. Albans," to the Transylvania University Library. Her buying during the 1960s and 1970s continued to focus on rural life, birds, hunting, and, as always, horses. The remainder of the distinguished Peck collection went to Transylvania at the time of her death.

Bibliography

B. Wolf and Fleming, passim; Correspondence with Kathleen Bryson, archivist of Transylvania University, 1983; Correspondence with Fremont C. Peck, 1983.

PENNYPACKER, Samuel W. (b. April 9, 1843, Phoenixville, Pa.; d. September 2, 1916, Pennypacker Mills, Pa.). *Collection Disposition*: Henkels, December 14, 1905, April 25, December 5 and 6, 1906, April 24 and 25, November 26 and 27, 1907, April 16, November 27 and 28, 1908, October 18 and 19, 1909.

In his forthright autobiography, Pennypacker declared that although his formal education had ended at age seventeen he never stopped learning through books. After serving in the Civil War he studied law and was admitted to the Pennsylvania bar in 1866. As an extra source of income he began to edit a series of legal compilations, which brought him not only financial gain but also considerable professional recognition. His political career included appointments to the Philadelphia Board of Education, the judgeship of the Court of Common Pleas, and finally election to the office of governor. His chief outside interest was historical research, particularly as applied to early events in his own state. Since the materials for research were not readily at hand, he set about to find them.

From his earliest years, Pennypacker had been an imaginative and energetic collector, first gathering Indian artifacts from the fields around the family farm and then, when he moved to Philadelphia, turning to books. He was interested in Pennsylvania history in general, but with a particular fascination for the printing of Benjamin Franklin and Christopher Sower, the literature of the Mennonites and the Schwenkfelders, and the colorful German artwork known as Vorschrift. In addition to these specialties, he gathered the documents of the early colonial legislatures, court records, and long runs of Franklin's *Pennsylvania Gazette*. The Franklin holdings were truly distinguished and, according to Pennypacker, exceeded those of any other library in the country. In addition to Franklin's printing, Pennypacker owned books relating to him as well as books and papers from his personal library. While books and pamphlets came to Pennypacker from all over the world, he often found the best hunting close to home. He frequently went incognito to country sales and bought bushel bags full of books for little or nothing. Occasionally Franklin, Sower, or Ephrata imprints would turn up in the midst of these bundles of "rubbish." His knowledge of early printing and book values turned out to be as useful in the sophisticated Philadelphia bookshops as it was in country auctions. From the shelves of William Brotherhead's shop he purchased a unique edition of Edgar Allan Poe's poems for sixty cents. It was Brotherhead, in his charming reminiscence about Philadelphia collectors, who singled out Pennypacker as a true bibliomaniac. For his broad interests Pennypacker deserved Brotherhead's designation. When books became more of a burden than an asset, however, Pennypacker decided to sell. He had used his library for research and writing, but as governor he had no time for such diversions. Furthermore, the 10,000 volumes in the house in Philadelphia were in constant danger from fire and thieves. After saving a portion of the books relating to the Mennonites and the Schwenkfelders, Pennypacker turned the remaining collection over to Stan Henkels for auction. The sales disappointed Pennypacker, who believed he could have done better privately. His library was unique in its emphasis on local and regional printing and on local history.

Bibliography

A. *The Autobiography of a Pennsylvanian* (Philadelphia, 1918).

B. *DAB* 14, 447–448; *NCAB* 9, 487; Cannon, 254–259, A. S. W. Rosenbach, *Books and Bidders* (Boston, 1927), 8–9; William Brotherhead, *Forty Years Among the Old Booksellers of Philadelphia* (Philadelphia, 1891).

PENROSE, Boies (b. November 20, 1902, Philadelphia, Pa.; d. February 27, 1976, Greenwich, Conn.). *Education*: A.B., Harvard University, 1925. *Collection Disposition*: Sotheby (London), February 5, 1934; November 19, 1945, January 28, 1947, June 7 and 13, 1971, November 9, 1971.

The two most important personal influences on Penrose's book-collecting career were his grandfather Joseph W. Drexel* and his Harvard instructor George Parker Winship. From his grandfather, a prominent collector of the 1880s, Penrose inherited an impressive library of Americana and several incunabula. Included in this library were first editions of the travel narratives of Hakluyt, Purchas, and DeBry, Caxton's printing of Higden's *Polychronicon*, and Wynkyn de Worde's printing of Cicero's *Offices*. At Harvard, in Winship's fine arts class, Penrose became interested in early printing. For several years he bought fifteenth-century imprints as his budget allowed. By 1928, however, two events changed his collection pattern—the C.H.W. Leconfield sale, which offered a great travel library, and the Lionel Robinson catalog, with its rich assortment of early English books. From that time on, Penrose concentrated on English travel books and manuscripts covering a span of time from the Middle Ages to the Renaissance. Among his printed travel accounts of the fifteenth century were the works of Thomas Coryate, William Lithgow, Fynes Moryson, and Robert Sherley. In addition to those important but lesser-known figures, he had the early printed accounts of the voyages of Drake and Raleigh. Another rich section of the collection concerned the development of the East India Company and the opening of trade with the Orient. As for Americana, Penrose owned most of the standard works, supplemented by such rarities as the Basel "Columbus Letter" of 1494 and both the 1589 and 1598 editions of Hakluyt. In 1961 he estimated that the total size of his library would probably never exceed 500 volumes.

In addition to the books, however, the collection held a number of important early maps and atlases. Among these, Penrose had a 1513 Ptolemy atlas and a 1520 *Solinus*, the first map to include the printed designation "America." The aforementioned Leconfield sale supplied twenty-three of the most important travel books in the library, while the Henry Huth and Britwell sales accounted for thirty more. In order to carry out his commissions, Penrose employed several of the most astute dealers in the world, Bernard Quaritch and Lionel Robinson in London and Mabel Zahn of Sesslers in Philadelphia. Not content merely to collect, Penrose wrote a series of monographs on fifteenth- and sixteenth-century travel based on the holdings in his own library. These furnished a unique insight into the social life of the time. Although Penrose sold a few of his incunabula in 1934 and 1945, he kept the bulk of the collection together until 1971, when it too went to the auction block.

Bibliography

A. *A Selection of Rare Books, Manuscripts, Maps, and Prints from the Library of Boies Penrose of Barbados Hill, Devon, Pennsylvania* (New York, 1942); "The Library at Barbados Hill, Devon, Pennsylvania," *BC*, Autumn 1961, 301–310; "The Indiscreet History of a Bibliographic, and Antiquarian Tour Made in England in July 1938," *The Colophon*, Autumn 1938, 490–512.

B. *NYT*, February 28, 1976, 26; *Geographical Journal*, July 1976, 378.

PERKINS, John I. (b. June 4, 1863, Athens, Pa.; d. January 20, 1942, Los Angeles, Calif.). *Collection Disposition*: Scripps College.

In a series of tributes delivered in Perkins' honor in 1942, the speakers emphasized his extreme reticence, integrity, and great love of books. Perkins came from a family of ample means and was able to devote himself to collecting on a full-time basis for most of his life. His interests centered around what have been called the book arts—printing, binding, and illustration. For many years Perkins was one of the most favored customers in Ernest Dawson's bookshop in Los Angeles. It was one of Dawson's rules to close the shop exactly at 5:00 P.M., but when Perkins was in the store he extended the hours indefinitely. In the 1930s, when Dawson sent Dorothy Bevis abroad to hunt for rare books in Europe, Perkins' want lists were always in hand. Perkins also bought books from Alice Millard of Pasadena and other Los Angeles area dealers. His library, as it developed, was rich in examples of the work of famous printers from early times through the twentieth century. There were incunabula and Aldines, as well as works by Christopher Plantin, the Elzevirs, John Baskerville, Benjamin Franklin, and William Morris. The library held all but seven of the titles printed at Morris' Kelmscott Press. The English fine printing movement of the nineteenth century was also well represented, with copies of such works as the Doves Bible and the Ashendene edition of Spenser's *Faerie Queen*. Perkins was interested in fine binding and had examples of books bound in silver filigree, mother-of-pearl, and intricately carved leather. In another section of the library he gathered association books, illustrators, and autographed manuscripts. And this was not all. As he could find suitable copies, he acquired children's books, Californiana, and first editions of modern fiction. In 1938 Perkins met Dorothy Drake, Scripps College librarian, and through her developed a strong interest in the college and its library. He became convinced that his books would be used and enjoyed at Scripps as he wanted them to be. Perkins arranged for the books to go to the college, but such was his modesty that he asked that no publicity be attached to the gift during his lifetime. After presenting his gift Perkins continued to buy with enthusiasm, but now for the institution. Some of his finest volumes were acquired at this time.

Perkins was a devoted and knowledgeable book lover. He understood the importance of bibliography and maintained good relations with the book trade. His collection forms the backbone of the Special Collection Department of Scripps College.

Bibliography

B. Dorothy Drake, "John I. Perkins: The Man and His Books," Transcription of a talk on November 24, 1942; Sybil Fiedler, "From the Library," *Scripps Alumnae News* 6, 1949, 13–14; Ward Ritchie, *Bookmen and Their Brothels: Recollections of Los Angeles in the 1930s* (Los Angeles, 1970), 12–13.

PERRY, Marsden J. (b. November 2, 1850, Rehoboth, Mass.; d. April 15, 1937, New York, N.Y.). *Collection Disposition*: Brown University; Direct sale to A.S.W. Rosenbach; American Art—Anderson, March 11, 1936.

As an early entrepreneur in East Coast interurban rail lines, Perry amassed a considerable fortune. Along with these business responsibilities he developed a strong interest in amateur Shakespeare productions. Book collecting followed as a natural outlet for his fascination with Shakespeare and his times. By the time he was forty he had purchased sufficient Shakespeare materials to issue a "Preliminary List" of some 1,000 titles. In 1897 he bought the great J. O. Halliwell-Phillipps Shakespeare collection. Later he obtained the four notable folios from B. B. MacGeorge of Glasgow and six quartos from Sir William Penn. In a great coup he purchased two-thirds of the items from the Shakespeare catalog prepared by J. Pearson and Company in London. By this stroke Perry became one of the preeminent Shakespeare collectors in the country. However, financial reverses at the turn of the century made it necessary for him to reduce his collection drastically. In 1907 he was forced to sell the Halliwell-Phillipps books to Henry C. Folger*, and seven years later he lost a chance to own the famous "Devonshire Quartos" to high-bidding multimillionaire Henry E. Huntington*. Discouraged, Perry sold the remainder of his Shakespeare library to A.S.W. Rosenbach* in 1919, and from that shop the rarities found their way quickly into the private collections of Folger, Joseph Widener*, and John Pierpont Morgan Jr.*. In addition to the Shakespeare collection, Perry owned almost all the publications of William Morris' Kelmscott Press, a particularly choice gathering that contained Morris' personal copies, press ephemera, and proof runs.

In 1928 the Grolier Club of New York displayed the Morris materials and issued a handsome catalog edited by George Parker Winship. In one last collecting venture, Perry bought an impressive Rhode Island history collection, estimated at some 50,000 items. Appropriately, he gave the books to Brown University in Providence. Perry will be remembered as an important collector of Shakespeariana and as a generous contributor to Brown.

Bibliography

A. *A Preliminary List of Books and Manuscripts Relating to the Life and Writings of William Shakespeare Forming the Collection of Marsden Perry* (Providence, R.I., 1891); *A Chronological List of the Books Printed at the Kelmscott Press with Illustrative Material from a Collection Made by William Morris and Henry C. Marillier Now in the Library of Marsden Perry* (New York, 1928).

B. *NCAB* C, 361; Cannon, 326–328; *Grolier 75*, 61–63; "The World's Costliest Book," *Literary Digest*, November 15, 1919, 33.

PFORZHEIMER, Carl H. (b. January 29, 1879, New York, N.Y.; d. April 4, 1957, Purchase, N.Y.). *Collection Disposition*: Carl H. and Lily Pforzheimer Foundation; Sotheby's (London), June 12, 1978.

In storybook manner Pforzheimer rose from Wall Street clerk to Wall Street tycoon in a matter of only a few years. As his personal financial position grew, he began to invest in books and manuscripts. After making tentative purchases at the Henry Huth, Robert Hoe*, and Britwell Court sales, he appeared as a major buyer at the Henry Buxton-Forman auction in 1920. There, guided by A.S.W. Rosenbach*, he secured among other items Browning's *Pauline*, Fanny Brawne's own copy of Keats' *Poems*, and Shelley's rare *Posthumous Fragments of Margaret Nicholson*. With these purchases, Pforzheimer gave notice to the book world that he intended to become preeminent in the Victorian and Romantic periods, particularly with those materials relating to Shelley and his circle. At the same time, he began to acquire the famous Elizabethan authors as they came on the market. At the John Clawson* sale in 1926, for example, he spent more than $200,000 on Elizabethan and Tudor rarities. Three years earlier, at the Carysfort sale, he had acquired a Gutenberg Bible, the Fust and Schoeffer 1462 Bible, and two Caxton imprints. After the Jerome Kern* sale, at the end of the decade, his buying fell off, although from time to time he succumbed to Rosenbach "bargains." By 1939 economic indicators had started to move upward, and Pforzheimer heralded the new prosperity with a handful of purchases at the John Spoor* sale. The next year marked the publication of his impressive three-volume catalog covering English literature from 1475 to 1700. The extensive notes, supplied by bibliographer William A. Jackson, provided impeccable descriptions of the books in hand as well as comparative data on other copies. Although Pforzheimer stated that he had not attempted complete coverage on any particular authors, his holdings of Ben Jonson, Thomas Heywood, and Thomas Middleton were impressive. In the 1940s he continued to make additions to the Shelley collection whenever prices were reasonable.

At his death the administration of the library was turned over to the Carl H. and Lily Pforzheimer Foundation along with a substantial endowment for continued accessions. In 1978, in order to narrow the focus of the collection to the Romantic writers, the foundation sold thirty-five of the fifteenth-century Continental books, some of the early English titles, and the Gutenberg Bible. Pforzheimer showed what could be done with a combination of taste and means in the early part of the century.

Bibliography

A. *The Carl Pforzheimer Library: English Literature 1475–1700*, 3 volumes with an introduction by Carl H. Pforzheimer (New York, 1940).

B. Wolf and Fleming, passim; Carl Pforzheimer Jr., "Introduction," in *Shelley and His Circle: Additions to the Carl H. Pforzheimer Library 1957–1978* (New York, 1978); "Shelley as a Young Radical," *Gazette of the Grolier Club*, 1969, 25–29.

PIERSON, John Shaw (b. April 21, 1822, London, Eng.; d. July 2, 1908, Orange, N.J.). *Education*: A.B., Princeton University, 1840. *Collection Disposition*: Princeton University.

After graduating from college Pierson practiced law for a short time before accepting an appointment as marine agent for the New York Bible Society. In that capacity it was his job to place Bibles and other books on board ships sailing out of New York harbor. In over thirty years of service with the Society he became very familiar with the bookdealers and bookshops of New York. As a personal collector, he concentrated his energies on the literature of the Civil War. His attempts to gather background information on all phases of that conflict included social and economic studies and the military record. His collection of personal narratives by politicians and soldiers both Northern and Southern was extensive. Pierson was acutely aware of the value of ephemera and obtained many scarce pamphlets, broadsides, speeches, and sermons. By 1879 he had given 2,000 items to Princeton. In 1898 the college reported that there were 5,000 items in the collection, and by the time of Pierson's death there were almost 9,000. With only modest means Pierson made a scholarly contribution to the Princeton Library by assembling an important contemporary record.

Bibliography

B. "The Pierson Collection," *Princeton Alumni Weekly*, 1933; John Joline, "The Pierson Civil War Collection," *PLC*, April 1941, 105–110.

PLIMPTON, George A. (b. July 13, 1855, Walpole, Mass.; d. June 1, 1936, Walpole, Mass.). *Education*: A.B., Amherst College, 1876. *Collection Disposition*: Amherst College; Columbia University; Wellesley College.

After attending Harvard Law School from 1876 to 1877, Plimpton took a job as a salesman for the textbook firm of Ginn and Heath. He worked his way up through the ranks to the level of full partnership and later was appointed chairman of the board. When he joined Ginn, their line consisted chiefly of Greek and Latin classics. With the idea that a historical perspective would help in understanding the then-current market requirements, Plimpton began to collect early Greek and Latin texts. For forty years he continued to gather instructional materials and eventually owned the largest library of its kind in the country. His wide historical view encompassed manuscripts, incunabula, primers, and hornbooks, all the formats that provided instruction for children from medieval times to the middle of the nineteenth century. Plimpton argued that textbooks had played an important role in shaping society since they furnished the background for education. Textbooks, in his opinion, made civilization possible. The earliest manuscripts in the collection were a tenth-century "Arithmetic" by Boethius, several Euclid and Virgil texts, and a fourteenth-century Chaucer treatise on the astrolabe. The section of the library given over to hornbooks, those efficient colonial learning devices, was notable for both English and American examples. On another shelf, Lilly's *Latin Grammar* (1512) printed by Richard Pynson, fought for space with Clenardus' *Greek Grammar* (1570), printed by Aldus.

By 1935 the 15,000-item collection had completely overrun Plimpton's Park Avenue home. Fortunately a solution was available just uptown at Columbia University. The faculty of the Teachers College was delighted to receive the Plimpton library and have since relied on it as the backbone of their coursework in the history of education. Before the books were moved to Columbia, Plimpton used them as source material for *The Education of Shakespeare* and *The Education of Chaucer*, two lively and imaginative studies of early textbook use. While Plimpton's largest single gathering consisted of textbooks, he had several other interests. In 1900 he presented a large collection of Italian literature to Wellesley College in memory of his wife. Among the texts, which covered the period from 1400 to 1700, were notable works by Dante, Boccaccio, and Petrarch as well as a wide selection of medieval romances and burlesques. In the thirty-five years between the original gift and his death, Plimpton doubled the size of this collection. Finally, Plimpton built a sizable historical library on the French and Indian War, which he presented to Amherst College. This rich archive included letters, books, maps, newspapers, etchings, and relics evocative of the mid-eighteenth century. The focus of Plimpton's collecting was on the printed formats that contributed to the spread of humanistic thought. His gifts to Wellesley, Columbia, and Amherst have provided rich backing for the scholarly examination of that process.

Bibliography

A. *The Education of Shakespeare* (London, 1933); *The Education of Chaucer* (London, 1935); *Rara Arithmetica* (New York, 1908); "Grammatical Manuscripts and Early Printed Grammars in the Plimpton Library," *PAAS*, 1933, 150–178; *Catalogue of the Frances Taylor Pearsons Plimpton Collection of Italian Books and Manuscripts in the Library of*

Wellesley College (Cambridge, Mass., 1929); *The Plimpton Collection of French and Indian War Items* (Amherst, Mass., 1934).

B. *DAB*, Supp. 2, 532; *NCAB* 27, 274; Stanley King, "The Plimpton Years," in *The Consecrated Eminence: Story of the Campus and Buildings at Amherst College* (Amherst, Mass., 1951), 115–145; Thomas Lawler, *George Arthur Plimpton 1855–1936* (New York).

POOR, Henry (b. June 16, 1844, Bangor, Maine; d. April 13, 1915, New York, N.Y.). *Education*: A.B., M.A., Harvard University, 1865, 1872. *Collection Disposition*: Anderson, November 17, December 7, 1908, January 12, February 23, April 5, 1909.

After graduating from Harvard, Poor entered the family brokerage firm, where as part of his duties he supervised the publication of a survey of railway statistics. As *Poor's Railway Manual*, this guide became famous as the authoritative source for investors in the field. Poor's own financial career was marked with spectacular successes and equally spectacular failures. For a time at the turn of the century he had the means to employ experts to do his collecting. No less an authority than Stanford White bought art treasures for him, while Valentin Blacque secured his books and manuscripts. Poor thus amassed a lavish assortment of fine bindings, illuminated manuscripts, first editions, and press books. For example, he had the first edition of Thomas à Kempis' *De Imitatio Christi*, the inevitable signatures of the Presidents of the United States, and Caxton's printing of Higden's *Polychronicon*. In 1908, when Poor's financial structure collapsed, Arthur Swann of the Anderson Auction Company prepared a sumptuous sale catalog calculated to pull large bids out of sensitive buyers. The plan worked and the sale was a success. Walter T. Wallace* bought some of the English literature, but a new collector, Henry E. Huntington*, took away most of the prizes. With the irrepressible bookdealer George D. Smith leading the way, Huntington managed to capture almost one-third of the Poor library. For Poor this was the end, but for Huntington it was just the beginning.

Bibliography

A. *Catalogue of the Valentin Blacque Collection in the Library of Henry W. Poor* (New York, 1903); *American Bookbindings in the Library of Henry William Poor*, edited by Henri Pene DuBois (New York, 1903).

B. *NCAB* 16, 33; Wesley Towner, *The Elegant Auctioneers* (New York, 1970), 255–258; "A Record Year in Book Sales," *NYT*, April 10, 1909, 236.

POPE, Abbie Ellen Hanscom (b. May 13, 1858, Raynham, Mass.; d. August 24, 1894, Mechanic Falls, Me.). *Collection Disposition:* Dodd, Mead and Company, 1895, then sold *en bloc* to Robert Hoe III*; Anderson, May 12, 1910.

Although little is known of Pope's early years, by 1885 she was clearly a seasoned collector. In that year, through renowned bookdealer B. F. Stevens, she outbid the British Museum at the Osterley Park sale and obtained Malory's *Morte d'Arthur* (1485) printed by William Caxton. At the same sale she added another Caxton, Gower's *Confessio Amantis* (1483), one of five known copies. Through continued negotiations with Stevens, Pope obtained the four Shakespeare folios, thirteen quartos, and many other examples of Elizabethan and Jacobean drama, poetry, and prose. Following a popular trend of the day, Pope delighted in extra-illustrated extravaganzas such as a six-volume edition of Robert Burns which she expanded to thirteen volumes with portraits, manuscripts, letters, and ephemera all bound in crushed crimson levant morocco. She made up similar elaborate sets for many of the illustrious poets and dramatists of the Elizabethan period. The manuscript showpiece of her library was a Charles VI missal with 107 large miniatures and over 400 border drawings. With Pope's tastes for the sumptuous, it is not surprising that her library held examples of the work of the best-known binding craftsmen of the nineteenth century. In recognition of her knowledge, she was appointed chairman of the Bookbinding Committee for the 1892 World's Fair.

When Pope died suddenly at the age of thirty-six, Dodd, Mead and Company bought the books and issued a handsome sale announcement. New York collector Robert Hoe III* examined the books at Dodd's showroom and bought almost the entire collection, at a figure estimated at between $200,000 and $250,000. Much of Pope's reputation rested on her purchase at the Osterley Park sale. Years after her death the *New York Evening Post* would refer to her as "the most notable woman book collector America ever produced."

Bibliography

B. Charles Ryskamp, "Abbie Pope," *BC*, Spring 1984, 39–52; *New York Evening Post*, April 1, 1911.

PRINCE, Thomas (b. May 15, 1687, Sandwich, Eng.; d. October 22, 1758, Boston, Mass.). *Education*: A.B., Harvard College, 1707. *Collection Disposition*: Boston Public Library.

Reared in a prominent colonial New England family, Prince started life with a good education and ample financial means. He inherited an interest in books and collecting from his grandfather, Thomas Hinckley, the last governor of Plymouth Colony. Hinckley had a good library and impressed his grandson with the importance of saving letters and contemporary historical documents. By the time Prince entered Harvard, he had started what he called his New England library. This was a collection of books, pamphlets, and papers illustrative of the development of the history of New England. Shortly after graduating, Prince went to Europe, where he studied theology, served as pastor in several English churches, and augmented his personal library. On returning to Boston in 1717 he took up what became a lifelong appointment as assistant pastor of the Old South Church. At the same time he started a collection that came to be known as the South Church Library, consisting of theological classics in Latin, Greek, and Oriental languages. The two libraries were kept in separate quarters in the Old South Church, one for the use of historians, the other for ministers. Prince made abundant use of the historical material in writing his *Chronological History of New England*, which began to appear in 1737. The history was not popular, but it was a carefully documented sourcebook based on the materials built up over a period of thirty years of determined collecting. In addition to print sources, Prince acquired a number of manuscript collections, including the papers of colonial governors William Bradford and Thomas Hinckley and those of religious leaders Cotton Mather and John Cotton. A catalog prepared in 1846 showed that Prince owned five copies of the *Bay Psalm Book*, the first book printed in colonial America. Sadly, four of the five were either sold or lost during a number of changes in the library's location.

When Prince died he left all the books and papers to the South Church with careful instructions on housing and use. The British army, which occupied the building during the war, had little respect for colonial archives and used portions of the library to keep the stoves going. Other volumes were scattered throughout the countryside or were allowed to lie in disarray in the church. By 1814 the situation had become so bad that the Massachusetts Historical Society took over the remaining portions of the New England Library, removing the books to the Society's reading rooms. The final transfer took place in 1866, when the church officers agreed that the tracts and papers should be placed permanently under the jurisdiction of the Boston Public Library. A catalog assembled by Justin Winsor in 1870 showed 3,444 titles in the Prince library. A comparison of Prince's own manuscript catalog provided dramatic evidence of attrition suffered over the years. Prince was a scholarly collector who cared about the raw materials of colonial history. His library holds an important place in the Boston Public Library.

Bibliography

A. *The Prince Catalogue*, edited by Justin Winsor (Boston, 1870).

B. *DAB* 8, 232–233; *NCAB* 7, 144; Cannon, 1–14; "The Prince Library," *BBPL*, October–December 1922, 351–355. Peter Knapp, "The Reverend Thomas Prince and the Prince Library," *ABC*, October 1971, 19–23; Edwin Wolf II, "Great American Book Collectors to 1800," *Gazette of the Grolier Club*, 1971, 7–8. Horace Wadlin, *The Public Library of the City of Boston: A History* (Boston, 1911), 121–126.

Q

QUINN, John (b. April 14, 1870, Tiffin, Ohio; d. July 28, 1924, New York, N.Y.). *Education*: LL.B., Georgetown University, 1893; LL.B., Harvard University, 1895. *Collection Development*: New York Public Library; Anderson, November 12, December 10, 1923, January 14, February 11, March 17, 1924, February 8, 1927.

From the start Quinn was determined to make a place for himself in several worlds. With a driving ambition he completed a law degree while working for the secretary of the treasury and almost immediately set up a private practice in New York. His special interest was in tax law and the rights of artists and writers under the law. He waged a successful fight to have tariff duties reduced on the importation of artworks and thereby guaranteed himself a place of honor in the international art world. Toward the end of his career he defended James Joyce's *Ulysses* against the censors who would have banned it from importation into the United States. He was one of the chief backers of the 1913 Armory Show and was a leader in arranging for the 1921 exhibition of postimpressionists at the Metropolitan Museum of Art.

In 1902 Quinn traveled to Ireland, where he met the painter Jack Yeats, other members of the famous Yeats family, and a host of their friends. The ensuing correspondence with George Moore, Lady Gregory, George Russell, and others was a testimony to Quinn's charm. These friendships blossomed and provided Quinn with a continuing flow of letters, manuscripts, and books. When he traveled to Ireland again two years later, he went as an established friend of the literary community. He provided support for printing at the Dun Emer Press in Ireland and arranged to have small private editions of the works of J. M. Synge and W. B. Yeats brought out in America. In exchange for his help the writers supplied Quinn with manuscripts, proof copies, and limited rare inscribed editions. It was not long before Quinn's literary entrepreneurship became known across the water and provided him with easy introductions to a number of prominent English novelists and poets. Soon he was corresponding on a regular basis with May Morris, daughter of William Morris, Ezra Pound, Joseph Conrad, and James Joyce. Through his friendship with Conrad, for example, Quinn obtained all the author's existing manuscripts and typescripts at nominal cost. These documents later provided some of the most spectacular bidding at the Quinn auction sales. By 1923 Quinn's apartment had become so crowded with books, letters, paintings, and statuary that something had to go. Quinn decided to sell the books, since by that time he had become more interested in paintings. Through the early part of 1923 Quinn worked diligently on the five-volume sale catalog, which featured long and helpful sketches of the authors and a charming "Note" of introduction by Quinn himself. That "Note" concluded:

I cannot go through or attempt to write about or to tell what these books and manuscripts, which contain a world of beauty and romance or enshrine the records of friendships and of interests and enthusiasms have meant or mean to me, for they seem to me to be a part of myself, even though I may smile a little at my own feeling.

The first day of the sale was an unqualified success, with the Conrad material leading the way. On his investment of some $10,000 for Conrad, Quinn realized over $111,000 in return. A.S.W. Rosenbach* was the chief buyer. The rest of the sales were something of an anticlimax, with prices falling to unreasonably low levels. The manuscript of Joyce's *Ulysses*, for example, went for an astoundingly low $1,950. Rosenbach took that prize back to Philadelphia for his personal collection. By the end of the sale in March 1924, Quinn, now a sick man, wrote to tell Joyce how glad he was to see the last of the "mountain of books, that covered . . . the walls and shelves till they were like an incubus." Although the excitement of collecting was over, the importance of Quinn's library has assured him a place in the history of letters. A writer for the *New York Sun* identified Quinn's remarkable vision in one sentence: "He did not buy manuscripts or works of art to make a profit on them but because he loved good work and wanted to help those who created it."

Bibliography

A. "A Note," in *The Library of John Quinn*, Part One (New York, 1923).

B. *NCAB* 18, 39; Cannon, 228–230; B. L. Reid, *The Man from New York: John Quinn and His Friends* (New York, 1968); Harvey Simmonds, "John Quinn: An Exhibition to Mark the Gift of the John Quinn Memorial Collection," *BNYPL*, November 1968, 569–586; A. B. Saarinen, *The Proud Possessors* (New York, 1958), 206–237; "A Courageous Connoisseur," *New York Sun*, July 29, 1924; "John Quinn," *NYT*, July 29, 1924, 15.

R

RABINOWITZ, Louis (b. October 16, 1887, Rossane, Lithuania; d. April 27, 1957, New York, N.Y.). *Collection Disposition*: Yale University; New York Public Library; Jewish Theological Seminary.

After emigrating to the United States from Lithuania at the age of fourteen, Rabinowitz worked in a variety of jobs in the New York garment district. He became a manager in a dress factory and developed a number of inventions connected with the manufacture of clothing. As his means increased, he provided funds for a variety of philanthropic projects—an archaeological exploration in Israel under the direction of Hebrew Union College, a study of academic freedom conducted by faculty at Columbia University, and development of the Institute for Research in Rabbinics at the Jewish Theological Seminary.

Rabinowitz' interest in books was from the philanthropic rather than the personal point of view. His gifts to the Yale Library began in 1943 and included first editions and manuscripts of Clemens, Willa Cather, and Cooper. In the following year he provided funds for translation of various Hebrew classics, thus initiating an important scholarly project that came to be known as the Yale Judaica Series. At the same time, he presented Yale with the library of the writer Sholem Asch, a collection made up of the author's manuscripts and his personal Judaic reference collection. By his efforts, Rabinowitz made Yale one of the leading centers of Hebrew scholarship in the country. Through the 1940s Rabinowitz continued to give Yale outstanding examples of English literature, early printing, and Jewish studies. In 1947, for example, Thomas Marston, writing in the *Yale Library Gazette*, reported a gift of 196 incunabula and 60 volumes of Elizabethan poetry and drama. In the early 1950s Rabinowitz supplied over 100 more incunabula to Yale, including printings by Ulrich Zell and William Caxton. In this group Caxton was represented by his most famous work, the 1477 printing of *The Dictes and Sayengis of the Philosophers* in a contemporary binding. In 1956

Rabinowitz gave Yale the Gutenberg printing of the 1460 *Catholicon*. These gifts, impressive as they were, constituted only part of his philanthropy. In 1952, for example, he gave the Jewish Division of the New York Public Library fourteenth- and fifteenth-century illuminated liturgical manuscripts and a number of rare printed volumes, including a first edition of Maimonides' *Moreh Nevukhim*, a fifteenth-century commentary on Job. Although he bought some rarities from A.S.W. Rosenbach*, the majority of his purchases came from Quaritch. He knew the needs of his favorite libraries, and many of his purchases were made with these institutions in mind. He rarely kept volumes on his own shelves for long, preferring that they reach qualified scholars as soon as possible. In 1955, in an appropriate gesture of gratitude, Yale appointed Rabinowitz chairman of their Division of Semitic Languages. He continued to serve the university in that post until his death in 1957.

Bibliography

A. *Catalogue of Hebrew and Yiddish Manuscripts and Books from the Library of Sholem Asch*, presented to Yale by Louis Rabinowitz (New Haven, 1945).

B. *NCAB* 49, 199–200; M. Block, "Two Illuminated Manuscripts of Mahzor Given by Louis Rabinowitz," *BNYPL*, December 1952, 423–425; M. Davis, "Louis Rabinowitz," *Publications of the American Jewish Historical Society*, June 1958, 226–229; Thomas Marston, "A Fifteenth-Century Library," *YLG*, January 1947, 31–35; Thomas Marston, "A Group of Incunabula and Early English Books," *YLG*, April 1957, 172–175; "Louis M. Rabinowitz," *NYT*, April 30, 1957, 28.

RICE, John A. (b. February 22, 1829, Northborough, Mass.; d. April 19, 1888, Chicago, Ill.). *Collection Disposition*: Bangs, March 21, 1870.

By the time he was thirty-five, Rice had achieved some eminence in the Chicago hotel business as part owner of the famous Sherman House. From his substantial income he bought fine clothes, horses, and rare books. In 1868 for example, with the assistance of New York bookdealer Joseph Sabin, he acquired Eliot's "Indian Bible" and other fine items from the James Bruce sale. By 1869, however, Rice had overinvested in the grain market and had to sell the library to pay his debts. Again Sabin provided helpful expertise. He traveled to Chicago, cataloged the books, announced the sale in his house organ, *The American Bibliopolist*, and conducted the sale in New York. Since the Rice collection was well known, such important Americana collectors as William Menzies*, Edward Asay*, and George Brinley* were on hand to vie for rarities. With a return of more than $42,000, the Rice sale was one of the most profitable held in the United States up to that time. After the sale, Rice continued to buy books occasionally but never again considered himself a serious collector. Writing in 1899, Robert Roden praised Rice as a "man who felt keenly the love of books in all its phases."

Bibliography

B. Eugene Field, "Diagnosis of the Bacillus Librorum," *Love Affairs of a Bibliomaniac* (New York, 1896), 135–145; Robert Roden, "John A. Rice," in *Contributions Towards a Dictionary of English Book Collectors*, Part 13 (London, 1899); Robert Rosenthal, "Three Early Book Collectors of Chicago," *Library Quarterly*, July 1983, 373–376; Wallace Rice, "Eugene Field: Reader and Collector," *Reading and Collecting*, September 1937, 11–13; Joseph Sabin, "The Private Libraries of Chicago," *American Bibliopolist*, November 1869, 330.

RICHARDSON, William King (b. June 27, 1859, Boston, Mass.; d. January 28, 1951, Boston, Mass.). *Education*: A.B., Harvard University, 1880; B.A., Oxford University, 1884; Harvard Law School, 1884. *Collection Disposition*: Harvard University.

For over fifty years Richardson was known in Boston legal circles as an energetic and successful practicing attorney. He used his legal training and his scholarly inclinations to become a distinguished book collector. His tastes were diverse and included manuscripts, incunabula, Aldines, fine bindings, eighteenth-century French illustrated books, and fine printing. In developing his library, Richardson wisely placed himself in the hands of the most knowledgeable bookdealers in England and Europe. This practice allowed him to take advantage of many important turn-of-the-century auction sales. His manuscript holdings ranged from twelfth-century English missals to fifteenth-century French illuminated Books of Hours. Of his 109 incunabula, 53 were printed before 1480 and constituted one of the most distinguished holdings in America. Among them were examples of the work of Zainer, Mentelin, and Aldus. The Aldines, numbering over 135 items, were particularly notable for their high quality and remarkable provenance. The three volumes of Ovid (1533), for example, were the copies bound for Jean Grolier. The bindings in the Richardson library were spectacular. The interlaced sixteenth-century French bindings from the ateliers of Badier and Padeloup vied for attention with the works of the great English master Roger Payne. The provenance of these rare bindings was a major factor in their importance. The Richardson library held works done for Cardinals Richelieu and Mazarin, Archbishop William Laud, Prince Eugene of Saxony, and Napoleon.

Not limiting himself to bindings, Richardson collected a number of the highly regarded eighteenth-century French illustrated books. In many cases the plates in these books were issued in several states, and he made it his business to acquire as many of these variants as possible. From an interest in the illustrated French books, Richardson moved on to the products of the fine press movement in England as launched by William Morris and his followers. Eventually his library contained notable examples of the book arts ranging over a period of eight centuries. It had always been Richardson's intention to give the collection to Harvard, and when the Houghton Library opened in 1924 it seemed the right moment. A handsomely fitted "Richardson Room" provided an appropriate and supportive institutional setting. The collection remains a testament to the founder's scholarly judgment and good taste.

Bibliography

B. *NCAB* 39, 278; William Jackson, "The William King Richardson Library," *HLB*, Autumn 1951, 328–337; *The Houghton Library 1942–1967* (Cambridge, Mass., 1967), 35–45.

RICHMOND, Carleton Rubira (b. February 13, 1887, Boston, Mass.; d. December 13, 1975, Boston, Mass.). *Education*: A.B., Harvard University, 1910. *Collection Disposition*: Harvard University; Sotheby Parke Bernet, October 30, 1981, December 7, 1982.

With a mixture of determination and intelligence, Richmond rose from stock boy to president of a major Boston textile firm. Outside business hours he devoted himself to libraries and collecting. He was active in many scholarly organizations and served as president of both the Boston Athenaeum and the American Antiquarian Society. In his collecting Richmond followed two main lines of interest—the seventeenth-century English diarists John Evelyn and Samuel Pepys, and gardening. His Pepys and Evelyn collection included first editions, manuscripts, letters, and social history. Eventually all these materials went to Harvard's Houghton Library. Richmond's other interest, flower books, stemmed from his own hobby of gardening. He had sixteenth- and seventeenth-century illustrated herbals, printed texts on flower culture, and a remarkable collection of early botanical drawings and watercolors. After his death the books and plates on botanical subjects were dispersed at auction.

Bibliography

B. "Carleton Rubira Richmond," *PAAS*, April 1976, 38–40; Walter M. Whitehill, "Carleton Rubira Richmond," *PMHS*, 1975, 165–166.

ROLLINS, Philip Ashton (b. January 20, 1869, Somersworth, N.H.; d. September 11, 1950, Princeton, N.J.). *Education*: A.B., M.A., Princeton University, 1889, 1892. *Collection Disposition*: Princeton University.

When he was five years old Rollins traveled to Wyoming to spend the summer on his father's ranch under the care of the famous wilderness scout Jim Bridger. From that time until he entered Princeton he spent summers in the West and came to appreciate the realities of cowboy life. It was an introduction to the country that was to absorb his attention for fifty years. The West he knew was the West of vast ranches and the long trail drives all organized under the watchful eye of the foreman, the trail boss, and the cowhand. Rollins' memories of these men, and his desire to tell their story without Hollywood glamour, led to several excellent accounts. His first book, *The Cowboy*, reflected his precise knowledge of the working cattleman, as did his later volumes, *Jinglebob* and *Gone Haywire*.

Rollins started to collect books and manuscripts on the West several years before publication of *The Cowboy*. Since few collectors were interested in western books at that time, he was able to buy choice items in secondhand-book shops and from catalogs at reasonable prices. He was also able to secure source material from early settlers in his frequent travels across the western states. In addition to his cowboy and ranch life collection, Rollins developed an interest in the various mid-nineteenth-century accounts of overland travel to the Pacific. Of the 379 travel narratives listed in Wagner's *The Plains and the Rockies*, Rollins owned 179, a remarkable figure when one understands that he collected in only a few of the fields mentioned in the bibliography. Not wishing to limit his collection to monographs alone, Rollins gathered brand books, maps, advertising folders, cattle-sale posters and saddle catalogs—the ephemera of everyday life in the early West. Rollins' ties with Princeton were strong. He served as the first chairman of the Friends of the Princeton University Library and was a member of the Advisory Council. In 1945 he and Mrs. Rollins presented the Princeton Library with more than 3,000 volumes of western Americana. This collection was placed in a special room in the Harvey Firestone Library, where students and faculty could savor the true atmosphere of the Old West.

Bibliography

B. *Grolier 75*, 175–177; Esther Bentley, "A Conversation with Mr. Rollins"; Robert Cleland, "The Writing of Philip Ashton Rollins"; Harold Dodds, "Philip Ashton Rollins"; and Thomas Streeter, "Rollins Collection of Western Americana," all in *PLC*, June 1948.

ROSENBACH, A.S.W. (b. July 22, 1876, Philadelphia, Pa.; d. July 1, 1952, Philadelphia, Pa.). *Education*: B.S., Ph.D., University of Pennsylvania, 1898, 1901. *Collection Disposition*: Philip H. and A. S. W. Rosenbach Foundation; Free Library of Philadelphia; American Jewish Historical Society.

Known chiefly as a bookdealer—perhaps the most successful of the twentieth century—Rosenbach was also an avid collector. Beginning with his earliest days in the book trade, Rosenbach put aside certain special books and manuscripts for his own collection. Of these collections, one of the foremost was made up of early American children's books. The origin of this collection must be attributed to Rosenbach's uncle, Moses Polock, who at one time worked for one of the leading children's book publishing houses in Philadelphia. It was Polock's good fortune to find in stock pristine copies of unsold children's books that had been issued by the firm at the end of the eighteenth century. He added to the collection regularly until 1900, when he turned them over to his astute young nephew. Rosenbach continued to build the collection, adding catechisms, spellers, primers, Latin texts, sermons, and a smattering of fiction and adventure tales. Taken as a whole, the children's books provided a unique look at an important aspect of seventeenth- and eighteenth-century American social history. The juveniles also furnished a history of American printing with examples from the presses of Isaiah

Thomas, Benjamin Franklin, and Thomas Bradford. In 1933 a fully annotated catalog of the collection was produced and, as Ellen Shaffer said, it immediately became the standard by which all other collections were to be measured. Fourteen years later the 800 books were turned over to the Free Library of Philadelphia and remain one of their prize holdings.

Following another lifelong interest, Rosenbach assembled an impressive private collection of American Judaica. He wrote articles for the American Jewish Historical Society and collected manuscripts, diaries, and printed materials on the development of Jewish life on the American continent. In 1926 the Society published Rosenbach's lengthy *American Jewish Bibliography* and received from the collector the materials described. Rosenbach continued to give important documentary material to the Society throughout his life. Although the Free Library and the Jewish Historical Society received important materials, he kept the gems of his private library at the family home on Delancey Street. With impressive books and manuscript holdings, the library was a many faceted treasure. In 1973 a catalog listing over 200 items attempted to display the richness of the whole. As the compiler pointed out, each item listed in the catalog indicated a multitude of similar items not shown. So it was with Joseph Conrad and Robert Burns manuscripts, Cervantes first editions, and early American printing. Distinguished Americana holdings included the *Bay Psalm Book*, Eliot's "Indian Bible," the only known copy of Franklin's 1733 *Almanac*, Washington letters, and Lincoln manuscripts. For literary scholars, Delancey Street was the place to see the manuscript of Joyce's *Ulysses*, Wilde's *Salome*, or Douglas' *South Wind*. In early 1950 the Philip H. and A.S.W. Rosenbach Foundation was established as a museum-library, with appropriate housing for the brothers' personal collections of books, painting, and household furnishings. The Rosenbach library was the product of over fifty years of finely honed connoisseurship and in the words of Edwin Wolf II truly represented "the bestest of the mostest."

Bibliography

A. *An American Jewish Bibliography* (Philadelphia, 1926); *Books and Bidders* (Boston, 1927); *Early American Children's Books* (Portland, Maine, 1933); *A Book Hunter's Holiday* (New York, 1936); *One Hundred and Fifty Years of Printing in English America 1640–1790* (Philadelphia, 1940); *A Selection from Our Shelves: Books, Manuscripts, and Drawings from the Philip H. and A.S.W. Rosenbach Foundation Museum* (Philadelphia, 1973).

B. *DAB*, Supp. 5, 586–588; *Grolier 75*, 194–195; Ellen Shaffer, "The Rosenbach Collection of Early American Children's Books in the Free Library of Philadelphia," *ABC*, March 1956, 3–7; Edwin Wolf II, "Abraham Simon Rosenbach," *Pennsylvania Library Chronicle*, Winter 1952–1953, 45–50; Edwin Wolf and John Fleming, *Rosenbach: A Biography* (Cleveland, 1960); *To Doctor R.: Essays Here Collected and Published in Honor of the Seventieth Birthday of Dr. A.S.W. Rosenbach* (Philadelphia, 1946), 54.

ROSENBLOOM, Arthur M. (b. December 8, 1903, Pittsburgh, Pa.; d. July 21, 1979, Pittsburgh, Pa.). *Education*: A.B., Yale University, 1925. *Collection Disposition*: Yale University, private sale.

From his earliest days at Yale, Rosenbloom concentrated on collecting books by sixteenth-century Elizabethan dramatists and the English Romantic poets of the nineteenth century. Instead of following fads or working from lists, Rosenbloom collected only authors he liked: Shakespeare, Ben Jonson, Thomas Carew, Leigh Hunt, Shelley, Keats, and Byron. According to Herman W. Liebert, librarian of the Beinecke Library at Yale, Rosenbloom was a born connoisseur with an acute natural sense of quality. The Rosenbloom library was a tasteful and perceptive gathering of important books and manuscripts.

Bibliography

B. Herman W. Liebert, "Arthur M. Rosenbloom 1903–1979," *YLG*, January 1980, 147–148.

ROSENBLOOM, Charles J. (b. April 13, 1898, Steubenville, Ohio; d. April 1, 1973, Jerusalem, Israel). *Education*: A.B., Yale University, 1920. *Collection Disposition*: Yale University; Carnegie-Mellon University; National University of Jerusalem.

While some of his enthusiasm for book collecting can be attributed to a studious father, Rosenbloom often said he first learned to love books at Yale. There he was exposed to the resources of one of the finest libraries in the country, a highly stimulating faculty, and an exciting variety of speakers and exhibitions. His serious interest in collecting began when he obtained an autographed first edition of John Drinkwater's *Loyalties* directly from the poet. Over the years, he added works by other contemporary English authors as well as rare editions by the Elizabethans and Victorians. Rosenbloom was a perfectionist when it came to physical condition, admitting only those books to his shelves that qualified at the highest level. A Rosenbloom book was by definition a book in mint condition. In addition to forming a large personal library, Rosenbloom gave regularly to Yale, Carnegie-Mellon University, and the University of Jerusalem. On his death the bulk of the library was divided among these institutions. According to Herman W. Liebert, librarian of Yale's Beinecke Library, Rosenbloom was a lover of books and an assiduous collector.

Bibliography

B. Herman W. Liebert, "The Charles J. Rosenbloom Bequest," *YLG*, April 1975, 309–310; Suzanne Rutter and Donald Gallup, "A Checklist of the Bequest," *YLG*, April 1975, 311–345; Correspondence with Lucile Johnson Rosenbloom, July 1984.

ROSENWALD, Lessing J. (b. February 10, 1891, Chicago, Ill.; d. June 25, 1979, Jenkintown, Pa.). *Education*: A.B., Cornell University, 1912. *Collection Disposition*: Library of Congress.

Like many Philadelphia collectors, Rosenwald got his start at Sessler's Bookshop on Walnut Street. He had moved East from Chicago in 1920 to choose a site for a new Sears store, a family enterprise, and found Sessler's an oasis. Passing by the window one day in the early 1920s, he was attracted to a Scottish print by D. Y. Cameron, bought it, and took it home. That was the crucial first step in the formation of a collection that by 1979 numbered 25,000 engravings, etchings, lithographs, and woodcuts and more than 5,000 books—one of the most important gatherings of the graphic arts ever assembled in the United States. His interest in woodcuts led to an appreciation of early printed books, an enthusiasm nurtured by Philadelphia bookdealer A.S.W. Rosenbach*. Among his first purchases from Rosenbach were a 1493 Koberger printing of Schedel's *Liber Chronicarum* and the 1488 *Kolnische Chronik* of 1499. Eventually he owned 568 incunabula, including the 1462 Fust and Schoeffer Bible, the Psalter of 1457, and the *Canon Missae* of 1458. In 1929, with Rosenbach's help, he added three block books from the Holford collection and some of William Blake's illustrated works from the William A. White* estate. Later he added eighteenth- and nineteenth-century French illustrated books, Dutch and Flemish books of the fifteenth century, and a complete run of the Kelmscott Press. Although manuscripts were never a strong feature of the Rosenwald library, those present were outstanding. In 1952 he purchased the monumental two-volume manuscript "Giant Bible of Mainz" from H. P. Kraus. This Bible is notable for its border illuminations done by an anonymous artist known as "The Master of the Playing Cards," thought to be the first artist to work on copper. In 1952 the Giant Bible went on display in the Library of Congress, where it shared prominence with Gutenberg's printed work.

Rosenwald's first association with the Library of Congress came in 1943, when he gave some 400 books. Included with the gift was a proviso that he had the right to add to the collection whenever he wanted to. That proviso was acted on again and again in the remaining thirty-five years of his life. The 500-page published catalog of the Lessing J. Rosenwald Collection, edited by Frederick Goff, tells the story best. Those who have written about Rosenwald's accomplishments have characterized his collecting style as "brick by brick" rather than by mass purchases. He was a careful buyer, always conscious of condition and determined to have only the best. He was generous with his books, retaining custody during his lifetime but eager to have them displayed in libraries and museums. Adjoining his home he built a facility called the Alverthorpe Gallery, where some of his most precious volumes could be seen by the interested public. He enjoyed the chance to talk about books and the graphic arts with students from nearby colleges. According to William Matheson, Chief of Rare Books and Special Collections at the Library of Congress, Rosenwald was essentially an educator, a rare breed of collector who learned from his own experiences and had the ability and grace to share those experiences with others. The title of Matheson's article in the *Library of Congress Quarterly Journal*, "Lessing J. Rosenwald: A Splendidly Generous Man," is an apt characterization of a great collector.

Bibliography

A. "The Formation of the Rosenwald Collection," *QJLC*, October 1945, 53, 62; "The Mirror of the Collector," *QJLC*, July 1965, 160–169; "Experiences in Collecting," *Gleason Library Associates Record*, June 1972, 13–19; *Recollections of a Collector* (Jenkintown, Pa., 1976); *The Lessing J. Rosenwald Collection*, preface by Frederick Goff (Washington, D.C., 1977).

B. Wolf and Fleming, passim; H.P. Kraus, *A Rare Book Saga* (New York, 1978), 117–126; Frederick Goff, "The Rosenwald Library," *BC*, Spring 1956, 28–37; Frederick Goff, "Rosenwald and the Gift to the Nation," *AB*, September 26, 1981, 2003–2017; Frederick Goff, "The Gift of Lessing J. Rosenwald to the Library of Congress," *QJLC*, July 1965, 172–193; William Matheson, "Lessing J. Rosenwald: A Splendidly Generous Man," *QJLC*, Winter 1980, 1–24; Carl Zigrosser, "So Wide a Net: A Curator's View of the Lessing J. Rosenwald Collection, 17th to the 20th Century," *QJLC*, July 1965, 194–205; "Collector," *The New Yorker*, March 10, 1973, 30; *Rosenwald and Rosenbach: Two Philadelphia Bookmen*, Catalogue of an Exhibit at the Rosenbach Museum and Library from the Lessing J. Rosenwald Collection at the Library of Congress, April 30 to July 31, 1983 (Philadelphia, 1983).

S

ST. JOHN, Cynthia Morgan (b. October 11, 1852, Ithaca, N.Y.; d. August, 1919, Ithaca, N.Y.). *Collection Disposition*: Cornell University.

As a young girl growing up in rural New York, St. John became fascinated with the romantic poetry of William Wordsworth. Once, when the family was packing for an Adirondack Mountains trip, she set aside a plush new edition for leisure reading, but when a friend advised her to take a worn 1842 copy instead as more appropriate for camping, she complied. This event stimulated St. John to look for other old editions of the poet's work. She wrote to booksellers up and down the East Coast but without result. Few American dealers were interested in Wordsworth at that time. In 1883 St. John and her husband traveled to England, where they found a more hospitable environment for their search. The English scholar-collectors William A. Knight and Edward Dowden had already amassed solid Wordsworth libraries and were generous with advice and gifts for the enthusiastic American collector. John R. Tutin, a Hull bookseller, was particularly helpful and taught St. John the importance of original condition and advised her on values. She had a frugal nature and was quite capable of refusing even the most desirable items if the price seemed too high. On one occasion she turned down a copy of *Grace Darling* at $100, only to have another copy appear at a cheaper price from the library of Henry Reed, Wordsworth's first American editor. This brought St. John and Reed's daughter together in an amiable relationship that resulted in St. John's acquisition of the voluminous Reed-Wordsworth correspondence.

At one point in her collecting career, St. John had a brief encounter with English forger and bibliographer Thomas J. Wise. In a letter of 1916, Wise authenticated as genuine a copy of Wordsworth's *To the Queen* which St. John had purchased from Chicago dealer Walter Hill. In 1934 John Carter and Graham Pollard revealed *To the Queen* as one of the many Wise fabrications.

For a number of years St. John worked on a Wordsworth bibliography based on her own collection. In 1909 a fire destroyed her carefully accumulated notes, sparing only a fragment entitled "The Formation and Growth of the Collection." This manuscript remains in the Cornell archives and is a useful record for Wordsworth scholars. On St. John's death in 1919, since no buyer was present, the estate trustees authorized the preparation of a sale catalog. This was viewed as a serious loss by the members of the Cornell English faculty for whom the collection had long been a major resource. An appeal went out and Victor Emanuel, a wealthy alumnus, provided the funds for the purchase. Four years later the Cornell Wordsworth Collection was recognized as an official unit in the university library. A bibliography was published and support was provided to ensure the steady growth of the collection. Because of St. John's collecting enthusiasms and Emanuel's financial support, Cornell can boast one of the finest Wordsworth collections in the country.

Bibliography

A. *The Wordsworth Collection, formed by Cynthia Morgan St. John and Given to Cornell University by Victor Emanuel*, compiled by Leslie Broughton (Ithaca, N.Y., 1931) and *Supplement* (Ithaca, N.Y., 1942); *The Cornell Wordsworth Collection: A Catalogue of Books and Manuscripts Presented to the University by Mr. Victor Emanuel* (Ithaca, N.Y., 1957).

B. Leslie Broughton, "The Formation and Growth of the Collection," in *The Cornell Wordsworth Collection: A Brief Account* (Ithaca, N.Y., 1940), 3–17; G. H. Healey, "Cynthia Morgan St. John and Her Collection," in *Bicentenary Wordsworth Studies* (Ithaca, N.Y., 1970), 377–392.

SAKS, John A. (b. July 10, 1913, New York, N.Y.; d. May 30, 1983, Greenwich, Conn.). *Collection Disposition*: Parke-Bernet, December 10, 17, 1963; Christie's, April 7, 1978, April 20, 1979, October 1, 1980, May 22, June 10, 1981; Christie's (London), November 19, 1982, May 20, 1983.

From 1940 to 1980 Saks had few challengers to his preeminence in the field of collecting English private press books. He began to buy in 1936 at the Marsden Perry* sale, an excellent starting place since Perry owned one of the world's fullest sets of the Kelmscott Press books on vellum. Saks went on to acquire rarities at the Cortlandt Field Bishop* sale in 1938 and the John Gribbel* sale of 1940. As a result of these purchases and others, he developed notable holdings of the issues of the Cresset, Nonesuch, Essex House, Shakespeare Head, Doves, Ashendene, and Kelmscott presses. These holdings included not only the regular editions but also limited numbered issues and special bindings. Saks had, for example, 6 of the 122 books bound personally by nineteenth-century craftsman Thomas Cobden-Sanderson.

In one departure from his central interest in press books, he gathered a choice collection of eighteenth-century Venetian illustrated books. The sale of these books in London in the summer of 1981 almost doubled Saks' original investment of $75,000. As his health deteriorated, after 1980, Saks increased the momentum of his sales. He disposed of his holdings of the specially bound Gregynog Press books at a private treaty sale in 1980, the Doves books in 1981, and his unequaled Ashendenes in the winter of 1982. The best was left for last. His Kelmscotts and six medieval manuscripts were made available to Christie's for cataloging in December 1982. Saks offered the forty-nine Kelmscotts on vellum for a reserve of $500,000 while letting the remaining paper copies, association material, and special bindings go on an individual basis. The entire collection brought a most satisfactory $1,184,245. Throughout his life Saks had been an unostentatious buyer. The splendid returns on his books and manuscripts proved that he had been a wise one.

Bibliography

B. Stephen Massey, "The Library of John A. Saks," *Christie's Review of the Season 1983*, 170–174; Hans Fellner, "Venetian Illustrated Books of the 18th Century," *Christie's Review of the Season 1981*, 198–199.

SANG, Philip D. (b. November 27, 1902, Chicago, Ill.; d. May 16, 1975, Chicago, Ill.). *Education*: B.S., Illinois Institute of Technology, 1923. *Collection Disposition*: Brandeis University; Sotheby Parke Bernet, April 26, November 14, 1978, June 20, 1979, June 30, 1980.

While he was a student at the Illinois Institute of Technology, Sang developed an interest in American history and the documentary record of that history. He began acquiring letters and autographed photographs of such well-known figures as Clemens, Lincoln, and Webster. In an interview for the *Chicago Tribune*, Sang recalled one of his original treasures—a picture of Clemens on a steamboat, inscribed "Be good and you'll be lonesome." Sang sought out documents that reflected the growth of American democracy from earliest times to the late 1960s. Primarily interested in the lives of great leaders, Sang acquired strong archival collections centered around Washington, Lincoln, Jefferson, and John F. Kennedy. Although the major portion of the collection consisted of documents, he also bought books and pamphlets by authors that interested him. His holdings of early editions of Stowe's *Uncle Tom's Cabin*, for example, was exemplary and included more than a score of translations into foreign languages. Sang was imaginative in selecting symbols that would illustrate the struggle for human freedom. One of his collections included letters, photographs, drawings, and brochures on the construction of the Statue of Liberty. In another area of interest, Sang collected documents and reports having to do with Jewish history and tradition. Unwilling to keep his treasures in a bank vault, he made them widely available to colleges, universities, and museums. He gave Brandeis his Webster letters, a set of the signers of the Declaration of Independence, several medieval manuscripts, and a number of letters signed by the delegates to the Hartford Convention while keeping control of the bulk of the collection himself.

Three years after his death, Sotheby Parke Bernet issued a magnificent catalog, revealing the astounding breadth of his library. His second set of the signers of the Declaration of Independence brought a record price of $195,000, while other rarities followed suit. Sang was a discriminating and imaginative collector. His American document collection was one of the most distinguished of the twentieth century.

Bibliography

B. John Davies, "Book Collector's Hobby Is History," *Chicago Tribune*, October 27, 1968, 32; Robert Seligman, "Auction Notes," *Book Collector's Market*, September-October 1978, 28; Clyde Walton, "Philip David Sang," *Sotheby Parke-Bernet Catalog* (New York, 1978).

SCHEIDE, John Hinsdale (b. 1875; d. September 29, 1942, Titusville, Pa.). *Education*: A.B., Princeton University, 1896. *Collection Disposition*: Princeton University.

At Princeton, Scheide was strongly influenced by a professor who claimed that the two most important events in history were the invention of printing and the discovery of America. For a young man who had already learned to appreciate the significance of historical perspective from his father, the professor's remarks fell on receptive ears. At first Scheide concentrated his collecting activities around his father William's* interests—biblical and ecclesiastical history. His English Bible collection, augmented with colonial New England sermons, grew gradually over the first two decades of the twentieth century. In 1924 he expanded his collecting endeavors dramatically with the purchase of James W. Ellsworth's* copy of the Gutenberg Bible. Next he obtained the magnificent Holford copy of the 1460 *Catholicon*, the 1462 Fust and Schoeffer Bible, block books, several Caxton printings, and fragments from the earliest presses of Italy and the low countries.

By the beginning of the 1930s, Scheide had started to purchase manuscripts and autographs. In 1931 he secured the manuscript of the Wyclif Bible, and seven years later he acquired one of the great treasures of the manuscript period— the sumptuously illuminated eleventh-century "Blickling Homilies." To these texts he added an early third-century Ezekiel on papyri and a fourteenth-century Magna Carta. Another important area in his library consisted of Americana. Among his early purchases were a 1493 "Columbus Letter" printed by Silber, the first edition of Cortez' "Relacion" (1522), and the first and third "Vespucci Letters." Moving into the eighteenth century, Scheide purchased the "Lexington Alarm," a dramatic account of the spirit of the country just before the outbreak of the Revolutionary War. He also owned Washington's "Williamsburg Journal" (1754) and the first broadside printing of the Declaration of Independence. His texts on exploration of the interior of the New World included the 1807 Pittsburgh edition of Patrick Gass' *Journal of Voyages and Travels of Lewis and Clark* and works by Hennepin and Champlain. Few of the items in the Scheide library served a single purpose. Manuscripts, incunabula, Bibles, and Americana complemented one another in an archive that sketched the development of Western culture.

Bibliography

A. "Love for the Printed Word as Expressed in the Scheide Library," *PBSA*, 3rd Q, 1957, 214–226.

B. *Grolier 75*, 191–193; Wolf and Fleming, passim; Julian P. Boyd, *The Scheide Library: A Summary View of Its History and Its Outstanding Books* (Princeton, 1947); Mina Bryan, "Scheide Library," *BC*, Winter 1972, 489–502; John Fleming, "Old English Manuscripts in the Scheide Library"; Mary L. Gibbs, "Aldus Manutius as Printer of Illustrated Books"; Frederick Goff, "Johann Gutenberg and the Scheide Library"; Lewis Lockwood, "The Beethoven Sketchbook in the Scheide Library"; Bruce Metzger, "An Early Coptic Manuscript of the Gospel"; Paul Needham, "Incunabula, Bibles, and Early Americana"; and Edwin Wolf II, "In the Mainstream of American Book Collecting," all in *PLC*, Winter 1976.

SCHEIDE, William Taylor (b. 1847; d. 1907). *Collection Disposition*: John Hinsdale Scheide.

As a pioneer in the oil business in western Pennsylvania, Scheide combined engineering skill and executive ability to amass a considerable fortune. With this income he was able to retire at age forty-two and devote the rest of his life to travel and collecting. Although his most active period of collecting followed his retirement in 1874, his manuscript catalog indicated youthful interests in literature, philosophy, and religion. Later Scheide concentrated on biblical and ecclesiastical history. The volumes in the Scheide library were gathered to satisfy the intellectual needs of an omniverous reader. The enthusiasms he planted germinated in his son John* and in his grandson William, setting in motion a remarkable collecting dynasty.

Bibliography

B. Julian P. Boyd, *The Scheide Library: A Summary View of Its History and Its Outstanding Books* (Princeton, 1947). Mina Byran, "Scheide Library," *BC*, Winter 1972, 489–502.

SCHIFF, Mortimer L. (b. June 5, 1877, New York, N.Y.; d. June 4, 1931, New York, N.Y.). *Collection Disposition*: Jewish Theological Seminary; Sotheby's (London), March 1938.

Before finishing his studies at Amherst, Schiff was sent abroad to learn the international banking business. Once this apprenticeship was completed he returned to the United States and joined the New York investment firm of Kuhn, Loeb and Company, where his father, Jacob, was a senior partner. In addition to his business activities, Schiff interested himself in a wide variety of civic and educational institutions, principally the Boy Scouts of America and the Jewish Theological Seminary. To both these organizations he devoted large amounts of time and money. In 1921, for example, he presented the seminary with a collection of 3,000 rare books on Anglo-Judaic thought. In this philanthropy he followed the pattern established by his father, who had provided generous support for Hebraica collections at the New York Public Library, Harvard University, and the Library of Congress.

Although he had purchased a number of important books in the first few years of the century, the Robert Hoe III* sale in 1911 launched Schiff's collecting career. The bindings by Padeloup, Derôme, and Le Monnier and the tasteful illustrations of Boucher, Moreau le Jeune, Cochin, Eisen, and Gravelot all appealed to his love of the sumptuous. The 120 volumes he bought at the Hoe sale provided examples of the work of the finest artists and craft binders of sixteenth- and seventeenth-century Europe. For the next ten years he continued to buy selectively, securing seven Grolier bindings, three by Thomas Mahieu and two in Henry II style. In 1920, A.S.W. Rosenbach* sold Schiff a number of distinguished French illustrated books from the Robert Schuhmann library, including Graffigny's *Lettres d'une Péruvienne* with Lefèvre drawings and *L'Éloge de la Folie* with seventeen original sketches by Eisen. Other notable items in his library included a 1733 copy of Pine's *Horace* in a signed mosaic binding and the original Fermiers–Généraux edition of La Fontaine's *Contes* illustrated by Eisen in a special binding designed by Gravelot. Another great treasure in the Schiff library was the *Missale Parisienne* of 1777, stamped with the royal arms of Madame de Pompadour.

In 1935, four years after Schiff's death, Seymour De Ricci produced an elaborate catalog of the signed bindings in the library. The unique quality of the works described and the precise bibliographical notes by De Ricci made this catalog a valuable reference tool. Three years after publication of the catalog, the heirs disposed of the library in a disastrous auction in London. The only beneficiaries were collectors like Lessing J. Rosenwald*, who through Rosenbach found it possible to obtain rare binding and illustrated folios for bargain prices. Schiff is remembered as a connoisseur who brought together an unrivaled collection of decorative bindings and illustrated books.

Bibliography

A. Seymour De Ricci, *French Signed Bindings in the Mortimer Schiff Collection* (New York, 1935); *British and Miscellaneous Signed Bindings in the Mortimer Schiff Collection* (New York, 1935).

B. *Grolier 75*, 203–206; Wolf and Fleming, passim; *NYT*, June 5, 1931, 1.

SCHMULOWITZ, Nat (b. March 29, 1889, New York, N.Y.; d. February 25, 1966, San Francisco, Calif.). *Education*: A.B., University of California at Berkeley, 1910; LL.B., Hastings College of Law, 1912. *Collection Disposition*: San Francisco Public Library.

By profession Schmulowitz was a probate and trial lawyer, noted for his defense of such Hollywood personalities as "Fatty" Arbuckle and Mary Pickford.

His avocation—book collecting—led to the development of one of the best wit and humor collections in the country. During his college days Schmulowitz had been interested in musical comedy and wrote the lyrics for several amateur productions. Later he edited books on Jewish humor and contributed articles on humor to national magazines. The collection sprang from his interest in folktales and the transmission of humor from one culture to another. He searched bookshops for nearly forty years in order to represent humor in all its lively forms. A particular strength of the collection was its extensive holding of the various editions and translations of Joe Miller joke books. From 1941 to 1947 Schmulowitz was a member of the Library Commission of San Francisco, serving one year as president. On April Fools' Day 1947 he gave ninety choice books from his humor collection to the San Francisco Public Library and launched the Nat Schmulowitz Collection of Wit and Humor (''SCOWAH''). Once the collection was established, Schmulowitz added volumes at a rapid rate, sometimes over 100 a month. In 1962 the holdings numbered 11,000 items, a figure that climbed to 17,000 by 1977. The Schmulowitz collection has been a source of pride to the library and has provided raw material for numerous anthologists, editors, and lecturers. Perhaps the best use of the collection has been to demonstrate the continuing importance of humor as a positive force in human relations.

Bibliography

A. *Catalog of the Schmulowitz Collection of Wit and Humor* (San Francisco, 1961) and *Supplement I* (San Francisco, 1977).

B. William Ramirez, ''Nat Schmulowitz,'' *California Librarian*,April 1966, 94–95; William Ramirez, ''SCOWAH: The Schmulowitz Collection of Wit and Humor,'' *Folklore and Folk Music Archivist*, Summer 1963, 2–3.

SCHOMBURG, Arthur A. (b. January 24, 1874, San Juan, Puerto Rico; d. June 10, 1938, Brooklyn, N.Y.). *Collection Disposition*: New York Public Library.

At the age of sixteen, after growing up in Puerto Rico, Schomburg moved to New York. In later years he explained how a grade school teacher had introduced him to the importance of the black heritage and the pleasures of reading. In his spare moments he hunted for books in the secondhand-book stores of New York. It was a time when many Negroes were becoming interested in their past, and Schomburg found intellectual stimulation in that atmosphere. In 1911, with John E. Bruce, he helped found the Negro Society for Historical Research. Schomburg's library, as it developed, included documentary material on the Afro-American heritage and a print and manuscript archive on individual contributions of blacks. He owned papers and documents from the earliest era of the slave trade; sermons, addresses, and letters from prominent black leaders; manuscript poems of Paul Lawrence Dunbar; and original texts by Booker T. Washington. His collection included, among other treasures, first issues of the colonial poetry of Jupiter Hammon and Phillis Wheatley. Aided by this vast research library, Schomburg wrote articles for the two most important black journals of his day, *The Crisis* and *Opportunity*.

In 1925 the New York Public Library opened a Division of Negro Literature at the 135th Street branch and one year later acquired the Schomburg library, then comprised of 5,000 books, 3,000 manuscripts, and 2,000 etchings and drawings. This purchase was made possible through funds provided by the Carnegie Corporation. In 1932 the library used another grant from Carnegie to employ Schomburg as the first curator of the collection. In that position he was able to carry forward the bibliographic work that had absorbed most of his life.

Bibliography

A. *Calendar of Manuscripts in the Schomburg Collection of Negro Literature* (New York, 1942); "The Negro Digs up His Past," in *The New Negro*, edited by Alain Locke (New York, 1925).

B. *DANB*, 546–548; *DALB*, 461–463; Stanton Biddle, "The Schomburg Center for Research in Black Culture: Documenting the Black Experience," *BNYPL*, 1972, 21–35; Donald Joyce, "Arthur Alonzo [sic] Schomburg: A Pioneering Black Bibliophile," *Journal of Library History*, April 1975, 169–176; Elinor Sinnette, "Arthur A. Schomburg: Black Bibliophile and Curator" (Ph.D. dissertation, Columbia University, School of Library Science, 1977).

SHAW, Robert Gould (b. May 6, 1850, Parkman, Mass.; d. April 10, 1931, Boston, Mass.). *Education:* A.B., Harvard University, 1869. *Collection Disposition:* Harvard University.

Trained as an architect, Shaw practiced for only a few years before he decided to devote full time to management of his estate and to collecting. He had been a collector of theater material from the age of twelve, encouraged by his father to save playbills and other stage memorabilia. It was an interest that occupied him throughout his long life. Fortunately for Shaw, three extensive theater collections became available at important auction sales at the turn of the century. The first of these to come on the market, the library of John Augustin Daly*, contained just the kind of material Shaw liked—portraits, playbills, prints, letters, and extra-illustrated volumes. His success at the Daly sale was followed by substantial purchases at the auctions of the theatrical libraries of Thomas McKee* and Peter Gilsey. All the time Shaw was collecting new materials he was extra-illustrating the older sets he already had. For example, he enlarged the Brander Matthews and Laurence Hutton *Actors and Actresses of Great Britain and the United States* from five to eighty volumes with the insertion of playbills, portraits, letters, and prints. Soon the library outgrew his Brookline residence and the three rooms set aside for it in the Colonial Building in Boston. Initially Shaw favored the Boston Public Library as a permanent relocation, but Harvard theater professor George Pierce Butler convinced him that an academic setting would be a much better choice. The handsome new Harry E. Widener Memorial Library building became part of the inducement, as did the promised status as curator of the theater collection. With his own library now under institutional care, Shaw was able to go out and secure additional materials. In 1917 he helped Harvard acquire the extensive theatrical collection of Evert J. Wendell*. The two vast collections complemented each other nicely, with Shaw's emphasis on English and American theater and Wendell's on Continental productions and personalities. Through the Shaw and Wendell holdings it was possible to trace the careers of prominent and not so prominent actors and actresses, productions of specific plays, or the history of a particular theater. Shaw served as curator from 1915 to 1925 and then as emeritus curator up to the time of his death. As a final gift, Shaw provided Harvard with a sizable endowment so that it might add materials to the substantial base he had established.

Bibliography

B. *NCAB* 30, 243–244; Alfred Potter, *The Library of Harvard University* (Cambridge, Mass., 1934), 131–133; William Van Lennep, "The Harvard Theatre Collection," *HLB*, Autumn 1952, 281–301.

SHEA, Joseph B. (b. June 2, 1863, Allegheny, Pa.; d. January 6, 1930, Pittsburgh, Pa.). *Education:* B.A., Princeton University, 1885. *Collection Disposition:* American Art–Anderson, December 1, 1937, January 6, 1938.

Shea entered the retail store business in Pittsburgh in the late nineteenth century, following a line of work established by his father and grandfather. In 1901 he became director of Joseph Horne and Company, the largest department store in western Pennsylvania. From his father, who had gathered a library of American history and literature, he inherited an interest in collecting. At first he concentrated on Pittsburgh history—narratives of early settlement, business records, newspaper files, and imprints from the first presses of that city—but soon he expanded his scope to include the entire Trans-Allegheny area. Many of the narratives in his library dealt with Indian captivity and the French and Indian War. In his literature section he had first editions of many of the important nineteenth-century English and American poets and novelists. In addition to books by Hawthorne, Kipling, Shelley, and Thackeray he had an impressive collection of Kelmscott Press books. In all cases physical condition was important to Shea, and most of the books were clean, uncut copies. The library was dispersed at auction seven years after his death.

Bibliography

B. *NCAB* 21, 259.

SILVER, Louis H. (b. 1902, Chicago, Ill.; d. October 27, 1963, Chicago, Ill.). *Education:* B.A., University of Illinois, 1924; LL.B., University of Chicago, 1928. *Collection Disposition:* University of Chicago; Sotheby's (London), November 8, 1965; Sotheby Park Bernet, November 15, 1965.

After working for a short time as an engineer, Silver turned to law and real estate. As a result of several successful ventures, he accumulated large commercial holdings and at the time of his death was president of Gold Coast Hotels in Chicago. He was also active as a board member in a variety of Chicago cultural institutions including the Newberry Library and the Art Institute. Silver's tastes as a book collector were diverse and included incunabula, fine binding and printing, English literature, Renaissance history, and the history of science. During the 1930s Silver bought many books from the Rosenbach Company and continued to be one of their best customers for more than twenty-five years. After Rosenbach died, Silver directed his orders to John Fleming and continued to secure a steady stream of important volumes from that source. He also traded with H. P. Kraus in New York, Maggs in London, and Leo Olschki in Rome. While he was essentially a personal collector, he made occasional gifts directly to his alma mater, the University of Chicago. In 1958 he gave the university the library of the Leslie family of County Monaghan, Ireland. This 2,000-volume collection, obtained through the offices of critic and author Sir Shane Leslie, was rich in nineteenth-century belles lettres and Irish history. The following year Silver gave the university a sumptuous gift of early landmark volumes in the history of science and thought, including a 1481 Ptolemy, two seventeenth-century studies of mathematics by John Napier, and a 1612 edition of Humphrey Baker's *The Well Spring of Sciences*.

Many rumors concerning the disposal of the Silver library circulated during the later part of the 1960s. In May 1964, officers of Silver's estate announced that an agreement had been reached with the University of Texas, but in a dramatic last-minute turn of events the Newberry Library of Chicago matched the Texas bid and bought the library for an astounding $2,750,000. Reactions to this event in rare book trade varied from incredulity to anger. John F. Fleming, who had acted for Texas, filed a suit against the Silver estate claiming $412,000 in fees. Although the action failed, Fleming received considerable support in the antiquarian book journals. Shortly after the books were secured, the Newberry aggravated the situation further by announcing plans to sell duplicates and other items they deemed "irrelevant" to their collection. While some of the items were undoubtedly duplicates in the technical sense, the Silver copies placed for sale in London appeared to some expert observers as superior to the "home" copies retained in the Newberry. Among the rarities sold were a Nicolas Jenson Bible of 1476, an *Ars Memorandi* of 1470, George Bernard Shaw's manuscript of *John Bull's Other Island*, and letters by William Harvey, Lord Chesterfield, and Benvenuto Cellini. John Hayward, editor of *The Book Collector*, commented acidly on the attitude of greed and ruthlessness that seemed to pervade the entire transaction. Lawrence W. Towner defended the Newberry action, saying they had always planned to subsidize part of the purchase with a sale of items that fell outside their immediate collecting priorities. Financially the sale was a great success, netting the Newberry some $800,000. Although all the important European houses were represented, the American contingent of Kraus, Warren

Howell, and Fleming secured the most distinguished items. The *Ars Memorandi* went to Kraus for what he called the "modest price" of $81,000, while Howell paid slightly over $44,000 for a magnificent Coverdale Bible. One week after the London sale, Sotheby Parke Bernet in New York offered 200 lots of Silver books not included in the Newberry transaction. This sale, which boasted a Doves Bible, a Kelmscott Chaucer in pigskin, and a splendid Ashendene Malory on vellum, brought the estate $34,000. Although the Silver library was not large, it had enough items of quality to make it a distinguished collection.

Bibliography

A. *A Selection of the Books and Manuscripts from the Louis Silver Collection, Now in the Newberry Library* (Chicago, 1964); *A Catalogue of an Exhibition of Books and Manuscripts Selected from the Louis H. Silver Collection in Honor of a Visit of the Grolier Club to the Newberry Library* (Chicago, 1965).

B. Wolf and Fleming, passim; John Hayward, "Commentary," *BC*, Spring 1964, 14–15; Autumn 1964, 287–288; Autumn 1965, 297–301; H. P. Kraus, *A Rare Book Saga* (New York, 1978), 215–217; Lawrence W. Towner, "Every Silver Lining Has a Cloud," in A. N. L. Munby and Lawrence W. Towner, *The Flow of Books and Manuscripts* (Los Angeles, 1969).

SKIFF, Frederick W. (b. August 12, 1868, Kent, Conn.; d. March 15, 1947, Tillamook, Oreg.). *Education:* B.A., Yale University, 1888. *Collection Disposition:* Butterfield and Butterfield (San Francisco), September 15, 1947.

Trained in accounting, Skiff began his career with the Connecticut State Insurance Department. He moved to Oregon in 1905, joined the Olds and King Department Store in Portland, and rose in that firm from junior accountant to assistant treasurer. Throughout his life Skiff was intensely interested in documents and artifacts of the past. By the time he was twenty-five he had formed collections of pewter, guns, china, and furniture. In the 1890s, as he recounted in *Adventures in Americana*, it was possible to travel from farm to farm in New England and buy Chippendale mirrors, Hepplewhite chests, Staffordshire plates, flintlock muskets, prints, and old books at bargain prices. Skiff was, to say the least, an eclectic collector. Among his many literary interests were Holmes, Longfellow, Whittier, Alcott, and Emerson. In seeking these authors, he established close friendships with Jacob C. Chamberlain* and Frank Maier*, both active collectors of nineteenth-century American literature. From Chamberlain he learned the fundamentals of bibliography, and from Maier he learned the importance of physical condition. In many cases Skiff favored association copies, in which personal letters were included. As a boy he had lived near the estate of naturalist John Burroughs, and in later life he collected Burroughs first editions and autographs. After reading Burroughs' biography of Whitman, Skiff began an intensive hunt for variant editions of *Leaves of Grass*. Over a period of ten years he was able to secure most of the important American and foreign editions.

After Skiff moved to Oregon, his interests shifted to northwestern history. He began to acquire newspapers, diaries, law books, legislative journals, and city documents on the settlement of the western states. Using the same door-to-door technique he had found successful in New England, he located many scarce volumes in the homes of early settlers and their descendants. Along with rich stores of Oregon materials, he uncovered works on the gold rush, North American Indian culture, and early western travel. He collected books that interested him and never bought with profit in mind. In a published interview in the *Portland Oregonian*, Skiff said, "Never buy with speculative intent, but buy books for their reading value, their place in American literature, and their delight of ownership." The library was dispersed at auction after his death and provided West Coast collectors and dealers with a tasteful collection of literature and Americana.

Bibliography

A. *Adventures in Americana* (Portland, Oreg., 1935); *Landmarks of Literature* (Portland, Oreg., 1937).

B. Catherine Jones, "The Astounding Skiff Collection," *Portland Oregonian*, September 11, 1938, 5–8; "Frederick Skiff," *PAAS*, April 1947, 15–16.

SLOCUM, Myles S. (b. December 10, 1883, Ossining, N.Y.; d. June 9, 1956, San Marino, Calif.). *Education:* B.S., Princeton University, 1910. *Collection Disposition:* Princeton University; California Book Auctions, October 31, November 1, 1981. Christie's November 20, 1981.

After working for a few years as a design engineer, Slocum retired, moved to California, and began to collect books. He learned the fine points of bibliography as well as the importance of pristine condition from Pasadena bookseller Alice Millard. With her help, and that of Los Angeles bookdealers Ernest Dawson and Jake Zeitlin, he put together a distinguished library of English and American literature and fine printing. His Grabhorn Press imprints were particularly impressive, as were his holdings of Doves and Kelmscott books. According to California printer Ward Ritchie, Slocum was an enthusiastic buyer whose interests fluctuated from one press to another but whose devotion to fine printing never varied. He took great satisfaction in handling the crisp pages and polished leather bindings of a well-made book. The library reflected his varied tastes and interests. While his family was growing he collected children's books, and later, when he had more time to pursue his own hobbies, he added titles on hunting and horsemanship. No damaged or inferior book was ever admitted to his shelves. In maintaining this standard, and in other matters of bibliographic precision, he was supported by his colleagues in the Grolier Club in New York and the Zamorano Club in Los Angeles.

Not willing to simply gather books for his own private library, Slocum believed in sharing his collecting enthusiasm. While his daughters were in college at Scripps, he initiated a book-collecting competition with an annual award for the student with the best personal library. After his death this competition was carried forward by his daughters. Regarding the final disposition of the library, Slocum was as specific as he had been about its construction. He did not want his books sealed away in an institution, but rather placed for auction on the open market. His wishes were followed in sales conducted in Los Angeles and New York during the fall and winter of 1981. The opening page of the California Book Auction catalog carried the perfect tribute—the books offered were from "The Library of a Gentleman."

Bibliography

B. Ward Ritchie, *Bookmen and Their Brothels: Recollections of Los Angeles in the 1930s* (Los Angeles, 1970), 17–19; Correspondence with Judy Sahak, librarian at Scripps College, 1984; Correspondence with Florence Slocum Wilson, 1984.

SMITH, David E. (b. January 21, 1860, Cortland, N.Y.; d. July 29, 1944, New York, N.Y.). *Education:* Ph.B., Ph.D., Syracuse University, 1881, 1887. *Collection Disposition:* Columbia University.

During an active teaching career, Smith collected a large library on the history of mathematics. He was particularly interested in the sixteenth- and seventeenth-century contributions made by scholars in the Far East, India, and the Middle East. Always conscious of the importance of the graphic record, he promoted better library facilities for the American Mathematical Society, edited their *Bulletin*, and for twenty years served as librarian of that organization. In 1908 he and fellow collector George A. Plimpton* produced *Rara Arithmetica*, a catalog of mathematics books from early times to 1600. His most important publication, based primarily on his personal library, was *The History of Mathematics*, issued in 1923. As a faculty member at Columbia, it was natural that Smith gave his 11,000-item library to that institution. It stands as a scholarly archive on the history of mathematics.

Bibliography

A. *Rara Arithmetica: A Catalogue of the Arithmetics Written Before the Year MDCI with a Description of Those in the Library of George Arthur Plimpton of New York* (Boston, 1908).
B. *DAB*, Supp. 3, 721; *NCAB*, E218.

SMITH, Harry B. (b. December 28, 1860, Buffalo, N.Y.; d. January 1, 1936, Atlantic City, N.J.) *Collection Disposition:* A. S. W. Rosenbach, 1914; American Art—Anderson, April 8, 1936.

Although Smith's earliest experiences in the theater were as an actor and a newspaper critic, he became best known in the 1890s and the early twentieth century as a librettist. His long list of successful shows included many done with Reginald DeKoven, Flo Ziegfeld, and Victor Herbert. While he was employed with the *Chicago Daily News*, he got to know the paper's famous literary editor, Eugene Field*, and through him met the members of the legendary "Saints and

Sinners Corner'' of McClurg's Bookshop. It was there that his interest in rare books developed. He purchased an inscribed *Pickwick Papers*, and that started him on a lifelong quest for presentation copies. On his frequent trips east he became acquainted with the potentates of the New York book world, including the irrepressible dealer George D. Smith. With increasing royalties from his plays and the help of Smith, he bought a Keats manuscript at the Charles Foote* sale of 1894 and eleven Shelley letters at the Charles Frederickson* sale three years later. When the John Augustin Daly* library was sold in 1901, Smith secured a scrapbook containing some twenty love letters from Dickens to Maria Beadnell.

Smith withdrew from the market with the outbreak of World War I since he felt he could no longer compete with Henry E. Huntington* and John Pierpont Morgan*. He decided to place his books on the market and to that end had a handsome sale catalog produced with the evocative title *A Sentimental Library*. It was the kind of collection that included much to tempt an up-and-coming bookdealer. The dealer in this case was a young Philadelphia entrepreneur, A. S. W. Rosenbach*, showing an early flair for business that was to make his name a byword. Rosenbach used the Smith books to launch his career. Smith never stopped collecting. He kept accumulating literary items associated with Dickens, Shelley, and Lamb and developed a large archive of letters, manuscripts, and books on Napoleon. In 1921, deciding to act as his own bookseller, Smith issued an ambitious catalog and did very well. Still, he continued to buy for himself. Six months after his death the library provided the substance for an important New York sale. Buyers were attracted to such treasures as Dickens' own copy of *The Cricket on the Hearth* inscribed to Hans Christian Andersen and the proof sheets of Browning's *The Ring and the Book*. Smith expressed his own philosophy of collecting very well in the introduction to *A Sentimental Library*: "It is not yielding to temptation that oppresses me, but more the remorse for the times I yielded not."

Bibliography

A. *First Nights and First Editions* (Boston, 1931); *A Sentimental Library* (New York, 1914); "Gentlemen of the Old School," *The Colophon*, no. 3, 1930.

B. *NCAB* C, 159; Wolf and Fleming, passim.

SPARKS, Jared (b. May 10, 1789, Willington, Conn.; d. March 14, 1866, Cambridge, Mass.). *Education:* A.B., M.A., Harvard University, 1815, 1818. *Collection Disposition:* Cornell University.

As a historian, editor, teacher, and administrator, Sparks pursued a number of distinguished careers. He was editor of the *North American Review* and he published the multivolume sets *Diplomatic Correspondence of the American Revolution* and *Correspondence of the American Revolution*. In preparing these compilations, Sparks amassed a huge library on American history. In one case, he gathered books and papers for ten years to prepare a general history of the

Revolution. In 1871 a catalog of his library was prepared for auction, but at the last minute Andrew Dixon White*, president of Cornell, bought the lot for $12,000. The Sparks collection gave the new university in Ithaca a notable scholarly archive on American history.

Bibliography

A. *Catalogue of the Library of Jared Sparks with a List of the Historical Manuscripts Collected by Him* (Cambridge, Mass., 1871).

B. *DAB* 9, 430–434; *NCAB* 5, 433; H. B. Adams, *The Life and Writings of Jared Sparks* (Cambridge, Mass., 1893); "The Sparks Library," *American Bibliopolist*, 1872, 122.

SPECK, William A. (b. January 19, 1864, New York, N.Y.; d. October 9, 1928, New Haven, Conn.). *Education:* Certificate, New York School of Pharmacy, 1883. *Collection Disposition:* Yale University.

An aspiring collector looking for a model would do well to examine the career of Speck. What he began under the most unpromising circumstances developed into one of the world's great collections of material by and about Goethe. Speck was trained as a pharmacist and devoted thirty years of his life in a small New York town to the routine demands of that trade. At the age of nine in the Hoboken Academy he had been exposed to the rich dialogue of Goethe's *Götz von Berlichingen*, and that started him on a lifelong study and appreciation of Goethe. He frequented New York shops and twice made pilgrimages to Goethe's homeland in Weimar. Financing his purchases with short-term bank loans, Speck slowly accumulated a library of books, pamphlets, medals, and portraits that became known far beyond the limits of his hometown.

In 1912, representatives of Yale visited Speck and invited him to transfer the collection to New Haven and to act as its curator. This was an epochal event in Speck's life and at last allowed him the freedom he needed to pursue Goethe materials on a full-time basis—and of course now he had university funds at his disposal. There was no task too large nor detail too trivial for Speck if he believed following it up would increase the strength of the collection. Many Yale officers and alumni found it impossible to resist the curator's appeals to dig a little deeper into a budget in order to find the money for a favored purchase. His optimism was irresistible. In 1917, in recognition of his varied contributions to the library, he was appointed Assistant Professor of German. According to his colleagues, his knowledge of the collection was extraordinary, including information on the history and provenance of each item down to the most minute detail. One of his great achievements was the acquisition, in 1922, of the Ehrhardt Faust collection. This gathering consisted chiefly of playbills, newspapers, and magazine articles relating to Goethe's theatrical productions and complemented rather than duplicated Speck's own library. In yet another endeavor, Speck initiated a series of scholarly publications based on rare items in the Goethe collection. In many ways he was a quintessential collector, knowledgeable, devoted, and determined. In a memorial tribute Carl Schreiber summed up Speck's contribution to Yale as a priceless legacy. Certainly it was nothing less.

Bibliography

A. "The Goethe Medals and Medallions in Yale University Library," *YLG*, October 1926, 17–20.

B. *NCAB*, 29, 36; Anton Kippenberg, "Die Speckiche Goethe Sammlung in New Haven," *Jahrbuch der Sammlung Kippenberg*, 1922, 335–338; Christa Sammons, "The German Literature Collection," in *The Beinecke Rare Book and Manuscript Library* (New Haven, 1974), 92–95; Carl Schreiber, "William A. Speck: In Memoriam," *YLG*, January 1929, 55–59; Carl Schreiber, ed., "William Alfred Speck," in *Goethe's Works, with the Exception of Faust* (New Haven, 1946), xxi-xlii.

SPENCER, William Augustus (b.?; d. April 15, 1912, at sea on the *Titanic*). *Collection Disposition:* New York Public Library.

The son of a wealthy Newport family, Spencer was educated abroad and spent most of his life in Europe. While visiting New York in 1910, he was greatly impressed with the public library building then under construction and decided to give his private collection to the city. Under the terms of his will the original gift was supplemented with a generous endowment for the purchase of fine illustrated books, handsome bindings, etchings, drawings, and paintings. The Spencer collection contained some 232 French illustrated books done by the leading craftsmen of the late nineteenth century. One of the most unusual binding examples in the collection was the copy of *Aurora Australis*, published at the winter quarters of the British Antarctic Expedition bound in the wood from the expedition's packing cases. Among the noted European binders represented in the Spencer collection were Emile Mercier, Léon Gruel, and Marius Michel. The twenty-five volumes of Michel's work, covering the period 1896–1912, included many examples of his mosaic technique, while the volumes bound by Mercier show his impeccable gilding methods. The Spencer collection was significant because it included most of the influential French binding styles that evolved at the beginning of the century. Although most of the books were obtained directly from the artists themselves, a few carried the provenance of Robert Hoe III* and Henry Huth. The original Spencer gift and endowment provided the necessary support for the development of one of the most distinguished graphic arts collections in the country.

Bibliography

A. *Dictionary, Catalog, and Shelf List of the Spencer Collection of Illustrated Books and Manuscripts and Fine Buildings* (Boston, 1970); *Catalogue of Japanese Illustrated Books and Manuscripts in the Spencer Collection of the New York Public Library* (Tokyo, 1968).

B. Henry Kent, "The Spencer Collection," *BNYPL*, June 1914, 533–538, and "Catalogue,'' 540–572; Karl Kup, "The Spencer Collection of Illustrated Books in the New York Public Library," *Book Collector's Packet*, October 1945, 1–4; Harry Lydenberg, *History of the New York Public Library* (New York, 1923), 423–425.

SPINGARN, Arthur Barnett (b. March 28, 1878, New York, N.Y.; d. December 1, 1971, New York, N.Y.). *Education:* A.B., M.A., LL.B., Columbia University, 1897, 1899, 1900. *Collection Disposition:* Howard University; University of California at Los Angeles.

Shortly after he graduated from law school, Spingarn prepared a brief for a civil rights case. In the process he developed a lifelong interest in that area. In 1911 he was appointed chairman of the Legal Committee of the National Association for the Advancement of Colored People (NAACP) and from 1940 to 1965 served as president of that organization. His accomplishments in civil rights can be traced in a series of U.S. Supreme Court decisions that helped chart the way toward racial equality. From his earliest days at the NAACP, Spingarn had collected the writings of black authors and writings about blacks. What started as a small reference library grew into one of the largest collections in the United States. One especially strong area of the collection featured works of the poets and novelists of the Harlem Renaissance, with complete files of books and pamphlets by such authors as Langston Hughes, Countee Cullen, and Arna Bontemps. In addition to contemporary literature, Spingarn ransacked secondhand-book stores for the earliest known Negro writing in America, Africa, and the Caribbean. He owned first editions of the work of colonial poet Phillis Wheatley and had a wide selection of Afro-Cuban and Afro-Brazilian literature. From 1937 to 1968 he prepared the annual listing of books by black authors for *The Crisis*, a task that added many titles to his shelves. In addition to books, Spingarn's library contained journals, programs, playbills, mimeographed speeches, letters, and personal ephemera. In 1946, Howard University purchased the entire collection as an appropriate addition to its growing research facilities. It was combined with the library of Jesse E. Moorland* to form the Moorland-Spingarn Research Center.

Bibliography

A. "Collecting a Library of Negro Literature," *Journal of Negro Education*, January 1938, 12–18; *Dictionary Catalog of the Arthur B. Spingarn Collection of Negro Authors* (Boston, 1970).

B. *CB*, 1965, 34–35; Roger Daniels, "The Spingarn Collection: Its Historiographical Significance," *UCLA Librarian*, May 1966, 38; Beverly Gary, "White Warrior," *Negro Digest*, September 1962, 63–65; Michael Winston, "Moorland-SpingarnResearch Center: A Past Revisited, a Present Reclaimed," *New Directions: The Howard University Magazine*, Summer 1974, 1–6.

SPOOR, John A. (b. September 30, 1851, Freehold, N.Y.; d. October 15, 1926, Chicago, Ill.). *Collection Disposition:* Parke-Bernet, April 26, May 3, 1939.

As a prominent Chicago businessman, Spoor was connected with the growth of the city's transportation and banking facilities. He was at various times the chief officer of the Chicago Junction Railroad and the Chicago Surface Lines. His civic interests included the Chicago Historical Society, the Children's Hospital, and the Newberry Library, where he served as a trustee.

Like many other book collectors of his day, Spoor was interested in the English poets and essayists of the nineteenth century—Lamb, Shelley, Byron, and the Brownings. For example, Spoor had such rarities as the autograph album of Lamb's ward Emma Isola inscribed by Keats, Southey, Tennyson, and Wordsworth. His Shelley first editions included perfect copies of such gems as *The Necessity of Atheism*, *A Vindication of Natural Diet*, and *A Refutation of Deism*. For his purchases Spoor dealt chiefly with bookdealers Stevens and Brown in London and Walter Hill in Chicago. Spoor and his neighbor John Henry Wrenn* were bibliographic friends and sometimes rivals for certain nineteenth-century pamphlets. English bibliographer Thomas J. Wise alluded to this rivalry in letters to Wrenn, but fortunately Spoor never became a target for Wise's fabrications.

After Spoor's death his books were placed in the vaults of the First National Bank of Chicago. Speculation about their disposition became one of the favored topics of conversation among American bibliophiles. When the sale was finally announced for the spring of 1939, book reviewer John Winterich suggested that the event would be the "pyrotechnic climax" of an otherwise dull season. In spite of such claims, conditions surrounding the sale could hardly have been worse. The United States was just emerging from a long and draining economic depression, and World War II was beginning to erupt in Europe. On the first day of the sale, prices fell far below expectations. It was shocking to many that Elizabeth Browning's *Marathon* brought only $2,400 when thirteen years earlier a copy had sold for $17,500 at the Jerome Kern* sale. The chief beneficiaries were collectors Frank J. Hogan* and Carl H. Pforzheimer*, who with the help of A. S. W. Rosenbach* were able to pick up rarities at bargain prices. A copybook in which both Shelley and Mary Godwin had made notes went to Scribner's for $3,900, while Hill got a signed copy of Browning's *Pauline* for the same price. Prices fell far below the levels reached when comparable volumes had been sold at the Kern, Seth S. Terry*, and Cortlandt Field Bishop* auctions. Investors were simply not willing to put their money into rare books while the country was beginning to fight a global war. The Spoor library was characteristic of its time, but by 1939 that time had run out.

Bibliography

A. *A Bibliography of the First Editions in Book Form of the Writings of Charles and Mary Lamb, Published Prior to Charles Lamb's Death*, compiled by Luther Livingston (New York, 1903).

B. Philip Brooks, "Notes on Rare Books," *NYT*, June 11, 1939, VI, 18; John Winterich, "The Spoor Sale," *Saturday Review of Literature*, April 22, 1939, 18; Wolf and Fleming, passim.

SQUIER, E. George (b. June 17, 1821, Bethlehem, N.Y.; d. April 17, 1888, Brooklyn, N.Y.). *Collection Disposition:* Bangs, April 24, 1876; Anderson, April 23, 1917.

As a journalist, amateur archaeologist, diplomat, and author, Squier distinguished himself in a variety of areas. His numerous studies of Latin American history and archaeology were considered among the best commentaries of their time. In addition, his work as chief editor for Frank Leslie's publishing firm gave him a reputation for expertise in the history of the American Civil War, a subject treated in great detail in *Frank Leslie's Pictorial History of the American Civil War*. Squier's library reflected his interests in Latin America, United States history, and archaeological and ethnological subjects. At the sale of his books and manuscripts in 1876, Hubert Howe Bancroft* was one of the chief buyers. Thus the Squier collection formed part of the substance of Bancroft's great library of Mexican and Latin American history.

Bibliography

B. *DAB*, 9, 488–489; *NCAB* 4, 79; Cannon, 98–99; *NYT*, April 18, 1888, 8.

STEFANSSON, Vilhjalmur (b. November 3, 1879, Manitoba, Can.; d. August 26, 1962, Hanover, N.H.). *Education:* A.B., University of Iowa, 1903. *Collection Disposition:* Dartmouth College.

Chiefly known as an Arctic explorer, Stefansson was also an able writer and an avid book collector. While he was a student at Harvard and at Iowa he began a series of explorations that brought him international renown. He lived with the Eskimos during 1906 and 1907 and headed the Canadian Arctic expedition from 1913 to 1918. Stefansson's collection of books and maps grew steadily from a few shelves to one of the largest accumulations of Arctic studies in the world. All aspects of northern culture were of interest to Stefansson, and all were represented in his library. In 1933 he augmented his collection by obtaining a large number of rarities from the Nantucket Whaling Museum. Instead of accepting a check for a talk delivered at the museum, Stefansson asked for the equivalent value in books from their little-used library. The museum officers agreed and gave the explorer a valuable collection. As one observer commented, Stefansson obtained $10,000 worth of books for a forty-five minute talk.

Stefansson felt that the only way to collect was to buy everything. This was easy in the early years of the century because polar materials attracted little attention in the book markets. By 1930, however, a number of collectors and dealers had become interested, and Stefansson had a harder time finding books at prices he was willing to pay. As his collection grew, he was forced to move from one New York apartment to another, seeking space. Inquiries began to pour in from all over the world, and soon what had been a personal library became a public resource. Government agencies, private corporations, and independent scholars found the Stefansson collection a rich archive. By 1951, Stefansson decided that the library needed to be placed in a public institution.

Because of its emphasis on northern studies, Dartmouth College seemed to be the ideal location. Through the generosity of an alumnus the purchase was completed and the 20,000 volumes and supporting maps were moved to the Baker Library. In 1959, in honor of the founder, the Dartmouth Library produced the first issue of *Polar Notes*, a scholarly journal dedicated to Arctic research. The college has continued to support the growth of this preeminent collection with funds for materials and for professional staff. Stefansson once commented that he knew little of stocks and bonds but that he did know polar books. The Dartmouth collection attests to that knowledge.

Bibliography

A. *Discovery: An Autobiography* (New York, 1964).

B. *DAB*, Supp. 7, 715–717; *NCAB* A, 230; Evelyn Stefansson, "A Short Account of the Stefansson Collection," *Polar Notes*, November 1959, 5–12; Evelyn Stefansson, "The Bookman," *Polar Notes*, November 1962, 42–47; Charles Everitt, *The Adventures of a Treasure Hunter* (New York, 1951), 262–264.

STERN, Alfred Whital (b. June 10, 1881, New York, N.Y.; d. May 3, 1960, Chicago, Ill.). *Collection Disposition:* Library of Congress; Illinois State Historical Library.

Because of his extremely reticent nature, little is known about Stern's development as a collector. He was a Chicago businessman with a deep interest in the Civil War period, particularly in Abraham Lincoln. Over a period of thirty-five years he acquired books, pamphlets, broadsides, documents, letters, and association pieces, many of them rare and all in excellent physical condition. The range of his Lincoln collection was extraordinary. He acquired legal documents issued as part of Lincoln's early law practice, texts of the Lincoln-Douglas debates, campaign biographies, state papers from the presidential period, assassination literature, memorial sermons, and letters. In addition to the Lincoln items, Stern acquired collateral material on the slavery question, the Civil War period, and the period of the reconstruction. He had the standard works as well as ephemeral pamphlets on all the major military and political figures of the era. Not satisfied to collect rarities in book form only, Stern had sheet music, broadsides, prints, cartoons, newspapers, and photographs. One section of the library consisted of Lincoln joke books. Attempting coverage as comprehensive as possible, Stern gathered every unique edition or printing he could find of such well-known Lincoln items as the Cooper Institute speech, the Lincoln-Douglas debates, and the Gettysburg Address. All this went to form one of the most remarkable Lincoln collections in the country.

In 1943 Stern made himself known to David C. Mearns at the Library of Congress. Stern wanted to know what arrangements might be made if on his death he wished to bequeath Lincoln's famous letter to General Hooker to the library. In a continuing series of negotiations carried on by librarians Archibald McLeish and Luther Evans, Stern agreed to present the letter along with some of his Lincoln books. By 1950 Stern had decided to turn over his entire Lincoln collection, some 5,000 items, to the Library of Congress as a gift to the American people. Along with the library, Stern established an endowment for continued purchases and for the publication of appropriate catalogs and bibliographies. He continued to make personal additions to the collection up to the time of his death. Established as a separate area in the Library of Congress, the Alfred Whital Stern Collection of Lincolniana was accurately characterized by Mearns as the "greatest Lincoln library ever formed by a single man."

Bibliography

A. *Catalog of the Alfred Whital Stern Collection of Lincolniana*(Washington, D.C., 1960).

B. *SCLC*, 341; Vincent L. Eaton, "Some Highlights of the Alfred Whital Stern Collection," *QJLC*, February 1952, 65–73; J. M. Edelstein, "Lincoln Papers in the Stern Bequest," *QJLC*, December 1961, 7–14; David C. Mearns, "Alfred Whital Stern and the Hoof Prints," *QJLC*, February 1952, 57–64.

STETSON, John B. (b. October 11, 1884, Philadelphia, Pa.; d. November 15, 1952, Elkins Park, Pa.). *Education:* A.B., Harvard University, 1907. *Collection Disposition:* Anderson, April 20, 1920; American Art, April 17, 1935; Parke-Bernet, February 25, March 10, April 14, 1953.

It would be difficult to imagine a career more diverse than that followed by Stetson. He began by working in the family hat company in Philadelphia, managed a bleaching plant in Massachusetts, owned a New York book and art auction firm, served as envoy extraordinary to Poland, and finally worked in a brokerage firm in Philadelphia. He was an officer in both world wars and culminated those assignments with an appointment as director of the Federal Bureau of Supplies.

Stetson's book-collecting activities were nearly as eclectic as those in his business careers. He was an early customer of A. S. W. Rosenbach*, buying a variety of French literature, eighteenth-century color-plate books, tales of chivalry, and Americana. Among his rarities were Caxton's 1520 *Lanclot du Lac*, a fourteenth-century manuscript of the "Roman de la Rose" once owned by John Ruskin, the second Madrid edition of Part I of *Don Quijote*, and an autographed manuscript of Sir Richard Burton's "Terminal Essay" from *The Thousand and One Nights*. In his Americana section Stetson acquired the 1555 edition of de Vaca's *Relacion* and the Menzies-Cooke-Ives copy of the 1663 Eliot Bible. In 1910, working through Rosenbach, he bought an extensive collection of Oscar Wilde first editions and later obtained the notorious "Dear Bosie" letters sent by Wilde to the young Lord Alfred Douglas. With a decline of the family fortunes, Stetson had to retrench and sell the Wilde materials. Most of them went to William Andrews Clark Jr.*, a new collector on the Los Angeles scene. Shortly after the disposition of the Wilde collection, Stetson began to concentrate on Spanish and Portuguese materials. From 1922 until the time of his death, he served as honorary curator of the Portuguese literature collection at Harvard. His chief gift to that institution was the 6,000-volume historical library of Fernando

Palha, an important member of the Lisbon Academy of Science. During his period of service to Harvard, Stetson became a close working colleague of Library Director Archibald Cary Coolidge, aiding him in the selection of French, Spanish, and Portuguese literature. At the same time, Stetson became involved in a self-serving negotiation with English bibliophile Henry Buxton Forman. Representing himself as a private buyer interested in giving books to an institution, Stetson obtained a good price on Forman's private library, then turned it over to Mitchell Kennerley, his business partner at the Anderson Gallery. Forman was angry and took pains to see that the entire book world heard of his displeasure.

In 1935, when portions of Stetson's own library came up for sale, depression prices prevailed. Rosenbach, who had sold the books to Stetson in the first place, bought actively for new customers like Philip Hofer*, Lucius Wilmerding*, and Tracy W. McGregor*. The final sales of the Stetson books in 1953 brought an end to a remarkable collection.

Bibliography

B. *NCAB* 42, 67; Wolf and Fleming, passim; "John B. Stetson," *PAAS*, April 1953, 18–20; *New York Post*, April 10, 1920, 10.

STOCKHAUSEN, William E. (b. 1912; d. April 4, 1974, Hudson, N.Y.). *Education:* A.B., LL.B., Yale University, 1935, 1938. *Collection Disposition:* Sotheby Parke Bernet, November 19, December 14, 1974.

Among those who influenced Stockhausen on the development of his personal library were Yale professor Chauncey Brewster Tinker*, collector Waller Barrett, and bookdealer Michael Papantonio*. Stockhausen discovered the lure of bibliomania in Tinker's classroom. Later Barrett carried him farther along the bibliographic trail into the realm of first editions, and finally bookdealer Papantonio showed him where to buy the books. Stockhausen began collecting seriously around 1959 and, as a disciple of Barrett, concentrated on twentieth-century American literature. He started with William Faulkner and moved on to New England poet Robert Frost, the author who became his primary interest. Stockhausen's Frost collection was distinguished by a number of inscribed copies, letters, and manuscripts. In one case Stockhausen obtained a collection of letters from Frost to Wade Van Dore, a friend for whom the poet provided considerable literary advice. Many of the Frost books contained lengthy inscriptions to his early publisher, Mark DeWolf Howe, and his biographer Lawrence Thompson. Encouraged by his success with Frost, Stockhausen broadened his field of interest to include Cather, Hemingway, Steinbeck, E. A. Robinson, and other moderns. Then, remembering his undergraduate classes with Tinker, he began to acquire English literature. He bought a number of significant titles at the Barton Currie* and Robert Esty sales of 1963. Among the gems added at that time were Dickens' "Pickwick" in parts, Austen's *Pride and Prejudice* in original boards, the Kilmarnock Burns, Boswell letters, Keats and Shelley first editions, and Shakespeare folios.

As his new author collections developed, the old ones had to go. He had formed a solid Emily Dickinson library, but subsequent lack of interest prompted him to sell it off. He traded Dickinson's lyrics for Poe's ringing verses. These were not the minor works but the rarest of the rare, the first editions of *Tamerlane* (1827) and *Al Aaraaf, Tamerlane, and Minor Poems* (1829). At the Grolier Club exhibition in late 1966, members had a chance to examine some of the highlights in the collection. When the library was brought to auction in 1974, all the chief American dealers were on hand. The honors for securing the most important sale items went to John F. Fleming of New York and Warren Howell of San Francisco. It was Fleming who stole the headlines with his successful bid of $123,000 for *Tamerlane*. The Stockhausen library had been built lovingly over a period of years, based on an excellent working relationship between a sophisticated collector and sophisticated bookdealers. Its sale offered collectors an unusual opportunity to obtain rare and significant items from an important gathering of American and English literature.

Bibliography

B. "English and American Literature from the Collection of William E. Stockhausen," *Gazette of the Grolier Club*, 1967, 28; Michael Papantonio, "William E. Stockhausen 1912–1974," in *Sotheby Parke Bernet, Catalogue*, November 1974.

STONE, Wilbur Macey (b. 1862; d. December 21, 1941, East Orange, N.J.). *Collection Disposition:* American Antiquarian Society; Anderson, January 26, 1925, April 12, 1926, Parke-Bernet, January 16, 1940, April 10, 1943.

In the early decades of the twentieth century, Stone was well known as an expert on children's books and a connoisseur of bookplates. Between 1900 and 1935 he wrote a number of short studies on these topics and formed several impressive personal collections. He was chiefly interested in the history of children's literature and wrote about the contributions of such eighteenth-century figures as Isaac Watts and John Taylor. By 1938 Stone had a collection of 200 various editions of Watts' charming collection of verses entitled *Divine Songs Attempted in Easy Language for the Use of Children*. He also had large holdings of chapbooks, battledores, grammars, fairy tales, miniature Bibles, and New England primers. One important section of his library featured the English children's books printed by John Newbery. Since Newbery was the first publisher to offer a variety of books for children, this collection was of great historical interest. Over the years many authors took advantage of Stone's collection to support their research. Collector and bibliographer d'Alte A. Welch* recalled visiting Stone's library and seeing the walls lined with children's books, each with its own brightly colored paper cover. It was, according to Welch, an exciting place to work. Although many of the books were dispersed at auction, the exemplary collection of Watts' *Divine Songs* was preserved as a unit by gift to the American Antiquarian Society. As an author and collector, Stone contributed significantly to the appreciation of the history of children's literature.

Bibliography

A. *The Divine and Moral Songs of Isaac Watts* (New York, 1918); *Four Centuries of Children's Books from the Collection of Wilbur Macey Stone* (Newark, N.J., 1928); *The Gigantic Histories of Thomas Boreman* (Portland, Maine, 1933); *The History of Little Goody Two-Shoes* (Worcester, Mass., 1940); "Collections of Rare Children's Books: A Symposium," *Library Journal*, March 1, 1938, 192–193.

B. d'Alte A. Welch, *A Bibliography of American Children's Books* (Worcester, 1972), xiii; *NYT*, December 22, 1941, 17.

STREETER, Edward C. (b. November 10, 1874, Chicago, Ill.; d. July 17, 1947, Stonington, Conn.). *Education:* A.B., Yale University, 1898; M.D., Northwestern University, 1901. *Collection Disposition:* New York Academy of Medicine; Yale University; Cleveland Academy of Medicine.

As a student at Yale, Streeter was deeply interested in both literature and history. He served as editor of the literary magazine and was an avid student of both Latin and Greek. After working in Chicago clinics for five years he moved to New England, where he spent the remainder of his professional life. His early exposure to the humanities was a major factor in directing his later academic interests toward the history of medicine, a subject he taught at Harvard from 1921 to 1933. He was particularly interested in such significant sixteenth-century figures as the medical humanist François Rabelais and the Belgian anatomist Andreas Vesalius. Always attracted to the graphic arts, Streeter wrote a study in 1916 describing the influence of certain sixteenth-century painters on anatomical drawing. After retiring from Harvard he moved to Yale, where he continued to lecture on medical history. His personal library began to take shape after several extended trips to Europe. There he was able to locate the monumental works of the early anatomists, some of the first books on syphilis, and a unique gathering of the works of Ambroise Paré, the father of surgery. In an important block purchase, Streeter obtained the library of Nicholaus Pol, chief surgeon to Maximilian I of Austria. Books and manuscripts were not the only objects of Streeter's widening interests. In the 1930s he began to buy antiquarian weights and measures and apothecary implements to illustrate another facet of medical history. When shelving space became a problem at home, Streeter placed some of his library up for sale.

In 1927 a large part of the historical collection, including eighty-three incunabula, went to A. S. W. Rosenbach*, while the Pol books were given to the Cleveland Academy of Medicine. As soon as the Rosenbach purchase became known, a number of institutions began to look for support to enable them to meet the substantial asking price—$185,000. The New York Academy of Medicine, under the energetic direction of its president, Samuel W. Lambert*, moved with speed and determination. A prospectus was sent to members, soliciting funds for what was described as one of the finest private medical collections in the world. With the help of the Rockefeller Foundation and individual gifts from

Edward S. Harkness* and others, the collection was secured and placed in the Academy.

With his first collection out of the way, Streeter began to buy books again, this time materials for his ongoing studies in the history of medicine. His second collection was eventually placed with those of Harvey Cushing*, John F. Fulton*, and Anton Klebs to form at Yale one of the most distinguished medical collections in the country. The Streeter weights and measures also went to Yale, where they were given handsomely appointed facilities in the Medical Library. By pursuing his hobby with intelligence and energy, Streeter provided both Yale and New York with unique research facilities for the study of medical history.

Bibliography

B. *NCAB* 37, 253–254; "E. C. Streeter, 1874–1947: A Biographical Appreciation," *Yale Journal of Biology and Medicine*, December 1947, 203–211; Samuel Lambert, "Streeter Collection" (Circular letter to members of the Academy of Medicine, 1928).

STREETER, Thomas W. (b. July 20, 1883, Concord, N.H.; d. June 12, 1965, Morristown, N.J.). *Education:* A.B., Dartmouth College, 1904; LL.B., Harvard University, 1907. *Collection Disposition:* Yale University; American Antiquarian Society; Dartmouth College; Princeton University; University of Virginia.

Although trained as a lawyer, Streeter's financial ability soon led him away from the law and into management. His administrative record with major corporations was said to have been characterized by diligence and a deep sense of stewardship. The precision that made him an effective lawyer and businessman contributed to his success as a collector.

First and last, Streeter was attracted to American history. Even during his college days he enjoyed historical studies and had started to collect on a modest level. These books, according to Lawrence Wroth, were English and American "after-dinner" items gathered chiefly for display. By 1920, however, Streeter began to take collecting more seriously and started to work within a well-organized plan. He directed his efforts toward books that would reflect historical or cultural beginnings—the discovery of America, the opening of the western territories, the first newspapers, the first railroads—anything that spoke of the creativity and adventure of first things. With a sure sense of what he wanted, Streeter wisely placed himself in the hands of experts: bibliographer Henry R. Wagner* and bookdealers Lathrop Harper, Edward Eberstadt, and Henry Stevens. The Wagner bibliographies—*The Plains and the Rockies* (1920) and *The Spanish Southwest* (1924)—provided the bookish nourishment that Streeter needed to push forward his own collecting endeavors. The library grew rapidly in the early 1920s. After the 1929 stock market crash, Streeter was forced to sell rather than buy. Many of the books went back to Harper, who generously bought them at high prices. Streeter paid tribute to this act of kindness in a memorial published at the time of Harper's death. Never completely out of the book market, Streeter concentrated during the tight-money decade of the 1930s on canal and railroad reports. Since he was one of the few collectors looking for this ephemeral literature, he bought at bargain levels. Ultimately Streeter gave many of his books to academic institutions, where he believed they would serve as a scholarly archive. Within the broad range of his Americana holdings, Texas material loomed as a major unit. From 1927, when he had been involved in business negotiations in the Southwest, Streeter had gathered local history and literature. His goal was to develop a bibliography of Texas imprints and of books, broadsides, and maps about Texas during the period 1795–1845. This formidable task took twenty-seven years to complete and is a landmark in American bibliography.

Like other collectors before him, Streeter was less interested in the books once the collection was formed and the bibliography was under way. In a sense, the fun was over. The collection, of course, was highly desirable, and no one understood this better than Yale librarian James Babb. What better place for the Streeter books than beside the Wagner books in the Yale libraries? With this in mind, Babb launched a successful fund-raising drive and in 1956 brought the Texas collection to New Haven. The remainder of the Streeter library was dispersed at auction. Long before his death, Streeter identified books that would do well at the sale. When the books did become available at Sotheby Parke Bernet between October 1966 and October 1969, all Streeter's predictions came true. The auction set new records in many fields and brought the estate the astounding total of over $3 million.

Parallels have been drawn between Streeter and George Brinley*, one of the outstanding collectors of the nineteenth century. Some of the comparisons seem exaggerated, but in the final distribution of their books similarities did exist. Brinley set aside a fund of $25,000 to help five libraries make purchases at his sale. Streeter magnified this idea in scale and set up a fund of $400,000 for eighteen institutions. Chicago bookdealer Kenneth Nebenzahl remarked that, far from limiting purchases, such stimulation served to whet the appetites of the libraries involved, encouraging them to spend much more than they received in the gift. An examination of the sale catalog provides the best picture of Streeter's accomplished collecting goals—to form an integrated library reflecting the history and development of the United States from discovery to the opening of the West. Streeter set a standard for collecting Americana that may never be equaled.

Bibliography

A. *Bibliography of Texas 1795–1845* (Cambridge, Mass., 1955–1960); *Americana—Beginnings* (Morristown, N.J., 1952); "Lathrop C. Harper," *Bibliographical Society of America Newsletter*, May 1951, 4–5; "The Rollins Collection of Western Americana," *PLC*, 1947–1948, 191–204; "Henry R. Wagner: Collector, Bibliographer, Cartographer, and Historian," *QCHS*, March 1957, 165–175.

B. *NCAB* 51, 107–108; *NCAB* F, 422–423; James Alger, "Tom Streeter: A Gentleman of Books," *Hoja Volante*, February 1965; John Carter, "A Personal Appreciation of T. W. S.," *AB Bookman's Yearbook 1970*, 5–6; Howell Heaney, "Thomas W. Streeter, Collector, 1883–1965," *PBSA*, 3rd Q 1971, 243–256; Kenneth Nebenzahl, "Reflections on Brinley and Streeter,'' *PBSA*, 2nd Q 1970, 165–175; Frank Streeter, "Some Recollections of Thomas W. Streeter and his Collecting,'' *Gazette of the Grolier Club*, 1980, 40–50; Edward Eberstadt, "The Thomas W. Streeter Collection,'' *YLG*, April 1957, 147–153; Lawrence Wroth, "The Americana Library of Thomas Winthrop Streeter,'' *AB Bookman's Yearbook 1970*, 3–4; "Streeter Americana Highlights,'' *Bookman's Yearbook 1970*, 10–28.

SULZBERGER, Mayer (b. June 22, 1843, Heidelsheim, Ger.; d. April 20, 1923, Philadelphia, Pa.). *Collection Disposition:* Jewish Theological Seminary of America.

As a noted jurist, first president of the American Jewish Committee, and founder of the Jewish Publication Society, Sulzberger built a remarkable library. In addition to Hebraic books and manuscripts, he acquired English poetry, history, and philosophy. With the help of bibliographer-bookseller Ephraim Deinard he obtained a wide range of European studies on Jewish history, including an esoteric collection of Russian texts. In 1901 Sulzberger gave his collection of 2,400 books and 500 manuscripts to the Jewish Theological Seminary in New York, and in 1903 he added 5,000 liturgical texts and broadsides. For these important gifts Sulzberger was identified as the father of the Jewish Theological Seminary library.

Bibliography

A. *A Catalogue of the Old Hebrew Manuscripts and Printed Books of the Library of the Hon. Mayer Sulzberger of Philadelphia*, prepared by Ephraim Deinard (Philadelphia, 1896).

B. *NCAB* 15, 283; *Encyclopaedia Judaica*, 15, 509–510; Alexander Marx, *Studies in History and Booklore* (New York, 1944), 234–236; Adolph Oke, "Jewish Book Collections in the United States,'' *American Jewish Yearbook 1943–1944*, 67–96.

SUTRO, Adolph (b. April 29, 1830, Aix-la-Chapelle, Ger.; d. August 8, 1898, San Francisco, Calif.). *Collection Disposition:* State Library of California.

Born in Prussia, Sutro migrated with his mother to the United States in 1850 and one year later settled in California. After working for a number of years in San Francisco in the tobacco trade, he moved to Virginia City, Nevada, to try his luck in silver mining. His determination paid off, and by 1879 he had made a fortune. At that point he returned to San Francisco, where he spent the remainder of his life supporting a variety of philanthropies. Although he had a so-called "gentleman's library'' in Nevada, Sutro had never collected seriously until 1880. His objective, as it developed, was to build a library for the people of San Francisco modeled on the fine research libraries he had seen in Europe. Sutro bought history, political science, philosophy, literature, art, architecture, and science. His system was to buy in bulk. He would walk into a bookshop in London or Paris and take the entire stock, 15,000 to 20,000 volumes at a time. At the Sunderland sale in London in 1881, he acquired over 9,000 political pamphlets and broadsides covering the times of Charles I through the reign of

Queen Ann. Later he added an amazing 3,000-item incunabula collection from the Carthusian Monastery at Buzheim. In addition to his own buying, he employed agents to comb European shops for likely books and journals. In this way he acquired the four Shakespeare folios, manuscript notes from Shakespearean editor J. O. Halliwell-Phillipps, and first editions of works by Ben Jonson and John Milton. In 1889 Sutro bought 40,000 to 50,000 titles from the stock of Mexico City's oldest bookdealer, Libreria Abadiano. The particular strength of this stock was around its documentation of the period of the Spanish colonization and the Mexican struggle for independence.

At the time of Sutro's death, his library held some 125,000 bound volumes and 125,000 pamphlets, tracts, and broadsides. Sadly, Sutro's dream of providing a reference library for the people of San Francisco almost perished in the disastrous earthquake and fire of 1906. At least half the general collection and 90 percent of the incunabula were destroyed. Fortunately, the 40,000-volume library on Mexican history was spared, along with an important archive of eighteenth-century political and scientific manuscripts formed by Sir Joseph Banks, president of the Royal Society. After Sutro's death an involved legal contest delayed the settlement of the estate, but finally, in 1913, his daughter gave the 90,000-volume library to the state of California. Four years later, with the formal opening of the Sutro Collection, the founder's dream was realized.

Bibliography

B. *DAB* 9, 224; *NCAB* 21, 126; Richard Dillon, "A Peek at the Sutro Library," *QNLBCC*, Spring 1952, 27–32; Richard Dillon, "Adolph Sutro: Private and Institutional Collector," *QNLBCC*, Fall 1974, 86–91; Gary Kurutz, "The Sutro Library," *California History*, Summer 1980, 173–178; W. M. Mathes, "A Bibliophile's Dream: Adolph Sutro in Mexico," *QNLBCC*, Summer 1980, 73–75; Robert Stewart, *Adolph Sutro: A Biography* (Berkeley, Calif., 1962).

T

TAYLOR, Charles Henry (b. October 2, 1867, Charlestown, Mass.; d. August 18, 1941, Boston, Mass.). *Collection Disposition:* American Antiquarian Society; College of William and Mary.

For more than forty years Taylor worked on the *Boston Globe*, a newspaper founded shortly after the end of the Civil War by his father. By avocation he was an enthusiastic bibliophile. His interests were broad and included printing, shipwrecks, canals, railroading, Boston history, lithography, and novelist Herman Melville. In the early decades of the twentieth century he was a well-known figure in Boston bookshops and in the local bibliographic and literary societies. At one time he was president of the Club of Odd Volumes and chairman of the board of trustees of the Massachusetts State Library. His chief interest was in the activities of the American Antiquarian Society. Shortly after he was elected to membership in 1912, he presented the library of that institution with all his books on printing and journalism. For the next thirty years he kept adding valuable materials in an ever-growing stream. According to Director Clarence S. Brigham, Taylor's consistent, openhanded generosity in the 1920s and 1930s provided the library with a backbone of essential research materials. From 1927 to 1937 he also gave a number of books, pamphlets, and broadsides on American history to the College of William and Mary.

Bibliography

B. "Charles Henry Taylor," *PAAS*, October 1941, 237–241; Correspondence with Margaret Cook, Curator of Rare Books at the College of William and Mary, 1984.

TAYLOR, Henry C. (b. January 14, 1894, Brooklyn, N.Y.; d. May 1, 1971, New York, N.Y.). *Education:* A.B., Yale University, 1917. *Collection Disposition:* Yale University.

From his early interest in books by nineteenth-century English novelists, Taylor progressed to color-plate books on hunting and fishing and finally to early works on navigation. His collection was strongest in tales of English exploration but also contained French and Spanish accounts. He owned the 1494 Basel edition of the "Columbus Letter" as well as early printings of Blaeu, Ptolemy, Champlain, and Drake. One of the outstanding items in his collection was the so-called Drake "Silver Map," a medallion etched with the map of the world and struck to commemorate the 1577–1580 circumnavigation. The collection got its start in 1939, when Taylor bought a boat and tried to teach himself how to use it. In the process he bought a 1647 edition of Captain John Smith's *Sea Grammar* and found therein a list of eleven essential related titles. With the help of various bookdealers and librarians, he was eventually able to add all these titles. The Taylor library, consisting of 14 manuscripts, 22 incunabula, and some 370 books of the sixteenth and seventeenth centuries, was not large, but each item was well selected and significant. Yale received the Taylor library in 1971 and honored the gift by publishing a handsome descriptive catalog.

Bibliography

A. *The Henry C. Taylor Collection*, compiled by John S. Kababian (New Haven, 1971).

B. John S. Kababian, "The Henry C. Taylor Collection," *BC*, Spring 1965, 34–48; "Early Books and Manuscripts on Navigation from the Collection of Henry C. Taylor," *Gazette of the Grolier Club*, June 1970, 27–30.

TERRY, Roderick T. (b. April 1, 1849, Brooklyn, N.Y.; d. December 28, 1933, Newport, R.I.). *Education:* A.B., Yale University, 1870; D.D., Princeton University, 1881. *Collection Disposition:* American Art—Anderson, May 2, November 7, 1934; February 15, 1935.

From 1881 to 1905 Terry served as pastor of the South Reformed Church of New York. For the next twenty-eight years he resided in Newport, Rhode Island, and contributed actively to the civic and cultural life of that aristocratic community. It was during the Newport years that he began to devote attention to his lifelong interest in books and collecting. He became a member of the Grolier Club of New York and in that environment was able to enjoy the companionship of such avid collectors as Beverly Chew*, William A. White*, John B. Thacher*. His interests were varied and included early printing, English and American letters, and Americana. Ruth Granniss, librarian of the Grolier Club, identified Terry's richly diverse collection as "an old-time library." The incunabula period was represented by samples of printing from Germany, Italy, and England, but aside from several handsome Caxtons none was of the highest order. The quality of Terry's English literature, however, was unquestionable. He had the four Shakespeare folios, as well as distinguished first editions of Byron, Lamb, Spenser, and Milton. In many cases letters and manuscripts accompanied the printed texts. Terry had a special affection for autographs, and with the help of A. S. W. Rosenbach* he completed a set of the signers of the Declaration of Independence.

In general the Americana section of his library was strong, with the inevitable Eliot "Indian Bible," a first edition of Drake's "Voyages," a run of unique eighteenth-century Rhode Island broadsides, and a selection of Franklin imprints. When the library was sold in 1934, the country was still in the wake of the depression, so Rosenbach was able to get the items he wanted at the prices he was willing to pay. It was a buyer's market for such Rosenbach customers as Arthur Houghton, Frank B. Bemis*, and Frank J. Hogan*. Although the Terry sales netted some $270,000, that return was considerably below the prices paid by the collector. Terry was a connoisseur in the grand old tradition of the nineteenth century. His library reflected his eclectic tastes and cultivated good judgment.

Bibliography

B. *NCAB* 10, 233; *Grolier 75*, 48–50; Wolf and Fleming, passim.

TERRY, Seth S. (b. September 25, 1862, Rochester, N.Y.; d. December 19, 1932, East Aurora, N.Y.). *Education:* LL.D., Harvard University, 1886. *Collection Disposition:* American Art—Anderson, December 4, 1935.

Following his graduation from Harvard, Terry combined successful careers in politics and law. He was elected to the New York Commission on Accounts in 1894 and supervised many reforms in that city department. After he retired from active legal practice, he was able to devote himself to a number of humanitarian causes, book collecting, and travel. Terry's collecting activities, shared with his son, focused on English literature. Terry's objective was to obtain the first editions of those works in English literature which over the centuries had been most influential. For this purpose his collection was based largely on the Grolier Club listing *One Hundred Books Famous in English Literature*. The development of the Terry library followed the principles laid down by Frederick Locker-Lampson in building his Rowfant Library, that every book should have a special reason for its inclusion and that together all would make a logical whole. Each book in the Terry library was a showpiece both in provenance and in condition. They were pristine, with first state printing and original binding. Among the long list of English authors represented in the library were Arnold, Austen, Barrie, Carroll, Galsworthy, Beaumont and Fletcher, and Milton. Perhaps the most spectacular of the Milton items was the first edition of *Paradise Lost* (1667) in original sheepskin with protecting covers made from a rafter in the room in which the poet wrote his masterpiece. This remarkable book had progressed from the Lamport Hall library of Sir John Isham to the Britwell Court collection of S. R. Christie Miller before it was sold to Terry at the Robert B. Adam* auction. The period of the 1920s was a fortunate one for Terry because a number of notable libraries of English literature came on the market at that time. Through Rosenbach, Walter Hill, and Gabriel Wells, Terry was able to take advantage of a number of these offerings. He bought heavily at the Herschel V. Jones*, Winston Hagen*, and Beverly Chew* auctions. Terry had a particular affection for presentation copies, and many of the volumes in the library were enriched with intimate dedications to wives, mothers, and lovers.

When the Terry books came on the market in 1935, the devastating effects of the great depression were just beginning to lift. Rosenbach, who had sold many of the books to Terry, was an active bidder. In behalf of Arthur Houghton, he bought the Book of Common Prayer for $15,100 and *Paradise Lost* for $17,500. Coming when it did, the Terry sale did much to restore confidence of the book world in the continuing value of genuine rarities.

Bibliography

B. *NCAB* 26, 242; Wolf and Fleming, passim.

THACHER, John Boyd (b. September 11, 1847, Ballston Spa, N.Y.; d. February 25, 1909, Albany, N.Y.). *Education:* A.B., Williams College, 1869. *Collection Disposition:* Library of Congress; Anderson, October 30, 1913, January 8, March 13, October 22, 1914, May 13, November 3, 1915, January 10, 1916, December 1, 1920, December 4, 1922.

For thirty-five years Thacher was associated with business and politics in Albany, New York. He was a member of the Board of Health, a state senator, and twice mayor of the city of Albany. Four distinct but overlapping areas attracted his attention as a collector—incunabula, Americana, the French Revolution, and autographs. His fascination with first things led Thacher to form a collection of the earliest products of European printing presses. Between the years 1888 and 1899 he was able to secure examples of the work of 500 fifteenth-century presses. Certainly no other private collector in America could boast that sizable an accumulation. Thacher's deep interest in the fifteenth century led to formation of a collection on voyages and discovery. His extensive Columbus archive contributed directly to his massive three-volume *Christopher Columbus: His Life, His Work, and His Remains as Revealed by Original Printed and Manuscript Records* (1903). This book, along with *The Continent of America* (1896) and *The Cabotian Discovery* (1897), established Thacher's reputation as a sound historian and a bibliophile. During the last ten years of his life, Thacher formed a collection of books and papers on the French Revolution. He started by gathering autographed letters and documents from every important figure involved in the revolutionary movement. He wanted to produce a treatise that would reflect the exact impressions and words of those who had participated. Unfortunately, Thacher's death cut short this work in progress. Mrs. Thacher gave the incunabula and the French historical materials as a deposit to the Library of Congress, but bequeathed them outright on her death. The remainder of the books were sold in New York between 1913 and 1922. Thacher was an assiduous collector and a productive scholar. His collections enriched the Library of Congress and his writing illuminated the earliest period of American history.

Bibliography

A. *The Collection of John Boyd Thacher in the Library of Congress* (Washington, D.C., 1931).

B. *DAB* 18, 388; *NCAB* 7, 37; Cannon, 112; *Grolier 75*, 38–41; "John Boyd Thacher Collection," in *SCLC*, 346–347; "John Boyd Thacher," in *Catalogue of the John Boyd Thacher Collection of Incunabula* (Washington, D.C., 1915), 7–17; Edith Brinkmann, "John Boyd Thacher," *PBSA*, 1st Q 1920, 33–37.

THAYER, Sylvanius (b. June 9, 1785, Braintree, Mass.; d. September 7, 1872, Braintree, Mass.). *Education:* U.S. Military Academy, 1808. *Collection Disposition:* Dartmouth College.

After several years of study in France, Thayer was appointed superintendent of the Military Academy at West Point. During his fifteen years in that position he raised the standards of scholarship to the high level he had observed in similar European institutions. When he retired from West Point in 1833, he was placed in charge of harbor control in Boston. From the time of his student days he had been a book collector. His personal library reflected both his major interests: military tactics and professional engineering. He owned drill manuals, Napoleonic campaign literature, architectural plate books, and classic French civil engineering texts. In an effort to raise American engineering standards, he donated his entire library to Dartmouth College, where it provided support for the Thayer School of Engineering. Thayer's library was one of the important scholarly resources for the new school.

Bibliography

B. *DAB* 9, 410–411; *NCAB* 2, 37; Stanley Birch, "Notes on the Thayer Collection," *Dartmouth Library Bulletin*, November 1970, 50–53.

THOMAS, Isaiah (b. January 19, 1749, Boston, Mass.; d. April 4, 1831, Worcester, Mass.). *Collection Disposition:* American Antiquarian Society; Dartmouth College.

At the age of six, Thomas was taken into a Boston printing shop as an indentured apprentice. He learned the trade so well that, according to his biographer, Clifford Shipton, by the time he was forty-five he was the most important printer-publisher of his generation. He worked in Boston until his independent Whig political views made it expedient for him to take refuge in a nearby city. With the help of friends and under cover of night, he moved his press and type to Worcester on April 16, 1775. There his reputation as a craftsman spread and the business flourished. He published schoolbooks, almanacs, newspapers, dictionaries, bibles, and juveniles—a complete line of the most wanted and popular books of his day. By the 1790s, with a paper mill in Worcester and branch presses and bookstores throughout New England, Thomas had become a printing and publishing entrepreneur. He approached printing not only from the business point of view but also with a scholarly historical sense.

In order to improve his own work he collected a large library of typefounders' handbooks and manuals representing the best products of the British and European trade. He also obtained almanacs, broadsides, books, newspapers, and pamphlets from all the earliest American presses. These publications traced the development of printing and were individually important as documents of American history. In 1810 Thomas used his library to prepare a two-volume *History of Printing*, regarded as the standard in its field for over 100 years. His interest in the preservation of the historical record led to the formation of the American Antiquarian Society. Already a member of the existing learned societies, Thomas proposed that the new group concentrate on identification and preservation of the sources of American history. In 1812 the American Antiquarian Society was incorporated, with Thomas elected as the first president. The next year Thomas gave the Society his extensive historical library, said to have been the largest of its kind in existence. To that initial deposit he added a collection of philosophy, religion, and scientific treatises that had been part of the Mather* library. Finally, he gave funds for a library building and established an endowment for the library's future growth. Although Thomas is chiefly remembered as a printer, he also deserves attention as a collector.

Bibliography

A. *The History of Printing in America* (Worcester, Mass., 1810); "The Diary of Isaiah Thomas 1805–1828," *Transactions of the American Antiquarian Society*, 1909.

B. *DAB* 9, 435–436; *NCAB* 6, 264; Cannon, 50–56; Charles L. Nichols, *Isaiah Thomas: Printer, Writer, and Collector* (New York, 1912); Clifford Shipton, *Isaiah Thomas: Printer, Patriot, and Philanthropist 1749–1831* (Rochester, N.Y., 1948); Ray Nash, *The Isaiah Thomas Donation* (Hanover, N.H., 1949).

TICKNOR, George (b. August 1, 1791, Boston, Mass.; d. January 26, 1871, Boston, Mass.). *Education:* A.B., Dartmouth College, 1807. *Collection Disposition:* Boston Public Library; Harvard University.

Ticknor's family background and early training destined him for a life of scholarship. His father and mother were both teachers, and they provided their son with a classical education at home. The proof of the effectiveness of this training came when Ticknor applied to Dartmouth and was admitted at the age of fourteen. After completing two years at Dartmouth and some study in the law, Ticknor decided to pursue a European education. From 1815 to 1819 he studied and traveled extensively in Germany, Spain, and England. During the last two years of his stay in Europe he spent much of his time learning Spanish and building a library of Spanish literature. He needed the training because he had been asked to assume a professorship of French and Spanish languages at Harvard. Fortunately Ticknor had the advice of specialists—Don José Antonio Condé, to teach him the history of the literature, and Obadiah Rich, consul to Spain, to get him books.

After a fifteen-year career at Harvard, Ticknor decided to abandon teaching and follow his writing interests on a full-time basis. The object of his research was nothing less than a comprehensive history of Spanish literature. Having ample financial resources, Ticknor was able to build a library of primary and secondary sources. Again help was forthcoming from European literary scholars and bookdealers. He was particularly fortunate to be able to enlist the help of Don Pascual de Gayangos, a translator who was well versed in the intricacies of Spanish manuscript and print materials. Gayangos not only provided suggestions on difficult bibliographical problems but also bought books for Ticknor in the European markets. Ticknor also gave Obadiah Rich carte blanche to buy manuscripts and books. After his monumental history was published to universal acclaim in 1849, Ticknor found himself an international literary figure.

Two years after the publication of the history, Ticknor became involved in the movement to establish a public library in Boston. His scholarly reputation and knowledge of the book trade made him an ideal proponent for library service. In 1856 he again traveled to Europe in quest of books, this time for the benefit of the public library. Four years later he gave the library several important collections from his own holdings: 143 volumes of Molière and 160 volumes of Provençal literature. Finally, Ticknor gave his great collection of Spanish and Portuguese materials, which had served as the foundation for his own writing, to the Boston Public Library in 1871. Ticknor's will also provided a trust fund to keep the collection current. The Ticknor library was not an accumulation of designated rarities or fine bindings, but rather the working collection of a diligent scholar. As such it stands as one of the great repositories of Spanish literature and history in the United States.

Bibliography

A. *Life, Letters, and Journals* (Boston, 1876); *Catalogue of the Spanish Library and of the Portuguese Books Bequeathed by George Ticknor to the Boston Public Library* (Boston, 1879).

B. *DAB* 9, 525–528; *NCAB* 6, 477, Cannon, 57–63; Walter Whitehill, *Boston Public Library: A Centennial History* (Cambridge, Mass., 1956), 49–50, 62–64; "The Ticknor Library," *BBPL*, October-December 1921, 301–306.

TILDEN, Samuel (b. February 9, 1814, New Lebanon, N.Y.; d. August 4, 1886, Yonkers, N.Y.). *Collection Disposition:* New York Public Library.

Shortly after his admission to the bar in 1841, Tilden was appointed to the Corporation Council of New York City, a post that launched his successful political career. In 1876 he was nominated as a candidate for President of the United States but was defeated in a controversial vote count. Throughout his life, Tilden gathered books, journals, and newspapers in the areas of politics and finance. As New York Public Library Director Harry M. Lydenberg pointed out, this was not a bibliophile's library but a politician's working collection. In addition to his law books, Tilden had 15,000 to 20,000 books and pamphlets dealing with English banking, natural history, the theater, and currency reform.

He also had long runs of nineteenth-century biographies of famous actors and actresses. As a hobby he practiced the popular art of extra-illustration and embellished texts with the addition of prints, portraits, and letters. In the case of Sir Walter Scott's *Waverley Novels*, for example, he created an elaborate thirty-five-volume set from an original twelve-volume edition. On his death the library materials were turned over to the Tilden Trust, an organization formed to make the materials available to the people of the city of New York. After five years of legal complications, Tilden's intent was realized and the city received the library along with a $2.5 million endowment. This bequest was linked with the Lenox and Astor libraries and eventually formed the basis of the present New York Public Library system. Although Tilden is remembered more as a politician than as a collector, his large personal library was significant.

Bibliography

B. *DAB* 7, 537–541; *NCAB* 3, 53; John Bigelow, *The Life of Samuel J. Tilden* (New York, 1895); Phyllis Dain, *The New York Public Library* (New York, 1972), 36–77; Harry M. Lydenberg, *History of the New York Public Library* (New York, 1923), 301–348; "The Library of Samuel J. Tilden," *BNYPL*, January 1899, 4–8.

TINKER, Edward Larocque (b. September 12, 1881, New York, N.Y.; d. July 6, 1968, East Setauket, Long Island, N.Y.). *Education:* A.B., LL.B., Columbia University, 1902, 1905; Ph.D., University of Paris, 1933. *Collection Disposition:* American Antiquarian Society; University of Texas.

Trained as a lawyer, Tinker gained prominence as an expert on Louisiana history and the cowboy. On both these topics he collected books, wrote scholarly articles, and delivered lectures and seminars. Beginning in 1924 with the publication of *Lafcadio Hearn's American Days*, he produced a series of well-received monographs on New Orleans literary and historical backgrounds. His *Bibliography of French Newspapers and Periodicals*, published by the American Antiquarian Society in 1932, demonstrated his ability to do meticulous research, while his column "New Editions, Fine and Otherwise," which ran in the *New York Times Book Review* from 1937 to 1942, established his reputation as a knowledgeable bookman. During the 1940s he gave the American Antiquarian Society his collection of French-language newspapers and early Louisiana imprints. By that time he had become more interested in the American cowboy, the *gaucho* of Argentina, and the *vaquero* of Mexico. Tinker believed that these horsemen had a common heritage that made them particularly attractive as folk heroes. He studied their songs and stories and collected their artifacts—saddles, bridles, spurs, and ropes. In 1953 he published *The Horsemen of the Americas and the Literatures They Inspired*, a major historical study. Subsequently he gave his library—some 3,000 books—and his artifacts to the University of Texas. The Tinker Foundation, which he endowed, has continued to supply the university with funds for the purchase of important archival materials.

Bibliography

B. *PAAS*, October 1968, 232–236.

TINKER, Chauncey Brewster (b. October 22, 1876, Auburn, Maine; d. March 16, 1963, New Haven, Conn.). *Education:* A.B., A.M., Ph.D., Yale University, 1899, 1900, 1902. *Collection Disposition:* Yale University.

Tinker's enthusiasm for learning, collecting, and teaching came together to produce the model scholar-bibliophile. His career as a student at Yale focused on English literature and led naturally into teaching. After teaching one year at Bryn Mawr, Tinker returned to Yale, where he served as Professor of English literature for more than forty years. His specialties were the eighteenth and nineteenth centuries, with emphasis on such figures as Johnson, Arnold, Tennyson, Browning, Trollope, and their associates. Tinker's reputation was founded in the 1920s on his studies of James Boswell, and those studies in turn were founded on manuscript and book materials from the scholar's personal collection. He had based his career on books, he told Yale alumni in 1924, because books were the essential mark of scholarship and the basis of a great university. He urged his listeners to contribute their own collections to the library and to provide whatever financial aid they could. The talk hit the mark and under the energetic direction of Frank Altschul* led to the founding of the Yale Library Associates.

In 1930 Tinker was appointed Keeper of Rare Books in the new Sterling Library, a post that gave him an opportunity to combine his enthusiastic belief in learning with his knowledge of the importance of rare and primary materials. Never a wealthy man, he kept in friendly contact with bookdealers A. S. W. Rosenbach and Gabriel Wells and added nineteenth-century items as he could afford them. In 1941 he made a number of significant purchases of Blake and Johnson material at the sale of the A. Edward Newton* library. His interests were so well known that rare books frequently came to him as gifts from such collector friends as Robert B. Adam* and Harvey Cushing*, and even occasionally from Rosenbach himself. The record of his many happy bibliographic associations can be read in the provenance notes included in the printed catalog of his library. As James Babb pointed out in the preface to that volume, although Tinker never allowed Yale to publicize his gifts they provided a magnificent archive on English literary achievement. Tinker was much more than an ambitious and knowledgeable private collector. He was an author, a bibliographer, an inspiration as a teacher to generations of Yale students, and an energetic spokesman for the importance of books and learning.

Bibliography

A. "The Asperities of Book Collecting," *Yale Review*, 1919, 207–209; "Reflections of a Curator," *YLG*, July 1948, 8–18; *The University Library: An Address on Alumni University Day* (New Haven, 1924). "The Caliph of Books: A. E. N.," *Atlantic Monthly*, December 1943, 102–106; *The Tinker Library* (New Haven, 1959).
B. James Babb, "Preface," in *The Tinker Library* (New Haven, 1959), vii-viiii; A. T.

Hazen and E. L. MacAdam, "First Editions of Samuel Johnson: An Important Exhibition and a Discovery," *YLG*, January 1936, 45–51; Herman W. Liebert, "Chauncey Brewster Tinker 1876–1963," *Yale Alumni Magazine*, May 1963, 18–20; Wilmarth S. Lewis, "Chauncey Brewster Tinker," *YLG*, July 1963, 1–2.

TONER, Joseph M. (b. April 30, 1825, Pittsburgh, Pa.; d. July 30, 1896, Cresson, Pa.). *Education:* M.D., Vermont College of Medicine, 1850; M.D., Jefferson Medical College of Philadelphia, 1853. *Collection Disposition:* Library of Congress.

By the time he was thirty-five, Toner had established himself as one of the leading physicians in Washington, D.C. He took a strong interest in public health and spent a great deal of time advocating the benefits of pure water and inoculation. His study of public health led him to the history of medicine, particularly to the backgrounds of prominent eighteenth-century American physicians. He started a clipping file, and when the task became too burdensome he employed an assistant to copy biographical information from the *Pennsylvania Gazette* and other colonial papers. In the 1850s and 1860s he was a familiar figure scouring Washington bookshops, buying pamphlets and journals by the pound in the hope of securing a few useful historical items. By 1870 his library had grown to 6,000 titles and was increasing at the rate of 800 to 1,000 volumes a year. The clipping files, which once included only deceased physicians, came to hold information on famous men and women from every age, nation, and profession. Questions began to come to Toner from small-town practitioners and from the office of the United States surgeon general. His personal archive had become a national resource.

In addition to collecting, Toner encouraged the American Medical Association and the American Public Health Association to start professional libraries. As president of both organizations, he was in a position to see that his suggestions were followed. By 1880 Toner started to think about the disposition of his library. He offered it to a number of cities if they would provide a fireproof building. Only Philadelphia responded. As an alternative, Toner's friend Ainsworth Spofford, the Librarian of Congress, suggested the advantages of the national library. Toner agreed, and in 1882 he presented his entire collection—28,000 books, 18,000 pamphlets, and more than 1 million clippings—to the Library of Congress. In addition to his extensive holdings on medical history, Toner had strong peripheral collections on George Washington, the District of Columbia, and western exploration and settlement. Toner was an avid and generous bibliophile.

Bibliography

B. *DAB* 9, 586–587; *NCAB* 7, 539; *SCLC*,356–357; *ARLC*, 1897, 37–38; Whitfield Bell, "Joseph M. Toner, 1825–1896, as a Medical Historian," *Bulletin of the History of Medicine*, January-February 1973, 1–24; Morris Fishbein, *History of the American Medical Association 1847–1947* (Philadelphia, 1947), 623–624.

TRENT, William P. (b. November 10, 1862, Richmond, Va.; d. December 6, 1939, Hopewell Junction, N.Y.). *Education:* B.Litt., A.M., University of Virginia, 1883, 1884. *Collection Disposition:* Boston Public Library.

After reading the law for a short time, Trent decided to devote himself to literary studies. He served as the first editor of the *Sewanee Review* and made extensive contributions to the *Cambridge History of American Literature*. Of his many interests, seventeenth-century English novelist and essayist Daniel Defoe became a specialty. For over twenty years Trent made it his task to collect everything by and about Defoe. This search involved serious bibliographical problems because Defoe had issued an avalanche of pamphlets, broadsides, and editorials, many under assumed names. It was part of Trent's task to trace the true authorship of hundreds of ephemeral pieces. Once this was done he had the research materials for a definitive study of Defoe's career. Poor health, however, forced him to turn the task over to one of his students. After Trent's death the remarkable Defoe library was put up for sale. The Boston Public Library made the best offer and obtained one of the finest Defoe research collections in the country.

Bibliography

A. *A Catalogue of the Defoe Collection in the Boston Public Library* (Boston, 1966).

B. *DAB*, Supp. 2, 666–667; Zoltán Haraszti, "A Great Defoe Library," *BBPL*, January 1931, 1–14.

U

ULIZIO, B. George (b. February 2, 1889, New Haven, Conn.; d. 1969, Haddonfield, N.J.). *Collection Disposition:* American Art—Anderson, January 28, 1931, October 30, 1935; Kent State University.

After attending parochial schools in New Haven, Ulizio took a job as a runner in the New York Stock Exchange. Following his natural bent toward business, he became a successful manager and worked in a variety of executive positions.

Although the origins of Ulizio's collecting interests are unknown, he was almost certainly influenced by a trio of his Philadelphia bibliophilic friends: A. Edward Newton*, John Eckel, and Morris L. Parrish*. Ulizio's acquisitions of the Victorians matched those of Parrish almost author for author. He bought chiefly from the Philadelphia firms of Charles Sessler, and A. S. W. Rosenbach* and from the Mannados Book Shop, Arthur Swann, and James Drake in New York. Through them he secured first editions of Kipling, Meredith, Reade, Stevenson, and Dickens. His holdings of the latter two authors were particularly distinguished. From the George Barr McCutcheon* sale of 1925 he obtained an immaculate copy of Stevenson's first book, *The Pentland Rising*, along with a remarkable copy of Dickens' *Pickwick Papers* in parts. This set was in original wrappers and enshrined in the Eckel bibliography as one of the fourteen best copies. Sadly, financial pressures made it necessary for Ulizio to sell his library just as it was beginning to achieve real strength. In the 1931 catalog Eckel pointed out the similarities between the Ulizio library and that sold two years earlier by Jerome Kern*. The "Pickwick" was the chief topic of conversation among bookmen for weeks before the sale. How high would it go? Few guessed it would reach $13,000—more than double what Ulizio paid six years earlier. Other Victorian first editions brought equally high prices as the avid New York dealers Jerome Brooks, James Drake, and Barnet Beyer outdid themselves.

As soon as the sale was over, Ulizio began to gather a second library, but after a few years financial pressures made it impossible for him to keep those books, and again he put them up for auction. Undaunted by the loss of two fine libraries, Ulizio began a third collection. In a shrewd negotiation he traded a number of his early children's books to the Library of Congress for fifty-five rare copyright deposit volumes. Among the titles secured in this exchange were the first editions of Harte's *The Luck of Roaring Camp*, Bellamy's *Looking Backward*, and Whitman's *Two Rivulets*.

In another phase of his collecting Ulizio obtained presentation copies from living authors. He wrote to Sandburg, Dreiser, and others, obtaining letters, autographs, and inscribed first editions. In his earliest collecting efforts Ulizio had concentrated on English writers, but in later years he turned more to Americans, particularly those listed in Merle Johnson's *High Spots in American Literature* and Jacob Blanck's *Bibliography of American Literature*. In the 1950s and 1960s the American side of his library grew rapidly, with acquisitions ranging from Cooper's frontier tales to Hemingway's realistic novels. His energetic collecting activities brought him to the attention of other collectors, among them Kent State University's Matthew Bruccoli and C. E. Frazier Clark Jr. Shortly before his death Ulizio sold his library to Kent State. Ulizio was a determined collector whose interests in books endured for over fifty years.

Bibliography

A. *The George B. Ulizio Collection of English and American Literature: An Exhibition on the Occasion of the Dedication of the Kent State University Library* (Kent, Ohio, 1971).

B. P. DuBois, "The Ulizio Collection: A Catalogue of Deposit Copies," *The Serif*, September 1970, 35–51; Correspondence with Dean Keller, Special Collections Librarian, Kent State University, July 1982.

UPDIKE, Daniel Berkeley (b. February 24, 1860, Providence, R.I.; d. December 29, 1941, Boston, Mass.). *Collection Disposition:* Providence Public Library; Henry E. Huntington Library; Boston Athenaeum; Grolier Club.

According to his biographers, Updike was the most distinguished American printer during the first half of the twentieth century. He started working at the Houghton Mifflin publishing company in Boston in 1880 and thirteen years later decided to go into business for himself. Updike's accomplishments at the Merrymount Press are well known to anyone who has followed the history of American printing. From the execution of single-sheet advertising announcements to the production of full-scale books, Updike's goal was always the same— unequaled excellence. Merrymount books have the quality of correctness and unity that sets them apart from ordinary contemporary printing.

In order to assist with questions that arose in his daily work and to supply background for his own writing, Updike built a large personal library. He owned type handbooks, works on papermaking, treatises on lettering, printer's manuals, and specimen sheets dating back to the sixteenth century. This collection, as

Updike once explained to Paul Standard, was a working library. After reserving the books he needed for regular consultation, Updike deposited the rest of his collection in the Providence Public Library. In 1911 he had helped the library buy a collection of more than 1,000 volumes on printing from the St. Bride Foundation in London. The books arrived but languished in storage. In 1937, under pressure from Yale's printing chief Carl Rollins, the "Updike Collection of Books on Printing" was dedicated, with new quarters for display and storage. It was the kind of collection, Updike claimed in his opening-day remarks, that would help a conscientious printer improve his work and make a lazy printer uncomfortable. On his death the remainder of his personal library and all his notes for many publications went to the Providence Library.

Bibliography

B. *DAB* 10, 120–121; *Grolier 75*, 102–104; Zoltán Haraszti, "Daniel Berkeley Updike," *BBPL*, May 1935, 157–173; Clarence Sherman, "The Updike Collection of Books on Printing," *Print*, Spring 1942, 55–56; Paul Standard, "A Printer's Library," *The Dolphin*, Fall 1940, 41–47; George Parker Winship, *Daniel Berkeley Updike and the Merrymount Press* (Rochester, 1947); Lawrence C. Wroth, "Daniel Berkeley Updike," *Print*, Spring 1942, 52–54.

V

VAN DUZER, Henry Sayre (b. February 26, 1853, New York, N.Y.; d. March 1, 1928, New York, N.Y.). *Education:* A.B., Harvard University, 1875; LL.B., Columbia University, 1877. *Collection Disposition:* Anderson, February 17, 1919, February 6, 1922.

Van Duzer was a New York lawyer who devoted himself to collecting the nineteenth-century English novelist William Makepeace Thackeray. Although Van Duzer's early interests had included Lamb and Goldsmith, he soon limited his quest to Thackeray alone. His collection consisted of books, articles, letters, manuscripts, portraits and sketches by the author, and critical materials by others. Among the many rare printed items in the collection were a copy of the illustrated edition of *The Exquisites*, an unproduced farce, and the pseudonymous *Flore et Zephyr*, Thackeray's first appearance in print. Many of the finest items in the library had come to Van Duzer from the William Lambert* sale in 1914. As the collection grew, Van Duzer worked on a definitive bibliography. When this was published in 1919 it provided a carefully organized outline of publication details for Thackeray's major novels.

When the Van Duzer Thackeray collection was placed up for sale in 1922, it attracted some of the leading figures of the book world—Henry E. Huntington*, Jerome Kern*, William Randolph Hearst*, A. S. W. Rosenbach*, and John Pierpont Morgan Jr.'s* librarian, the flamboyant Belle da Costa Greene. All were on hand to see that their interests were well served. Hearst took many of the drawings and first editions, while Huntington had to be satisfied with a few oddments and a marble bust copied after the original in Westminster Abbey. The Van Duzer sale is remembered as a high water mark for Thackeray enthusiasts.

Bibliography

A. *A Thackeray Library* (New York, 1919).
B. Cannon, 224–235; *NYT*, January 22, 1922, 10.

VICKERY, Willis (b. November 26, 1859, Bellevue, Ohio; d. September 26, 1932, Cleveland, Ohio). *Education:* LL.B., Boston University, 1889. *Collection Disposition:* American Art—Anderson, March 1, 1933.

Vickery was a Cleveland judge who collected English literature. His library included some 20,000 items, with over a quarter of that total given over to Shakespeare studies. In 1911 he supported the publication of a lavish limited edition of *The Tempest* and in later years contributed a number of rarities to the New York Public Library's tercentenary exhibition of Shakespeare's death. He owned the four folios, an edition of Blake's *Songs of Innocence and Experience* handcolored by Blake, Kelmscott Press books, and first editions of the works of Keats, Shelley, Spenser, and Wilde. The Rowfant Club of Cleveland, where he was an active member, published his talks on books and collecting. His library was sold at auction in New York six months after his death.

Bibliography

A. *A Search for a First Folio* (Cleveland, 1905); *Three Excessively Rare and Scarce Books* (Cleveland, 1927).

B. *NCAB* A, 209.

VON FABER DU FAUR, Curt (b. July 5, 1890, Stuttgart, Germany; d. January 10, 1965, New Haven, Ct.). *Education*: Ph.D., University Giesen, 1921. *Collection Disposition:* Yale University.

According to the introduction to his *German Baroque Literature*, Von Faber began to collect at the age of twenty-two. It was an unsystematic beginning, as he recalled later, but one that became more structured over the years. By the time he was thirty he had decided to form a library representing the Baroque period in German literature from its beginnings around 1575 down to its last vestiges in 1740. The emphasis in the collection was on the seventeenth century and featured complete holdings of such writers as Opitz, Harsdörfer, Moscherosch, Grimmelshausen, and von Logau. As Von Faber pointed out, books and pamphlets from the seventeenth century were so rare that the term "first edition" had relatively little meaning. The later Romantic period was also well covered in his library, with complete runs of poetry, fiction, humor, philosophy, and drama. Printed materials from the Romantic period were much easier to find. In 1944 Von Faber sold his library, some 7,500 items, to Yale, where it has served as a complement to the magnificent Goethe collection developed by William A. Speck*. In recognition of his various contributions to Yale, Von Faber was appointed assistant curator of German literature from 1944 to 1954 and selected curator in 1955.

Bibliography

A. *German Baroque Literature* (New Haven, 1958); "The Faber du Faur Library," *YLG*, July 1945, 1–6; "The Collection of German Baroque Literature in the Yale Library," *YLG*, July 1955, 1–9; "The German Literature Collection," *YLG*, April 1964, 138–150; "The Faber du Faur Collection," *Philobiblon*, March 1958.

W

WANGENHEIM, Julius (b. April 21, 1866, San Francisco, Calif.; d. March 10, 1942, San Diego, Calif.). *Collection Disposition:* San Diego Public Library; University of California at Berkeley; Scripps College.

In 1895 Wangenheim moved from San Francisco to San Diego to help his father-in-law manage a prosperous grocery business. Later he turned to finance and was an important figure in San Diego banking and real estate. His civic interests included the Park Commission, the Water and Harbor Commission, the Fine Arts Society, and the public library. Always an avid reader, he was one of the strongest proponents of open stacks for the city library system. His personal library focused on the history of books and printing and included such landmarks as an Egyptian papyrus, a Mongolian woodblock, several medieval manuscript leaves, a Kelmscott Chaucer, an Ashendene Dante, and a Doves Bible. He owned mother-of-pearl and tortoise-shell bindings and signed works by Zaehnsdorf, Sangorski, and Sutcliffe. His literary collection ran to nineteenth-century American and English novelists and poets. He bequeathed a number of works on the history of science to the University of California at Berkeley, but the bulk of the collection went to the San Diego Public Library. There a separate room, furnished as a private library, is maintained in honor of his generosity and love of books.

Bibliography

A. "Julius Wangenheim: An Autobiography," *QCHS*, June 1956, 119–144; September 1956, 253–274; December 1956, 345–366; March 1957, 63–78; June 1957, 149–164.

B. Correspondence with Eileen Boyle, Librarian of the Wangenheim Room, San Diego Public Library, 1981; Clara E. Breed, *Turning the Pages, San Diego Public Library History 1882–1982* (San Diego, 1983), 169–171.

WAGNER, Henry R. (b. September 27, 1862, Philadelphia, Pa.; d. March 28, 1957, San Marino, Calif.). *Education:* A.B., LL.B., Yale University, 1884, 1886. *Collection Disposition:* Yale University; Henry E. Huntington Library; Pomona College; Bancroft Library; California Historical Society; American Art, March 17, 1922; direct sales to bookdealers Lathrop Harper in New York and Glen Dawson in Los Angeles.

Although he was trained in the law, Wagner never practiced for any length of time. He became interested in mining and taught himself both the technical and management aspects of that business. In 1898 he went to London as an ore buyer for the Guggenheim firm. His assignments for the next thirty years took him to South America, Spain, and Mexico—in fact, anywhere his astute management expertise was needed. At the age of sixty he retired, moved to California, and devoted the next thirty-five years to collecting and writing. In Wagner's case, collecting was a dominant force. In London in 1903, on his first trip abroad, he discovered the endless fascination of bookshops and auction rooms. He obtained technical books on mining, but more interesting to Wagner were the historical studies on the influence of silver and gold on world trade. He formed a sizable collection of sixteenth- and seventeenth-century tracts and pamphlets on the influence of precious metals on the Irish economy. When his collection reached 10,000 items he made a brief checklist and presented the entire lot to Yale. This system of gathering and dispersing books was to become his hallmark. Once he had built a collection and written it up, he moved on to something else. This was partially a matter of space and money but more directly an indication of Wagner's restless intellectual curiosity.

After the London assignment, Wagner was sent to Mexico, where he started a new collection—Mexican history. He was particularly interested in Mexico's nineteenth-century revolution and subsequent relations with the American border states. The Texas portion of the library grew rapidly and was distinguished by a number of important manuscripts. Choice among these were the papers of French botanist Jean Berlandier, who had traveled in Mexico in 1828 and 1829 as a member of the Mexican Boundary Commission. Not wishing to limit himself to the Southwest, Wagner began to acquire journals, diaries, and maps that reflected the opening of the Midwest and the Far West. Many of these materials came from the two most respected dealers in western Americana, Edward Eberstadt and Lathrop Harper. When in 1915 sacrifices because of space problems were called for, Wagner sold the Mexican and South American library to Yale, and followed four years later with the Texas and Midwest items. This shelf-cleaning was concurrent with the publication of Wagner's first great bibliography, *The Plains and the Rockies* (1919). Because of numerous errors, the first issue was withdrawn; a final version was delayed until 1921. Eight years after the bibliography came out, Wagner sold the backbone of the collection to Henry E. Huntington* for his library at San Marino. With part of the money received from Huntington, Wagner began to buy sixteenth-century Mexican imprints and materials on the Spanish Southwest. He quickly abandoned the idea of gathering the Mexican documents, however, when a Maggs catalog forced prices to astronomical heights.

Wagner was never one to be bamboozled by artificial rarities or by manufactured trends in collecting. He continued to buy southwestern materials, however, and in 1924 published another master work, *The Spanish Southwest 1542–1794*. Again, after the bibliography was printed, Wagner sold the books, this time to Lathrop Harper. Other historical collections and publications followed—first *Spanish Voyages to the Northwest Coast of America in the Sixteenth Century*, then *Cartography of the Northwest Coast of America to the Year 1800*. All Wagner's cartography books and maps went to Pomona College, while the narratives of De Las Casas and Cortez found a hospitable home in the Bancroft Library at Berkeley. Other collections included Grabhorn Press books and an old and cherished library on metallurgy.

Throughout his life, Wagner devoted considerable time to the California Historical Society, the Zamorano Club of Los Angeles, the Southwestern Museum, and the Historical Society of Southern California. In all these associations he held offices, edited publications, and acted as an intellectual spur. Thomas Streeter*, eminent Texas collector, identified Wagner as a pioneer who avoided the pitfalls of fashion and provided scholars with a variety of reliable guides. Librarians and scholars are in his debt.

Bibliography

A. *Bullion to Books* (Los Angeles, 1942); *Collecting, Especially Books* (Los Angeles, 1941); *Sixty Years of Book Collecting* (San Francisco, 1952).

B. *NCAB* 45, 522; *Grolier 75*, 118–120; Cannon, 267–270; Ruth F. Axe, "Henry R. Wagner: An Intimate Profile," *AB Bookman's Yearbook*, 1979; Edwin H. Carpenter, *Henry R. and Blanche C. Wagner* (Santa Ana, Calif., 1964); Charles Camp, "Our Founder, Henry R. Wagner, Is Dead," *QCHS*, March 1957, 79–82; Lawrence Clark Powell, *Viva Wagner* (Los Angeles, 1964); Lawrence Clark Powell, "Henry R. Wagner," *Hoja Volante*, May 1952; Thomas Streeter, "Henry R. Wagner and the Yale Library," *YLG*, October 1957, 71–76; Thomas Streeter, "Henry R. Wagner: Collector, Bibliographer, Cartographer, Historian," *QCHS*, June 1957, 165–175.

WAGSTAFF, David (b. October 1, 1882, Babylon, N.Y.; d. June 6, 1951, Tuxedo Park, N.Y.). *Education:* A.B., Harvard University, 1905. *Collection Disposition:* Yale University; University of Virginia.

As a collector of sporting books and manuscripts during the 1930s and 1940s, Wagstaff had few peers. His interests included hunting, fishing, horse-breeding, falconry, and boating. He enjoyed the historical perspective and acquired a number of classical and medieval manuscripts that touched on sporting activities. Among his prize possessions were a fifteenth-century manuscript on the care of horses and one on the sport of falconry. Another unique item in the Wagstaff library was a thirty-three-volume diary of Colonel Peter Hawker, an ardent nineteenth-century English sportsman. While hardly a scholarly work, Hawker's diary was delightful social history, as it included a vivid record of the hunting and fishing customs of the day. In addition to the manuscript material, Wagstaff collected an assortment of books and journals treating every topic of sporting interest from big-game hunting to mountain-climbing. Between 1940 and 1950 the *Yale Library Gazette* recorded a steady flow of materials from Wagstaff's shelves to New Haven. In 1945 Yale library officers appointed him Curator of Sporting Books, an appropriate honor for a discriminating collector. After his death, with the exception of a few rarities that went to the University of Virginia, Yale received the remainder of the library.

Bibliography

B. *NCAB* 46, 145; Edmund Silk, "The Wagstaff Collection of Classical and Medieval Manuscripts," *YLG*, July 1944, 1–9; Marjorie Wynne, "The Wagstaff Sporting Books and Manuscripts," *YLG*, July 1945, 6–14; Marjorie Wynne, "The Boke of St. Albans," *YLG*, July 1951, 33–36.

WAKEMAN, Stephen H. (b. 1859, New York, N.Y.; d. January 4, 1924, New York, N.Y.). *Collection Disposition:* American Art, April 28, May 8, 1924.

After working in the family produce business for twenty years, Wakeman retired to devote himself to book and manuscript collecting. He was one of the first to focus serious attention on American literature. From the beginning he decided to limit his collecting endeavors to nine prominent authors: Bryant, Emerson, Hawthorne, Holmes, Longfellow, Powell, Poe, Thoreau, and Whittier. With these authors Wakeman attempted to be complete not only for first editions but also for pamphlets, journal appearances, broadsides, and translations. In addition to printed sources, he made a specialty of manuscripts, letters, presentation copies, and association items—the kind of "sentimental library" that was dear to the heart of a contemporary, collector Harry B. Smith*.

Although Wakeman bought from several agents, his chief source was Boston dealer P. K. Foley. In 1897 Foley issued the first well-organized bibliography to cover American literature. This list, *American Authors 1795–1895*, supplied the bibliographic information Wakeman needed. He is remembered as the collector who once owned the only surviving parts of the manuscript of Hawthorne's *Scarlet Letter*, complete manuscripts of his *Blithdale Romance* and *Dr. Grimshawe's Secret*, the surviving portion of Holmes' *Autocrat of the Breakfast Table*, Longfellow's manuscript for "The Children's Hour," and thirty-nine volumes of Thoreau's *Journal*. In 1909 bookdealer George Hellman asked Wakeman to consider selling his manuscript library to John Pierpont Morgan*. In the Morgan collection, Hellman pointed out, the manuscripts would be well administered and would complement print materials and other manuscripts already on hand. After lengthy negotiations Wakeman and Morgan settled on an agreement whereby 260 manuscripts changed hands for $165,000. Wakeman continued to collect letters and manuscripts until his death, but not on his earlier scale. When the collection was brought to auction in 1924, the print materials attracted considerable interest. The Poe items in particular brought good returns. A presentation copy of *The Raven* reached $4,200, and Poe's own copy of *Tales of the Grotesque and Arabesque*, with revisions in his hand, went for $3,400—both to A. S. W. Rosenbach*. The Wakeman sale had the effect of confirming American literature as a legitimate collecting area.

Bibliography

B. *Grolier 75*, 95–98; Cannon, 179–180; George Hellman, *Lanes of Memory* (New York, 1927), 42–47; "J. P. Morgan Buys Rare Manuscripts," *NYT*, October 27, 1909, 1.

WALLACE, Walter T. (b. 1866; d. 1922). *Collection Disposition:* American Art, March 22, 1920.

In the early years of the twentieth century, Wallace formed one of New York's finest libraries. According to historian Carl Cannon, it was an "old fashioned library" in the sense that it included a wide range of literary first editions and association copies from all periods of English and American literature. Wallace obtained most of his books between 1900 and 1910, when a number of important private libraries were dispersed in New York auctions. He acquired an extensive Dickens collection, including a famous "Pickwick" in parts, at the Edwin Lapham* sale, a Caxton printing, some distinguished Coleridge items, and several Byron pamphlets from the Henry Poor* sale. In 1909 he bought many choice American literary items from the Jacob C. Chamberlain* and the Frank Maier* sales. While most collectors forwarded their bids through established bookdealers, Wallace chose to avoid the middleman and bid for himself. Bookdealers were unwilling to let his independence go without challenge, so in retaliation they often pushed the bids higher than usual when Wallace was known to be interested. In spite of such obstacles, Wallace obtained some extraordinary items.

Although any attempt to list the Wallace high points would be doomed to failure, a few titles stand out. He owned Lord Amherst's copy of the Coverdale translation of the Bible, the four Shakespeare folios, a long set of Lamb and Byron first editions, and Caxton's printing of Higden's *Polychronicon*. In many cases Wallace secured letters and manuscripts as embellishments for the printed texts. One remarkable item was a letter from Thackeray to Elizabeth Barrett Browning in which he turned down a poem she submitted for the *Cornhill Magazine*.

When the Wallace books came on the market in 1920, bookdealers had their revenge. According to A. Edward Newton* writing to Amy Lowell*, "bloody work was done." Poe rarities went for under $500, while the Thackeray letter to Mrs. Browning achieved only $1,710. The *New York Post* described the sale as a "disaster without parallel." The chief benefactors were, of course, dealers like James Drake, Gabriel Wells, and A. S. W. Rosenbach*, who were able to get Wallace's fine books at bargain-basement prices.

Bibliography

B. Cannon, 151–152, Goodspeed, 199–200; Luria Maxwell, "Miss Lowell and Mr. Newton: The Record of a Literary Friendship," *HLB*, January 1981, 5–34; "The Amazing Wallace Sale," *New York Evening Post*, April 3, 1920, sec. 3, 10; "The Wallace Sale," *NYT*, March 23, 1920, 6; March 24, 1920, 12; March 25, 1920, 11; March 26, 1920, 7; "The Walter Thomas Wallace Library of Rarities," in American Art Association, *Catalogue* (New York, 1920).

WALLCUT, Thomas (b. August 16, 1758, Boston, Mass.; d. June 5, 1840, Boston, Mass.). *Collection Disposition:* American Antiquarian Society; Bowdoin College; Massachusetts Historical Society.

Although he lacked the traditional advantages of a higher education or extensive financial means, Wallcut developed an impressive personal library. For thirty-eight years he worked as a scribe in the Massachusetts State House, but his avocation was history. He was one of the founding members of the Massachusetts Historical Society and contributed frequently to *American Apollo*, the Society's journal. As part of his job as secretary for the Society, Wallcut bought appropriate material for the library from book sales and auctions. In this way, and through exposure to political events at the State House, he developed an interest in colonial history. Many of the events of the time were recorded in tracts and pamphlets, an ephemeral record that Wallcut collected in depth. He was a steady customer in Boston secondhand-book shops and auction rooms. Some of his important religious tracts came from the 1790 Mather Byles sale. Since Byles was the grandson of Increase Mather, many of these items had a distinguished provenance.

From the time he attended a charity school in Hanover, New Hampshire, Wallcut had maintained a close friendship with Eleazar Wheelock and his son-in-law William Allen, the founders of Dartmouth College. In 1817 Wallcut gave 500 books on religion and language to the new college. Two years later he transferred the gift to Bowdoin College when Allen moved to the presidency of that institution. He gave the bulk of his library, some 10,000 pamphlets and tracts, to the American Antiquarian Society in 1834. In a last act of benefaction, Wallcut gave the Massachusetts Historical Society a small collection of early American and continental religious studies. Wallcut was an avid collector, devoted to learning and generous in his contributions to scholarly institutions.

Bibliography

B. Earl Taylor, "Thomas Wallcut 1758–1840," *BC*, Summer 1983, 155–170; Robert Wallcut, "Memoir of Thomas Wallcut," *PMHS*, 1841, 193–208; Edwin Wolf II, "American Book Collectors to 1800," *Gazette of the Grolier Club*, 1971, 20–22.

WALTERS, Henry (b. September 26, 1848, Baltimore, Md.; d. November 30, 1931, New York, N.Y.). *Education:* B.A., M.A., Georgetown University, 1869, 1871; B.S., Harvard University, 1873. *Collection Disposition:* Walters Art Gallery; Parke-Bernet, April 23, 1941.

As a young man, Walters lived with his parents in Paris and developed a keen interest in all forms of art. Walters' father, William, was a devoted collector and friend of many well-known continental artists and art dealers. In order to document his holdings, the elder Walters commissioned a number of handsome catalogs describing his paintings and ceramics. After his father's death, Walters saw several of these catalogs through the press, an experience that heightened his own interest in collecting.

Beginning in 1894, Walters set out to collect on his own terms, with emphasis on illuminated manuscripts and incunabula. Over a period of thirty-five years, and with the help of the members of the international book trade, he built one of the most spectacular manuscript collections in the country. He specialized in European Books of Hours, Byzantine and Armenian illumination, fine bindings, and calligraphy. His Books of Hours made up a major portion of the exhibition "Illuminated Books of the Middle Ages and Renaissance" shown at the Baltimore Museum of Art in 1949. Shown at the same time were his eleventh-century "Four Gospels" from the Benedictine abbey at Reichenau, a twelfth-centuryNew Testament from the Canterbury school, and a psalter from the Benedictine monastery in Westphalia. Usually Walters bought his rarities book by book, but in 1902 he made an exception and bought 1,200 incunabula from Italian bookdealer Leo Olschki. In one stroke Walters placed his library among the very few that could boast substantial holdings of fifteenth-century printing. He acquired, among other prizes, the works of Fust and Schoeffer, Ratdolt, Zainer, Amerback, and Jenson. Walters never bought simply to acquire "collectors items," but rather concentrated on works he liked. As Lillian Randall has pointed out, his chief concern was to develop a library that would complement the art collections.

After Walters died in 1931, his widow inherited the bulk of the estate, most of which was turned over immediately, with a substantial endowment, to the Walters Art Gallery in Baltimore. Some of the fine bindings and manuscripts, however, remained in the possession of the family, a fact that many overlooked, until they appeared for sale in April 1941. It was a time of national emergency, and few collectors were willing to invest large amounts of money in rare books. Dealers like A. S. W. Rosenbach* and Gabriel Wells, did much of the buying because they knew a bargain when they saw one. The magnificent collections in Baltimore speak for themselves. Under the intelligent guidance of curators like Dorothy Miner, the legacy of William and Henry Walters has continued to stimulate investigation in countless areas of humanistic research.

Bibliography

A. *Incunabula Typographica: A Descriptive Catalogue of the Books in the Fifteenth Century in the Library of Henry Walters* (Baltimore, 1906); *Illuminated Books of the Middle Ages and Renaissance: An Exhibition Held at the Baltimore Museum of Art, January 27-March 18, 1949* (Baltimore, 1949).

B. *DAB* 10, 399–400; *NCAB* 37, 288; Cannon, 194–195; *Grolier 75*, 42–44; Dorothy Miner, "The Publishing Ventures of a Victorian Connoisseur: A Sidelight on William

T. Walters," *PBSA*, 3rd Q 1963, 271–311; Lillian Randall, "Henry, Son of William: The Walters Rare Book Collection," *Gazette of the Grolier Club*, 1977, 46–57; Lillian Randall, "Manuscripts in the Walters Art Gallery," *Manuscripts*, Fall 1980, 298–302. Correspondence with Lillian Randall, Librarian of Walters Art Gallery, June 1983.

WASON, Charles W. (b. April 20, 1854, Cleveland, Ohio; d. April 15, 1918, Cleveland, Ohio). *Education:* B.ME., Cornell University, 1876. *Collection Disposition:* Cornell University.

Applying his engineering education to city transportation, Wason followed a successful business career with various Cleveland rail lines. He became interested in China and its varied cultures in 1903 after he returned from an extended Far Eastern tour. As a result he began to collect books and journals on that country's history. With the help of Cleveland publisher Arthur H. Clark, he accumulated an impressive library of some 9,000 volumes on China. In addition to books, he secured maps, manuscripts, pamphlets, and 60,000 journal articles. He also had unique runs of over thirty English-language newspapers, starting with those issued during the period of the earliest British colonization.

In 1914 Wason drew up a trust agreement with Cornell by which the university would receive the library and a $50,000 endowment on his death. When the books went to Cornell in 1919, Yale scholar Kenneth Scott Latourette delivered the dedicatory address. He praised the gift for its depth and recommended it to those wishing to study China from a scholarly point of view. If expanded, he declared, it could become a mecca for sinologists. Cornell administrators augmented the original holdings, added professional staff, and set aside excellent physical quarters. As a direct result of the Wason gift, Cornell can boast one of the finest Far Eastern collections in the country.

Bibliography

A. *The Catalog of the Wason Collection on China and the Chinese*, compiled and edited by Paul Cheng (Washington, D.C., 1978).

B. *NCAB* 33, 280–281.

WELCH, d'Alte A. (b. April 9, 1907, New York, N.Y.; d. January 4, 1970, Cleveland, Ohio). *Education:* B.A., M.A., Ph.D., Johns Hopkins University, 1929, 1931, 1937. *Collection Disposition:* American Antiquarian Society; University of California at Los Angeles.

By profession Welch was a research biologist and taught at John Carroll University in Ohio. By avocation he was one of the country's leading collectors of English and American children's books. From the time he was a teenager, and a regular patron at the Forty-second Street New York Public Library, Welch had been fascinated by children's stories and nursery rhymes. On a trip to England in 1924, he visited the secondhand-book shops, acquired over 200 juveniles, and laid the basis for his collection. Shortly after his return to the United States, he met renowned author Wilbur Macey Stone* and had a chance to see Stone's splendid collection of miniature children's books, thumb Bibles, and John Newbery imprints. At about the same time, he discovered the tempting Boston bookshops of Charles Goodspeed and P. K. Foley.

In 1945 Welch met Clarence S. Brigham, director of the American Antiquarian Society, and with his encouragement decided to compile a bibliography of American children's books printed before 1821. The bibliography, as it appeared in the *Proceedings* of the Society over the years 1963–1967, was a meticulous enumeration of titles with ample identification of locations in both private and public collections. This work, which was revised and issued in separate form in 1972, stands as the definitive bibliography on early American children's books. Before his tragic death, Welch had bequeathed his American imprints to the American Antiquarian Society but had not determined the disposition of his English books. Because of Welch's long and amiable relationship with the University of California at Los Angeles, the family decided to sell them to that growing institution. For his outstanding personal library and his exemplary bibliography, Welch is remembered as one of the most important children's book collectors of the twentieth century.

Bibliography

A. *A Bibliography of American Children's Books Printed Prior to 1821* (Worcester, Mass., 1972).

B. "James d'Alte Aldridge Welch," *PAAS*, April 1970, 20–23; Wilbur Jordan Smith, "UCLA's Trove of Rare Children's Books," *Wilson Library Bulletin*, October 1975, 149–153; Correspondence with Wilbur J. Smith, Curator Emeritus of Special Collections, University of California, at Los Angeles, 1984.

WELLS, Carolyn (b. June 18, 1862, Rahway, N.J.; d. March 26, 1942, New York, N.Y.). *Collection Disposition:* Library of Congress; Anderson, October 18, 1923.

Wells had a literary career that spanned almost sixty years. She began contributing humorous verse to newspapers while she was in grade school and was still writing in her seventies. She wrote successfully in several genres— children's literature, light verse, and detective fiction. In all these she had an easy, popular touch that won her a circle of devoted readers. Perhaps her most lasting contribution was a series of well-edited anthologies of light verse, parody, and nonsense.

Wells became interested in collecting around 1920, when she was given a volume of Walt Whitman's poems. After corresponding with collector A. Edward Newton* on the difficulties of securing early Whitman books, she decided to make that author her particular province. With the help of bookdealer Alfred F. Goldsmith, she soon had an impressive Whitman library. In 1922 she and Goldsmith published a checklist of the collection, which included, among other items, over 100 variant editions of *Leaves of Grass*. To these holdings she added letters, manuscripts, photographs, etchings, books from Whitman's library, and a vast array of critical analysis. In several of her published articles, Wells described book collecting in less than reverential terms. It was, she declared, an "idiot's delight" since "collected books are not read and not meant to be read." These barbs stirred Vincent Starrett to characterize Wells as frivolous and naive about the true nature of collecting. That ended the debate, since Wells never defended her position in print. In general, she took the view that a library ought to please its owner and that if it grew too large it should be sold or given away. It was the same pragmatic philosophy that Henry R. Wagner* followed throughout his distinguished collecting career. Wells enjoyed the hunt and was pleased when rarities fell into her net. At the same time, she could ridicule poorly informed collectors who bought showy first editions by authors they never read. Wells' refreshing essays and her Whitman collection, now at the Library of Congress, have assured her a place in the history of American book collecting.

Bibliography

A. *A Concise Bibliography of the Works of Walt Whitman, with a Supplement of Fifty Books About Whitman*, compiled by Carolyn Wells and Alfred P. Goldsmith (New York, 1922); "On Finishing a Collection," *The Atlantic*, November 1926, 623–632; "On Collecting Whitman," *The Colophon*, Fall 1940; *The Rest of My Life* (Philadelphia, 1937), passim.

B. *NCAB* 13, 213; *SCLC* 377; A. Edward Newton, *End Papers* (Boston, 1933), 108–116; Vincent Starrett, *Penny Wise and Book Foolish* (New York, 1929), 109–114.

WENDELL, Evert J. (b. December 5, 1860, Boston, Mass.; d. August 27, 1917, Neuilly, France). *Education:* A.B., Harvard University, 1882. *Collection Disposition:* Anderson, May 4, May 19, 1905; American Art, October 15, 17, 20, 22, and 24, 1919; Harvard University.

Known for his athletic prowess as well as his theatrical abilities, Wendell was reported to be one of the most popular of all the Harvard undergraduates of his day. His early enthusiasm for good sportsmanship spilled over into philanthropy; particularly in support of homeless city children. Born into a family with considerable means, he used his resources to help others. Throughout his life he was known to be passionately fond of the stage, a friend of theatrical people, and a better-than-average amateur actor. This interest led him to collect books on the theater and theater memorabilia. Wendell was not a discriminating collector, like his friendly rival Robert Gould Shaw*, but rather an accumulator. This meant that he bought playbills, letters, clippings, prints, and books by the bundle, seldom checking to see what they might contain. This practice resulted in the acquisition of many duplicates, sometimes as many as three and four copies, of a given work. Like Shaw, Wendell was one of the chief buyers at the turn-of-the-century Augustin Daly*, Thomas McKee*, and Peter Gilsey sales. He secured manuscript materials, books, photographs, and engravings of theatrical interest.

After Wendell's death, Harvard was given first choice from his library as well as any profits derived from the sale of duplicates. The transaction, involving some 300 cases of material, constituted the largest single bequest Harvard's library had ever received. The sale of the duplicates alone brought in enough to defray the costs of cataloging the remainder of the collection. Wendell's gift was not limited to theatrical materials alone but included books, pamphlets, and ephemera on sports, the history of New York City, murder trials, biography, and politics. Fortunately the Wendell and Shaw theatrical holdings complemented each other perfectly. Where Shaw had emphasized quality and concentrated on American and British sources, Wendell had taken the shotgun approach and bought everything, including a large representation of continental materials. The combination of the two collections established the Harvard library as one of the foremost theatrical archives in the country. All accounts of Wendell refer to his youthful charm and his desire to please, characteristics that never deserted him, even in later years. His loyalty to Harvard was underlined by the gift of his magnificent theater collection.

Bibliography

B. *NCAB* 20, 378; Cannon, 331–333; Alfred Potter, *The Library of Harvard University* (Cambridge, Mass., 1934), 134–135; L. P. Marvin, "Evert Jansen Wendell," *Harvard Alumni Bulletin*, November 1917, 29–31; William Van Lennep, "The Harvard Theatre Collection," *HLB*, Autumn 1952, 281–301; Owen Wister, "Evert Jansen Wendell," *The Harvard Graduates Magazine*, March 1918, 345–356.

WHITE, Andrew Dixon (b. November 7, 1832, Homer, N.Y.; d. November 4, 1918, Ithaca, N.Y.). *Education:* A.B., M.A., Yale University, 1853, 1856. *Collection Disposition:* Cornell University.

The son of a New York banker, White was educated at Yale where he distinguished himself by winning the DeForest Gold Medal for a paper on diplomatic history and by serving as editor of the *Yale Literary Magazine*. After traveling in Europe, he became interested in politics and was elected to the New York state legislature. There he met Senator Ezra Cornell and with him drew up plans for a new university to be located in Ithaca, New York. White was elected first president of Cornell University and served in that capacity until 1885.

According to White's autobiography, books and reading had been important since his early school years. His travels in Europe heightened his interest in history and furthered the development of his personal library. White took advantage of the relatively low prices and bought heavily in history, particularly those books that treated the French Revolution. He gathered original documents by Marat and Robespierre as well as printed reminiscences of French generals and patriots. He had a variety of interests, his collecting enthusiasms spilling over into the history of the inquisition, witchcraft, and scientific discovery. Because White believed that original documents vivify classroom lecturers, he used the purchases to support his teaching.

White's vigor in building a personal library was matched by his efforts in building the Cornell University library collections. With his enthusiasms for learning he was able to attract outstanding scholars and to secure important gift collections. Not the least of his achievements was securing the services of Daniel Willard Fiske* as the first university librarian. This appointment laid the groundwork for acquiring the Fiske collections of Dante, Petrarch, and Icelandic studies. On leaving the office of the presidency in 1885, White turned over his personal library to the university with the stipulation that it be provided separate housing and professional maintenance. By 1892, when he presented a large collection of Mormon books, his total gift had reached approximately 30,000 volumes. White was both a personal collector and an institutional collector, a reader, and a productive scholar. His support of the Cornell library established it as an important facility for ongoing research.

Bibliography

A. *Autobiography* (New York, 1906).

B. *DAB* 10, 88–93; *NCAB* 4, 476; Cannon, 136–138; Glenn Altschuler, *Andrew D. White: Educator, Historian, Diplomat* (Ithaca, N.Y., 1979).

WHITE, John G. (b. August 10, 1845, Cleveland, Ohio; d. August 27, 1928, Jackson Lake, Wyo.). *Education:* A.B., Western Reserve, 1865. *Collection Disposition:* Cleveland Public Library.

Trained in the law, White became best known to many Cleveland citizens as the donor of valuable chess and folklore collections to the city's public library. One account of White's early interest in chess refers to the "intellectual walks" he took with his father—one day they would speak in Latin, another in Greek, and finally in chess, playing each move and countermove without board or pieces. This may have been the stimulus that prompted White to start collecting chess literature. He was interested in the historical, artistic, and social aspects of the game from early times to the present. This included books in foreign languages, journals, tournament records, newspaper columns, manuscripts, and chess ephemera. The White library was built day by day, item by item over a period of fifty years with the assistance of bookdealers and chess connoisseurs all over the world. As his collections grew, White became more and more drawn to the literature about backgrounds of the game and almost incidentally to Oriental studies and folklore. In 1889, as chairman of the board of the Cleveland Public Library, he proposed a plan to develop a special department of folklore based on his collections. White's motivation stemmed from his wish to help the library during a budget crisis and to call attention to worldwide cultural beliefs. The Oriental and folklore collections complemented each other nicely, for they both focused on the humanistic elements in world civilization. White gathered materials on non-Western peoples in original languages, wishing to have native authors speak to readers directly rather than through translators. The folklore collection included materials on witchcraft, gypsy lore, superstition, and folk medicine.

In addition, White gathered thousands of ballads, medieval romances, and legends of chivalry.

Between 1899 and 1928 White gave over 50,000 items of Oriental and folklore interest to the Cleveland Public Library, retaining the chess and checker books for his own research. In 1926, when he felt English dealers were charging unreasonable prices, he shifted his accounts to Germany and France, where books seemed more reasonable. He once reminded Bernard Quaritch, the London bookdealer, that he was only a poor lawyer, not a Morgan, Rockefeller, or Ford. Toward the end of his active collecting career White remarked that while some of his colleagues seemed to collect for the sake of collecting, he gathered books and manuscripts for those who could "interpret and use them."

On his death, White's family turned the 12,000 item chess and checker collection over to the library with a sizable endowment for maintenance and future development. The motto on White's bookplate, "Devoted to Chess," was an appropriate legend for a collector who had built one of the outstanding libraries in the world.

Bibliography

A. *Catalog of Folklore, Folklife, and Folksongs*, 2nd edition (Boston, 1978).

B. *NCAB* 22, 376; Walter Green, "The Chess Collection," *The Gambit*, June 1930, 13–19; Alice Loranth, "The John G. White Collection," *Michigan Chess*, August 1975, 3–10; Alice Loranth, "Mr. White and the John G. White Collection" (Talk to the Rowfant Club, November 1978); Alice Loranth, "The European Ethnic Folklore Resources of the White Collection" (Talk to the Ohio Folklore Association, Fall 1972); Ina Roberts, "Biography of John Griswold White," *The Gambit*, June 1930, 1–6.

WHITE, William Augustus (b. December 12, 1843, Brooklyn, N.Y.; d. May 6, 1927, Brooklyn, N.Y.). *Education:* A.B., Harvard University, 1863. *Collection Disposition:* Harvard University; Princeton University; Grolier Club; Anderson, October 27, 1911, February 6, 1920; Direct sales to A. S. W. Rosenbach.

Although known chiefly as a collector of Shakespeare and Blake, White was also interested in the Romantic poets of the early nineteenth century, the Elizabethans, and early American drama. His first rarities came from the 1889 Frederick Perkins sale, which he followed, in 1903, with the purchase of the Monckton Milnes library. Acquisition followed acquisition until, like many another collector, White faced a shortage of space. In 1911 the Anderson Auction Company listed 175 lots as available from the "private library of a Brooklyn collector." With shelf-room to spare, White was able to move enthusiastically into the Elizabethan era, adding titles by Decker, Jonson, Drayton, and others. By 1914 White had enough distinguished volumes to prompt publication of his *Hand-List of Early English Books*. Two years later the *Catalogue of the Exhibition of Shakespeariana*, issued by the New York Public Library, featured a large number of rarities from White's collection. Bibliographer Henrietta Bartlett claimed that White had suggested the exhibition, and then made it a success with his contributions. As his interest in the Elizabethans grew, White found he had less time for American literature. In 1917 he presented the American first editions to Harvard and sold the drama collection to his friend Dr. Fred Atkinson. Even the Elizabethan literature was not immune to weeding. In 1920 the Anderson Galleries offered "Rarities of English Literature" from the White collection. At about this time White began to sell some of his choicest rarities to Henry E. Huntington* and Henry C. Folger*. The Blake materials however were preserved. In *A Bibliography of William Blake* (1921) Geoffrey Keynes paid special tribute to the White collection and to White himself for his "inestimable aid," in the compilation. White was less concerned with profit, although profit there was, than with a sense of fulfillment in knowing his research materials would be located where they would do the most good.

When White received an honorary Doctor of Letters at Princeton in 1926, the citation mentioned both his scholarship and his liberality in making that scholarship readily available. The Shakespeare folios went to Princeton and a large number of Elizabethan reference books to the Grolier Club of New York. The remainder of the library was turned over to the Rosenbach Company.

Bibliography

A. *Hand-List of Early English Books* (New York, 1914); *Catalogue of Early English Books, Chiefly of the Elizabethan Period*, catalogued by Henrietta Bartlett (New York, 1926).

B. *NCAB* 23, 376; Cannon, 329–331; *Grolier 75*, 35–37; Wolf and Fleming, passim; "Notes on Rare Books," *NYT*, August 15, 1926, 18.

WIDENER, Harry E. (b. January 3, 1885, Philadelphia, Pa.; d. April 15, 1912, at sea, on the *Titanic*). *Education:* A.B., Harvard University, 1907. *Collection Disposition:* Harvard University.

The son of an affluent and cultured Philadelphia family, Widener grew up surrounded by books and art. From the time he graduated from Harvard until his untimely death, he devoted himself to collecting. As Widener pursued his studies at Harvard he became more and more interested in collecting and bibliography. At home he was exposed to the bookish interests of his cousin William Elkins*, his grandfather P. A. B. Widener, and most important to the finely honed expertise of Philadelphia bookseller A. S. W. Rosenbach*. The influence of the scholarly faculty at Harvard along with the biblio-magic created by such dealers as Rosenbach and Bernard Quaritch exerted a powerful pull on young Widener, drawing him further into the world of rare books. Mrs. Widener, delighted by the direction of her son's interests, urged him on with gifts of sumptuous books illustrated by Cruikshank and Rowlandson, costume books, and Shakespeare folios.

By the time Widener was a senior he had become a knowledgeable collector. His tastes led him to literature and, whenever possible, to fine association copies. In this regard he was influenced by A. Edward Newton*, writer and spiritual leader for a generation of early-twentieth-century bibliophiles. Among the many rarities in the Widener library, one of the most distinguished was the Countess of Pembroke's elaborately bound copy of Sir Philip Sidney's *Arcadia*(1613). Also notable were extensive collections of rare first editions by Robert Lewis Stevenson and Charles Dickens. Widener's resources were almost unlimited. From the John Augustin Daly* sale he obtained a number of extra-illustrated volumes, among them Daly's own copy of *Woffington: A Tribute* (1888) with bound-in portraits, watercolors, and playbills. The strength of the library, however, was in the association items from such literary giants as Robert Browning, Charlotte Brontë, and Swinburne. He also acquired Rowlandson and Leech plates, Shelley rarities, and much more. In addition to buying from Rosenbach and Quaritch, Widener was an assiduous book scout on his own behalf. He prowled the shops and auction rooms of New York and London, making good use of his extraordinary memory to locate treasures. Frequently he was successful. He did not do as well, however, at the Robert Hoe III* sale in 1911, when George D. Smith carried off almost all the important books for Henry E. Huntington*. After this sale Widener is reported to have told Newton that he did not want to be remembered simply as a collector, but hoped for recognition in association with a great library. He believed that association would never be, because it seemed that Morgan, Huntington, and Frank B. Bemis* were buying up all the best books and manuscripts. Widener went to London a year later to attend the Huth sale and on the return voyage became one of the victims of the *Titanic* disaster.

After his death Mrs. Widener continued to buy books along the lines she felt he would have followed. At the same time, she began to develop plans with Harvard officers for the funding of a library building to be built in memory of her son. This building, dedicated in June 1915, houses the rare book collections of the university and includes, among other treasures, the distinguished gathering of some 3,000 books and manuscripts brought together by Widener and his family. Although developed over a period of less than ten years, the Widener literature collection was remarkably rich. It continues to make an impressive contribution to humanistic scholarship.

Bibliography

A. *A Catalogue of Some of the More Important Books, Manuscripts, and Drawings in the Library of Harry Elkins Widener* (Philadelphia, 1910); *A Catalogue of the Books and Manuscripts of Robert Lewis Stevenson in the Library of the Late Harry Elkins Widener*, with a memoir by A. S. W. Rosenbach (Philadelphia, 1913); *A Catalogue of the Writings of Charles Dickens in the Library of Harry Elkins Widener* (Philadelphia, 1918); *Catalogue of the Works Illustrated by George Cruikshank and Isaac and Robert Cruikshank in the Library of Harry Elkins Widener* (Philadelphia, 1918).

B. *DAB* 10, 184–185; *NCAB* 15, 12; Cannon, 209–212; *Grolier 75*, 221–223; Arthur Freeman, "Harry Widener's Last Book, Corrigenda to A. E. Newton," *BC*, Summer

1977, 173–185; A. E. Newton, "A Word in Memory," in *The Amenities of Book Collecting* (Boston, 1918), 343–355; Alfred Potter, *The Library of Harvard College* (Cambridge, Mass., 1934), 135–138; Wolf and Fleming, passim.

WIDENER, Joseph E. (b. August 19, 1872, Philadelphia, Pa.; d. October 26, 1943, Philadelphia, Pa.). *Education:* B.A., University of Pennsylvania, 1892. *Collection Disposition:* National Gallery, Washington, D.C.; Parke-Bernet, November 28, 1944; Free Library of Philadelphia.

As a member of a wealthy Philadelphia family, Widener was exposed to books and art from his earliest years. His father, P. A. B. Widener, architect of a giant transportation empire, collected paintings, prints, extra-illustrated sets, and fine bindings. His nephew, Harry E. Widener*, was an avid collector of literary first editions. Clarence S. Bement*, a close family friend, collected illuminated manuscripts, early prayer books, and English literature. Acting as a catalyst for these Philadelphia collectors was the ebullient bookdealer A. S. W. Rosenbach*. When Widener started buying from Rosenbach, he favored nineteenth-century English sporting books with colored plates by Leech, H. K. Browne, and Henry Alken. He also acquired impressive holdings of early English, French, and American sporting journals, stud books, and turf registers—the colorful record of horse-racing and horse-breeding.

After this initiation, Widener plunged ahead to other and more exotic purchases. With a nudge from Rosenbach and an investment of $60,000, he picked up the splendid set of first folios that had once belonged to Marsden Perry*. Once that purchase was digested, he began to build his distinguished collection of eighteenth-century French illustrated books and prints. The timing could not have been better. In 1920 Rosenbach had concluded an agreement to acquire the eighteenth-century French library of Robert Schuhmann and needed buyers. Widener promptly carried off $150,000 worth of beautifully bound and printed rarities for his growing library at Lynnewood Hall. According to Wolf and Fleming, this purchase gave Widener instant claim to a collection of international stature. In 1923, after long negotiation, the Louis Olry-Roederer French books, drawings, and proof plates came into Rosenbach's hands, and again Widener was there to select choice items. He added a signed mosaic binding by Derôme and drawings by Eisen, Boucher, and Moreau le Jeune. Widener's splendid French drawings, prints, and books went to the National Gallery in Washington, D.C., his Shakespeare folios and illuminated manuscripts to the Free Library of Philadelphia. The remainder of his library was sold at auction in New York.

Bibliography

B. Wolf and Fleming, passim; A. S. W. Rosenbach, *A Description of the Four Folios of Shakespeare, 1623, 1632, 1663–64, 1685, in the Original Bindings*, the gift of Mr. P. A. B. Widener and Mrs. Josephine Widener Wichfeld to the Free Library of Philadelphia in memory of their father, Joseph E. Widener (Philadelphia, 1945).

WILLIAMS, John Camp (b. September 6, 1859, Utica, N.Y.; d. February 26, 1929, Utica, N.Y.). *Education:* A.B., Amherst College, 1882. *Collection Disposition:* American Art—Anderson, November 6, 1929.

An easterner by birth, Williams moved to Chicago in 1880 to pursue a career in the iron and steel business. He was associated with several firms before he and a number of colleagues started the Western Tool Company. He retired in 1899 and devoted the rest of his life to collecting and to the study of New York history.

The well-annotated catalogs of the Williams sale indicated several interests—Americana, book illustration, and English literature. Although the books of American interest constituted a small portion of the entire library, they offered some enticing items: a beautifully bound copy of Hariot's "Virginia" (1590), a set of the *Royal American Magazine* from 1774 to 1775 with plates by Paul Revere, an early-nineteenth-century manuscript account of one of the first mission visits to Hawaii, pamphlets on Freemasonry, and a collection of early imprints from Utica, Schenectady, and Albany, New York. One of the most important sections of the library was composed of books displaying engraved copperplate technique. In an introduction to the 1929 sale catalog, bibliographer Henrietta Bartlett identified Williams as the leading American authority on this style of illustration. His library included Bettini's *Monte sancto di Dio* (1477), from the Robert Curzon collection, the first printed work to include copper engravings, and Roesslin's *The Byrth of Mankynde* (1540), the first English book to use that medium.

Another high point in the Williams library was the Sir Thomas Brooke copy of Henry Holland's *Baziliologia* (1618), bound in crushed red-levant morocco by Bedford. This was identified as one of ten known copies and judged by bibliographer H. C. Lewis to be the finest in existence. As for Shakespeare, Williams owned the second, third, and fourth folios, Henry Willobie's *Avisa* (1594), the first text to provide direct mention of the playwright, and John Hall's *Select Observations* (1657), the first book to give a contemporary account of Shakespeare's family. The library also held a number of distinguished incunabula, including Alexander De Ales *Summa Universae Theologiae* (1482), printed by Koberger and the editio princeps of Cicero's "Rhetoric" (1470) printed by Jenson. Williams had also secured a wide assortment of first editions by Milton, Spenser, Wither, Crashaw, and other luminaries of the seventeenth and eighteenth centuries.

The Williams sale attracted all the major New York bookdealers, although according to one observor bids were conservative, based on the mediocre condition of some of the books. The second and third folios, for example, brought only $525 and $625 respectively, while the third folio, in slightly better condition, sold for $1,000. The highest price paid for any book was $13,000, given by A. S. W. Rosenbach* for *Baziliologia*. Lathrop Harper took Smith's *General History of Virginia* for $1,000, while Charles Heartman paid $7,300 for a handsome copy of Hariot's "Virginia." James Drake was one of the heaviest buyers, including among his purchases the *Royal American Magazine*, a Poe letter, and Spenser's *Complaints* (1591) in crimson crushed levant morocco. The Williams library was a well-conceived collection of books and prints, particularly notable for its attention to copperplate illustration.

Bibliography

B. *NCAB* C, 458–459; "The Sale of the John C. Williams Library," *PW*, November 16, 1929, 2407–2410.

WILMERDING, Lucius (b. January 24, 1879, New York, N.Y.; d. July 15, 1949, Far Hills, N.J.). *Education:* A.B., Harvard University, 1901. *Collection Disposition:* Grolier Club; New York Public Library; Parke-Bernet, November 27, 1950, March 5, October 29, 1951.

After graduating from Harvard, Wilmerding joined a brokerage firm in New York. He was involved with a number of civic and charitable organizations and was active in service to the Grolier Club and the New York Public Library.

The Grolier *Yearbook* of 1950 paid tribute to Wilmerding as a fastidious collector with an important library of French literature and fine bindings. Many of the important books and manuscripts in the collection came through purchases made at the Seth Terry* and John Stetson* sales of 1935 and from the Cortlandt Field Bishop* sale of 1938. Wilmerding used New York bookdealer Gabriel Wells as his agent in many of these sales, and it was Wells who secured the famous "Olive Branch Petition" for him at the Lothian sale of 1931. This document, addressed to George III and signed by the members of the Continental Congress in 1775, now forms a part of the distinguished manuscript collection of the New York Public Library, a gift from Wilmerding. In all his purchases Wilmerding was a close student of provenance, state, and issue. He was an authority on Renaissance binding and could often supply the date of a work and the name of the craftsman. His shelves held outstanding examples of the work of Derôme, Padeloup, Gruel, Le Gascon, and Nicholas Eve as well as elaborate commissioned bindings made for such sixteenth-century patrons as Jean Grolier and Marcus Fugger.

To all his collecting Wilmerding brought a scholar's respect for history. He collected a set of the *Almanachs Royaux* to study the lives of the French nobility. His love of association books was manifest in such holdings as a collection of Keats and Stevenson presentation copies and in a unique autobiographical memoir by Michael de Montaigne. The most important American and European dealers were on hand when Wilmerding's library was offered at auction in New York in 1950 and 1951. High prices were the rule as the fine bindings and rare literary items brought record bids from A. S. W. Rosenbach*, Maggs, Berès, and others. The enthusiastic level of bidding had not been seen since the Jerome Kern* sale of 1929. Wilmerding's intelligent approach to collecting was justified by the results in the auction rooms. He is remembered as a knowledgeable and generous bookman.

Bibliography

B. *Grolier 75*, 210–212; *NCAB* 39, 525–526; *Grolier Yearbook*, 1950, 123–127; C. W. Wickersham, "The Olive Branch," *BNYPL*, November 1952, 539–543; Wolf and Fleming, passim.

WILSON, Carroll A. (b. May 12, 1886, Benton Falls, Maine; d. June 27, 1947, New York, N.Y.). *Education:* B.A., Williams College, 1907; Oxford University, 1908–1911. *Collection Disposition:* Williams College; Scribner's Book Store; Parke-Bernet, January 25, 1945.

After completing his studies at Oxford, Wilson entered legal practice in Boston. In 1921 he joined the Guggenheim Corporation as their chief legal counsel. Few collectors have documented the beginning of their avocation as specifically as Wilson. In his copy of Anthony Trollope's *The Warden*, a penciled inscription reads, "The purchase of this book began my serious book-collecting. I bought it as a birthday present to myself in May 1925, and thereby opened the door to some of the pleasantest hours of my life." This note, written with a mixture of businesslike detail and literary grace, was characteristic. In working out his particular collecting style, Wilson decided to limit his library to a select number of nineteenth-century authors and to try to cover those authors completely. *The Catalogue of the Grolier Club Centenary Exhibition of the Works of Thomas Hardy* (1940) and *Catalogue of the Collection of Samuel Butler* (1945), both based on Wilson's holdings, were meticulous and complete. These were not mere checklists but well-annotated compilations complete with bibliographic detail.

Wilson was profoundly influenced by the work done by Alfred C. Chapin* in forming a library of rare books for students at Williams College. He decided to supplement Chapin's efforts and to prepare a complete Thomas Hardy library for the college. The object, according to Wilson, was to show the students how such a collection could be made and how it could be used. Although Hardy, Butler, and Trollope attracted Wilson, his predominant interest was in American authors. When he went after Alcott, Emerson, Hawthorne, Holmes, Irving, Poe, or Thoreau, no scrap of information was too minute for his net. He obtained first appearances, variant bindings, individual magazine publications, pamphlets, letters, theater programs—everything. This was no mere accumulation but rather an intelligently organized bibliographic taxonomy.

Wilson's expertise was in constant demand. He was the collaborator, with Richard Curle, on *Collecting American First Editions* (1931) and a contributor to a score of other texts and reference books on American literature. The second volume of Jacob Blanck's *Bibliography of American Literature* was dedicated to Wilson's memory. His associations with fellow collectors were remarkably amiable considering the intense rivalry common among those following overlapping fields. Morris Parrish*, Robert Taylor, and Waller Barrett, among others, shared a deep respect for Wilson's bibliographic expertise. He was active in the Grolier Club of New York and the Bibliographical Society of America and was a longstanding chairman of its Committee on Publications. On Wilson's death, Scribner's purchased the library and issued an annotated two-volume catalog, *Thirteen Author Collections of the Nineteenth Century and Five Centuries of Familiar Quotations*. It was, as David Randall pointed out, "a monument to Wilson," including, as it did, his extensive notes and comments. For his wide-ranging scholarship, generosity, and aptitude for bibliography John Carter was correct in identifying Wilson as "one of the most distinguished book collectors of our time."

Bibliography

A. *First Appearances in Print of Some Four Hundred Familiar Quotations* (Middletown, Conn., 1935); *Catalog of the Grolier Club Centenary Exhibition of the Works of Thomas Hardy* (New York, 1940); *Catalogue of the Collection of Samuel Butler* (New York, 1945); *Thirteen Author Collections of the Nineteenth Century and Five Centuries of Familiar Quotations* (New York, 1950).

B. *NCAB* 37, 137; *Grolier 75*, 224–227; John Carter, "Carroll Atwood Wilson," in *Books and Book Collecting* (London, 1956), 31–38. Charles Goodspeed, "Carroll A. Wilson," *PW*, November 22, 1947; David Randall, "Carroll Atwood Wilson," *Dukedom Large Enough* (New York, 1969), 303–307; *PAAS*, October 15, 1947, 261–262.

WING, John M. (b. April 7, 1845, N.Y.; d. March 14, 1917, Chicago, Ill.). *Collection Disposition:* Newberry Library.

All Wing's professional life centered on printing. As a boy he worked in small print shops and newspaper offices in western New York State. In 1866 he moved to Chicago and founded two profitable trade journals. At the age of forty-three he retired to devote himself to travel and collecting. Considering his background, it is not surprising that Wing concentrated on the graphic arts, calligraphy, early printing, and the aesthetics of book design. He was particularly fond of extra-illustrating and embellished many books in his collection with watercolors, drawings, portraits, and letters.

On his death the Newberry Library in Chicago received the collection and a sizable endowment for additional purchases and maintenance. The John M. Wing Foundation is a typographical library within the Newberry Library and one of the country's richest archives on the history of printing. According to Pierce Butler, the foundation's first custodian, the archive would follow the goals set by its doner and devote itself to the accumulation of "such things as will instruct, correct and inspire the makers and users of books in the higher aspects of the typographic art."

Bibliography

A. *Dictionary Catalogue of the History of Printing, from the John M. Wing Foundation in the Newberry Library* (Boston, 1961) and *Supplement* (Boston, 1970).

B. Cannon, 192–193; Pierce Butler, "A Typographical Library," *PBSA*, 2nd Q 1921,

73–87; James Wells, "The Wing Foundation," *Print*, March 1953, 157–162; James Wells, "The John Wing Foundation of the Newberry Library," *BC*, Summer 19–59, 156–162; George B. Utley, *Handbook of the Newberry Library* (Chicago, 1933), 61–70.

WINTHROP, James (b. March 28, 1752, Cambridge, Mass.; d. September 26, 1821, Cambridge, Mass.). *Education:* A.B., Harvard College, 1769. *Collection Disposition:* Allegheny College.

As the member of one of the oldest and most distinguished colonial families, Winthrop was exposed early in life to the benefits of books and reading. Shortly after graduating from Harvard he was appointed librarian and served in that capacity until 1787. Subsequently, he acted as judge of common pleas for Middlesex District and worked on various municipal and regional land surveys. He was interested in the natural sciences, history, theology, and languages and was one of the founding members of the American Academy of Arts and Sciences. According to one account, he published somewhat dubious scientific and mathematical investigations in the *Memoirs* of the Academy, much to the embarrassment of the other members. In the course of his studies, Winthrop amassed a large personal library, one of the finest in the colonies. When his friend Timothy Alden founded Allegheny College in Meadville, Pennsylvania, Winthrop donated his books to that institution. With this library combined with the one already given by William Bentley*, Allegheny opened with one of the largest and best academic collections in the country.

Bibliography

B. *DAB* 10, 407–408; E. A. Smith, *Allegheny: A Century of Education* (Meadville, Pa., 1916), 43–49; Edwin Wolf II, "Some Books of Early New England Provenance in the 1823 Library of Allegheny College," *PAAS*, April 1963, 13–44.

WOLFF, Robert Lee (b. December 22, 1915, New York, N.Y.; d. November 11, 1980, Cambridge, Mass.). *Education:* A.B., M.A., Ph.D., Harvard University, 1936, 1937, 1947. *Collection Disposition:* Harvard University.

While Wolff was a student at Harvard, he heard a senior member of the History Department say he expected his students to read and appreciate the adventure novels of G. A. Henty. This started Wolff on a search that developed into a passion for the Victorian novel. Wolff was not completely drawn to collecting until he saw a handsomely bound first edition of Henty's *With Buller to Natal*. When he found a copy of the three-decker *Dorothy's Double*, he was ensnared. Reading Michael Sadleir's *Excursions in Victorian Bibliography* strengthened his resolve to make the Victorian novel his own province. Where Sadleir had gone, he would go also—only further. As his interests became known, catalogs poured in. These made entertaining reading, but with a Harvard professor's salary Wolff could consider only bread-and-butter purchases. Early in the chase Wolff decided to concentrate on the lesser novelists rather than the established writers. Books by Anna Bray, William Kingston, W. E. Norris, and Charlotte

Yonge began to fill his shelves, names that were important in their day but remained only as curiosities in the twentieth century. In some cases this made hunting easier, but more often the search for a certain Bray novel about the Devon coast could go on for years. The matter of securing binding variants was another intriguing element in collecting Victorian fiction. Few examples ever turned up in original paperboards. When copies did appear, they often included library stigmata—labels, numbering, and stampings. Naturally Wolff wanted only pristine copies. He also began to look for presentation copies and, when the price was not too high, letters and manuscripts. The objective of his hunt was to produce a mirror of Victorian social life in all its many aspects.

As the library developed in strength and quality, it became Wolff's working tool for the production of articles and books on Victorian literature. Among the many association books in the Wolff collection, there were some half-dozen that he lovingly referred to as *the* copy. This was a super-category that he reserved for those rare items that so evoked the author and his times as to be absolutely unique. The copy often contained a warmly personal inscription from the author to some choice recipient. George du Maurier's *Peter Ibbetson*, presented to his daughter—"To Sylvia du Maurier from the author of her being (and this book)"— was one of these. For Wolff the compelling quality of the dedication was heightened by his knowledge that Sylvia and her children eventually came under the financial protection of master storyteller James M. Barrie. It was a direct line, according to Wolff, between the father of Peter Ibbetson to the mother of Peter Pan, a never-to-be-equaled association. By Wolff's standards, books of this kind marked the difference between a collection that was simply good and one that was superlative. Throughout his collecting career Wolff took careful notes on each book he acquired, recording variants that might distinguish it from all other copies. He included these notes in a massive bibliography planned to rival the more limited work issued by Michael Sadleir. The first volume came out in 1981, a year after Wolff died. Wolff summarized the rewards of his own collecting activities by saying that he enjoyed hunting and cataloging books but that his greatest pleasure came from reading.

Bibliography

A. *Nineteenth Century Fiction: A Bibliographic Catalogue* (New York, 1981); "Some Pleasures of the Chase," in *Strange Stories and Other Explorations in Victorian Fiction* (Boston, 1971), 3–67; "Nineteenth Century Fiction," *BC*, Autumn 1965, 335–347, "Nineteenth Century Fiction," *BC*, Winter 1965, 511–522.

B. Walter E. Smith "Nineteenth Century Fiction: A Bibliographic Catalogue," *PBSA*, 4th Q 1982, 481–488.

WRENN, John Henry (b. September 11, 1841, Middletown, Ohio; d. May 13, 1911, Los Angeles, Calif.). *Collection Disposition:* University of Texas.

After several years working as a bookkeeper in his father's paper mill in Ohio, Wrenn moved to Chicago, where he entered the brokerage business. His earliest collecting interests were the New England poets and novelists of the nineteenth century. In 1892, on a trip to England, Wrenn met bibliographer Thomas J. Wise, and from that meeting sprang one of the most notorious dealer-customer relationships of all time. Wise quickly took over the formation of Wrenn's library of eighteenth- and nineteenth-century English literature with a series of ingratiating letters and offers. He moved from bibliographic "friend" to bookdealer in an extraordinarily careful and sophisticated manner. At first Wise supplied Wrenn with facsimile copies of the early works of Swinburne, Ruskin, and William Morris as a function of his position as secretary of the Shelley Society. In 1897 Wise offered Wrenn a copy of the "first edition" of the *Vicar of Wakefield* in red morocco for £50—since, as he reported, he already had a "better copy." From that point until Wrenn's death Wise sent a stream of letters, and "rare books" across the Atlantic from Ashley House to Chicago. Between 1898 and 1910 Wise supplied Wrenn with manufactured first editions of Ruskin, Tennyson, Browning, and a host of other nineteenth-century authors. During this time Wrenn and Wise started vacationing together on the continent, attending sales and cementing their bibliographic friendship. Through Wise, Wrenn met such literary giants as Edmund Gosse, Henry Buxton Forman, and William Rossetti, brother of the poet. One of the most important collections transferred to Wrenn came from "The Pines," where Swinburne had lived his last years under the protection of Theodore Watts-Dunton. Wise had been able to secure entry into this stronghold and provided his Chicago friend with legitimate books, manuscripts, and letters. Wrenn had no idea that many of the rarities he bought from Wise were pure fabrications. It was not until the publication of John Carter and Graham Pollard's meticulous *Enquiry into the Nature of Certain Nineteenth Century Pamphlets* in 1934 that the full story of Wise's duplicity became known.

The subsequent publications about Wise have produced a vivid chapter in the history of book collecting. As Texas rare book librarian Fanny Ratchford has pointed out, the forgeries, with all the attention they have received, accounted for only a small part of the 6,000-volume Wrenn library. Many of the basic author collections—Pope, Defoe, Swift, Fielding, Goldsmith, and Walpole, to name only a few—were deep and sound, richly preserved in full or nearly full runs. After Wrenn's death the library remained in Chicago for a time, although aggressive bookdealers made a number of preliminary offers. In 1918, through the lobbying of English Professor R. H. Griffith, the library was purchased for $225,000 by the University of Texas. There, according to a specific agreement with the family, it was organized in a separate facility and maintained by a professional staff. Two years after the books had been moved to Texas, a five-volume catalog bound in primrose-yellow buckram was issued by Wrenn's son and edited by Wise. It was appropriate that Wise have his hand in at the last, since by Ratchford's estimate he had provided almost 80 percent of the books. The Wrenn library was clearly a product of the London bibliographer-salesman.

Bibliography

A. *A Catalogue of the Library of the Late John Henry Wrenn*, 5 volumes (Austin, 1920).

B. Appleton 8, 486–487; Cannon, 200–205; *Grolier 75*, 31–34; J. W. Draper, "A Catalogue of the Library of the Late John Henry Wrenn" (review) *Modern Language Notes*, 1921, 237–243; John Carter and Graham Pollard, *An Enquiry into the Nature of Certain Nineteenth Century Pamphlets* (London, 1934); Wilfred Partington, *Forging Ahead* (New York, 1939); Fannie Ratchford, "Thomas J. Wise to John Henry Wrenn on Nineteenth Century Bibliography," *PBSA*, 1st Q 1942, 215–228; William B. Todd, "The Wrenn Library," *Texas Library Chronicle*, Fall 1974, 73–79; T. J. Wise, *Letters of Thomas J. Wise to John Henry Wrenn* (New York, 1944).

WYLES, William (b. 1857; d. January 23, 1946, Santa Barbara, Calif.). *Collection Disposition:* University of California at Santa Barbara.

Before he moved to California in 1887, Wyles had tried his hand at herding sheep in Montana, working for a railroad, and managing hotels in Chicago. He continued in the hotel business in Santa Barbara, augmenting those activities with real estate ventures in Los Angeles. Late in life he began to collect books on Abraham Lincoln and the Civil War. As a boy he had known men who had fought in the war, and he remembered their stories. Once started as a Lincoln collector Wyles spread a wide net, buying books, posters, broadsides, and ephemera wherever he could find it. One of the most valuable single items in the collection was an autographed photograph of Lincoln that had been used to raise money for the Union soldiers. A special section included books from Lincoln's own library, some Lincoln had owned as a lawyer in Illinois and others he read after he became President.

In another collecting path, Wyles gathered books and pamphlets on the development of the American West. Here he concentrated on diaries and overland journals—the authentic accounts of those who first saw the western areas. Finally, Wyles rounded out his library with a collection of materials dealing with American expansion in the Orient. Again he concentrated on the first things—the narratives of those who made their journeys before 1900. In a pattern familiar to many collectors, books began to overflow the Wyles home. Fortunately the University of California at Santa Barbara was able to provide the necessary space and administrative services. Wyles bought books as long as he lived and in his will included an endowment that has allowed continued acquisitions. The Wyles collection is one of the strongest West Coast resources for the study of Lincoln and his times.

Bibliography

B. Jay Monaghan, *William Wyles and the William Wyles Collection*(Santa Barbara, Calif., 1980).

Y

YOUNG, Owen D. (b. October 27, 1874, Van Hornesville, N.Y.; d. July 11, 1962, Saint Augustine, Fla.). *Education:* A.B., Saint Lawrence University, 1894; LL.B., Boston University, 1896. *Collection Disposition:* New York Public Library.

Growing up in rural New York State and later as a student at Saint Lawrence University, Young had no money to invest in books. When he started to practice law in Boston, however, he began to make regular purchases at Goodspeed's and at the Old Corner Bookstore. In these locations he whetted an appetite for literature that led him to develop an impressive library. In 1912 Young moved to New York as chief counsel and vice-president of the General Electric Company. This appointment and subsequent promotions gave Young the financial means to indulge his bookish interests. During a long stay in London in 1924, Young became a steady customer of bookdealer Walter T. Spencer. Here the collector found a mouth-watering array of literary manuscripts, pamphlets, and books with drawings and prints. From Spencer's back room and cellar Young dug out rarities by Thackeray, Lamb, Dickens, Bacon, Milton, Smollett, and others. Shortly New York and Philadelphia dealers became familiar with Young's hunger for literary manuscripts and rare editions. A. S. W. Rosenbach* supplied over 100 letters exchanged between Hawthorne and his publisher, while Goodspeed's sold him one of the five known copies of Poe's *Tamerlane*.

The 1920s were the years of important book-sales, and Young took advantage of every opportunity. He obtained Milton's *Comus* from the John L. Clawson* sale of 1926 and added other rarities from the collections of Herschel V. Jones*, Winston Hagen*, and W. K. Bixby*. When the Jerome Kern* books came on the market in 1929 Young made some of his most important purchases. Working through Rosenbach and other dealers, he spent more than $375,000 adding notable items by Byron, Keats, Pope, Sterne, Tennyson, Charlotte Brontë, and others. One of his most outstanding purchases at that time was the 1865 *Alice in Wonderland* inscribed by Lewis Carroll to Alice Liddell, the original Alice of the story.

During the depression Young began to sell parts of his collection, and by 1941 he was ready to dispose of the entire lot. To his delight the books fit perfectly into a substantial gift that Albert Berg* was putting together for the New York Public Library. Berg agreed to purchase an undivided half-interest in the books if Young would present the remainder as a gift. The negotiations worked, and in December 1941 the officers of the library jubilantly announced the acquisitions of the Berg-Young collection. It was, as reported in the *New York Times*, a gift of "almost fabulous proportions." For Young the disposition of the books to the New York Public Library was singularly appropriate. In a charming short essay Josephine Young Case, the collector's daughter, remembered the sense of trusteeship with which her father gathered books. He felt, she reported, like a "volunteer" who had only a temporary right to own precious books and whose duty it was to pass them along to another volunteer. Patrons of the New York Public Library can be deeply grateful to Young for his philanthropic point of view.

Bibliography

B. *NCAB* A, 81; *CB*, 1945, 701–704; Wolf and Fleming, passim; New York Public Library, *Guide to the Research Collections* (Chicago, 1975), 79–80; Lola Szladits, *Owen D. Young, Book Collector* (New York, 1974); Josephine Young Case, "The Volunteer," in *Owen D. Young, Book Collector* (New York, 1974); *NYT*, July 12, 1962, 28; Josephine Young Case and Everett Needham Case, *Owen D. Young and American Enterprise* (Boston, 1982), 401–415.

Appendix I
Areas of Collector Specialization

This listing attempts to reflect major collecting interests. A collector such as Jacob Chester Chamberlain, who gathered works by Bryant, Emerson, Hawthorne, Holmes, Irving, Longfellow, Poe, Thoreau, and Whittier is simply listed under American literature. One-author and one-subject collectors are listed under the most appropriate specific entry. This listing is intended to be suggestive rather than complete.

Aeronautics

Richard Gimbel

Alaska

Hubert Howe Bancroft
Valerian Lada-Mocarski

Aldine Editions

William Loring Andrews
John Carter Brown
William E. Burton
Templeton Crocker
Robert Hoe III
William King Richardson

Aldrich, Thomas Bailey

Frank Maier

American Literature

Owen F. Aldis
Frank B. Bemis
Albert A. Berg
William D. Breaker
Jacob C. Chamberlain
Beverly Chew
Walter P. Chrysler Jr.
Evert A. Duyckinck
Charles B. Foote
Albert Gorton Greene
Frederick R. Halsey
Caleb Fiske Harris
Parkman Dexter Howe
William T. H. Howe
Henry E. Huntington
Marshall C. Lefferts
Josiah K. Lilly

Thomas Lockwood
Cyrus H. McCormick
William E. Stockhausen
Stephen H. Wakeman

Americana

Edward G. Asay
Thomas Aspinwall
Samuel L. M. Barlow
J. Carson Brevoort
George Brinley
John Carter Brown
Elihu Dwight Church
William L. Clements
Joseph J. Cooke
Edward A. Crowninshield
Charles Deane
Henry F. Depuy
Wilberforce Eames
James W. Ellsworth
William B. Osgood Field
Peter Force
Almon W. Griswold
Henry E. Huntington
John F. Hurst
Thomas Jefferson
Herschel V. Jones
Matt B. Jones
Grenville Kane
Levi Z. Leiter
James Lenox
Cotton Mather
Increase Mather
Richard Mather
Cyrus H. McCormick
Tracy W. McGregor
Thomas Jefferson McKee
William Menzies
Henry Cruse Murphy
Isaac Norris
Thomas Prince
John A. Rice

Thomas Wallcut
John Camp Williams

Americana—Midwest

Clarence M. Burton
Edward Caldwell
George W. Paullin

Americana—Voyage and Discovery

Samuel L. M. Barlow
Edwin J. Beinecke Sr.
James Ford Bell
George Brinley
John Carter Brown
William Byrd
Alfred C. Chapin
Elihu Dwight Church
William L. Clements
Frank C. Deering
Wilberforce Eames
William M. Elkins
John Work Garrett
Ogden Goelet
Henri Harrisse
Brayton Ives
Charles H. Kalbfleisch
Grenville Kane
Levi Z. Leiter
James Lenox
Josiah K. Lilly
Tracy W. McGregor
Henry Cruse Murphy
Boies Penrose
John Hinsdale Scheide
Henry C. Taylor
John Boyd Thacher

Americana—Western Movement

Hubert Howe Bancroft
Frederick W. Beinecke
William Robertson Coe

Everitt DeGolyer
Robert S. Ellison
Herbert Evans
Donald McKay Frost
Everett D. Graff
William J. Holliday
C. G. Littell
William Smith Mason
Winlock Miller
Philip Ashton Rollins
Thomas W. Streeter
Henry R. Wagner
William Wyles

Andersen, Hans Christian

Jean Hersholt

Architecture History

Samuel Putnam Avery
Laurence H. Fowler

Arctic

Vilhjalmur Stefansson

Arizona

Joseph A. Munk

Asch, Sholem

Louis Rabinowitz

Association Books

William K. Bixby
Eugene Field
Frank J. Hogan
Parkman Dexter Howe
Adrian H. Joline
Jerome Kern
Frederick W. Skiff
Harry B. Smith
Lucius Wilmerding

Austen, Jane

C. Beecher Hogan

Baskerville Editions

Moncure Biddle

Beardsley, Aubrey

Albert Eugene Gallatin

Beerbohm, Max

Albert Eugene Gallatin

Bibles

Moncure Biddle
John Carter Brown
Estelle Doheny
William Kurrelmeyer
James Lenox
George Livermore
Cotton Mather
Increase Mather
Richard Mather
John Hinsdale Scheide

Bierce, Ambrose

Estelle Getz

Bindings

William Loring Andrews
Samuel Putnam Avery
Doris L. Benz
Cortlandt Field Bishop
Matthew C. D. Borden
Morgan Gunst
Robert Hoe III
Philip Hofer
Edwin B. Holden
Lowell Kerr
John Pierpont Morgan

Michael Papantonio
John I. Perkins
Henry W. Poor
Abbie Ellen Hanscom Pope
William King Richardson
John A. Saks
Mortimer L. Schiff
Louis H. Silver
William Augustus Spencer
Julius Wagenheim
Henry Walters
Lucius Wilmerding

Black Life and Culture

C. Glenn Carrington
Jesse E. Moorland
Arthur A. Schomburg
Arthur Barnett Spingarn

Blackstone, William

Hampton Carson

Blake, William

Cortlandt Field Bishop
A. Edward Newton
Lessing J. Rosenwald
Chauncey Brewster Tinker
William Augustus White

Boccaccio, Giovanni

Harold C. Bodman

Bonaparte, Napoleon

Andre DeCoppet

Book Papers

see Decorated Book Papers

Boston

Charles Henry Taylor

Boswell, James

Ralph H. Isham
Chauncey Brewster Tinker

Botanical Illustration

Rachel McMasters Miller Hunt

Botany

Oakes Ames
Rachel McMasters Miller Hunt

Boyle, Robert

John F. Fulton

Bradford, William

Henry F. Depuy
Henry Cruse Murphy

Bridges, Robert

Frederick Coykendall

Browne, Thomas

LeRoy Crummer

Browning, Robert and Elizabeth

A. Joseph Armstrong
George Herbert Palmer
Harry E. Widener

Burke, Edmund

James M. Osborn

Burney, Charles

James M. Osborn

Burns, Robert

John Allan
John Gribbel

Burroughs, Edgar Rice

J. Lloyd Eaton
C. Beecher Hogan

Butler, Samuel

Carroll A. Wilson

Byron, George Gordan

Luther A. Brewer

Byzantine Art

Robert Woods Bliss

Byzantine History

Robert Woods Bliss

California

Hubert Howe Bancroft
William Robertson Coe
Robert E. Cowan
Templeton Crocker
Estelle Doheny
Jennie Crocker Henderson
William J. Holliday
Henry E. Huntington
C. G. Littell
William Smith Mason
William McPherson
Henry R. Wagner

Calligraphy

Henry S. Borneman
John Frederick Lewis
Henry Walters
John M. Wing

Canals

Charles Henry Taylor

Carroll, Lewis

Harcourt Amory
Solton Engel
John Gribbel
Eldridge R. Johnson
Morris L. Parrish

Cartography

Henry R. Wagner
see also Americana—Voyage and
  Discovery

Caxton, William

John Pierpont Morgan
Abbie Ellen Hanscom Pope

Cervantes, Miguel de

Carl Tilden Keller

Chandler, Raymond

E. T. Guymon

Chess

John G. White

Children's Books

Elisabeth Ball
George H. Hess
Irvin Kerlan
Edgar S. Oppenheimer
A. S. W. Rosenbach
Wilbur Macey Stone
d'Alte A. Welch

China

Charles W. Wason

Civil War, American

James W. Bollinger
Wymberley Jones DeRenne

Caleb Fiske Harris
Harlan H. Horner
Levi Z. Leiter
Josiah K. Lilly
Tracy W. McGregor
John Shaw Pierson
Alfred Whital Stern
William Wyles

Classical Philology

Stewart Irvin Oost

Clemens, Samuel

Walter P. Chrysler Jr.
Franklin J. Meine
Willard S. Morse

Cobden-Sanderson, T. J.

John A. Saks

Codes

George Fabyan

Conrad, Joseph

John Quinn
A. S. W. Rosenbach

Cookbooks

see Gastronomy

Copperplate Engraving

John Camp Williams

Costume Design

John Frederick Lewis

Cowboys

Edward Larocque Tinker

Cruikshank, George

Frederick W. French
William F. Gable
Robinson Locke

Cuneiform Writing

John Frederick Lewis

da Vinci, Leonardo

Elmer Belt

Daniel Press

Alfred C. Berol

Dante Alighieri

Harold C. Bodman
Daniel Willard Fiske

de Bury, Richard

Hamilton Cole

Decorated Book Papers

Rosamond Bowditch Loring

Defoe, Daniel

William P. Trent

Denmark

Jean Hersholt

Detective Fiction

Adrian H. Goldstone
E. T. Guymon

Detroit

Clarence M. Burton

Dibdin, Thomas F.

John Allan
Hamilton Cole

Dickens, Charles

Cortlandt Field Bishop
Barton Currie
William M. Elkins
DeCoursey Fales
Richard Gimbel
Ogden Goelet
Frederick W. Lehmann
George Barr McCutcheon
George B. Ulizio
Walter T. Wallace
Harry E. Widener

Dictionaries

Warren N. Cordell

Dime Novels

George H. Hess

Doolittle, Hilda

Norman Holmes Pearson

Doyle, Arthur Conan

J. Lloyd Eaton

Dryden, John

William A. Clark Jr.

East India Company

Boies Penrose

Economics

Henry R. Wagner

Egan, Pierce

John G. Heckscher

Elzevir Editions

William Loring Andrews
Junius S. Morgan

Engineering

Sylvanius Thayer

English Literature

William H. Arnold
Thomas P. Barton
Clarence S. Bement
Albert A. Berg
Edward Hale Bierstadt
William K. Bixby
William E. Burton
William Byrd
Alfred C. Chapin
Beverly Chew
John L. Clawson
Alexander Smith Cochrane
Templeton Crocker
John Augustine Daly
Estelle Doheny
Herman L. Edgar
Henry Clay Folger
Frederick W. French
Horace H. Furness Sr.
John Work Garrett
Winston Hagen
Robert Hoe III
Frank J. Hogan
Edwin B. Holden
William T. H. Howe
Henry E. Huntington
Theodore Irwin
Brayton Ives
Herschel V. Jones
Jerome Kern

Edwin N. Lapham
Marshall C. Lefferts
Paul Lemperly
James Lenox
Josiah K. Lilly
Thomas Lockwood
Amy Lowell
Cyrus H. McCormick
George Barr McCutcheon
John Pierpont Morgan
John Pierpont Morgan Jr.
James M. Osborn
George Herbert Palmer
Morris L. Parrish
Carl H. Pforzheimer
Henry W. Poor
Louis Rabinowitz
Arthur M. Rosenbloom
Charles J. Rosenbloom
Louis H. Silver
Myles S. Slocum
John A. Spoor
Roderick T. Terry
Seth S. Terry
William Augustus White
Carroll A. Wilson
James Winthrop
John H. Wrenn
Owen D. Young

Esperanto

George Alan Connor

Evelyn, John

Carleton Rubira Richmond

Extra-Illustration

Robert B. Adam
John Allan
Matthew C. D. Borden
John Carter Brown

William E. Burton
Hamilton Cole
John Augustin Daly
Ferdinand Julius Dreer
Frederick W. Lehmann
William Menzies
Abbie Ellen Hanscom Pope
Robert Gould Shaw
Samuel Tilden

Faulkner, William

Linton R. Massey
William E. Stockhausen

Field, Eugene

Frank Maier
Willard S. Morse

Fielding, Henry

Frederick S. Dickson
Donald F. Hyde

Fishing

Daniel B. Fearing
John G. Heckscher
Samuel W. Lambert
Clara S. Peck
David Wagstaff

Fletcher, John Gould

Norman Holmes Pearson

Folklore

Franklin J. Meine
John G. White

Fore-Edge Painting

Estelle Doheny
Estelle Getz

Franklin, Benjamin

John F. Hurst
William Smith Mason
Henry Cruse Murphy
Samuel W. Pennypacker

Freemasonery

Henry S. Borneman
John Camp Williams

French and Indian War

George A. Plimpton

French History

John Adams
Andre DeCoppet

French Illustrated Books

Frank Altschul
Edwin B. Holden
William King Richardson
Lessing J. Rosenwald
William Augustus Spencer
Joseph E. Widener

French Literature

William A. Clark Jr.
Dannie N. Heineman
Lucius Wilmerding

French Revolution

William Maclure
John Boyd Thacher
Andrew Dixon White

Frost, Robert

H. Bacon Collamore
William E. Stockhausen

Gardening

Robert Woods Bliss
Carleton Rubira Richmond

Gardner, Earl Stanley

E. T. Guymon

Gastronomy

Katherine Golden Bitting

Gay, John

Ernest Lewis Gay

Geology

Everitt DeGolyer

Georgia

Wymberley Jones DeRenne

German Literature

Dannie N. Heineman
William Kurrelmeyer
Adolph Lewisohn
Leonard L. Mackall
William A. Speck
Curt Von Faber du Faur

Goethe, Johann Wolfgang

Leonard L. Mackall
William A. Speck

Goldsmith, Oliver

William M. Elkins

Grabhorn Press

Myles S. Slocum
Henry R. Wagner

Greek Classics

Edward Alexander Parsons

Greenaway, Kate

William F. Gable

Haggard, H. Rider

Frederick Coykendall
J. Lloyd Eaton

Hardy, Thomas

Richard Gimbel
Paul Lemperly
George Barr McCutcheon
Carroll A. Wilson

Harte, Bret

Jennie Crocker Henderson
Frank Maier

Harvey, William

Harvey Cushing

Herbals

Rachel McMasters Miller Hunt

Herbert, George

George Herbert Palmer

Hogg, James

Robert B. Adam

Horace

Moncure Biddle
Horace H. Furness Sr.

Hornbooks

Elisabeth Ball
Irvin Kerlan

Edgar S. Oppenheimer
George A. Plimpton
Wilbur Macey Stone
d'Alte A. Welch

Horsemanship

Clara S. Peck
David Wagstaff
Joseph E. Widener

Houseman, A. E.

H. Bacon Collamore

Hudson Bay Company

James Ford Bell

Hughes, Langston

Arthur Barnett Spingarn

Humor

Franklin J. Meine
Nat Schmulowitz

Hunt, Leigh

Luther A. Brewer

Hunting

Clara S. Peck

Iceland

Daniel Willard Fiske

Illuminated Manuscripts

William Loring Andrews
Edwin J. Beinecke Sr.
Clarence S. Bement
Robert Garrett
Robert Hoe III

John Frederick Lewis
John Pierpont Morgan
John Pierpont Morgan Jr.
Henry Poor
Henry Walters

Illustration

John I. Perkins
Lessing J. Rosenwald
John A. Saks
William Augustus Spencer

Incunabula

Frank Altschul
Edwin J. Beinecke Sr.
Cortlandt Field Bishop
Alfred C. Chapin
Estelle Doheny
Joseph W. Drexel
James W. Ellsworth
Paul Louis Feiss
Howard L. Goodhart
Mary S. Harkness
Rush C. Hawkins
Robert Hoe III
Henry E. Huntington
Theodore Irwin
Grenville Kane
James Lenox
John Frederick Lewis
William Mackenzie
John Pierpont Morgan
John Pierpont Morgan Jr.
Louis Rabinowitz
William King Richardson
Lessing J. Rosenwald
John Hinsdale Scheide
Louis H. Silver
Adolph Sutro
John Boyd Thacher
Henry Walters

Indians

see North American Indians

Inquisition

George Lincoln Burr
Henry Charles Lea
Andrew Dixon White

Irving, Washington

George S. Hellman

Italian Literature

Howard L. Goodhart
George A. Plimpton

Italian History

H. Nelson Gay

Jackson, Andrew

Henry F. Depuy

Jeffers, Robinson

C. Beecher Hogan
John S. Mayfield

Jenner, Edward

LeRoy Crummer
Harvey Cushing

Johnson, Samuel

Robert B. Adam
Donald F. Hyde
Ralph H. Isham
A. Edward Newton
Chauncey Brewster Tinker

Joyce, James

Harley K. Croessmann
John Quinn

Judaeus, Philo

Howard L. Goodhart

Judaica

Louis Rabinowitz
A. S. W. Rosenbach
Mortimer L. Schiff
Mayer Sulzberger

Keats, John

Luther A. Brewer
Amy Lowell

Kelmscott Press

Doris L. Benz
William W. Clary
Carl Edelheim
Frederick W. French
Estelle Getz
John Pierpont Morgan
Marsden J. Perry
John Quinn
William King Richardson
Lessing J. Rosenwald
John A. Saks

Kentucky

J. Winston Coleman
Ruben T. Durrett

Kipling, Rudyard

Ellis A. Ballard
Solton Engel
William B. Osgood Field

Lamb, Charles

Charles Frederickson
John A. Spoor

Landscape Architecture

Robert Woods Bliss

Landscape Gardening

Rachel McMasters Miller Hunt

Lang, Andrew

William W. Clary

Latin American History

E. George Squier

Law, History

Hampton Carson

Lawrence, D. H.

Elmer Belt
H. Bacon Collamore
Thomas E. Hanley

Lawrence, T. E.

Thomas E. Hanley
Bayard L. Kilgour Jr.

Leach, John

William B. Osgood Field

Lear, Edward

William B. Osgood Field

Lenin, Nikolai

Valerian Lada-Mocarski

Lewis, Sinclair

Adrian H. Goldstone
Jean Hersholt

Lincoln, Abraham

James W. Bollinger
Harlan H. Horner
William Harrison Lambert
Alfred Whital Stern
William Wyles

Linnaeus, Carolus

Thomas Jefferson Fitzpatrick

London

Horace H. Furness Sr.

Louisiana

Charles E. A. Gayarre
Edward Alexander Parsons
Edward Larocque Tinker

Lovecraft, H. P.

J. Lloyd Eaton

Lowell, James Russell

Edward Hale Bierstadt
Parkman Dexter Howe

Machen, Arthur

Adrian H. Goldstone

Magic

Harry Houdini

Manuscripts

see Illuminated Manuscripts

Markham, Edwin

John S. Mayfield

Maryland

John Work Garrett

Masefield, John

Frederick Coykendall

Mathematics, History

David E. Smith

Mather, Cotton

Tracy W. McGregor

Medicine, History

John Redman Coxe
LeRoy Crummer
Harvey Cushing
Herbert Evans
John F. Fulton
Edward C. Streeter
Joseph M. Toner

Melville, Herman

Charles Henry Taylor

Mennonites

Samuel W. Pennypacker

Meredith, George

Frank Altschul

Merrymount Press

George L. Harding

Metallurgy

Henry R. Wagner

Mexico

Hubert Howe Bancroft
Everitt DeGolyer

Adolph Sutro
Henry R. Wagner

Michigan

Clarence M. Burton

Milton, John

William W. Clary
Thomas Lockwood

Mining

Eckley B. Coxe

Mitchell, S. Weir

Elmer Belt
Willard S. Morse

Mormonism

Herbert S. Auerbach
William Robertson Coe
Thomas Jefferson Fitzpatrick
Andrew Dixon White

Morris, William

see Kelmscott Press

Mountaineering

Francis P. Farquhar

Music, History

Joseph W. Drexel
Dannie N. Heineman

Nash, John Henry

Estelle Getz

Navigation

James Ford Bell
Henry C. Taylor

New Orleans

Edward Larocque Tinker

New York City

William Loring Andrews

Newbery, John

Wilbur Macey Stone

Newton, Isaac

Frederick E. Brasch

Nightingale, Florence

Elmer Belt

North American Indians

Edward E. Ayer
William C. Braislin
Elihu Dwight Church
Frank C. Deering
Everitt DeGolyer
Henry F. Depuy
Wilberforce Eames
Robert S. Ellison
Thomas W. Field
Thomas Gilcrease
Henry Cruse Murphy
George W. Paullin

Nuttall, Thomas

Thomas Jefferson Fitzpatrick

Orchids

Oakes Ames

Oregon

Frederick W. Skiff

Ornithology

Edward E. Ayer
William C. Braislin
William Robertson Coe
Ralph Ellis
John Work Garrett

Overbrook Press

Frank Altschul

Oxford University

William W. Clary

Paine, Thomas

Richard Gimbel

Pennsylvania

Harvey Bassler
Henry B. Borneman
William M. Darlington
Samuel W. Pennypacker

Pepys, Samuel

Carleton Rubira Richmond

Persius

Daniel B. Fearing

Petrarch

Harold C. Bodman
Daniel Willard Fiske

Physiology

John F. Fulton

Pittsburgh

William M. Darlington
Joseph B. Shea

Poe, Edgar Allan

Charles Foote
Richard Gimbel
Frederick R. Halsey
Frederick W. Lehmann
Josiah K. Lilly
William E. Stockhausen
Stephen H. Wakeman

Pope, Alexander

Marshall C. Lefferts

Portuguese Literature

John B. Stetson
George Ticknor

Potter, Beatrix

H. Bacon Collamore
William M. Elkins

Pound, Ezra

Norman Holmes Pearson

Printing History

Elmer Adler
Frank Altschul
George Allison Armour
Edwin J. Beinecke Sr.
Albert Bender
Doris L. Benz
Hamilton Cole
Theodore Low DeVinne
Carl Edelheim
Burton Emmett
Morgan Gunst
George L. Harding
Mary S. Harkness
Robert Hoe III
John I. Perkins
Lessing J. Rosenwald

John A. Saks
Isaiah Thomas
Daniel Berkeley Updike
John M. Wing

Pyle, Howard

Willard S. Morse

Rackham, Arthur

Alfred C. Berol
Frederick Coykendall

Rafinesque, C. S.

Thomas Jefferson Fitzpatrick

Railroading

Henry F. Depuy

Ray, John

Thomas Jefferson Fitzpatrick

Rhaeto-Romanic Language

Daniel Willard Fiske

Rhode Island

Joseph J. Cooke
Marsden J. Perry

Riley, James Whitcomb

Josiah K. Lilly

Robinson, E. A.

H. Bacon Collamore
C. Beecher Hogan

Rogers, Bruce

George Allison Armour
William W. Clary

Rousseau, Jean J.

William Maclure

Rowlandson, Thomas

Dickson Q. Brown
Harry E. Widener

Ruskin, John

Robert B. Adam
Marsden J. Perry

Russian Literature

Bayard L. Kilgour Jr.

Science Fiction

J. Lloyd Eaton

Science, History

Frederick E. Brasch
Everitt DeGolyer
Herbert Evans
Dannie N. Heineman
Josiah J. Lilly
James Logan
Louis H. Silver

Scott, Walter

DeCoursey Fales

Seager, Alan

Thomas E. Hanley

Serials

George Arents

Servetus, Michael

Leonard L. Mackall

Shakespeare, William

Thomas P. Barton
William E. Burton
William A. Clark Jr.
John Augustin Daly
Henry F. Durant
Henry Clay Folger
Horace H. Furness Sr.
Henry E. Huntington
Herschel V. Jones
Thomas Lockwood
John Pierpont Morgan
Marsden J. Perry
William Augustus White

Shelley, Percy Bysshe

Luther A. Brewer
William W. Clary
Charles W. Frederickson
Thomas Jefferson McKee
Carl H. Pforzheimer

Sheridan, Richard Brinsley

James M. Osborn

Shipwrecks

Charles Henry Taylor

Sinclair, Upton

Elmer Belt
Willard S. Morse

Soviet Union

Valerian Lada-Mocarski

Spanish Literature

John B. Stetson
George Ticknor

Spiritualism

Harry Houdini

Sports

Clara S. Peck
David Wagstaff
Joseph E. Widener

Steinbeck, John

Adrian H. Goldstone

Stevenson, Robert Lewis

Edwin J. Beinecke Sr.
Charles B. Foote
George Barr McCutcheon
B. George Ulizio
Harry E. Widener

Strawberry Hill Press

Wilmarth S. Lewis

Sullivan, Arthur S.

Edwin J. Beinecke Sr.

Surtees, Robert Smith

John G. Heckscher
Clara S. Peck

Swinburne, Algernon Charles

Lowell Kerr
John S. Mayfield

Tarkington, Booth

Barton Currie

Tennessee

Calvin M. McClung

Texas

Thomas W. Streeter
Henry R. Wagner

Thackeray, William M.

Barton Currie
Herman L. Edgar
DeCoursey Fales
Ogden Goelet
William Harrison Lambert
Henry Sayre Van Duzer

Theatre, History

Robinson Locke
Thomas Jefferson McKee
Robert Gould Shaw
Evert J. Wendell

Thomas, Isaiah

Charles Lemuel Nichols

Tobacco

George Arents

Torrey, John

Thomas Jefferson Fitzpatrick

Trade

James Ford Bell

Trollope, Anthony

A. Edward Newton
Morris L. Parrish

Typography

Theodore Low DeVinne
George L. Harding
Daniel Berkeley Updike

John M. Wing
see also Printing History

Updike, Daniel Berkeley

George L. Harding

Utah

Herbert S. Auerbach
Thomas Jefferson Fitzpatrick

Vesalius, Andreas

LeRoy Crummer
Harvey Cushing
Samuel W. Lambert
Edward C. Streeter

Virgil

Junius S. Morgan

Wallace, Lew

Josiah K. Lilly

Walpole, Horace

Wilmarth S. Lewis

Walpole, Hugh

Jean Hersholt

Walton, Izaak

Daniel B. Fearing
John G. Heckscher
Samuel W. Lambert
Clara S. Peck

Washington, George

William Menzies
Joseph M. Toner

Wells, H. G.

J. Lloyd Eaton

Whaling

Daniel B. Fearing

Whitman, Walt

William F. Gable
Carolyn Wells

Whittier, John Greenleaf

Edward Hale Bierstadt
Parkman Dexter Howe
Frederick M. Meek

Wilde, Oscar

William A. Clark Jr.
Donald F. Hyde
John B. Stetson

Williams, William Carlos

Norman Holmes Pearson

Witchcraft

George Lincoln Burr
Henry Charles Lea
Andrew Dixon White

Women

Miriam Y. Holden

Woodcuts

Sinclair Hamilton
Philip Hofer

Wordsworth, William

Cynthia Morgan St. John

Appendix II

Notable American Book Auctions

1860	October	William E. Burton (Sabin)
1864	May	John Allan (Bangs)
	November	John Redman Coxe (Thomas)
1865	May	Almon W. Griswold (Bangs; sale continued to 1880)
1869	March	Albert Gorton Greene (Bangs)
1870	March	John A. Rice (Bangs)
1871	December	Edward G. Asay (Bangs)
1875	May	Thomas W. Field (Bangs)
1876	April	E. George Squier (Bangs)
	November	William Menzies (Leavitt)
1879	March	George Brinley (1st) (Leavitt)
	June	Thomas Aspinwall (Leonard)
1880	March	George Brinley (2nd) (Leavitt)
1881	June	George Brinley (3rd) (Leavitt)
1883	March	Joseph J. Cooke (Leavitt)
	April	Caleb Fiske Harris (Leavitt; sale continued to 1884)
1884	March	Henry Cruse Murphy (Leavitt)

Two sources that provide further information on American book auctions are Clarence Brigham's "History of Book Auctions in America," which appeared as a lengthy introduction in George McKay's *American Book Auction Catalogues 1713–1934* (New York, 1937) and Robert Roden's "Books of Highest Price" which appeared in the *New York Times Review of Books and Arts*, April 2, 1898. *American Book Prices Current* has supplied an annual report of the sale of books, manuscripts and autographs at auction since 1895. William Hallam Weber's privately printed *An Alphabetical List of the Named Book Auction Sales as Recorded by the American Book Prices Current from the Beginning of 1935 to August 1982* is also a useful list.

1886	April	Charles W. Frederickson (Bangs; sale continued to 1897)
	November	George Brinley (4th) (Leavitt)
1887	March	Rush C. Hawkins (Leavitt)
	November	Henry Ward Beecher (American Art)
1890	February	Samuel L. M. Barlow (American Art)
	April	Hamilton Cole (Bangs)
1891	March	Brayton Ives (American Art)
1893	April	George Brinley (5th) (Libbie)
1894	November	George Livermore (Libbie)
	November	Charles B. Foote (Bangs; sale continued to 1895)
1897	April	Edward Hale Bierstadt (Bangs)
	May	Charles W. Frederickson (Bangs)
1898	March	Charles Deane (Libbie)
1900	March	John Augustin Daly (American Art)
	March	Carl Edelheim (American Art)
	November	Thomas Jefferson McKee (Anderson; sale continued to 1905)
1901	January	William H. Arnold (Bangs)
	April	Frederick W. French (Libbie)
1902	April	Marshall C. Lefferts (Bangs)
	October	Frank Maier (Anderson)
1904	May	John F. Hurst (Anderson; sale continued to 1905)
1905	May	Wilberforce Eames (Anderson; sale continued to 1907)
	December	Samuel W. Pennypacker (Henkels; sale continued to 1910)
1906	April	Herschel V. Jones (Merwin)
1908	November	Henry W. Poor (Anderson; sale continued to 1909)
	December	Edwin N. Lapham (Anderson)
1909	February	John G. Heckscher (Merwin)
	November	Frank Maier (Anderson)
	November	Jacob C. Chamberlain (Anderson)
1910	April	Wilberforce Eames (Anderson; sale continued to 1911)
1911	April	Robert Hoe III (Anderson; sale continued to 1912)
1912	November	Daniel B. Fearing (Libbie)
1913	February	Matthew C. D. Borden (American Art)
	April	Ferdinand Julius Dreer (Henkels)
	October	John Boyd Thacher (Anderson; sale continued to 1922)
1914	January	William Harrison Lambert (Metropolitan)
	December	Adrian H. Joline (Anderson; sale continued to 1915)
1915	January	John L. Clawson (Merwin)
	April	Brayton Ives (American Art)
1916	March	William K. Bixby (Anderson)
	March	Henry E. Huntington (Anderson; duplicates; sale continued to 1923)

	November	Herschel V. Jones (Anderson)
1917	January	John L. Clawson (Anderson)
1918	May	Winston Hagen (Anderson)
	December	Herschel V. Jones (Anderson; sale continued to 1919)
1919	February	Frederick R. Halsey (Anderson)
	October	Evert J. Wendell (American Art)
	November	Henry F. Depuy (Anderson; sale continued to 1920)
	November	Samuel Putnam Avery (Anderson)
1920	January	Theodore Low DeVinne (Anderson)
	February	William Augustus White (Anderson)
	March	Walter T. Wallace (American Art)
	April	Edwin B. Holden (American Art)
	October	Samuel W. Pennypacker (Freeman)
	November	John L. Clawson (Anderson)
1921	April	Robinson Locke (American Art)
	April	William Loring Andrews (Anderson)
1922	February	Henry Sayre Van Duzer (Anderson)
1923	February	Clarence S. Bement (American Art)
	October	Carolyn Wells (Anderson)
	November	William F. Gable (American Art; sale continued to 1925)
	November	John Quinn (Anderson; sale continued to 1924)
	December	Eugene Field (Anderson)
1924	April	Stephen H. Wakeman (American Art)
	December	Beverly Chew (Anderson; sale continued to 1925)
1925	March	Luther A. Brewer (American Art)
	April	George Barr McCutcheon (American Art; sale continued to 1926)
1926	February	Robert B. Adam (Anderson)
	May	John L. Clawson (Anderson)
1927	March	Marshall C. Lefferts (Anderson)
	March	William C. Braislin (Anderson)
1929	January	Jerome Kern (Anderson)
	November	John Camp Williams (American Art)
1931	January	B. George Ulizio (American Art/Anderson)
1933	February	Levi Z. Leiter (American Art/Anderson)
	March	Willis Vickery (American Art/Anderson)
1934	April	William K. Bixby (American Art/Anderson)
	November	Roderick T. Terry (American Art/Anderson; sale continued to 1935)
1935	January	Ogden Goelet (American Art/Anderson; sale continued to 1937)
	April	John B. Stetson (American Art/Anderson)
	November	William D. Breaker (Rains)
	December	Seth S. Terry (American Art/Anderson)

1936	April	Harry B. Smith (American Art/Anderson)
	November	Estelle Getz (American Art/Anderson)
1937	April	George Allison Armour (American Art/Anderson)
	December	Joseph B. Shea (American Art/Anderson)
1938	May	Cortlandt Field Bishop (Anderson)
	November	William Randolph Hearst (Parke-Bernet; sale continued to 1939)
1939	April	John A. Spoor (Parke-Bernet)
1940	January	Wilbur Macey Stone (Parke-Bernet)
	January	Paul Lemperly (Parke-Bernet)
	February	Adolph Lewisohn (Parke-Bernet)
	October	John Gribbel (Parke-Bernet; sale continued to 1947)
1941	April	A. Edward Newton (Parke-Bernet)
1942	January	Ellis A. Ballard (Parke-Bernet)
1944	November	Joseph E. Widener (Parke-Bernet)
1945	February	C. G. Littell (Parke-Bernet)
	April	Frank J. Hogan (Parke-Bernet; sale continued to 1946)
	December	Grenville Kane (Parke-Bernet)
1946	April	Eldridge R. Johnson (Parke-Bernet)
1947	September	Frederick W. Skiff (Butterfield)
	October	Herbert S. Auerbach (Parke-Bernet; sale continued to 1948)
1950	November	Lucius Wilmerding (Parke-Bernet; sale continued to 1951)
1952	February	Walter P. Chrysler Jr. (Parke-Bernet; sale continued to 1955)
1953	March	John B. Stetson (Parke-Bernet)
1954	March	Jean Hersholt (Parke-Bernet)
	April	William J. Holliday (Parke-Bernet)
1955	February	Andre DeCoppet (Parke-Bernet; sale continued to 1958)
1963	May	Barton Currie (Parke-Bernet)
1965	November	Louis H. Silver (Sotheby Parke Bernet)
1966	October	Thomas W. Streeter (Sotheby Parke Bernet; sale continued to 1969)
1967	November	Charles E. Feinberg (Sotheby Parke Bernet; sale continued to 1968)
1974	November	William E. Stockhausen (Sotheby Parke Bernet)
1977	March	Jonathan Goodwin (Sotheby Parke Bernet; sale continued to 1978)
	November	David Borowitz (Sotheby Parke Bernet; sale continued to 1978)
1978	April	Philip D. Sang (Sotheby Parke Bernet; sale continued to 1980)
	April	John A. Saks (Christie; sale continued to 1983)
	September	Arthur Haddaway (Christie)
1981	October	Carleton Rubira Richmond (Sotheby Parke Bernet; sale continued to 1982)

	October	Myles S. Slocum (California Book Auction)
	November	Myles S. Slocum (Christie)
	December	Adrian H. Goldstone (California Book Auction)
1984	November	Doris L. Benz (Christie)

Index

About the Author

DONALD C. DICKINSON is Professor of Library Science in the Graduate Library School, University of Arizona. He is the author of *Bio-Bibliography of Langston Hughes* and *Hellmut Lehmann Haupt: A Bibliography* and has contributed articles and essays to *American Writers, American Libraries, Wilson Library Bulletin,* and the *American Book Collector.*